# Conjuring Hitler

# Conjuring Hitler

## How Britain and America Made the Third Reich

Guido Giacomo Preparata

Pluto  Press

LONDON • ANN ARBOR, MI

First published 2005 by Pluto Press
345 Archway Road, London N6 5AA
and 839 Greene Street, Ann Arbor, MI 48106

www.plutobooks.com

British Library Cataloguing in Publication Data
A catalogue record for this book is available from the British Library

ISBN   978 0 7453 2182 0 hardback
ISBN   978 0 7453 2181 3 paperback
ISBN   978 1 8496 4225 5 PDF


Library of Congress Cataloging in Publication Data applied for


10   9   8   7   6   5   4   3   2   1

Designed and produced for Pluto Press by
Chase Publishing Services, Fortescue, Sidmouth, EX10 9QG, England
Typeset from disk by Stanford DTP Services, Northampton, England
Printed and bound by CPI Group (UK) Ltd, Croydon, CR0 4YY

*For Suzanne*

# Contents

*List of Figures*                                                          ix
*A Chronology of Germany's Undoing, 1900–45*                               xi
*Preface*                                                                  xiv

1. **Introductory: The Eurasian Embrace. Laying Siege to Germany**
   **with World War I, 1900–18**                                            1
   The Second Reich: The Tragedy of an Imperial Upstart                     1
   The Heartland, the Crescent and the Nightmare of British
   Geopolitics                                                              8
   The Blood of the Romanovs and the Encirclement of Germany               15
   The 'Useful Idiots' of Sarajevo                                         20
   Besieging Germany                                                       22
   Conjuring Lenin                                                         27
   The Last Days of America: from Republic to Truculent Empire            38

2. **The Veblenian Prophecy. From the Councils to Versailles**
   **by Way of Russian Fratricide, 1919–20**                              42
   The Impossible Revolution                                              42
   Inducting Hitler into the Mother Lodge                                 57
   The Allied Betrayal of the Russian Whites                              60
   The Peace Treaty That Was Too Harsh                                    74
   Dreaming of Hitler and Deciphering Versailles                          80

3. **The Meltdown and the Geopolitical Correctness of**
   ***Mein Kampf* Between the Kapp and the Beerhall Putsch,**
   **1920–23**                                                            89
   Erzberger: One Man Alone against the Inflation                         89
   Hiring Trebitsch-Lincoln to Foil the Kapp Putsch                       98
   Rathenau, The Reluctant Victim of the Russo-German Pact               112
   The Hyperinflationary Purge of 1923                                    121
   The Maiden Storm of the Nazi Fundamentalists                          130

4. 'Death on the Installment Plan', Whereby Governor Norman
   Came to Pace the Damnation of Europe, 1924–33                    138
   The Banking 'Grid' and the Rules of the Gold Game                138
   Montagu Norman and the 'Nationalization' of the Bank             147
   The Dawes Bailout and the Hierodule Schacht                      159
   I. G. Farben and Germany's First Five-Year Plan                  165
   Britain's Grand Charade to Crash the New Gold Standard           171
   The Last Scheme of Kurt von Schleicher and the End of Weimar     181

5. The Reich on the Marble Cliffs. Fire, Legerdemain and
   Mummery all the Way to Barbarossa, 1933–41                       202
   Nazi Coup d'Etat                                                 203
   Money Magic, Work Creation and Foreign Aid                       211
   A British Masquerade to Entrap the Germans Anew                  228
   A Soviet Tale of Madness and Sacrifice                           244
   Fake War in the West, True Push in the East                      254

6. Conclusion                                                       263

Notes                                                               269
Select Bibliography                                                 295
Index                                                               305

# List of Figures

1. Eurasia and the Fault-Line 11
2. White Nests in the Russian Civil War 67
3. The London/New York Tandem Discount Policy, 1919–32 155
4. Sterling-Dollar Exchange, 1919–33 156
5. The Cycle of Work Creation 219
6. The Masquerade of His Majesty's Stewards and Diplomats 230
7. Alliances and Threats on the Eve of the Czechoslovak Crisis, 1938 240

# Acknowledgments

I wish to thank first of all my institution, the University of Washington, Tacoma for the unwavering support it afforded me in conducting research on this theme and developing it in the course of a five-year long series of lectures. In particular my thanks go to Director and Professor Bill Richardson, Professor Anthony D'Costa and Professor Michael Allen. I am also greatly indebted to Professor Zarembka for the warm endorsement of my project, and to Roger van Zwanenberg at Pluto Press for taking his chances with me, shaping the script, and purging many a noxious metaphor. No less vital have been the help and protection of a thick cohort of guardian angels led by: Dr. Faride Motamedi and Professor John Elliott, who shielded me always and Professor Monika Sudjian, who opened *Deutschtum* to me, and shared the anguish of the exile. Family and friends in Italy, France and Tacoma are in my thoughts – a special salute goes to my companion Andrea.

# A Chronology of Germany's Undoing, 1900–45

**1900**  The construction of the German Imperial fleet proceeds apace.

**1904**  Strategic allegiance between Britain and France.

**1907**  Triple Entente of Britain, France and Russia, designed to encircle Germany.

**1914**  Outbreak of World War I.

**1916**  Russian attempts at a separate peace with Germany.
*December*: murder of Rasputin.

**1917**  *March*: deposition of the Czar.
*April*: the US joins the war.
*October*: Bolshevik takeover.

**1918**  *March*: peace between the Reich and the Bolsheviks.
*November*: capitulation of the Reich.

**1919**  *January–May*: civil tumult in Germany; beginnings of the Weimar Republic.
*June*: ratification of the Versailles Treaty.
*September*: Hitler becomes a politician.

**1920**  Allied sabotage of the Russian counter-revolutionaries.
*March*: Kapp putsch.
*September*: Veblen casts his prophecy.

**1921**  *August*: assassination of Erzberger.

**1922**  *April*: Russo-German pact.
*June*: assassination of Rathenau.

**1923**  Inflationary debacle in Germany.
*January*: French invasion of the Ruhr.
*November*: the Hitlerites' Beerhall putsch.

**1924**  *April–September*: Announcement and implementation of the Dawes bailout.
*December*: Hitler is amnestied.

**1925**  *April*: Britain goes back to gold.

**1927**  *July*: central bankers' conference at Long Island.

**1928**  *May*: the Nazis gather 2.6 percent of the vote in the national elections.

**1929**  *September*: London precipitates the crash in New York. Extinction of the steady financial transfer from America to Germany.

**1930** *September*: soaring unemployment; Nazi breakthrough at the elections: 18.7 percent.

**1931** *March*: aborted project for an Austro-German Union.
*May*: Collapse of the Creditanstalt in Austria.
*July*: German banking crisis.
*July–September*: Britain wrecks the Gold Standard.
*October*: Hitler encounters Hindenburg.

**1932** *May*: Baronial Cabinet of Papen.
*June*: End of Reparations.
*July*: the Nazis garner 37.3 percent of the ballot.
*November*: the Nazis lose 2 million votes; Hindenburg refuses to make Hitler chancellor.
*December*: Schleicher becomes Chancellor; unemployment in Germany at 40 percent.

**1933** *January*: meeting at Schröder's on the 4th; Hitler sworn in on the 30th.
*February*: Reichstag fire.
*March–August*: Nazi consolidation of power; promotion of work creation under Schacht.

**1934** *June*: Röhm purge.
*July*: Anglo-German financial agreement.
*August*: Hitler is acclaimed Reichsführer; rearmament is launched in earnest; heavy Anglo-American investment in Germany.

**1935** *June*: Anglo-German Naval Pact.

**1936** Peak of British appeasement.
*March*: Militarization of the Rhineland.
*September*: Lloyd George visits Hitler.
*December*: the 'pro-Nazi' King Edward VIII abdicates.

**1937** *October*: the Windsors tour Germany.
*November*: Lord Halifax flies to Germany to give Hitler the green light.

**1938** Culmination of Nazi boom: erasure of unemployment.
*March*: annexation of Austria.
*September*: emasculation of Czechoslovakia at Munich.

**1939** *March*: Nazi seizure of Czechoslovakia; official split of the British establishment in dealing with Germany; British unilateral guarantee to Poland.
*August*: Russo-German pact for the partition of Poland.
*September*: the 'phoney war' begins.

**1940** *April–June*: Nazi offensive in the West and capitulation of France.

*July*: secret talks with Windsor in Spain.

*August–September*: failed aerial campaign versus Britain.

*December*: Preparation completed in Germany for the invasion of Russia (Barbarossa).

**1941**  *March–May*: German success in the Mediterranean basin.

*May*: Hess vanishes.

*June*: the Nazis invade the USSR.

**1943**  *January*: German surrender in Stalingrad.

*May*: the Axis capitulates in North Africa.

*July*: the Allies land in Sicily.

**1944**  *June*: Allied debarkation in Normandy (D-Day).

**1945**  *March*: the Americans cross the Rhine.

*May*: Germany is finished.

# Preface

Nazism. For many this topic is a fixation, especially for the peoples that suffered defeat and utter disfigurement because of it. Being Italian, I remember clearly my paternal grandfather reminiscing interminably about the days of Fascism, echoed by my grandmother; he never seemed able to untangle within himself the knot of sentiments towards Mussolini, the Germans, the war, and the horror of it all. At times he wished the Axis had won the war, at others he fancied France had not fallen so fast as to precipitate Italy in her catastrophic downfall – he would eventually experience combat in the Balkans, survive and remain indissolubly tied to the old world till his death, long after 1945. My father and I – the 'modern ones' – would listen to these tirades, rolling our eyes, and excusing the impropriety of even alluding to a possible Nazi victory on account of grandfather's earnest but essentially 'screwed-up' worldview. A worldview that, as we moderns had come to learn, had spelled the damnation of Europe and justified the Americanization of the vanquished.

But the Pax Americana that followed, deep down, was itself of dubious value: it began with a nuclear holocaust, brought affluence to the West perhaps, but gave very little by way of peace to the rest of the world. And what was left to feel of the defeated West was dismal: Germans and Italians had been reduced to a couple of emptied out, identityless tribes.

Presently, in the collective imagination of the West, there is nothing worse than Nazism. No greater sacrilege, no greater manifestation of brutality, inhumanity, and deception than the rule of this unique regime that held sway over Central Europe for a dozen years. The Nazis violated life in ways unseen, and the record of their atrocities during the war grew to be such that after their defeat, Germany was prostrated by a moral lapidation on the part of the victors, which still hasn't ceased. Ever since, a continuous torrent of books, articles, instruction and films, crafted by the Anglo-Americans, and diffused by their acquired minions in Europe, has flooded the venues of debate, impeding any views other than the 'truth' of the establishment. This truth being that Europe had been compromised by the belligerence of the outcast in her fold: the accursed Germans, who plunged their European brethren into war, and deservedly suffered thereby, all of them, the benign domination of their 'American uncles.'

I wanted to understand how all this came to pass. I wondered how Europe could commit such a messy suicide as to give herself to a foreign ruler possessed by a worldview different from the old one, yet equally violent and barbarous. And to answer the question it was obvious that I had to turn to the recent origin of the story, and that is to the Nazi curse itself. Why did it happen?

Being an economics graduate, I began by directing my interest to the Nazi boom of the 1930s and the financial contrivances employed to fuel the recovery, which later formed the topic of my doctoral dissertation. The research expanded around that core over the course of nearly a decade.

In this study there is no desire to reassess the record of the German cruelties: these have been sufficiently scrutinized, although only with anatomical (thus voyeuristic) fascination. Rather, it is my intent to push back the point of attack of this story by a few years: for the official 'narratives,' which are for the most part biased either by excessive contrition or apologia if written by Germans,[1] and more or less subtle execration if written by Anglo-Americans,[2] generally course through the gestation of Nazism only to dismiss it as a confused interlude marked by the raving vengefulness of the old Germany, and by the alleged effects of 'great historical forces' and 'irrationalism' – two half-baked and substantially meaningless notions, in fact.

The poor treatment of the Nazi gestation is due to two factors: first, the historical interval that covers the breeding of Hitlerism is notoriously complex, and that does not make for 'good cinema': for instance, when the Crisis hit the West in 1930, and the Nazis began to gather votes, Liberal historians hand the narration over to their fellow economists, and the economists, who understand famously nothing of the Crisis, throw it back to the historians, who are thus saddled with the last and sadly disappointing word in the current, miserable explication of the Nazis' rise to power.

Second, a detailed analysis of the emergence of Nazism is generally shunned so it seems, for it might reveal too much; in truth, it might disclose that the Nazis were *never* a creature of chance. The thesis of the book suggests that *for 15 years (1919–33)*, the Anglo-Saxon elites tampered

---

1. Ernst Nolte's *Der europäische Bürgerkrieg, 1917–1945: Nationalsozialismus und Bolschevismus (The European Civil War, 1917–1945: National-socialism and Bolshevism* (Berlin: Propyläen Verlag, 1987) is a fair instance of a mitigatory approach to the rise of Nazism.
2. A literally stereotyped production stretching from, say, William Shirer's *The Rise and Fall of the Third Reich* (New York: Simon & Schuster, 1960) to Michael Burleigh's *The Third Reich, A New History* (New York: Hill and Wang, 2000), or Ian Kershaw's recent biography of Hitler (in two volumes: *Hubris*, 1998, and *Nemesis*, 2000. New York: W.W. Norton & Company).

with German politics with the conscious intent to obtain a reactionary movement, which they could then set up as a pawn for their geopolitical intrigues. When this movement emerged immediately after World War I in the shape of a religious, anti-Semitic sect disguised as a political party (that is, the NSDAP), the British clubs kept it under close observation, proceeded to endorse it semi-officially in 1931 when the Weimar Republic was being dismantled by the Crisis, and finally embraced it, *with deceit*, throughout the 1930s. This is to say that although England did not conceive Hitlerism, she nonetheless created the conditions under which such a phenomenon could appear, and devoted herself to supporting financially the Nazis and subsequently arming them to the teeth with the prospect of manipulating them. Without such methodical and unsparing 'protection' on the part of the Anglo-American elites, along with the complicit buttress of Soviet Russia, there would have been no Führer and no Nazism: the political dynamism of the Nazi movement owed its success to a general state of instability in Germany, which was wholly artificial, a wreckage engineered by the Anglo-American clubs themselves.

By 'clubs' and 'elites' I mean the established and self-perpetuating fraternities that ruled the Anglo-Saxon commonwealths: these were (and still are) formed by an aggregation of dynasts issued from the banking houses, the diplomatic corps, the officer caste, and the executive aristocracy, which still remains solidly entrenched in the constitutional fabric of the modern 'democracies.' These 'clubs' act, rule, breed and think like a compact oligarchy, and co-opt the middle class to use it as a filter between themselves and their cannon fodder: the commoners. In fact, in the so-called 'democratic constituency,' which represents to date the most sophisticated model of oligarchic rule, the electorate wields no clout whatever, and political ability is but another expression for the powers of persuasion needed to 'build consensus' around (momentous) decisions already taken elsewhere.[3]

3. So-called 'democracy' is a sham, the ballot a travesty. In modern bureaucratized systems, whose birth dates from the mid-nineteenth century, the feudal organization has been carried to the next level, so to speak. A chief objective of what Thucydides referred to in his epoch as *synomosiai* (literally 'exchanges of oaths'), that is, the out-of-sight fraternities acting behind the ruling clans, has been to make the process of the exaction of rents from the population (a 'free income' in the form of rents, financial charges and like thefts) as unfathomable and impenetrable as possible. The tremendous sophistication, and the propagandistic wall of artfully divulged misconceptions surrounding the banking system (we will return to this theme in Chapter 4), which is the chief instrument wherewith the hierarchs expropriate and control the wealth of their supporting community, is the limpid testimony of this essential transformation undergone by the feudal/oligarchic organization in the modern era. The West has moved from a low-tech agrarian establishment built upon the backs of disenfranchised

The story told in this book is the story of the British empire, which by 1900, fearing the rising power of the young German Reich, contrived in secrecy a plan for a giant encirclement of the Eurasian landmass. The main objective of this titanic siege was the prevention of an alliance between Germany and Russia: if these two powers could have fused into an 'embrace,' so reasoned the British stewards, they would have come to surround themselves with a fortress of resources, men, knowledge and military might such as to endanger the survival of the British empire in the new century. From this early realization, Britain embarked upon an extraordinary campaign to tear Eurasia asunder by hiring France and Russia, and subsequently America, to fight the Germans. The vicissitudes of the first half of the twentieth century made up the epic of the great siege of Europe.

As will be shown in Chapter 1, World War I completed the first act of the attack, which was crowned by the imperial ingress of the United States on the grand chessboard. Germany had lost the war, but she had not been defeated on her own territory; Germany's elites, her political and economic structure had remained intact. Thus after 1918 began the second act of the siege: that is, an astounding political maneuver willingly performed by the Allies to resurrect in Germany a reactionary regime from the ranks of her vanquished militarists. Britain orchestrated this incubation with a view to conjuring a belligerent political entity which she encouraged to go to war against Russia: the premeditated purpose was to ensnare the new, reactionary German regime in a two-front war (World War II), and profit

---

serfs to a highly mechanized post-industrial hive that feeds off the strength of no less disenfranchised blue- and white-collar slaves, whose lives are mortgaged to buy into the vogue of modern consumption. The latter-day lords of the manor are no longer seen demanding tribute since they have relied on the mechanics of banking accounts for the purpose, whereas the sycophants of the median class, as academics and publicists, have consistently remained loyal to the *synomosiai*. The other concrete difference between yesterday and today is the immensely increased throughput of industrial production (whose potential level, however, has always been significantly higher than the actual one, to keep prices high). As for the 'democratic participation' of the ordinary citizens, these know in their hearts that they never decide anything of weight, and that politics consists in the art of swaying the mobs in one direction or another according to the wishes and anticipations of the few having the keys to information, intelligence and finance. These few may at a point in time be more or less divided into warring factions; the deeper the division, the bloodier the social strife. The electoral record of the West in the past century is a shining monument to the utter inconsequence of 'democracy': in spite of two cataclysmic wars and a late system of proportional representation that yielded a plethora of parties, Western Europe has seen no significant shift in her socio-economic constitution, whereas America has become, as time progressed, ever more identical to her late oligarchic self, having reduced the democratic pageant to a contest between two rival wings of an ideologically compact monopartite structure, which is in fact 'lobbied' by more or less hidden 'clubs': the degree of public participation in this flagrant mockery is, as known, understandably lowest: a third of the franchise at best.

from the occasion to annihilate Germany once and for all. To carry out these deep and painstaking directives for world control, two conditions were necessary: (1) an imposing and anti-German regime secretly aligned with Britain had to be set up in Russia, and (2) the seeds of chaos had to be planted in Germany to predispose the institutional terrain for the growth of this reactionary movement of 'national liberation'. The first objective was realized by backstabbing the Czar in Russia in 1917 and installing the Bolsheviks into power; the second by drafting the clauses of the Peace Treaty so as to leave the dynastic clans of Germany unscathed: indeed, it was from their fold that Britain expected the advent of this revanchist movement (Chapter 2).

What unraveled in Germany after the Great War was the life of the Weimar Republic, the puppet regime of the West, which incubated Nazism in three stages: a period of chaos ending with the hyperinflation and the appearance of Hitler (1918–23, dealt with in Chapter 3); a period of artificial prosperity during which the Nazis were quiet and the future war machine of Germany was in process of being assembled with American loans (1924–29); and a period of disintegration (1930–32) paced by the financial mastermind of the twentieth century: Montagu Norman, the Governor of the Bank of England (Chapter 4).

After the incubation was completed and the Hitlerites obtained with the aid of Anglo-American financial capital the chancellorship of the Reich (January 1933), the formidable recovery of Germany began under the Nazi wing, British loans, and the financial artistry of Germany's central banker: Hjalmar Schacht, Montagu Norman's protégé. There followed the unbelievable 'dance' of Britain and Nazi Germany (1933–43), led by the former to push the latter to go to war against Russia. And Russia, too, acting in sync with London, appeased the Nazis in order to lure them into the trap of the Eastern Front. England put out a mesmerizing show by feigning before the world that her ruling class was divided between pro-Nazis and anti-Nazis, and that such a scission accounted for the apparent lack of commitment to fight Hitler on the Western Front after the invasion of Poland had triggered World War II. The truth was quite different: a bargain was being transacted behind the scenes; Britain calculatingly prevented the Americans from opening a western front for three years so as to allow the Nazis to penetrate and devastate Russia undisturbed in exchange for the prompt evacuation of German forces from the Mediterranean basin, which was one of Britain's zones of vital interest. In the end, after this spectacular feat of dissimulation, Britain dropped the mask and closed in on the duped Nazis, who would be crushed on two fronts by the colluded Soviet and Anglo-American forces (Chapter 5).

To annihilate the German threat, the British ruling elites had gambled for high stakes; for over 30 years (1914–45) they had woven a web of financial machinations, international complicities, intelligence conspiracies, diplomatic devilry, military savvy, and inhuman mendacity, and they finally succeeded. This game for Anglo-American supremacy came at the cost of approximately 70 million lives (two world wars): a holocaust whose nature is beyond words. Both conflicts were willed and set off by Britain. In the first one, it was political incapacity that lost Germany, in the second there was no longer a Germany worth speaking of: all we see is a benumbed population harnessed to a native automaton fitted, armed and wound up by the British (and the Soviets).[4]

So the West has to think again – to think, in fact, that there *is* something far worse than Nazism, and that is the hubris of the Anglo-American fraternities, whose routine is to incite indigenous monsters to war, and steer the pandemonium to further their imperial aims.

4. The leitmotiv of this book is the conscious nature of the effort expended by the British clubs to preserve the empire, it being understood that such an effort was worthwhile even if it meant surrendering leadership to the American brethren, whom the London clubs cultivated as their spiritual heirs. The message conveyed here is that Britain's imperial way was possibly the most atrocious manifestation of machiavellism in modern history for she stopped at nothing to defend her dominant position; she knew of no means that could not justify the end. To achieve world hegemony, Britain did not retract from planning in Germany an interminable season of pain and chaos to incubate an eerie, native force, which she thought of manipulating in a second world conflict – that too a British idea. All of this was, from the beginning in 1919 till the end in 1945, a cool-headed, calculated plot. Needless to say, I am well aware that such a thesis might too easily lend itself to being booed by the patriotic 'experts' of Western academia as yet another grotesque conspiracy theory; but in fact this thesis provides no more than a thread with which one may finally string together a collection of clues and solid evidence, which have been available for years, and have formed ever since a platform for dissenters, that is, for those students of history and economics that have had the candor to acknowledge that the central tenet of international relations was, then as now, *secrecy*. One need only think of the multibillion-dollar budgets devoted in our time to so-called 'intelligence', managed by non-elected 'officials' and earmarked for undisclosed acts of sabotage and disinformation perpetrated at home and abroad, nebulous 'surveys', mercenary commissions, and god-only-knows what else, of which the taxpayers themselves have naturally no knowledge whatsoever. Again, the democratic public is to have no say, yet is enjoined to pay for allowing the absentees to conspire behind closed doors. True, not all conspiracies succeed – some are riper 'for the times', as they say, than others – but all great historical developments, good or ill, are unfailingly animated, fought and countered by the initiates of the several antagonistic 'societies'; and the herds, despite themselves, always follow. In the twentieth and early twenty-first centuries, it is the Anglo-American clubs that have carried the day, and their tenure has little to do with human rights, free markets and democracy, regardless of what they may shamelessly profess. What follows is the story of the most important battle they victoriously fought so far: the horrifying campaign against Germany.

# 1 Introductory: The Eurasian Embrace

## Laying Siege to Germany with World War I, 1900–18

'A petty Navy Royall of three score tall ships or more, but in case fewer...
seemeth to be almost a mathematical demonstration, next under the
merciful and mighty protection of God, for a feasible policy to bring
and preserve this victorious British monarchy in a marvellous security.
Whereupon the revenue of the Crown of England and wealth public
will wonderfully increase and flourish; and then...sea forces anew to be
increased proportionately. And so Fame, Renown, Estimation and Love,
and Fear of this Brytish *Microcosmus* all the whole of the great world over
will be speedily and surely be settled.'

John Dee *The Brytish Monarchy* [1577][1]

### The Second Reich: the tragedy of an imperial upstart

The sudden growth of the German Reich during the second half of the
nineteenth century compelled the British Commonwealth to launch a
sweeping maneuver against the world's continental landmass. The chief
objective was the prevention of a durable alliance between Russia and
Germany. Britain proceeded to deter the union by signing a triple alliance
with France and Russia designed to encircle the German Reich (1907).
After the outbreak of war, the operation was deepened by enlisting the
aid of the United States in a phase during which the Russian link of the
alliance seemed to be giving (1917). As a perilous gap opened in the East,
Britain hastened to fix it by encouraging a Liberal experiment under a
straw man, a barrister by the name of Kerensky, which dissolved in a
few months. Meantime, as a possible alternative, revolutionary nihilists
– the so-called Bolsheviks commanded by the intellectual radical Lenin
– were transferred to Russia through a labyrinthine network of organized
subversion by obscure 'agents' such as the Russian Parvus Helphand, with
the expectation that out of such inflow would emerge a despotic regime,
whose polarity (materialist, anti-clerical, and anti-feudal) was the inverse
of that of the German Reich. The involvement of the United States became

1

part of a broader deployment ranging from a military reinforcement on the Western Front to Zionist propaganda for the joint (with Britain) occupation of Palestine, which loomed as a vital geopolitical zone on the East–West divide. The Reich's surrender at the end of World War I (1918) completed the initial stage of Germany's annihilation.

If we are to understand the rise of the Nazi era and the conflict between Britain and the German Reich, we must first examine the international relations of the new German nation from 1870 onwards.

\* \* \*

By 1900 it was all clear.

Improbable as it might have appeared, a German empire had emerged from the post-Napoleonic morass: a nation culled from a garbled constellation of feisty principalities had at last coagulated, 'by blood and iron,' round the martial core of its feistiest province, the kingdom of Prussia. And so, in the 1870s, there it stood before the eyes of the West: the Second German Reich.

An unstable compound: a coupling of feudal hunger and formidable scientific achievement. After all, this was the uncouth matrimony of the unfailing Prussian armies with the best music, physics, chemistry, political economy, historiography, philosophy, and philology the West had to offer. A formidable beginning.

And soon enough, this German dynastic state, conscious of its potential and bursting with overconfidence, enticed the curiosity of the great British Commonwealth.[2] In those early days, England had paid scarce attention to German politics, preoccupied as she was with French colonial rivalry and the 'Great Game' in Central Asia that pitted her military forces against czarist Russia.[3] Germany had been too fragmented to claim a piece of the geopolitical surveys of the British generals. Not that German commerce did not matter to Britain: the opposite was true. But when, under the leadership of the master tactician and Chancellor of the Empire, Otto Bismarck (1870–90), the nature of the trade between Britain and Germany was gradually reversed; that is, when Germany ceased to act vis-à-vis the United Kingdom as the mere supplier of foodstuffs and recipient of her manufactures, to become, in turn, a growing industrial power in her own right, the British Foreign Office and the subsidiary clubs began to ponder the matter over with some apprehension.[4]

Evidently, the Germans were benefiting from the merits of borrowing: they had had the opportunity to snap up a panoply of technological know-how ready-made from their European counterparts, and perfect it dramatically, without the encumbrances and sunken costs of pioneering. Yet even if untrammeled industrial production remained problematic: if manufactures were to yield a profit, national business could seldom rely on the local markets – they might be too narrow, they saturated fast. Where was one to dump the surplus at a profit? Where did Britain unload hers? In her colonies. Hence Germany too pushed for 'a place in the sun.'

The bill for national expenses incurred in outfitting warships and consular administration overseas, which as a rule far outweighed the pecuniary gains of the protected concerns, was, and has been, naturally footed by the public. Indeed, colonies also served as a comfortable springboard for imperial intrigue. Though the imperial chancellor Bismarck had preferred to consolidate Germany's continental, that is, Middle-European position, by weaving a steady and diplomatically criss-crossed reticulation of arrangements in the midst of the other 'big players' (Britain, Russia, Austria-Hungary, and France), the vested interests of commercial enterprise became persuasive enough to change the iron chancellor's mind, and induce him to bless the Reich's colonial bid. This took place in the first half of the 1880s.

As was to be expected, the costs associated with the Reich's penetration of Africa (southwest Africa, Togoland, the Cameroons, a stake in Tanganyika), the Pacific (part of New Guinea, the Solomon, Marshall and Caroline Islands), and the Far East (the outpost on the Kiao-Chao bay, with its state-of-the-art colonial architecture, masterful civil engineering, and the fashionable beach resort of Tsing-Tao), were, gauged against the profitable extraction of raw materials and foodstuffs, somewhat disproportionate. Germany acquired 'colonial territories some four times as large as herself.'[5] Notwithstanding (1) the public outlay for shielding commerce with 'the flag,' (2) the earnest commitment of the Deutschkolonialer Frauenbund (colonial women's league of Germany) to supply Teutonic females to the meager German corps of settlers[6] (they were 25,000, including the soldiers, by 1914), and (3) the rather speedy turnover of German investments in hemp, phosphates, cocoa and rubber, these territorial acquisitions were rated by the ruling circles a 'sad disappointment.'[7] Too costly, too thorny: the Germans lacked that imperial *désinvolture* with the natives, they knew nothing of that calm poise wherewith the British sahib seeped into the 'local mind' to lay a firmer hold of it.

Naturally, the Germans faced a number of violent insurgencies amongst their indigenous subjects – other than repress them ruthlessly, they did nothing more. Bismarck grew impatient, the great Berlin banks showed no interest in these exotic experiments, and in the interlude, the British empire was resenting ever more such German intrusion at the periphery: for all its flamboyant *Kultur*, the Reich was evidently the imperial *parvenu* of the world. Herbert Bismarck, the chancellor's son, in his capacity of insider, confessed that embarking on a colonial policy 'was popular and conveniently adapted to bring [Germany] into conflict with England at any given moment.'[8]

So the Germans wanted attention; they were keen to share with their British cousins the condominium of the world, and eventually clash with them, though it would assumedly have to be a collision of short duration. It appeared Germany desired competition for its own sake – a competition which, in the imagination of German rulers and nationalist intellectuals alike, should historically have led to a theoretical 'change of the guard' between Britain and Germany, something akin to the transition from the Spanish to the British empire in the seventeenth century.

And so while Bismarck junior did not conceal his imperialistic enthusiasm, the late chancellor Bernhard von Bülow (1900–09) would years later decry in his memoirs that the German people had no political ability whatever.[9] Possibly it was all true, but it did not bode well for Germany's national security. The ablest student of the era, Nowegian-American social scientist Thorstein Veblen, remarked in 1915:

Doubtless, a penchant for profundity and deliberation bulks large among the habits of those who cultivate [German] culture. But nothing can be more profoundly and meticulously deliberate than the measured footsteps of the man who no longer knows where he is going, though he is on his way.[10]

Because it knew not precisely where it was going, German imperial policy might have been judged amateurish, but the facts facing external observers persisted: here was an educated 'anthill', replete with technique and presumption that was seeking to expand. And expand it did: despite its naivety in the arts of imperial scheming, the Reich laid rail – the most sophisticated – everywhere it could, established an enviable network of commercial stations, introduced impeccable administration, and eventually hoped to crown it all with the diffusion of its unsurpassed arts and sciences. Not as politically experienced as the British, but nonetheless a competitor of disturbing brilliance. To restrain, challenge, and defeat the Germans would be no simple task.

By 1890, admittedly not even the master strategist, Bismarck himself, who was now being dismissed by the new Emperor, Wilhelm II, had been capable of identifying a 'new course' for Germany. He clearly comprehended, as will be emphasized hereafter, the importance of not antagonizing Russia, though that proved extremely difficult, considering that Germany's closest ally, the Austrian empire, was perennially at odds with Russia's aspirations in Eastern Europe. Hence, Bismarck's cherished goal, a solid alliance of the three continental sovereigns (the *Dreikaiserbund*), never materialized. Then, the tentatively 'friendly' feelers he had sent toward England had always been received with suspicion in London, for the Reich had been for some time unabashedly fashioning itself as a rival – there only remained to assess its degree of hostility. But that, as mentioned above, was a matter fuzzy to Germany herself.

What was certain was that France, within the shifting circles of alliances, was for Germany 'hopeless': in 1871, after the Franco-Prussian War, the newly proclaimed Reich had annexed industrially-rich Alsace and Lorraine, and thenceforth it was sworn hate between the two powers. By the time Bismarck left, he had done precious little to allay the discomfort of Britain.

Collectively, the gist of all such interminable diplomatic jockeying consisted in the Germans' unresolved complex of political inferiority vis-à-vis the British: Kaiser Wilhelm, the grandson of Queen Victoria; Bismarck, Admiral Tirpitz, the future father of the German Imperial Navy; and a slew of German grandees were all fluent in English, and educated in the ways of the British gentleman of leisure: the German attraction to Britain, the fascination with her mastery of power, were *strong*. But the German Reich was altogether a 'different' creature: it only wished it possessed an equal level of imperial savvy to make itself heard. And so it tried, with whatever it had – which was much, as the Allies were to realize two decades later, but not enough.

Thereafter, with Wilhelm II, came the *neuer Kurs*: and this 'new course,' which was in truth but the continuation of the old one, brought in relief the former orientation and unveiled its blurred medium-term aim: in brief, antagonism with Britain; antagonism to be settled by naval skirmishes, bold diplomacy, and commercial and technological swagger.

In the voluminous stream of scholarly production dealing with the Second Reich and the *Gründerzeit* (the 'founding epoch' of German imperial hegemony in the late nineteenth century) much has been made of Wilhelm II's infantile antics and capricious shallowness; much catastrophic action ascribed to the Kaiser's neurotic shame for his withered left arm and hand.

Leaving aside such psychologistic etiology *à bon marché*, which is graciously passing out of vogue, it may be more to the point to remark that the abiding tendency of Germany's new course appeared to be nothing more than a disquieting drift to dissolution. As one German historian recently observed, Wilhelm II was not the creator of German hubris, simply its most conspicuous functionary.[11]

Thus by the end of the nineteenth century, economically speaking, Germany and America were breathing down Britain's neck. But this elementary recognition on Britain's part hardly exhausted the matter. America spoke passable English, could be 'Liberal', and most important, was, like Britain herself, an island: she could not represent a threat. But the German language was as remote from the English as Wilhelmshaven was close to Dover. Germany was at hand, on the continent. And there was more.

Naval skirmishes...

It became apparent by the end of the century that Wilhelm II was enthusiastically supporting the project of expanding the Imperial Navy. At home, the cosmopolitans, the Socialists and the Liberals, were wary – of course, such a move would have meant a positive confrontation with Britain – but so were the conservative agrarians: a great Navy signified some form of open trade, and heavy taxes. The Reich silenced its landlord class – the so-called Junkers* – with protective tariffs, and set out to ratchet up the maritime effort, cheered by the vast majority of the country – Liberals, Catholics, pan-Germans, the rich absentee owners and not so rich Socialist underclass, all, in one shape or another, 'nationalists': at the time it seemed indecorous not to wear some of that collective pride for the so many astounding achievements of the young Reich.

Propaganda, public rallying and, to respond to German jingoism, whipping the average Briton into patriotic frenzy by feeding him a 'good hate' amounted to so much routine for the British governors and their dependable press organs: these things could be effected effortlessly, if the need arose.[12] But the German intrusion upon the waters of the North Sea, and therefrom the new fleet's predictable reach for the maritime expanses of the globe constituted for Britain, to put it mildly, a grave worry. This time the Reich had gone too far. It was encroaching upon the very means of British imperial management, the hallowed 'Royall Navy,' which had been the chief instrument of Great Britain's conquest of the world since

---

* That is, the landed aristocracy, which rules from the bastion of the agrarian class, the Junkers, from the Old High German *Juncherro*, 'young lord.'

the prophetic Elizabethan days of John Dee, the Queen's astrologer, cartographer, occultist, and intelligence officer.

The Germans were intuiting one thing too many: they were slowly understanding that if they successfully coupled continental might – which they could readily wield, being the Prussian divisions, solidly planted in the heart of Europe, the best in the world – with a powerful fleet, their military *force de frappe* would assuredly overpower that of Britain.

So then the issue of alliances came to the fore. Intuitively, the Germans knew since the epoch of Bismarck that it would not do to find themselves trapped between the 'hopeless' French, and the ambivalent Russians. A prolonged war, if fight one must, on two fronts had to be avoided. This was why Bismarck never sought to alienate Russia entirely; but the clumsy anti-Slav intrigues of the Austrian partner in the Balkans stood in the way: the Austro-Hungarian empire was the weak appendage of the Reich; the German General Staff was conscious of this burden. And would live to regret it – 'we are fettered to a corpse,' they would wail a mere month after the beginning of the war.[13] But for the time being, Austria remained the natural ally because she afforded a continuum of Germanic control upon the southeastern reaches of Europe, and, moreover, Austrians spoke beautiful German. That *fin de siècle* Vienna, though showing spreading symptoms of decadence, was one of the vanguards, if not *the* vanguard of 'German' artistic expression – a crucible of extraordinary inventiveness, second not even to Paris – is an important consideration in this regard.

Austrians spoke German, and the Prussians were convinced they could bring off the great European race in any case; they thought they could abundantly make up for the heavy military deficiencies of the Hapsburg empire. All such expectations were clearly misplaced. But while the Reich wallowed in its imprecision, Britain lost no time.

By 1900 it was clear to the British that the Reich could indeed 'pull it off'. It could overwhelm Britain and cause an advantageous (to the Reich), yet temporary, paralysis of European affairs, during which it might turn against France again to subdue her once and for all, and then direct her gaze at Russia...Russia could either be inveigled by Germany into a binding alliance, in which the latter would obviously dominate the former, or, alternatively, the Russians could be slowly mangled into submission by the Prussian armies. In either case, the British *cauchemar* would come true: if Germany and Russia united in one form or another, the Eurasian Embrace would come into existence: that is, a concrete Eurasian empire at the center of the continental landmass, which would come to rest on an enormous Slav army and German technological mastery. And that, the British elite sentenced, was never to be, for it would have mortally threatened the supremacy of the British empire.

## The heartland, the crescent, and the nightmare of British geopolitics

The 'heartland' was a hypothetical area centered in Eurasia, which would be so situated and catered to by resources and manpower as to render it an unconquerable fortress and a fearsome power; and the 'crescent' was a virtual semi-arc encompassing an array of islands – America, Britain, Australia, New Zealand and Japan – which, as 'Sea Powers,' watched over the Eurasian landmass to detect and eventually thwart any tendency towards a consolidation of power on the heartland.

This lingo was coined by the pioneers of Geopolitics, a new-fangled discipline developed at the turn of the twentieth century: on the surface, it consisted of a systematic and semi-erudite compilation of geography, elementary logistics, economic lore, and Machiavellian mystagogy collated *ad usum Delphini*. But its ulterior motive was a transliteration of individual human conduct into the dynamics of social aggregates: a political likening of nations to organic, willed, living creatures.[14] Because of this, geopolitics was likely to reveal in clear terms what the political agenda of a certain power might have been at a given point in time. A revelatory and much influential testimony was drafted during these times of anti-German conspiracies by Sir Halford Mackinder (1861–1947), a professor at the London School of Economics and one of Britain's founding fathers of geopolitics, in a piece entitled 'The Geographical Pivot of History,' which was published in the *Geographical Journal* of the Royal Society in 1904. This article illustrated in unequivocal terms the nature of the coming engagement.

Mackinder envisioned the alternatives and enumerated the stakes of the game. This was a public document, telling a simple story. Its drift was a fair exposition of the policy of the British Commonwealth, and subsequently of that of its spiritual heir, the American empire: indeed, up until the present time, the international policy of the US Administration has been waged seamlessly and coherently in the spirit of Mackinder's vision.

By 1900, the writing was on the wall.

The conception of Euro-Asia to which we thus attain is that of a continuous land, ice-girt in the north, water-girt elsewhere, measuring twenty-one million square miles, or more than three times the area of North America, whose centre and north, measuring some nine million square miles, or more than twice the area of Europe, have no available water-ways to the ocean, but on the other hand, except in the subarctic forest, are very generally favorable to the mobility of horsemen and camelmen. To east, south, and west of this *heart-land* are marginal regions, ranged in a vast *crescent*, accessible to shipmen. According to physical conformation, these regions are four in number, and it is not a little remarkable that in a general way they respectively coincide with the spheres of the four great religions – Buddhism, Brahaminism, Mahometanism, and Christianity... Britain, Canada, the United States, South Africa, Australia, and Japan, are now a ring of outer and insular bases for sea-power and commerce, inaccessible to the land-power of Europe...The spaces within the Russian empire and Mongolia are so vast, and their potentialities in population, wheat, cotton, fuel, and metals so incalculably great, that it is inevitable that a vast economic world, more or less apart, will develop inaccessible to oceanic commerce...In the world at large [Russia] occupies the central strategical position held by Germany in Europe. She can strike on all sides, save the north. The full development of her modern railway mobility is merely a matter of time...The oversetting of the balance of power in favor of the *pivot* state, resulting in its expansion over the marginal lands of Euro-Asia, would permit of the use of vast continental resources for fleet-building, *and the empire of the world would then be in sight. This might happen if Germany were to ally herself with Russia.* The threat of such an event should, therefore, throw France into alliance with the over-sea powers, and France, Italy, Egypt, India and Korea would become so many *bridgeheads* where the outside navies would support armies to compel the pivot allies to deploy land forces and prevent them from concentrating their whole strength on fleets.[15]

What this signified was that henceforth the modern struggle for world power would come to be driven by the images of a British nightmare. And these were the dreaded insights:

1. Britain feared most of all the possible emergence of a 'heartland' or 'pivot' as the nave of a land-fastness, impregnable behind bastions of ice, moated by uninviting shores, and towering in the midst of a continental space traversed by an extensive network of transportation – a chilling dream of Cossacks at a gallop, bullet trains and shadowy Huns blazing the highways of Central Asia. The earliest formulation of Mackinder's plan was the product of Britain's inveterate enmity towards Russia rather than a warning issued directly against Germany: it was in the plains of Russia that the heartland was initially identified.

After World War I, as Germany became the cynosure of international checkmating, Mackinder, in a successive version of the original 1904 article, updated his theory in keeping with British imperial designs by shifting the pivot along a southwestern trajectory, from the steppes of Siberia down to a nondescript midpoint along the great fault line that divides the West from the East, and which later came to coincide with the Churchillian 'iron curtain' separating Eastern from Western Europe. This virtual boundary may be imagined as a meridian issuing from the shores of the Red Sea, which meets the Black Sea by way of Palestine and shoots through the Balkans and the Baltic, all the way north to Murmansk in Russia (see Figure 1.1). Conceptually, the 'fault line' is the great divide that roughly sets Muslim Arabs in the south and Orthodox Slavs in the North, apart from the Modern Europeans in the West.

The fault line ideally bisects the heartland, which is located within Eurasia. The heartland is the islands' island; Mackinder's motto thus intimated that 'whoever rules the heart-land, rules the world island; whoever rules the world island, rules the world.'[16] In the northwest this came to mean that *if Germany would find ways of bridging the fault line by cementing the technological strength of the European West with the geographical immensity of the East via Russia, she would become the unconquerable head of the dreaded fortress looking over the Eurasian heartland.*

2.  The immediate revelation of such a nightmare was that no forces were to be spared to obstruct political let alone military coalitions of any form across the heartland, beginning with the plausible Russo-German alliance. And this Britain could best achieve by marshaling a league of sister islands, which she could dispose against Eurasia as a besieging crescent of Sea Powers. Excepting the Japanese trump, sea-power is Anglo-Saxon through and through; all the challenging isles listed by Mackinder are emanations of Britain herself: from America, with the addition of Canada, all the way round to Australia, including New Zealand – the empire's white dominions.

3.  Should Europe, the Near East, and Central Asia have been capable of coalescing into a solid confederation, their combined mineral, hydric, and natural resources (oil, grain, steel, water, lumber, and so on) would have afforded this enormous Eurasian League a defensive advantage such as would have nullified any prolonged blockade of the Sea Powers. Eurasia could then resist a British embargo *à outrance*.

4.  From this it followed that such a wealth of resources on the heartland could have been naturally channeled, in the face of overt naval aggression, to the launch of a defensive Eurasian fleet. The combined

Map by Sergei Domashenko and Jessica Graybill

*Figure 1.1*   Eurasia and the Fault Line

shield of land and sea forces from the continent against the crescent of maritime foes would have not only repulsed easily the onslaught from the sea, but in all likelihood ended with the utter defeat of the Sea Powers and their concomitant subjugation to the hypothetical joint command of the heartland.

5. The sudden appearance of the Prussian Reich had turned this Eurasian chimera into a tangible eventuality: this time the menace was *real*; the great enemy could come into being through a genial amalgam of Russian vitality and German sophistication. *The Eurasian Embrace is the consummation of a Russo-German political, military and spiritual fusion.* Against such a fusion, Mackinder seemed to suggest, Britain would have found herself powerless in the long run.

6. Hence the strategy of Britain became crystal clear: in order to deter the emergence of this threatening rival on the heartland, *she would have no alternative but to encircle the heartland in a permanent siege.* This would be effected by driving wedges (the bridgeheads) in the vital nodes of the continental body. In such areas the land armies could be trapped in perennial warfare, and their generals would be so engrossed by the exertion as to deflect their attention from the keen urgency to arm a Eurasian fleet and drive out the foreign (seafaring) aggressor.

The remarkable character of this piece, aside from its fastidious prescience, was its openly aggressive tenor. Though it was written in the shade of a Russian menace, its reasoning seemed to suggest that Britain had to favor the line of least resistance, and single out Germany as the proximate adversary because: (1) the Reich was the dynamic half of the Russo-German threat, and, (2) it could be surrounded and blockaded by an entente of neighboring parties with somewhat greater ease, hence Britain's forthcoming rapprochement with Russia, her traditional antagonist.

Naturally, such warming of Anglo-Russian relations led to no permanent settlement of the Eurasian question, nor was it its purpose to do so: the issue, overwhelming as it was from the British standpoint had to be tackled one bridgehead at a time; the détente with Russia served as a mere prelude to a general stratagem seeking the destruction of Germany. Britain could not, and possibly did not wish to foresee the unfathomable costs that she, and the world at large, would have to incur in order to accomplish this stratagem, but the empire took its chances nonetheless.

The evidence that the destruction of Germany became Britain's chief objective after 1900 is provided by the elaborate diplomatic activity that she would weave to provoke the world war, as will be recounted in the subsequent sections of this chapter.

In fact, it is one of the tenets of Anglo-American historiographical catechism that Germany had always been the incorrigible aggressor of the Pax Britannica.

The rhetoric prevailing in Germany in the first decade of the twentieth century about *Einkreisung* (encirclement) and the consequent popular appeal to wage a 'righteous defensive war' to break out of this 'encirclement,' accompanied by the irresponsible magniloquence of the military-industrial and imperial cliques led by Wilhelm II, as well as the drunken claims of so many nationalists about 'Germany's historical mission' and her 'duty to wage war,'[17] have all been summarily singled out as so many definitive and screaming proofs of Germany's indisputable guilt for triggering the first world conflict. But these meager elements prove nothing other than the malign influence of Germany's archaic nationalism and the utter confusion amongst her rulers as to the country's immediate strategic imperatives: stacked against the lucid analysis of Mackinder, which contemplated already in 1904 a massive pre-emptive strike against threatening rivals in Eurasia, German bombast shrank into insignificance: a prolonged world confrontation could have never been the idea of an isolated, and also inexperienced, German government. *In Mackinder's paper there was little if any indication that Germany was going to attack.*

Rather, Germany's boisterousness was no more than a heartening cry in the face of uncertainty. Nervous rather than cocky, the Reich prepared for war with stage fright, cheering itself up, cursing its good fortune, and damning everything, specially the day it had started gambling its fate on the grand chessboard. Undoubtedly, if left to herself, Germany would have never made the first move and opened the hostilities: she had too much to lose. Germany had to be driven to it. In truth, her sole concrete goal, had Britain kept out of Europe, never went beyond the wish to consolidate a 'Middle-European Empire of the German Nation', that is, an *ante diem* German-led European customs union, severed from Russia, and such an arrangement was something England could cohabit with.[18]

Five years after the end of World War I, a US Senator, Robert Owen, would undertake a deep, dispassionate study of the war's origins and present his finding to the American people on December 18, 1923: the several claims of Allied propaganda, namely that the Entente had to fight (1) to thwart the Kaiser's plan to dominate the world by force, (2) to make the world safe for democracy, and (3) to defend American ideals, Owen construed respectively as 'false', 'ludicrous', and 'untrue'.[19] He found that:

Neither the Russian or the French government was really believed that the German government intended aggressive war on them but the military preparedness of Germany and the bombast of some of its chauvinists laid a convenient but false foundation for the French and British propaganda that the German leaders had plotted the brutal military conquest of the world...In 1914 Germany had no reason for war, no terra irredenta, no revenge and knew that a general European war might easily destroy its merchant marine, its commerce, both of which were rapidly expanding, and cause the loss of its colonies.[20]

The Germans were new to the heady breeze of world success – their imperial tenure had yet to harden into maturity – but with their British enemies it was a different story.

The last thing Britain would want to do at this early stage was to give any inkling to the public, the enemy, or potential allies, of her desire to strangle Germany in a permanent siege. Instead, in public she set out to treat her nascent antagonism to the Reich as if it boiled down to a mere matter of business: the British thus affected the irked demeanor of jealous proprietors rushing to defend their commercial interests against the provocation of the German upstart.

This justification was a full-fledged travesty, though it appears still to be the explanation favored by the historians of the victorious West.[21]

*Yet in fact, the deep worry and restlessness caused by the German unknown amongst the stewards of the British empire marked an epochal divide in the overall strategy of Britain. By 1904, as revealed by her pattern of alliances, Britain appeared to have resolved for the all-out encirclement of the heartland, and the phenomenal, if half-blind, growth of Germany during the last two decades of the twentieth century provided her with the occasion.*

From the beginning Britain was the aggressor, not Germany.

Years later, in 1916, as Wilhelm brooded over the unspeakable butchery at the front, he whimpered in a letter he sent the mother of a fallen officer that he had never wanted *this* war, by which he meant a massacre of global magnitude. 'This is exactly right,' rejoined the British Prime Minister, Lloyd George, in a public response to the Kaiser's lament, 'The emperor Wilhelm did not want *this* war. He wanted another war, one that would have allowed him to dispatch France and Russia in two months. We were the ones that wanted *this* war, as it is being fought, and we shall conduct it to victory.'[22]

Britain's – and later on America's – drive to conquest was foreshadowed unmistakably by Mackinder's cursory yet almost oracular mention of the several bridgeheads that the Sea Powers needed to graft unto the heartland to draw out its armies in a deliberate sequence of separate clashes. To isolate each conflict, the targeted territorial portion had to be severed from its adjacent district, and bled white by prolonged strife waged in the name of political, religious, or ethnic diversity. Thus the Anglo-Americans have always acted: in Europe by spinning everybody against Germany (1904–45); in the Near East, by jamming Israel in the heart of the Arab world (1917–present); in the Far East, by planting thorns in the side of China: Korea, Vietnam, and Taiwan (1950–present); in Central Asia by destabilizing the entire region into tribal warfare with the help of Pakistan to prevent the Caspian seaboard from gravitating into the Russian sphere of influence (1979–present).

Most importantly, in such trying games of conquest, results might never be expected to take shape quickly, but might take a matter of weeks, months or even decades. Imperial stratagems are protracted affairs. The captains of world aggression measure their achievements, or failures, on a timescale whose unit is the generation. It is within such a frame that the incubation of Nazism should be gauged: it was a long and elaborate plan to eliminate the possibility of German hegemony over the continent. And the stewards of the empire took their time.

### The blood of the Romanovs and the encirclement of Germany

Germany and England prepared for war; the former looking forward to a limited engagement, the latter to an all-out siege. In 1898, the German Reich began to expand the Imperial Navy in earnest; by 1906, it had the second-biggest fleet in the world. In 1900–02, Britain shifted her strategic focus away form the outmoded anti-Russian intrigues in Central Asia, and the petty African jealousies versus France, and narrowed it on the progressive encirclement of Germany, with a view to directing upon her at the propitious moment the first, northwestern land-bridge of the comprehensive attack.

In 1904, by diplomacy, Britain drew France closer – according to the deal, or the *Entente Cordiale*, as it came to be known: to the tricolore went Morocco: Egypt to the Union Jack.[23]

In March, Helmuth von Moltke, the commander in chief of the Germany army, who would later bear the blame for losing the war after the first collapse on the River Marne (September 1914, discussed below), fearing the coming tempest, noted: 'No one has any idea what thunderstorms are forming above us; instead of preparing in solemn earnestness for the serious times ahead the nation is tearing itself to pieces.'[24]

In July of 1904, after four girls, a boy – an heir, the Czarevich Alexi was finally born to the Romanovs, Nicholas and Alexandra. The doctors noticed suspicious bleeding from the infant's navel, but the matter was promptly dismissed. One year later, to the month, Alexei suffered the first bout of what was, to the terror of his mother and father, diagnosed as hemophilia. 'Since the blood would not clot, the slightest cut endangered his life.'[25] Conventional medicine was powerless against the disease.

Six months prior to the Czarevich's first hemorrhage, in January 1905, Russia witnessed her first and last spontaneous, popular uprising: it was not led by self-styled 'irreconcilable atheists' like the Communist Trotsky, who would have joined the ebullient flow shortly thereafter,[26] but by a priest, pope Gapon. Protesting food shortages, low wages, and tyranny, thousands marching behind the pope reached the Winter Palace, to be shot at and dispersed by Cossacks and police officers: the day was remembered as 'Bloody Sunday.' There followed strikes and mounting tension. The Czar made concessions; the St. Petersburg Soviet (Russian for 'Council') came into existence as the spontaneous institutional embodiment of the local interests of the community, along with the emperor's reluctant assent to the formation of an advisory body, the Duma.

Throughout the year, in this ambiguous intermission of illusory reform, many future leading revolutionaries partook in the fervor of the newly founded Soviet, but their agitation was repressed: the Czar had indeed bluffed, and many such disturbers of the imperial peace were arrested and sent to Siberia, whence, one by one, they would all escape. Russia had been shaken within. Without, a few months after the popular sedition, she was beaten in Korea and Manchuria by Japan in a distant colonial dispute. The defeat was unprecedented.

In the midst of the Russian debacle Wilhelm, at last, attempted the Eurasian rapprochement; in July 1905 he lured the Czar to Björkö, on the Gulf of Finland, and succeeded in obtaining the approval of Nicholas to a treaty, whereby (1) the two powers were bound to mutual support in the case of war, and (2) Russia committed herself to informing France of the agreement with a view of involving the latter in the alliance.[27]

But as the Germans failed to grasp until the very last that Great Britain was orchestrating a monumental siege against them – the ultimate political misjudgment that would spell the ruin of Germany – a late alliance with Russia could not be concluded. Probably, by 1905 it was too late. Indeed, when Germany could have tied Russia to herself by accepting Russian securities (that is, extending her loans), as the occasion arose in 1887, piqued by Russia's economic antagonism, she had refused. The financial interests of France, and to a lesser extent Britain, had moved in at once to advance the money, and thereby fastened resolutely the fate of the Russian empire to their imperial policies.

Bismarck had merely toyed with Russia; he had never bound her to Germany, as he ought to have done. The Eurasian embrace could have only come into being through a German composition of Austrian and Russian ambitions in *Mitteleuropa*, with or without France. This was at heart the Central Powers' geopolitical mission, as a counter to the Sea Powers' forthcoming siege; in that, from Bismarck to Bethmann-Hollweg, the last pre-war Reich chancellor, they failed utterly. There lay the seeds of Europe's past and present dissolution.

The treaty of Björkö was never ratified. Upon returning home, Nicholas was severely dressed down by his ministers, who sobered him up by recalling the Czar to his commitments vis-à-vis France, which in turn, after having been informed of Nicholas's disquieting escapade, vetoed categorically any participation in an entente with the Reich – it seemed that Wilhelm had forgotten that the French were 'hopeless'. So Nicholas retracted and the Kaiser protested vehemently, but in vain, for by September it was all over. If deep Anglo-French money and German obtuseness had alienated Russia from an understanding with the Reich, likewise time-honored and intense Franco-Russian military cooperation definitively impeded any belated German wish to remedy the irremediable; the Germans had missed their opportunity, long before Björkö.[28]

In October 1905, the Czar recorded in his diary his first encounter with a 'Man of God.' Rasputin had landed in St. Petersburg. The circumstances surrounding his introduction in the imperial circle are still obscure, but between this first meeting and 1907, Rasputin must have been summoned to court during one of the Czarevich's hemophiliac attacks, and brought it to a miraculous end.[29] By touch and prayer, the Siberian healer alone could keep the Romanov heir alive. Alexandra, thanking the heavens for the auspicious appearance of this wandering monk, took him in as the spiritual guide, and let his unquestioned ascendancy grow upon her. The Czarina was in Rasputin's thrall, as the Czar was in hers. Thus the fate of the Russian empire fell into the hands of a peasant magus.

On Britain's agenda, after France came Russia: the *Entente Cordiale* (*à deux*) with France became the Triple Entente of Britain, France and Russia. In 1907, the mastermind of Germany's entanglement in the first world conflict, Lord Grey, Britain's Foreign Secretary, negotiated with Russia a partition of Iran in exchange for Afghanistan and the surrender of Tibet. 'The Great Game [in the East] had seemingly been brought to an end'[30] and a war on two fronts predisposed against Germany.

Meanwhile, the naval race continued. Between 1907 and 1909 Britain invited Germany twice to agree to a general curtailment of construction, provided that Britain was assured numerical superiority in this respect. Twice Germany refused: France and Russia might as well have been permitted to enjoin the Reich to limit its own land forces, quipped Wilhelm.[31] And he added:

> We simply *are* Central Europe and it is quite natural that other and smaller nations tend toward us. To this the British object because it absolutely knocks to pieces their theory of the Balance of Power, i.e. their desire to play off one European power against another at their own pleasure, and because it will lead to the establishment of a united continent.[32]

The premise was, from Germany's angle, correct, but the inference erroneous: again, Britain had been fatally underestimated. Germany counter-proposed twice in 1909: first, in April, the diplomats of the Wilhelmstrasse* suggested that the parties seal a naval convention, provided that Britain acquiesced to a 'benevolent neutrality' in case of Germany's engagement in a continental war. In other words, the Reich demanded that Britain play the role of the passive spectator; second, in December, the Germans offered anew to trade a limitation of tonnage for British neutrality and the agreement on fixed naval ratios. Twice Britain refused. And what was more, she resolved to scale up production so as to assemble two Dreadnoughts, Britain's new, much perfected destroyers, for every German warship.

One last overture was made to Russia in 1911 during the parleys at Potsdam, which had been officially scheduled to deal with the penetration of German capital in the Middle East, and lasted several months: Germany declared herself willing to rein in Austria's intrigues in Eastern Europe if Russia proved amenable to withdrawing her support from an eventual hostile policy instigated by Britain against Germany.

The Kaiser obtained a stretch of railway in Mesopotamia – the other, broken, tracts of Germany's long-sighted and formidable blueprint were bartered away to Britain and France – but no guarantee of neutrality on the part of Russia.

---

\*   The domicile of Germany's Reich Chancellery and ministerial offices; by metonymy it came to indicate the German Foreign Ministry.

Presently the margin for additional diplomatic maneuvering was exhausted. From this time onward Europe was on the path to war. The more the Kaiser had tardily sought to weaken the Triple Entente, the more Britain strengthened it: in 1912 Britain signed a secret naval convention with France, and the latter did likewise with Russia. Secretly, unbeknownst to the Houses and most ministers, Lord Grey of the Foreign Office exchanged with Cambon, the French ambassador in London, a series of letters in which, on the basis of classified military conventions drafted by the General Staff of both countries, Britain, in case of war, pledged intervention on the side of France.[33]

In these days, the strategists of Germany's General Staff were at work rehearsing and fine-tuning the Schlieffen Plan.[*] This plan had been drawn up in 1905, and, after 1906, modified by Schlieffen's successor, the younger Helmuth von Moltke, the nephew of the victorious general at Sedan in 1871.

The plan aimed at settling the war with a single, potent, blow. Schlieffen assumed that Germany would be engaged on two fronts: France to the West, Russia to the East; the former having to be annihilated before the latter could mobilize. Any fighting of extended duration, which would have predictably drained the embattled and resource-poor Reich, was to be avoided, and replaced instead by a stubborn resistance in the East, and a stationary contingent facing France, to make room for the pearl of the plan: 'a great wheeling wing going through Holland and Belgium and coming down on the flank and rear of the French armies by passing west of Paris.'[34]

The British had intelligence of the plan, down to its minute details: 'unbeknown to anyone in Berlin, [the Schlieffen Plan] had come into the possession of the French army in 1906, thanks to a traitor bought for sixty thousand francs.'[35] Indeed, Belgium was going to provide the cornerstone of Britain's diplomatic pretext for the commencement of hostilities.

Britain counted on Germany's inevitable violation of Belgian neutrality as soon as Moltke was to launch the Schlieffen blitzkrieg. Already, in 1906, the British General Staff, with the full logistical, and secret, cooperation of its Belgian counterpart, was involved in simulated maneuvers across Belgium featuring the deployment of a British Expeditionary Force on the continent – which, indeed, would have been regularly fielded in August 1914 under the command of Sir John French to aid the French armies against Germany's Parisian offensive. The public was never informed of such plans.[36]

---

[*]   After Count von Schlieffen, chief of the General Staff from 1891 to 1905.

From then on (1911–14) the series of crises had been almost uninterrupted:[37] incidents in North Africa, intrigue and tugs-of-war in the Balkans, warnings, defiance, and counter-warnings from all sides.

By the spring of 1914 the Entente was ready to ambush the Germans. On May 29, 1914, Edward House, President Wilson's chief advisor from Texas and America's *éminence grise* behind the Anglo-American imperial covenant, reported from Europe: 'Whenever England consents, France and Russia will close in on Germany and Austria'.[38]

## The 'useful idiots' of Sarajevo

Now, with an excuse or an 'incident,' one merely had to ignite this great and patiently amassed bonfire of pent-up hostility in the heart of Europe. What was wanting for sparking a war was a timely 'act of terror.' And a terrorist to effect it. It was rather easily found in the inconspicuous figure of a Serb student by the name of Gavrilo Princip. The occasion? Sarajevo.

On June 28, 1914, the legitimate heir to the Hapsburg throne, Archduke Ferdinand, and his consort Sophie descended on an official visit to the new province's capital.

As a retaliatory act against Austria's 1908 single-handed annexation of Bosnia-Herzegovina, which the Serbs had claimed for themselves, Cabrinovic, abetted by Grabez – two militants of a secret Pan-Serbian organization suggestively called 'The Black Hand', whose motto was 'Union or Death!' – hurled a bomb at the vehicle carrying their Royal Highnesses, and missed.

The bomb went off and wounded a few passers-by. The carriage moved on, and the visit proceeded as scheduled.[39] When the reception at the town hall came to an end, the Archduke and his wife boarded the car anew; suddenly Gavrilo Princip, the third party to the commando, came swinging to the right side of the vehicle; as he approached he fired at Ferdinand and his wife and killed both.

At the time, all three 'terrorists' were not even 20 years old.

The inciting incident that would have triggered the imbricate system of alliances and eventually dragged their signatories into battle had happened, at last.

This was an instance of terrorism: namely, a deed of violence, which, at best, was devoid of any appreciable political gain or motive, and at worst, as it elicited a far bloodier reprisal, was entirely deleterious to the terrorists themselves. An act of terror generally takes the form of a spectacular feat of devastation capable of rippling waves of public indignation, and accordingly provides the adversarial faction(s) with the pretext for commencing war. Recruiting terrorists never seems a problem: these appear at the basic level to be a loose collection of desperadoes, who end up being easily trained, provisioned, and oriented by the undercover intelligence services of the home country.

Thus, on the face of it, a senseless crime; in substance, a political gambit orchestrated elsewhere. Where? The covert role of Serbian intelligence in casting the three teenage students for the assassination was widely acknowledged, but 'the real director of the conspiracy had been Russia's military attaché, Colonel Victor Artamanov, who had told [the chiefs of Serb intelligence] in the early stages: 'Go ahead. If attacked you will not stand alone.'[40]

In general, the art of terror entails the (state's) underground promotion of a fractious grouping: say, an 'ethnic army of liberation,' or a radical militia, whose vanguard – the expendable fringe – numbers so many Princips as are readied for gaol or the gallows. Meanwhile the higher levels of this conspiratorial franchise feature a mix of intelligence officers in charge of disinformation, organization and cover-up, and hired 'consultants' – themselves intelligence officers 'on loan' from other state agencies, foreign and otherwise, or former soldiers of fortune, whose expertise runs the gamut of recruitment, financial shuffle, subversive methods and like techniques of destabilization.

In the simplest configurations, the subterranean instruction of the terrorist 'cell' by the state's secret services is part of a maneuver aimed at implicating this phantom 'organization' into a more or less spectacular act of sabotage. Sabotage either against the state itself, or against the 'targeted enemy', that is, a nation whose ruling clans are to be antagonized by the terrorist recruits in the name of ethnic or religious rivalry. In the first case, while the wounded government in the vengeful heat of retaliation 'clamps down on the terrorists,' a variety of prearranged ends, all congruent in point of social control and surveillance, is swiftly implemented.[*]

---

[*]   This seems to be the stable pattern of terrorist activity throughout the twentieth century, from the plot of the Black Hand in Sarajevo to the political assassinations carried out by European revolutionary cells in the 1970s (for instance, the Meinhof gang in Germany, or the Red Brigades and their various counterparts of the extreme Right in Italy. By striking panic among the population, Italian terrorist squads progressively fomented a state of collective psychosis, which came to be perceived popularly as 'the strategy of tension' of Italy's 'deviated secret services', and which ultimately corroborated the grip on the country of then tottering US-backed Christian-Democrat mafia), up to the carnage perpetrated by the Islamist Front in Algeria (1992), and the recent lurking 'threat' of Bin Laden's Al-Qaeda – a true 'Godsend' for America's imperial Establishment (as known, the evanescent Bin Laden and his lieutenants are from the start an invention of the CIA).

Sarajevo's example was a 'standard terrorist act' of the second kind; in fact, it did not fail to achieve all the objectives expected from such enterprise, namely, to (1) bring Germany into the war by way of Austria, the enemy of Russia, who in turn protected Serbia; (2) advance the cause of Serbia by harnessing her to the chariot of the Triple Entente; (3) sacrifice the material perpetrators by condemning them to imprisonment and capital execution; and (4) keep well hidden from historical memory the identity of the plot's *commanditaires*.

Gavrilo Princip was the first of a long sequence of 'patsies,' 'pawns,' or 'useful idiots,'[41] whose individually unflattering but politically expeditious task is to bring to a head decisions matured beforehand by the Elder Statesmen. Many such 'useful idiots' will be encountered in this narrative in connection with significant episodes: Felix Youssoupov[*] (the agony of Rasputin, 1916), Anton von Arco-Valley[†] (the shooting of Kurt Eisner, 1919), Oltwig von Hirschfeld, Heinrich Tillesen and Heinrich Schultz (the attempted assassination, 1920, and final dispatch of Erzberger, 1921[‡]), Erwin Kern, Hermann Fischer and Ernst von Salomon (the trio behind the death of Rathenau, 1922[**]), Martin van der Lubbe[††] (the Reichstag fire, 1933), and Alexei Nikolaev[‡‡] (the killing of Kirov, which triggered the anti-Troskyist purge, 1934).

## Besieging Germany

In the summer of 1914, Germany stood behind Austria, Russia behind Serbia. British diplomacy could now entrap both: the ally and the enemy alike.

On July 6, Britain's Foreign Secretary, Lord Grey, informed the German ambassador that Russia was yet unprepared to intervene, and that Britain had no binding obligation vis-à-vis either Russia or France: a deliberate lie.[42]

Two days later, the British Foreign Minister assured the Russians that, according to 'very reliable military sources', the Germans were rapidly conveying divisions to the East, and that the situation looked upon the Reich with disfavor: an even bigger lie.[43]

All such deceiving signals issued by the Foreign Office in cross-directions behind closed doors were accompanied in Britain by a public show of

---

[*]   See below, p. 28.
[†]   Chapter 2, p. 55.
[‡]   Chapter 3, pp. 96, 112.
[**]  Chapter 3, pp. 118–19.
[††]  Chapter 5, pp. 208–9.
[‡‡]  Chapter 5, pp. 245–6.

phoney attempts at mediation in the name of peace, initiated with an eye to deceiving the multitudes.[44] Britain had always been careful to spin the international tangle so as to drive the opponent in the position of the assailant, and reserve for herself the role of the peace-loving defender. This was a psychological artifice tailored for mass seduction, and the Germans had no knowledge or understanding of such tricks.

Austria issued the ultimatum to Serbia: a comprehensive injunction to annihilate any form of anti-Austrian propaganda in Serbia, and to open a formal investigation into the assassination, in which delegates of the Austrian empire were to partake.[45] Serbia accepted all points but the last one, which, in a theatrical diplomatic counter-move, she offered to submit to international arbitration at the international court of The Hague. Clearly, she had been instructed to turn down the ultimatum by her patrons, who had been waiting a long time for this moment: already on July 25, the British Treasury began printing special Notes, non-convertible into gold, marked for war expenses.[46]

The war against Serbia into which Austria was deliberately incited by the ruinous intrigues of Serbia at the instigation of Russia *was a trap* into which Austria fell, not knowing it was fomented by Russia to create a pretext of general mobilization and war and to make Austria and Germany appear to the world as the willful originators of the great conflict.[47]

The armies of Franz Josef prepared the attack against Serbia, Wilhelm was overjoyed – heedless of the consequences. After one more round of perfunctory diplomatic waltzes between London, Berlin, Paris, and St. Petersburg, Austria-Hungary went ahead and on July 28 bombarded Belgrade. The war had begun.

Russia, secretly goaded by France, who promised her support,[48] mobilized along her western frontier, and the German generals nervously awaited the green light from the Kaiser to launch the Schlieffen offensive. Pourtalès, the German ambassador in St. Petersburg, rushed to the foreign ministry, and asked its head, Sazanov, to halt the Russian mobilization. He implored three times. And when the Russian minister refused for the last time, Pourtalès handed him, with a trembling hand, Germany's declaration of war. It happened on August 1.

However, upon hearing the news of Russia's massing of troops, Wilhelm somewhat broke out of his stupor and commiseratively brought himself to acknowledge the truth of the situation:

In this way the stupidity and clumsiness of our ally is turned into a noose. So the celebrated encirclement of Germany has finally become an accomplished fact...The net has suddenly been closed over our heads, and the purely *anti-German policy* which England has been scornfully pursuing all over the world has won the most spectacular victory which we have proved powerless to prevent while they, having got us despite our struggles all alone into the net through our loyalty to Austria, proceed to throttle our political and economic existence. A magnificent achievement which even those for whom it means disaster are bound to admire.[49]

Indeed it was, and for such a disaster, the Germans had only themselves to blame.

At the outbreak of war, Rasputin brooded: 'No more stars in the sky...An ocean of tears...Our Motherland has never suffered a martyrdom as that which awaits us...Russia will drown in her own blood.'[50]

In yet another sudden *coup de théâtre*, as Germany prepared to unleash the onslaught on the Western Front, Britain issued one last cunning call for peace by informing the soon-to-be-warring parties that she was willing to guarantee her neutrality and provide assurances that France would not join the side of Russia in an eventual Russo-German conflict, provided Germany did not attack France. This last mischievous prank, which Wilhelm, with diabolical perseverance, took for a British accolade to his eastern invasion, nearly caused the already shaken Chief of the German General Staff, Helmuth von Moltke, to break down: the German mobilization was complete; the armies had to push forth, he insisted.

Pressured by the general, the German government as a brash counter-bargain demanded no less than the acquisition of two French fortresses (Toul and Verdun) as 'security' for France's neutrality. France naturally rejected the offer. On August 3, Germany declared war upon France. Staggering from one pitfall to another, Germany had turned herself into the world aggressor. Abel Ferry, the French Under-Secretary of State, wrote in his notebook: 'The web was spun and Germany entered it like a great buzzing fly.'[51]

Finally, as her turn was next, Britain came full circle: knowing that Moltke was ready to thrust Ludendorff's fusiliers through Belgium, the British government solemnly declared that it could not possibly tolerate the violation of Belgium's neutrality; it then professed its unconditional adherence to peace, and, shameless, assured the public that it had signed no secret compacts with either France or Russia.[52]

When the Schlieffen Plan was enacted and the Reich's armies crossed into Flanders, Britain sent Germany an ultimatum, which she knew the

Reich would have ignored; but to avoid surprises (it expired at midnight) the British Cabinet exploited the time lag between London and Berlin, and shortened the waiting by an hour.

Sitting in silence round a large circular table covered with a neat green cloth, the ministers furtively eyed the big clock until it struck 11:00. Twenty minutes later Winston Churchill, the First Lord of the Admiralty, walked into the hall to inform his colleagues that a telegram had been dispatched across the empire summoning the Royal Fleet to begin operations.[53]

And where did the summer of 1914 find Adolf Hitler? At 25, already a veteran of Viennese flophouses – one amongst many bourgeois *ratés* – young Hitler joined, with a profound sense of deliverance and expectancy a Bavarian regiment with the rank of private. A man that enlists, said Pasternak, is not a happy man:

> A few day later I was wearing the tunic which I was not to doff until nearly six years later. For me, as for every German, there now began the greatest and most unforgettable time of my early existence. Compared to the events of this gigantic struggle, everything past receded to shallow nothingness.[54]

Hitler would fight on the Western Front and earn several decorations for bravery.

The German March through Belgium and the initial clashes against the French, who lost 300,000 men in less than two weeks, were entirely successful for the Germans. Victory seemed assured. Paris was only 30 miles away. But then the Schlieffen Plan went awry. Moltke, believing victory certain, sent two corps to the East, for 'the Russians,' as he explained in his memoirs a year later, 'had been able to invade East Prussia quicker than expected, and before we had been able to achieve a decisive victory against the Anglo-French armies'; he then concluded: 'I recognize that this was a mistake, and one that we would pay for at the Marne.'[55]

What really came to pass in the course of the offensive on the River Marne, during which Moltke allegedly lost his wits, and communication broke down among the several corps of the otherwise unfaltering German war machine, remains a mystery. But for one reason or another, Germany, overwhelmed by her rivals to a degree far deeper than expected, ultimately faced the impossibility of carrying out the Schlieffen Plan as rapidly as she had originally intended in the unfamiliar environment of modern industrial warfare.

The German advance in the West came to a halt, and

in the next few months the French tried to dislodge the Germans from their positions. Neither was able to make any headway against the firepower of the other. A succession of futile efforts to outflank each other's position merely succeeded in bringing the ends of the front to the English Channel on one extreme and to Switzerland on the other. In spite of millions of casualties, this line, from the sea to the mountains across the fair face of France, remained almost unchanged for over three years.[56]

Caught between the wedge of trench warfare in the West and the stifling naval blockade – which Britain was tightening all around the Fatherland, including neutral outlets, thus violating international conventions – the Germans tried to break free. Neither Germany's resistance on the home front, nor the unrestricted submarine warfare of 1917 would slacken the siege.

As for the eastern theater of war, things in late summer had gone badly for the Reich: the front was broken.

General Hindenburg was 'a retired officer, whose principal occupation for some years had been sitting at a marble-topped table outside a café in Hamburg, making puddles with his beer'. 'To the amusement of young German military cadets who regarded him as half-witted, [he explained] that these puddles were the Masurian Lakes in which he would drown the enemy if he ever had the good fortune to command an army in that area'.[57] He had volunteered to serve in the army at the outbreak of hostilities, but was subsequently rejected. Yet his good fortune came nonetheless when Headquarters suddenly recalled him on account of his profound familiarity with the terrain upon which combat was being waged against the Russians.

Hindenburg reversed the outcome of the engagement swiftly; accompanied by Ludendorff, who had been dispatched by Moltke from Belgium to eastern Prussia (now northeastern Poland) to assist the German counter-offensive, he directed during September 8–15 the battle of the Masurian Lakes and its last stages were fought on Russian soil.

Whether other generals – German and Russian, the former for sagacity, the latter for incompetence – should have claimed authorship for such victories[58] is a matter of minimal import if weighed against the implacable German successes in the East throughout 1915. Though it had failed to cause a complete collapse of the enemy, Germany's eastern advance so alarmed the Russians that Czar Nicholas II assumed the superior command of the armed forces.

The Germans were flattered by the panicked resolution.

In June of 1916, running westward from the Romanian frontier, the Russian General Brusilov, who had become a hero for smashing the Austrian armies in Galicia at the inception of the war, attempted one massive offensive against the Austro-German forces. Over the course of three months, the outcome of the onslaught remained indecisive, but the losses were unheard of: the Central Powers lost 600,000 men, and the Russians over 1 million.

### Conjuring Lenin

Suddenly, in 1916 the Russian rulers began to ask themselves: what did they stand to gain from all this? What was there to be had from Germany's enmity? That Russia could occasionally teach the Hapsburg emperor Franz Josef a lesson in those eastern European and Balkan stockades that Russians and Austrians were vying to control? At these costs?

Though Britain might claim that she was fighting for her empire, France for her honor, and Germany for her survival, what could Russia advance to justify the holocaust? That such misgivings would have soon preyed on the Russians had been a predictable affair in London; for that reason in 1915 the Czar had been promised by the British, as a tempting bait, Costantinople and the Straits (yet to be wrested from Turkey) – no less facile was the suspicion in St. Petersburg that the British promise was empty, which indeed it was.

The year 1916, despite the human losses and the resurfacing restlessness of the hinterland (starvation and political agitation), had not witnessed catastrophic setbacks for the Russian army; *therefore from a position of relative strength, Russia could afford to initiate parleys conducive to a separate peace with the Germans.* Rasputin certainly wanted peace, and if he did, so did Czarina Alexandra, who, with her husband away at the front, was left in charge of the internal affairs of Russia.

Rumors started to circulate to the effect that Alexandra, being a 'German' (her mother, Alice, a daughter of Queen Victoria, had married the Grand Duke of Hesse, Louis IV), was conspiring with German agents to surrender Russia wholesale to her enemy. 'Down with the German woman!,' the populace clamored.[59] Yet the Czarina was embroiled into something altogether different. 'That [Alexandra] became an instrument in the hands of men who sought to bring about a separate peace with Germany is probable.'[60] And Britain now had to make sure that such 'men' ceased this activity forthwith.

In December 1916, a cabal of blue-blooded rakes and shady bureaucrats lured Rasputin into an evening feast, accompanied by opera singing. In the midst of such merriment, the healer gulped down a poisoned drink that could have sucked the life out of a regiment. Manifesting no visible distress from the ingested bane, Rasputin, before he was given time to regain the live music show, was repeatedly shot, stabbed, and beaten into a pulp by the scion of one of Russia's most prestigious families, Prince Felix Youssoupov, with a violence that petrified his accomplices. These then rushed to throw the body of the healer, still breathing, into the icy waters of a canal. A transvestite since the age of twelve, bordello impersonator in drag and petulant libertine, Youssoupov had convinced himself, by 1916, that Rasputin, through his magnetic hold on the Czarina, was driving Russia to perdition.

On February 1, the *Daily Mail*, uniting its voice to the chorus of the Russian mob, rejoiced at the magus's death.[61]

To the Romanovs the healer had prophesied: 'If I die or you abandon me, you will lose your son and your throne within six months.'[62]

War debts: in 1916–17 Russia owed to Britain a sum that was roughly a third of her annual income,[63] which was more than what Britain owed the United States; and what Russia owed to France was half of what she owed to Britain. Identifying what party benefited from the Russian holocaust presents no difficulty: Britain obviously did. The conduct of the war in Russia was no more in the Czar's hands than in those of Rasputin: rather, orders were dictated by the British Treasury.[64] In Russia it was said at the time that 'England and France will fight to the last Russian man.'[65]

On January 12, 1917, Lord George Buchanan, British ambassador in St. Petersburg, conferring with the Czar, was informed by the latter that a peace conference, 'the final one,' was to be expected soon. Buchanan rejoined that the Czar should take after the British government, and draw into the Imperial Cabinet an exponent of the 'moderate Left' so as to reach the twofold objective of soothing social disquiet while pursuing the offensive against the Germans. The Czar did not seem to decipher the message, and reiterated his intention of seeking the peace with Wilhelm II. Veiling a threat, Buchanan alluded mysteriously to the possibility of revolution and dropped the hint that he had had foreknowledge, by a week, of Rasputin's assassination. Nicholas paid no heed.[66] Like his German counterparts, he could not fathom how determined Britain was to prevent any form of dialogue between Russia and Germany.

The British ambassador in Russia himself was at the center of the scheme to overthrow the czar if he ever should lose his stomach for war...[To that end, he] had gathered a coterie of wealthy bankers, liberal capitalists, conservative politicians, and disgruntled aristocrats.[67]

Violent strikes erupted in the Russian capital a month after the *entretien* between the Czar and Buchanan: the turmoil would turn into Russia's famed February Revolution. When it exploded, Buchanan was 'out of the office,' on holiday: safely withdrawn from the scene of a tumult that he had contributed to kindle.

Undismayed at the thought of eventually facing 70 German divisions wheeling into the Western Front, the British War Cabinet instead received the news with satisfaction; Lloyd George, the Prime Minister, exclaimed: 'One of England's goals had been achieved!' Likewise, sharing Britain's expectant mood, US President Woodrow Wilson in an address to Congress acclaimed on April 2, 1917, the deposition of the Czar, speaking of 'those marvelous and comforting events' in Russia, where 'autocracy' had finally been struck down.[68]

This was truly absurd: in the midst of an unprecedented world war, the Allied public was to believe that its rulers were worried about the 'democratic temperature' of Russia far more than they were about the risk of losing the Russian ally altogether! Yet the public should have known that of all scenarios it was a Russo-German peace that the Anglo-American clubs feared the most, and that it was precisely to avoid this occurrence that the war was being waged. And the Liberal press was surely not going to enlighten its readers on the matter. Thankfully for these clubs, in 1917 Eurasia miscarried: Russia and Germany were, yet again, successfully kept separated.

The overthrow of the Czar was no minor achievement. Indeed it must have been part of a far wider scheme that had its significant counterpart in a parallel mission conducted on the other side of the Russo-German border (the 'fault line' proper) from a network connecting Berlin to the Scandinavian capitals. Working assiduously against the Eurasian embrace was another exceptional set of capable individuals. Their leader, Alexander Israel Helphand (1867–1924), better known by his sobriquet, Parvus, had started his modern adventure by joining the ranks of the revolutionaries. From Odessa, his Russian hometown, he had gravitated naturally towards the German-speaking world, and after earning a doctoral degree in economics at the University of Basle, he had become politically active on the side of the German Socialists. Around 1910, disillusioned by organized socialism's impotence, and having fallen foul of Germany's Leftist elite, Parvus had disappeared from the chronicles. Inconspicuous and modest, he had left Berlin...and resurfaced in Istanbul, transformed into a rich, extravagant merchant with a knack for international intrigue.

That Helphand, on account of his multiple talents – as an energetic, but disenchanted polyglot, deeply acquainted with the whole wide spectrum of Socialist agitation, and wielding a fluent pen and economic sense – must have been inducted into some form of 'network' can scarcely be doubted. However, other than a passing allusion of the German Minister Brockdorff-Rantzau to the nondescript 'powers ranged behind Helphand' (see below), historical documentation affords no material wherewith the contours of such an organization may be drawn with precision.

When the war came, Parvus was operative. In Istanbul, by guaranteeing a steady supply of armaments and war materials to the government of the Young Turks, he appeared to have played a significant role in securing Turkey's entrance in the war on the side of Germany. Thereafter, as Russia began to suffer the vertiginous reversal on the Eastern Front and the Entente powers feared that the Czar might have renounced the fight, he was selected for the top mission to Germany.

Effortlessly, he managed to come into immediate contact with the highest levels of the German Foreign Ministry. His proposal: to invite the gentlemen of the Wilhelmstrasse to finance and supervise the creation of a destabilizing movement within Russia that could have toppled the czarist regime and brought about a separate peace with the Reich. On the face of it, this plan seemed a variation on the theme of Eurasian cooperation. But the intent was the opposite.

Parvus would have later claimed that he had maneuvered the Germans to foment a general revolutionary wave in Russia, which would have hopefully spilled over to Germany and the rest of Europe, in the name of his long cherished dream: the international Socialist alliance of the world. His sincerity in this regard is hard to assess. The German diplomats, on the other hand, were convinced that *they* were spinning the game; they had naturally no curiosity for revolutionary experiments, and sought to 'use' Parvus's 'Red' network of Communist agitprops as 'a means of exerting pressure on the czar, and thus speeding diplomatic negotiations.'[69]

It was precisely these separate negotiations between the German and Russian empires that Parvus was expected to sabotage. Until the last stages of the Bolshevik seizure of power, Helphand's chief assignment would be to steer the Germans so as to ruin their chances of communication with the czarist empire. While the hired assassins of Rasputin and the British ambassador, Buchanan, supported by a team of professional spies sent from London, burned the bridges from St. Petersburg to Germany, Parvus et al. burned those from Berlin to Russia. The task facing Parvus would be greatly facilitated by the helpless naivety of his special interlocutor within the German Foreign Ministry: Count Brockdorff-Rantzau, German ambassador in Copenhagen.

The Danish capital, along with Stockholm, was selected as Parvus's Scandinavian base of intrigue between Berlin and Russia. From there Helphand ran an active and most profitable import-export company, as well as a research institute and its associated newsletter, as fronts for his circle of espionage. Suspended, like most aldermen of the Reich, between patronizing benevolence and provincial presumption, Brockdorff-Rantzau – a superb expression of Germany's despairing political ineptitude – left posterity a record of his thoughts as he stepped into the trap that Parvus laid out for him:

> It *might perhaps* be risky to want to use the powers ranged behind Helphand, but it would *certainly* be our admission of our own weaknesses if we were to refuse their services out of fear of not being able to *direct* them...Those who do not understand the sign of our times will never understand which way we are heading or what is at stake in this movement.[70]

He, least of all, understood the sign of the times. It is evident from this important passage that Brockdorff, and the German Foreign Ministry in general, was incapable of identifying the nature of 'these powers ranged behind Helphand', and that such a fact naturally caused Brockdorff anxiety. Given the stakes, a lacuna of such depth was, from the German standpoint, absolutely inexcusable. Nonetheless, stubbornly refusing to fathom the danger, and certainly encouraged by more than a few of his superiors, Brockdorff persevered, convinced that he was the master of the game. Little did the German diplomat perceive that, having succumbed entirely to the seduction of the tireless Parvus, he was in fact allowing these enigmatic 'powers' backing Helphand to undermine the life-saving (for Germany) peace talks with Russia, and quicken thereby the disintegration of the German imperial establishment.

The message conveyed in the 1915 memoranda penned by Parvus for Brockdorff and the Foreign Ministry was unequivocal: czarist Russia was the irredeemable enemy of the Reich. Parvus admonished the Germans that, if they resolved to sign a contract with Nicholas, the likely outcome would have been the formation in Russia of a reactionary government, which, on the strength of its repossessed armies (freed from the war engagement), might have circumvented the agreement and turned once more against the Reich. *The party they should have wagered on, Parvus insisted, was that of the Bolsheviks,* a determined, if somewhat meager, group bent on peace, and the resolute enemy of Czar Nicholas. Lenin was the name of their leader. Brockdorff was thoroughly captivated by the plausibility of such utterly deceptive arguments.[71]

In 1915 Germany started to pay. In two years the Reich allegedly devoted over nine tons of gold to the subversive effort against the Czar.[72] Parvus provided the business channels and the banking connections for remitting the sums, which were devoted to fitting the revolutionary militia and funding a sweeping propaganda apparatus, *Pravda* being the most notorious organ originating from the gift. After such profuse immobilization of resources, the Germans waited impatiently for these to bear fruit, but nothing stirred. Parvus pacified the *Herren* at once and assured them that the investment would yield. He then promised: they should have expected a quake on January 9, 1916; 'the organization,' he told them, had scheduled a mass strike on the eleventh anniversary of 'Bloody Sunday.'

Then, on January 9, the czarist regime recorded without particular alarm isolated acts of insurgency and sabotage, the sinking of a warship, and scattered hiatuses caused by labor demonstrations, which were all brought under control by the police without great difficulty. Von Jagow, the German Foreign Minister, did not conceal his irritation, and a few other, more alert diplomats, grew suspicious and begged their chief to terminate the intrigue with Parvus. But Brockdorff vouched passionately for him, and the top generals were not willing to discard the Bolshevik trump just yet: agog, they kept on dreaming of a merciless peace and vast annexations in the East – the granary of Ukraine, the Baltic seaboard, and indemnities in gold.

However, it was evident by then that, contrary to Parvus's tendentious claims, czarist Russia, despite the country's innumerable infirmities – such as her large debt, retarded industrial adoption, rural misery, or the unspeakable squalor of her city slums – was not a bankrupt concern, a rotten fruit about to decompose, but rather an economic unit with enormous manufacturing potential that was already exporting a third of the world's grain.[73]

Notwithstanding, the Germans, blinded by greed, resolved to wait a day longer, and continued to pay until, from the East, the signal was given in February, merely two months after the death of Rasputin.

The February Revolution of 1917 was never a German affair, and least of all a Bolshevik production. Lenin, when it erupted, was caged like a lion in Zurich, while Trotsky – the other protagonist of the subsequent November takeover – was agitating in Manhattan. The latter, on the basis of several testimonies, would expatiate in his lengthy history of the revolution on the presumed genuineness ('namelessness') of the February uprising, which he reconstructed in his narrative as the authentic proletarian prelude to the forthcoming Bolshevik rumble.[74] It was nothing of the sort.

In February 1917, as the mob was cued once again to take to the streets, seven of Russia's foremost generals and several garrisons of the capital forsook the Czar, who, bereft of military authority, was *de facto* forced to abdicate.[75] After placing themselves at the front of the protesting cohorts, the mutinous officers headed for the Duma – Russia's surrogate State Council – where they formally surrendered the 'revolutionary' will of the masses to the bourgeois exponents of the assembly, that is, to the Liberal conspirators (and interlocutors of Buchanan), with whom they (the seditious military) colluded.

The Liberals, in turn, were ready to hand over the scepter of power to Nicholas's brother, the Grand Duke Michael. But the Grand Duke did not want anything short of popular investiture: he thus refused. So the Liberals alone were saddled with the burden of command. There was no paradox in this ramshackle devolution of power, as Trotsky would claim – as power bounced from the masses back to royalty by way of the soldiery and the conniving bourgeoisie. The February Revolution was in truth a misbegotten Liberal putsch, designed to retain the Russian armies on the Eastern Front under the aegis of a constitutional regent. But as the royalty withdrew, the matter nested uncomfortably in the widening gulf formed by the uneasy coupling of bourgeois with Socialist leaders. The equilibrium was precarious, to say the least.

For the time being, out of the putschist Duma was carved the nucleus of Russia's new executive: the Provisional Government. It was oddly complemented by the resurrected Soviet, which was rapidly attracting Russia's motley wing of revolutionaries: the Bolsheviks were itching to capture it.

So at long last the time came to implement Parvus's masterstroke: in April 1917, with the agreement of the German authorities, he secured Lenin's passage through Germany in an armored train, from Switzerland to Finland, and thence to St. Petersburg.

Once alighted from the car, Lenin proclaimed his 'April Theses' (the Bolshevik program): peace with no annexations; no parliamentary republic, but a republic of Soviets; confiscation of all landed estates and the establishment of 'Model Farms'; one bank under the control of the Soviets.

Under German, and thus treasonous, sponsorship, Lenin returned; so did the Menshevik Plekhanov, who would support the pro-war Provisional Government, escorted to Russia by British destroyers.[76] En route from New York with an American passport, Trotsky, after being intercepted aboard a Norwegian liner and detained in Halifax by Canadian naval officers on legitimate suspicion of traitorous and subversive activities (that is, to conspire against Russia's new Provisional Government, a fighting member of the Entente), was inexplicably released upon orders from London and allowed in May to join his comrades in the Russian capital.[77]

Admittedly, this was for Britain the delicate piece of the great siege. The czarist regime had proved too unreliable and weak to play along the British directives since 1914. Before the dreaded (by Britain) prospect of a separate peace with the Reich materialized, the Czar was successfully ousted from the stage. This was the dynamics behind the February Revolution. Then Britain contemplated three possible courses of action:

1. The continuation of the February plot. According to its original architecture, the plan envisaged the creation of a Liberal Cabinet, buttressed by the Soviet (a parliament of sorts), and formally bound to the Royal House. The February episode was, in short, designed to implement at once Britain's political structure – a constitutional monarchy – in Russia. Evidently, the grafting was impracticable, but the coup, by repatriating pro-war Marxists like Plekhanov and other Mensheviks, who could be counted on to legitimate in the Soviet the Cabinet's protracted war effort, and by salvaging the royal superstition in the figure of a Romanov, was not lacking in brilliance. In fact, *Allied power, beginning with the United States on March 9, had promptly accorded the new government diplomatic recognition.* It remained to be seen whether the Provisional Government, even if shorn of imperial galloons, because of Grand Duke Michael's defection, could foster the cohesion necessary to pursue the war.

2. If the Provisional Government failed, the Bolshevik card could have been played, for which Britain could also thank Parvus and the unwittingly self-serving dealings of the German rulers, and attempt the social experiment in *terra nova*: for no one, despite the April Theses, could clearly foresee what sort of regime Lenin and his associates would have erected if they were to take power.

This second eventuality evidently presented a higher degree of risk, because the Bolsheviks had vowed to withdraw Russia from the conflict. The advantage of their takeover, however, resided in their congenital aversion to the German dynastic spirit, which was capitalist and imperialist.

Colonel House, privy councilor of US President Wilson and always a pragmatic supporter of Bolshevism, offered in late 1917 the rationale for the West's conspiratorial endorsement of the otherwise repugnant (to Western Liberalism) Bolshevik Communism:

> It is often overlooked that the Russian revolution, inspired as if by deep hatred of autocracy, contains within it…great motives of serious danger to German domination: [for example], anti-capitalist feeling, which would be fully as intense, or more intense, against German capitalism…[78]

Though the Leninists would have made peace – to withdraw the peasants and workers from the front – so went the British reasoning, imperial Germans and Bolshevized Russians could hardly fuse into the embrace: 'A treaty means nothing,' Lenin would tell his followers after signing the peace with Germany in March 1918, 'there is no justice that can exist between two classes.'[79]

In years to come, through financial manipulation – especially military aid – and fine diplomacy, one could hope to instigate a vast Communist state against the Reich: the path was indeed fraught with mortal hazards, but well worth the walk.

3. Again, were Russia's Provisional Government to fall, a coalition of 'White,' czarist, counter-revolutionary generals could plunge Russia into civil war and tame the country thereby. A meeting of like minds between Russian Whites and the *Reichswehr* generals, greatly facilitated by spiritual and class affinity, would have become, in time, an embrace.

Of the three possible developments, this last was for Britain the least desirable. And if it came to pass, no choice was left to the Sea Powers other than attempting to bribe the Whites away from the German embrace, which in turn carried even more risk than the Bolshevik option.

In the eight months of uncertainty between February and October 1917, the Provisional Government legislated much, but effected little. Populist barrister Kerensky assumed the role of prime minister; thereupon he rushed to the front to enhearten the faltering troops. In June, the Russian army ventured one last sally against the Austrians, who were forthwith adjoined by supporting divisions of Germans. At the sight of the German *Feldgrau* (field-gray) uniforms, the Russians threw down their shields and fled in panic. In July the Bolsheviks bungled a putsch. The Provisional Government responded with firmness. Lenin disappeared in Finland; Trotsky and other Communist ringleaders were thrown in jail. Informed of the Parvus connection, Kerensky was about to arraign the Leninst gang on charges of treason and conspiracy as 'German agents,' but as the White counter-insurgency (the czarist loyalists) appeared to stir in several districts, he refrained from persecuting the Bolsheviks and let them loose instead. Desperate logic brought him to think he could use the Red agitators as allies against czarist counter-revolutionaries.

Meanwhile, the Sea Powers deemed it was time to switch program, drop Kerensky, and opt for second best (Bolshevism).

Germany and 'the powers ranged behind Helphand' had paid in the West, and evidence suggests that Wall Street paid in the East: behind the humanitarian facade of a 'Red Cross War Council,' American capitalists had been conveying sums earmarked for the Russian Revolution. J. P. Morgan associates and interests linked to the Federal Reserve Board of New York fronted such a Council, which paid Kerensky after May 1917, and according to an article of the *Washington Post* (February 2, 1918), successively shifted the funding to the Bolshevik cause.[80] In September of 1917,

> Buchanan, the British ambassador, told his government that the Bolsheviks 'alone have a definite political program and are a compact minority...If the Government are not strong enough to put down the Bolsheviks by force, at the risk of breaking with the Soviet, the only alternative will be a Bolshevist government.'[81]

One month later, the Bolsheviks, a fringe movement with no popular backing, which in May had run 'a poor third to the socialist parties,'[82] seized power without firing a shot.

> [On] the day of the revolution, the fashionable people were on the Nevsky Prospect* as usual, laughing together, and saying that the Bolshevik power would not last more than three days. Rich people in their carriages were scolding the soldiers, and the soldiers 'argued feebly, with embarrassed grins'.[83]

---

* St. Petersburg's main artery.

Five years of civil war lay ahead.

In March 1918, Bolshevik Russia signed a harsh peace with the German generals at Brest-Litovsk,[†] and, fulfilling the rapacity of these, ceded to them the Ukraine, the Baltics and gold. The Eastern Front was now quiet and the Reich divisions in the East could be rolled back to France...but the Sea Powers had acted with prudence.

As they soberly pondered over the scenarios outlined above and waited to see which would have come to a boil first, they took no chances, and jammed into the Western Front the American infantry. Not coincidentally, America formally joined the war, in April 1917, when the Russian front appeared to be creaking. 'The important fact was that Britain was close to defeat in April 1917, and on that basis the United States entered the war.'[84]

America's intervention to the side of Britain was effected rather adroitly. Pressured by the Germans to plead with Britain in order to make her desist from the illegal blockade of the Reich, the Americans refused. By doing so, they left Germany no option but to engage in unrestricted submarine warfare, which was officially declared on January 31, 1917. The anticipated sinking of American cargoes, which were profusely refurbishing the Allied military engagement, would have then yielded the suitable pretext to break off diplomatic relations with the German Reich, and in fine wage war against it. The spectacular precedent for the *casus belli* (to rouse the patriotic masses) had been previously engineered with the sinking of the British cruiser, the *Lusitania*, which was made to yaw deliberately into the maws of German submarines in May 1915.[85]

Germany had managed to delay America's intervention from 1915 to 1917. Submarines had been withheld from combat, apologies given and reparations paid, but [by 1917] time had run out.[86]

The sequence of events in flashes: on February 22 revolution broke out in Russia, the czar fell on March 2, Lenin's passage was scheduled for March 27, Trotsky was intercepted on April 1, President Wilson declared war on Germany on April 6 and Lenin shipped on the 9th, Trotsky disembarked at St. Petersburg on May 18, US Commander Pershing sailed for Europe on May 29, 1917. Russia and Germany signed the peace on March 3, 1918; thereafter American soldiers – build-up completed – reached the European shores in waves of 330,000 per month.[87] By November 1918 they numbered over 2 million.[88]

---

[†]   Now in Poland.

## The last days of America: from republic to truculent empire

By the last quarter of 1916, the Allies had become dependent upon the United States not only for supplies but also for financing.

And it was in 1917 that Britain, who was nearly bankrupting herself in the first onslaught against the heartland, gradually passed on the military command of the great siege to the far fitter and greener might – military and economic – of the United States. This was done with the understanding, however, that Britain, being the experienced player, always retained an exclusive right to the strategic command of this siege.

By accepting the responsibility and committing her troops to the European fight, America took on consciously the duty of an imperial power. This was an ominous relay between the two English-speaking islands, and a decision that would have radically disfigured the complexion of America, and eventually that of the world at large.

The United States was not prepared to take over control of the sea herself, therefore she could not allow the defeat of Britain – nor did she trust Germany in the least. America's elites were Anglophile, and the American public, who had lent millions of dollars to Britain, saw the world through the lens of British propaganda: if the boom of inflation and prosperity sparked by the enormous Entente purchase of war *matériel* had collapsed because of an Allied defeat, the money loaned in Wall Street would have been as good as gone. All these factors demanded that the United States, beckoned by Britain, throw her imperial lot in with the vicissitudes of the heartland.[89]

The days of a great confederation of free cities in free states, the reverence due to Virginian gentlemen of letters, the reconciliation with Nature, and the pioneering spirit of the communes, that is, all the American treasures that could have afforded Old Europe and the world a kingdom of peace were abandoned remorselessly. A studied hunger for more time and space, and the irresponsible pursuit of bellicose vainglory – the late trademarks of the British empire– were being purchased by America at the expense of her youth. In the United States, the mood changed.

In 1914 90 percent of the American people had been against joining the war;[90] presently such temperance had to make room for aggressiveness: it was soldiers and cheering crowds that the US needed. The clubs saw to it that the shift was a fast one, *through fear*. Armaments were scaled up and punitive expeditions were hatched in the midst of 'a popular fear of aggression from without.'[91] Imbued with 'a spirit of particularism...and animosity between contrasted groups of persons,' America turned *patriotic*.[92] Now it was all about the gung-ho 'love for one's country,' which was not love at all, but the readied call to hurt the 'enemy,' whoever he was, wherever he lurked, anyhow, any time. Riding the wave of this induced, collective dementia, the citizen came to see himself and his folks as victims of plots, which were rumored to feed his credulity and strengthen within him the new idolatry of the red, white, and blue, 'American Pride,' and the 'Star Spangled Banner'.[93]

> From 1917 the public was fed fantastic stories dressed up as news, such as the 'discovery' that the Germans had secret gun emplacements in the United States ready to bombard New York and Washington. This alarming 'news' had been planted by the Allies as early as October 1914 and had succeeded in finding its way into presidential intelligence reports...[94]

Beyond the appeal to geopolitical likeness, cultural kindred, the threat of German submarine warfare, and the jumbo loans to the Entente, there was one more means whereby the United States could be baited to share the burden of the great siege, and this was Palestine.

Within the British Cabinet, the Prime Minister, Herbert Asquith, and the War Minister, Earl Kitchener, did not wish to fragment the European offensive for the sake of a Middle Eastern adventure. But the vanguard of imperial stalwarts, who were ranged behind the charismatic figure of Lord Alfred Milner, a former colonial officer turned oligarchical mastermind, thought otherwise.[95]

From the *Manchester Guardian*, in November 1915, recruits of the so-called Kindergarten – Milner's club, also known as the Round Table – intimated 'that "the whole future of the British Empire as a Sea Empire" depended upon Palestine becoming a buffer state inhabited "by an intensely patriotic race".'[96] Indeed, Palestine was 'the key missing link' that joined together the limbs of the British empire in a continuum stretching from the Atlantic to the middle of the Pacific.[97]

If World War I represented in fact the beginning of the heartland's great besiegement, the Milner faction thought it appropriate to seize the occasion and thrust, with the opening assault, two wedges at once: one at each extremity of the fault line. For that, America could be involved with troops in the Eurasian north (versus Germany), and the political campaigning of her Zionist lobby in the Middle Eastern south (versus the Arabs; see Figure

1.1, p. 11). But Asquith and Kitchener were not gazing that far. And the Kindergarten had no intention of letting the opportunity pass.

On 6 June, 1916, Kitchener drowned in a 'providential' shipwreck on his way to Russia in a mine-laden sea.[98] Betrayed in a backroom conspiracy of the Liberal Party, Asquith fell, and on December 7, 1916, David Lloyd George became Prime Minister. Exponents of the Round Table were forthwith raised to several high posts, and the master himself, Milner, was made into the chief strategist of the War Cabinet. Thereupon British troops were embarked for the Middle East to fight the Turks.

On December 11, 1917, General Sir Edmund Allenby and his officers entered the Holy City of Jerusalem at the Jaffa Gate, on foot.[99]

By August 1918 the first act of the great northwestern siege was brought to a close. After Ludendorff's last great attack in the spring, the Allies, bolstered by American manpower, repelled the infiltration, and beat the influenza-ridden Germans back to the 'Hindenburg Line.' Germany realized that she could not hold out any longer. She capitulated, and the armistice was signed in November.

> By August of 1918 Germany had given her best, and it had not been adequate. The blockade and the rising tide of American manpower gave the German leaders the choice of surrender or complete economic and social upheaval. Without exception, led by the Junker military commanders, they chose surrender...Looking back on the military history of the First World War, it is clear that the whole war was a siege operation against Germany.[100]

Ten million dead had not been sufficient to break the country and bring it amongst the satellites of the Sea Powers. Germany had not yet been vanquished on her own soil. To make her suffer a crushing and final defeat within her confines – the second and final act of the northwestern siege (that is, World War II) – the British schemers of the interwar period would apply themselves for the next 20 years to enforcing vis-à-vis the defeated Reich an ambivalent policy mix of sanctions and foreign direct investment. In fact, the obverse of this underhanded policy concealed the clubs' peculiar intent, which was to revamp the military and economic establishment of Germany while waiting to identify the 'right' sort of political leadership that could have 'used' this new, refitted Reich to Britain's advantage. In brief, the scheme consisted in rearming the enemy of yesterday, and so conspiring as to plunge Germany in another battle, which would offer (1) the pretext to annihilate Germany finally, and (2) the chance to take possession of Germany's geopolitical position. To this complex feat of provocation, which featured the incubation of Nazi Führer Adolf Hitler as the extraordinary 'drummer' of an unrecognizable, orientalized* Germany, the remainder of the present narrative is devoted.

---

*   See Chapter 5, footnote on p. 243.

# 2  The Veblenian Prophecy

## From the Councils to Versailles by Way of Russian Fratricide, 1919–20

MEPHISTOPHELES: Faust, stab thine arm courageously, And bind thy soul that at some certain day Great Lucifer may claim as his own.

FAUST: Lo, Mephistophiles, for love of thee [*stabbing his arm*]. I cut mine arm, and with my proper blood assure my soul to be great Lucifer's...

MEPHISTOPHELES: But, Faustus, thou must write it in manner of a deed of gift.

FAUST: Ay, so I will [*writes*]. But Mephistophile, my blood congeals and I can write no more.

MEPHISTOPHELES: I'll fetch thee fire to dissolve it straight.

FAUST: What might the staying of my blood portend? Is it unwilling I should write this bill? [*re-enter Mephistophiles with a chafer of coals*].

MEPHISTOPHELES: Here's fire; come, Faustus, set it on.

Christopher Marlowe, Dr. Faustus, Sc. V (58–91).[1]

### The impossible revolution

Germany surrendered in November 1918, Kaiser William II abdicated and the Reich imploded. From the interior of Germany's disarrayed society emerged for an instant, to demand 'change,' a diffuse and overall pacific procession of the underclass and its Bohemian phalanx – anarchists, intellectuals and artists. This manifestation was promptly quashed by the German elite's weakened yet spiritually intact military appendage with the tacit approval of the propertied middle class. The German armies marched back home to strangle the sedition were spearheaded by 'creatures of steel': young and merciless storm-troopers forged by war that commingled with ghostly formations of unyielding veterans in a novel alliance blessed by divinities theretofore unnamed. The country witnessed the birth of the so-called Conservative Revolution: a movement issued from the fathomless depths of Germanhood, drunk with the ecstasy of war, yet ferociously hostile to the modern pursuit of gain, as well as to the archaisms of royalty and hereditary nobility. Nazism was a very special offshoot of this 'revival from the deep,' which ramified in a tangled web of associations, parties, and secret orders – of such a revival writer Ernst Jünger, also a war veteran, became the celebrated troubadour. In one such order, lance corporal Hitler was inducted in late 1919. Meanwhile the Allies cleared the Russian stage of the last vestiges of czardom: actively funding the nihilistic dictatorship of the Bolsheviks, they allowed the latter to buy off the bulk of Nicholas's army and defeat the czarist White generals in Russia's civil massacre of 1919–22. Simultaneously, at Versailles, the Anglo-Americans laid the groundwork for the incubation of Russia's forthcoming enemy: by imposing reparations that did not seriously cut into the income of Germany's privileged classes, they induced a process of rehabilitation of the Reich's reactionary clans, with the secret intention of fostering a radical, anti-Bolshevik force, which could have been catapulted against the Russian ramparts and smashed thereafter in a repeated two-front global engagement. The only thinker of the age possessing the clairvoyant lucidity to assess and comprehend these transformations was the American Thorstein Veblen: after having examined the late development of the German Reich, he predicted its rout and, more importantly, he alone became alive to the reawakening of a peculiar sort of religious furor, which the war seemed to have unleashed all across Germany. Already in 1915, he depicted what was in fact an amazing sketch that foreboded the haranguing Führer; furthermore, in 1920, after the infamous Peace Treaty ratified in Versailles failed to carry out the dispositions which Veblen had thought necessary for disarming Germany and turning her into a peaceable partner of the Anglo-Saxon commonwealths, he prophesied by 20 years the forthcoming armageddon between Bolshevik Russia and Reactionary Germany (1941). This prophecy, uttered in a review of J. M. Keynes's best-selling book on the Parisian Peace Treaty, stands possibly as Political Economy's most extraordinary document – a testimony of the highest genius – and as the lasting and screaming accusation of the horrendous plot that was being hatched by the British during the six months of the Peace Conference following World War I.

Germany never experienced revolution. Much would be made of the alleged rift between Left and Right; many would account it as one of Hitler's ingredients for success. But the chasm dividing the kept from the proletarian classes was more apparent than real: the future clashes between the Nazi Brownshirts and the Red squads of the Communist Party were much more the effect of foreign intrusion into German politics than the result of a congenital antagonism gnawing at the foundations of the German order, as will be shown in Chapter 4. This is to say that, as for most of the 'democratic' West, Imperial Germany was overall a stable and cohesive society, and that whatever its sources of class contention and inequality, these were never articulated creatively and effectively by a true revolutionary movement. There was no true will to sedition in Germany before World War I, nor would there be afterwards. For six strange months between the surrender of November 1918 and the proclamation of the Weimar Republic in June of 1919, Germany would burn with the fever that follows a change of regime: a period of semi-benign protest, unorganized, which came soon to be marred by the interference of intellectual independents, private militias, foreign intrigue, and finished by the returning armies, which cleansed the isolated uprising in blood. This was the relatively unknown interval of the German Councils, after which Hitler came of political age.

We now turn to the narrative of the German revolution that was not meant to be – it never was for reasons that Veblen made manifest after he dissected the body of Europe's Labor movement at the end of the nineteenth century: on the basis of these early observations, which he coupled with his thorough study of the doomed Reich, Veblen would later have found himself ideally situated to cast the shocking prophecy of 1920.

*   *   *

At the turn of the twentieth century, save a few obdurate militants, orthodox Socialists in the industrialized West were giving up on 'Revolution.'

The working masses were somewhat less discontented with the room and board with which the establishment was providing them – the billeted quarters were, relatively speaking, growing somewhat larger, and the bill of fare more varied every year. *Panem et circenses* (the bread line and the movies) had contributed their satisfactory share to the capitalists' comprehensive effort to tame the unrest of the masses.

In Germany, by 1912, when the SPD (Sozalistische Partei Deutschlands) – the Socialist Party of Germany, the world's largest and most organized – became the leading political concern of the country with 34.8 percent of all votes in 1912,[2] the laborers' acquired distaste for the winds of change had found its most mature expression in August Bebel, the unchallenged Napoleon of German Socialism, who characterized Revolution as 'the great crashing mess' (*der grosse Kladderadatsch*).[3]

Plainly, the working ants of the German anthill harbored no keen desire to revolt, nor were their French and British counterparts any more willing to shake their own tree, so to speak. They merely wished to compromise and, like the polychrome crew of a whaling ship, went no further than chaffering with the captains over their due share.

But in principle, all Socialists were internationalists – brothers across borders – and pacifists. Then the war came, and the great cosmopolitan assembly of the world's Socialists, the so-called International, which had been poised to receive no less an award than the Nobel Prize for *peace*, was torn asunder by the pull of chauvinistic rage.[4]

In August 1914 the parliamentary faction of the SPD voted unanimously for the War Credits. In England and France, the proletarians likewise rallied behind the flag and readied themselves to slaughter their homologues athwart the firing line. The Kaiser in a felicitous rhetorical turn proclaimed that he no longer knew parties, but only Germans.

'This is betrayal!,' decried the sparse chieftains of the intransigent Left, who held the gentrified leaders of the SPD responsible for reneging on the internationalist and humane bent of the party. The revolution, they said, was being sacrificed by a posse of factory foremen-turned-bourgeois, whose co-opted role was that of shaping the workforce into a contented fixture of the capitalist stronghold.

And the denunciation was not far off the mark. More precisely the alliance of elite and proletarians, sealed in the name of patriotic superstition, was a peculiar consummation of conservatism. The kept class, headed by the emperor in Germany, and by the bureaucratic and business elite in the Liberal commonwealths, being in great measure 'sheltered from the stress of economic exigencies which prevail in any modern, highly organized industrial community,' was (and still is) by nature the standard-bearer of all those socially retarded (that is, barbarian) practices that breed in the shaded precinct of privilege and hereditary *fainéantise*: for example, sports, finance, and war.[5]

> The abjectly poor, and all those persons whose energies are entirely absorbed by the struggle for daily sustenance, are conservative because they cannot afford the effort of taking thought for the day after tomorrow; just as the highly prosperous are conservative because they have small occasion to be discontented with the situation as it stands to-day.[6]

Lodged in the urban slum, where the exercise of prevarication and brutality fashioned the mind, and suffering therefore deprivation and spiritual debilitation, the underclass was made to acquire great fluency in the language of invidious rivalry and clannish ferocity.

It cost the Junkers no time to clothe the masses in *Feldgrau*, the field-gray color of the Reich's uniforms. French, British, American, and Nipponese ardor in reaching the war front was likewise remarkable – less so that of the

Slavs, whose patriotic fitness, let alone business sensitivity, appeared to be never quite attuned to the governing passions of the times.

Exposed since birth to the violence of the ghetto, the German underclass was further 'sterilized' by the repeated practice of trade unionism, whose bargaining routines, by making membership exclusive, that is, 'scarce',[7] habituated the members to secure privileges at the expense of their fellow laborers: a business-savvy blue-collar chauvinist always made a 'good' army private.

The prolonged discipline of warlike stimulation and business chicane turned the laborer into a foolproof instrument of the Western hierarchies, and the great expectations of the revolutionaries into much regrettable disappointment. Veblen in 1907 noted:

> That part of the population that has adhered to the socialist ideals has also grown more patriotic and more loyal, and the leaders and keepers of socialist opinion have shared in the growth of chauvinism with the rest of the German people...[The SPD leaders] aver that they stand for national aggrandizement first and for international comity second...They are now as much, if not more in touch with the ideas of English Liberalism, than with those of Revolutionary Marxism.[8]

Barring the rashes caused by a few slipshod anarchists, Germany, in fact, possessed no rebellious core threatening to break out and consume her wholesale. Certainly the SPD suffered trouble and profound divisiveness over the war: in 1917, the splinter grouping of the 'Independents' seceded from the party's main body to form the USPD,* while strikes intermittently roiled the industrial performance of the Socialist electors throughout the conflict. Doubtless, dissent existed. But all in all, like Russia'a peasant wasteland, Germany's enchanted forest, tenanted by most obedient laborers, haughty bourgeois, and blind aristocrats, was easily domitable terrain – from within as well as from without. Tractable human material, despite the country's professed devotion to war, which was itself, quite aptly, a somnambulistic enterprise.

September 29, 1918, appears to be the point of attack in the script of Germany's so-called 'Revolution of 1918–19.'[9]

On September 13, Austria sent out an SOS; two days later, the defensive line of the Central Powers collapsed: the Allies had pierced the Balkan

---

* _Unabhängige Sozialistische Partei Deutschlands_, the Independent Socialist Party of Germany.

ramparts and forced the capitulation of Bulgaria. On the same day, the Allies in the West attacked the Hindenburg line on a wide front. It was Germany's last fortified line of defense and it began to give way.

For three years, Germany had been *de facto* ruled by her generals; by one in particular, Erich Ludendorff. It was he who contrived every spectacular attempt during the conflict to break loose from the siege: he launched the unrestricted submarine warfare, sent Lenin to Russia, foisted the 'predatory peace' on the Bolsheviks, and organized the last great assault of spring 1918. Presently, he was about to close the door on the Second Reich with another 'colossal' exploit.[10]

When he saw the Reich compromised, Ludendorff turned the unthinkable into a *fait accompli*: he ordered parliamentary democracy and took the SPD into the government. As he brought this about, he also made haste to inform the Kaiser and the Cabinet that the cause was lost, and urged that an armistice be sought with the Allies forthwith. 'So we have been lied to all these years!' howled the ministers. The emperor himself was quite incredulous, though no one could treasure the sentiment of a discredited mascot, least of all Ludendorff, who was taking aim to hit three targets with a single shot: (1) pacify the home front and soothe the Allies by setting up a parliamentary facade prior to the peace talks; (2) saddle the Socialists with the shame of defeat ('the poisoned gift' of command); and, most important, (3) save the army.

On October 5, the German public was finally apprised that it now had a parliamentary democracy under the Liberal Prince Max of Baden, and that as its very first act this government had addressed an immediate petition for peace and armistice to the American President.

On January 8, 1918, President Wilson had issued a loose platform for a new world order, the so-called Fourteen Points, based upon: transparent diplomacy, free trade and navigation, disarmament, and self-determination.

Between October 3 and 23, Wilson cabled the German Chancellery three notes, in which he demanded that the Reich (1) retreat from the occupied territories; (2) cease the U-boat war; and (3) force the Kaiser's abdication. Suddenly, on October 25, Ludendorff, on the basis of mixed information from the front, recanted it all: he hustled the Kaiser to break off the negotiations with Wilson and resume the fight; Wilhelm, and Germany, had had enough of the general: he was dismissed and replaced with General Groener, a logistics expert at the War Ministry. A chasm gaped in the foundations of the Reich.

Then the big mess came crashing down upon the Fatherland.

On Schilling Wharf, outside Wilhelmshaven, a corps of naval officers, in open defiance of the new government's orders, decided to launch the German flotilla, which throughout the war had lain at anchor and rusted by inanition, in a temerarious sortie against the archenemy, the Royal Navy – a mutiny, in short.

On October 30, 1918, the crews of the *Thüringen* and the *Helgoland* mutinied against their mutinous officers, in what amounted, in fact, to a pledge of allegiance on the sailors' part to the new government. The sea dogs' obstruction impeached the sortie. While the disobedient (to their immediate superiors), but law-abiding sailors were incarcerated, their shipmates of the Third Squadron staged a manifestation in Kiel protesting their incrimination. A lieutenant named Steinhäuser was sent to disperse the rally; facing non-compliance he ordered his platoon to fire on the protesters – 29 were mown down. But before the rest scattered, a sailor swung around, drew a pistol, aimed at Steinhäuser, and gunned him down. On November 3, 1918, it was Revolution in Germany.

On the morning of Monday, November 4, the sailors elected Soldiers' Councils (or Soviets),* disarmed their officers, armed themselves and ran up the red flag on their ships. The marines of the garrison declared their solidarity to the movement, and the dockers moved for a general strike.

> From the third day onwards it no longer took sailors to trigger off Revolution: it was spreading under its own impetus like a forest fire. As if by tacit agreement, the pattern everywhere was the same: the garrisons elected soldiers' councils, the workers elected workers' councils, the military authorities capitulated, surrendered or fled, the civil authorities, scared and cowed, recognized the new sovereignty of the workers' and soldiers' councils.[11]

After the officer caste, to which Germany had surrendered total command of herself even before the war, momentarily relinquished the helm with Ludendorff's dismissal, it was left, for a time, to the army's and the industry's rank and file to improvise in the rudderless nation a semblance of administrative emancipation: it irresistibly took the form of a 'council' – a spontaneous anarchoid life-form prone to jealous self-governance, whose ganglia fed off the associative limbs of the communal body: agriculture and artisanry.

It was 'wild' – chaotic, and scarcely representative – Soviets that Germany witnessed in these days: they were untamed by the suddenness of the

---

* The so-called *Räte* (sing. *Rat*), the German equivalent of 'Soviet.'

uprising, and the undeniable bullying of the underclass, which, as payback for years of resented regimentation, was avidly seeking to redress older torts and clamor its right to rule.

The aristocrats momentarily recoiled in their estates' subterranean corridors, while the bourgeois cast preoccupied glances from their windowsills. Von Bülow, the erstwhile chancellor of the Reich's apogee, looked on:

> In Berlin, on November 9, I witnessed the beginnings of a revolution... She was like an old hag, toothless and bald...I have never in my life seen anything more brutally vulgar than those straggling lines of tanks and lorries manned by drunken sailors and deserters...I have seldom witnessed anything so nauseating, so maddeningly revolting and base, as the spectacle of half-grown louts, tricked out with the red armlets of social democracy, who, in bands of several at a time, came creeping up behind any officer wearing the Iron Cross or the order *Pour le mérite*, to pin down his elbows at his side and tear off his epaulettes...[Quoting Napoleon] *Avec un bataillon on baleyerait toute cette canaille*\*...[12]

In less than two weeks Germany counted 15,000 of such soviets: they featured a simple hierarchical structure that was capped by an executive directorate of six members, the Council of the People's Commissars, led by SPD leader Friederich Ebert. Thus all decisions had in fact been remitted to a solid majority of non-revolutionary Socialists – overall, the uprising, at least in the beginning, was a pacific one. The fate of the 'Revolution' was in the hands of the SPD.

The 'mess' was not going to last long. But the pang of dissent of November 1918 was genuine: it appeared to have been unmarred by sooty conspiracies and Bolshevik agitation, whose exponents, by then grouped in the so-called Spartakus League, formed but a trifling minority of the movement. And yet the insurgents, most of them Socialists drawn from the proletariat, middle-class intelligentsia, and non-commissioned officers,[13] were now at a loss to make good of this exhilarating respite from the Junkers' *corvée*. Like his *confrère* in the Soviet of St. Petersburg in 1905, the Common Man of Germany's *Räterepublik* (Councils' Republic) of 1918 was meekly requesting benevolent stewardship from the top.

The rebellious lull was not going to last long because the workers controlled less than the soldiers commanded, which was nothing; and those with the keys to the financial network were obviously absent from

---

\*   'With a single battalion one could sweep all this rabble away.'

what turned out to be a convulsed village fair, overhung by unfavorable skies. Before these could so darken as to unleash a full-blown storm, a double betrayal was consummated at the Wilhelmstrasse: the aristocracy, in the guise of the army and the bureaucracy, agreed to throw the Kaiser overboard if the Socialists, in the name of 'order,' set out at once to smother the 'Revolution' – to betray, that is, blood of their own blood.

> The German revolution found an ignorant people and an official class of bureaucratic philistines. The people shouted for Socialism, yet they had no clear conception of what Socialism should be. They recognized their oppressors; they knew well enough what they did not want; but they had little idea of what they did want. The Social Democrats and the Trade Unions leaders were linked by blood and friendship with the representatives of the Monarchy and of capitalism, whose sins were their sins. They were satisfied with the juste milieu of the bourgeois; they had no faith in the doctrines they had proclaimed, no faith in the people who trusted them...They hated the revolution. Ebert had the courage to say so out right.[14]

On November 9, though the rattled Kaiser was still somewhat reluctant to dismount from the throne, the Chancellor Max von Baden issued a semi-mendacious announcement of Wilhelm's abdication. The emperor hesitated for a brief moment, then, fuming, he hurriedly boarded a train to Holland, wherefrom he would officially abdicate only three weeks later, and disappear from recorded memory. Thereafter, soon exhausted by the incipient intrigue, Prince Max washed his hands of the whole affair by nominating, unconstitutionally – for it was a prerogative of the emperor – the Socialist Fritz Ebert as Reich Chancellor, and fled to his domain on Lake Constance, never to be seen again.

It was during this time that, without knowing whether he represented a republic or an empire, Matthias Erzberger, a restless and notorious Catholic politico from Württemberg, accompanied by two officers and the German ambassador to Bulgaria, Count Obendorff, was sent as Governmental Representative on the Armistice Commission to the forest of Compiègne* to tender Germany's surrender to the Allies. Maréchal Foch, Erzberger's interlocutor, began to enumerate to the German legation what appeared to be the conditions of a *Diktat* rather than an armistice: evacuation of war zones; surrender of ports, war material, equipment, prisoners (without

---

*   Fifty miles north of Paris.

reciprocity), tonnage and vehicles; and annulment of the Soviet peace of Brest-Litovsk. General Hindenburg cabled Erzberger that for the sake of lifting the strangulating blockade the armistice had to be signed. Erzberger, a consummate haggler, succeeded in wresting from Foch a rebate on the weapons to be released and an extension on the evacuation deadline. The German signatures were affixed to the document of the armistice on November 11, 1918. The following day, upon his return to Germany, Erzberger was congratulated by Hindenburg and Groener on his performance.[15] World War I had formally come to an end.

When the news reached Adolf Hitler, he was recovering from temporary blindness at the military hospital of Pasewalk in Pomerania. After four years of unceasing activity on the western no-man's land, which he had zigzagged in a myriad of suicidal missions as *Meldegänger* (message courier), he was clouded by a blinding spray of mustard gas in Flanders during the last stages of the war. Upon learning from the hospital's chaplain of Erzberger's accomplishment, he despaired, and mused:

> Again, everything went black before my eyes; I tottered and groped my way back to the dormitory, threw myself on my bunk, and dug my burning head into my blanket and pillow...And so it had all been in vain. In vain all the sacrifices and privations; in vain the hunger and thirst of months which were often endless'...in vain the death of two millions who died...There followed terrible days and even worse nights – I knew all was lost. Only fools, liars and criminals could hope in the mercy of the enemy. In these nights hatred grew in me, hatred for those responsible for this deed.[16]

Now Fritz Ebert, the brand new Socialist chancellor, had to fulfill his half of the covenant with Groener and the army: he was to tame the Conciliar Movement, and lead it on, unawares, to the slaughterhouse. Meanwhile, the Councils' improvisation, performed with reckless underestimation of the forces of Reaction, was brought nonetheless to a higher pitch: when it first convened in Berlin on December 16, 1918, the First National Congress of the Workers' and Soldiers' Councils moved at once to reform the army: the supreme command, they proclaimed, was to rest with the People's commissars, disciplinary powers were to be wielded by the councils, insignia of rank abolished, and chiefs chosen by acclamation.

The generals could tolerate this circus no longer; Ebert and associates needed only to provide them with a pretext to suppress the show. On Christmas Eve, 1918, it was easily found by accusing, mendaciously, the

officious praetorian guard of the Revolution, the People's Naval Division
– a pell-mell but decently equipped aggregation of proletarian rebels in
arms – of foul play and conspiratorial subversion, and withholding its
pay accordingly. Violent confrontation ensued between the sailors and
the Socialist leaders. As Ebert refused to see its commander, the Division
occupied the Chancellery, thus offering the generals sufficient grounds
for the much desired military intervention. One such high officer at the
War Ministry, who, aside from Groener, promised Ebert immediate succor,
was General Kurt von Schleicher, a creature of shadows, who would haunt
henceforth the anguished *démarche* of German politics until the rise of
Nazism: incarnating despite himself the cursed fate of Germany, he would
rise to become Weimar's last chancellor.[*]

In the first clash that followed between regulars and Reds, the Reds, on
the brink of a scorching defeat, were suddenly rescued by swarms of popular
sympathy, which flooded the streets and held back the Reichswehr troops
from dealing the sailors the crushing blow. The rebels carried the day, and
got their pay; the number of dead remains unknown.

This was merely the prelude of the greater wave of repression that was
gathering at the gates of the German capital, and which would decide the
fate of the Revolution in the week of January 5–12, 1919.

On December 30, 1918, by further meiosis, The German Left (SPD),
through its 1917 filiation of the 'Independents,' spawned the extreme
nucleus of the KPD,[†] Germany's Communist Party, which did *not* at
first fashion itself after Lenin's dictatorial Bolshevik organization. Karl
Liebknecht and Rosa Luxemburg, who had drafted its manifesto, became
its icons.[17] Till the very end of parliamentary rule in 1933 the Communists
would antagonize the mother party (the SPD) for allegedly behaving as the
meretricious handmaiden of capitalism. Subsequently maneuvered from
Russia, the KPD would wage its Muscovite politics in an air of unreality,
and with such fractious obstinacy as to elicit the founded suspicion that
it came into being more as a tool of destabilization than as an organ of
proletarian representation. The KPD played no significant role in the
uprising of 1919.

In January the government finally acted: Ebert appointed his fellow
Socialist Noske commander in chief of elite squadrons of shock troops
(special forces) that had at long last returned from the front, loose gangs of
eternal lansquenets that showed no inclination to depose their weapons: the

---

[*]   See Chapter 4, pp. 196ff.
[†]   Kommunistische Partei Deutschlands.

Freikorps. For a Socialist tribune of 'the people' to preside over this sort of company had to have been a disquieting assignment, but Noske shrugged: 'It's all right by me,' he said, 'someone has got to be the bloodhound.'

The home front was now teeming with these marauding ghosts of the Thirty Years' War and the resurrected barbarian clans of Tacitus's *Germania*: splintered brigades of unshaven hunters – limbs of a single body blindly obedient to their fearless chief – were about to conquer the urban centers. 'Principes pro victoria pugnant, comites pro principe *(The chiefs fight for victory, but the retainers for the chief)*.'[18] The names of many such fearsome chieftains would inscribe themselves in the chronicles of the counter-revolution: Ehrhard ('The Consul'), von Epp, Reinhardt, von Stephani, Maercker, Pabst...

The Freikorps, recruited frantically at the end of the war and now numbering roughly 400,000 men, were unleashed upon Berlin and many other tumultuous German cities, which had seen the advent of Soviets. The so-called 'White' (that is, counter-revolutionary) repression was merciless. In Berlin, on the night of Jaunuary 15, Liebknecht and Luxemburg were knocked senseless with rifle butts and then shot in the head: they had had no part in the 'revolution', but their continual exposés on the KPD's press organ *Die rote Fahne* (*The Red Flag*) of Ebert's lurid compact with Quartermaster of the General Staff Groener had to cease. Good riddance even for Moscow, bent as it was on 'win[ning] dominant control...over the [newly formed Communist] Party,'[19] and purging it of its independent minds.

It was a new breed of men, 'slender, haggard...forged of steel,' that marched back home with a vengeance from the front.[20] Neither disconsolate monarchists nor rugged proletarians with nothing to come home to, these *Geächteten*, banished scavengers, who for the most part had once been part of the lettered bourgeoisie, had fallen prey to a different sentiment. It was as if the disintegration of the Reich's nobiliary scaffolding in November 1918 had uncorked a more ancient worship of the unfathomable idea of Germany.

> All of them were looking for something different...They still hadn't received the password. They foreboded this word; they would utter it, ashamed of its sound, tweak and eviscerate it with silent fear, and though they avoided it in the play of their various discussions, they always felt it hovering upon them. Eroded by time, mysterious, fascinating, intuited and not acknowledged, loved and not obeyed, the word radiated magic forces from the heart of deep darkness. The word was: *Germany*.[21]

Combat, 'the tempests of steel,' and the laceration of the Wilhelmine pretense had awakened a great many veterans to the exigency of building a new order. While they were convinced that Germany's Prussian humiliating past had to be repudiated entirely, the intellectual spokesmen of the Freikorps grappled uncomfortably with their middle-class heritage, whose custody of intellectual tradition they valued but whose philistinism they abhorred. In the course of numberless punitive raids conducted in the industrial slums, the White squadrons of the Freikorps surveyed the proles huddled in their feculent foyers and bunks with a blend of languor and excitable repulsion: the country was torn; to them this ghetto-humanity was one of aliens.

We marched in the suburbs, and from tranquil houses, elegant, ensconced in the foliage, cheers were echoed and flowers thrown at us. Many bourgeois were on the streets and waved at us, and some houses flew the flag. What hid behind those drawn blinds, behind those indifferent window panes, underneath which we passed haggard, exhausted, yet resolute, deserved, so we thought with conviction, our dedication. Here life had taken another course, reached another level; its intensity exuded an extreme sophistication that jarred with our rough jackboots and filthy hands. Our cupidity did not rise up to those houses, but they sheltered, we knew it, the fruits of a culture belonging to a century that had just run its course. The world of the bourgeois, the ideas created by the bourgeoisie, the worldly learning, personal freedom, pride in work, agility of the spirit: all of this was exposed to the assault of the bestialized masses and we stood as its defenders because it was irreplaceable...Yet it was we who fighting behind old banners saved the Fatherland from chaos. May God forgive us, that was our sin against the spirit. We thought of saving the citizen yet we saved the bourgeois.

Once even I went inside a proletarian dormhouse. I saw a room not larger than ten square feet, full of beds. Seven people, men, women, and children slept in that dump. Two women were lying in bed, each with a child; when we came in one of them burst out with a stridulous laugh and those that were loitering before the front door came streaming inside. The sergeant approached; swiftly, then, the woman lifted her blankets and gown, and a crackling erupted from her white buttocks. We startled back as the others doubled over in crass laughter, clapping their thighs, choked by guffaws; even the kids laughed: 'pigs!' would shout the women and children, and all of a sudden the room was full of screaming bodies; we backed up, slowly, until we found ourselves in the hallway again.[22]

Profiting from the middle class's apathy, the new lansquenets tamed the underclass and muffled in blood this brief civil war which, paradoxically, Social Democrcy waged against its very children – the working class – by the proxy of White counter-revolutionary brigades.[23]

In Munich, events had been no less extraordinary. Even before Erzberger signed the armistice, on November 7, massed on the Theresienwiese, a 150,000-strong crowd of children, men, and women, led by a blind peasant by the name of Gandorfer, acclaimed Kurt Eisner as leader of the Bavarian Republic, a former Berlin playwright of Jewish origin, and former USPD radical.

In harangues addressed to swarms of soldiers and civilians, Eisner envisioned a 'dictatorship of freemen' and railed against Liberalism's poisonous alchemy: how can one commix, he growled, brotherly love with the struggle for profit? That was like 'casting quicksilver in lead... Nonsense!'[24] Hardly a representative of South German rhythm, Eisner was rather 'one of those hybrid personages, such as arise in History births in times of chaos, an apparition conjured from some political Walpurgis to cast the anathema on the cadaver of the Second Reich.'[25]

With a view to manipulating the millenarian fervor of Munich's new apostles of radicalism and their desire to purge Germany's imperial past out of collective recollection, the US Administration seized the opportunity and invited Eisner to initiate a campaign, which, through the disclosure of classified government documents, should have ushered in the complete and public avowal of Germany's culpability for starting the war. Eisner complied by publishing duly edited – to enhance their sinister drift – excerpts of documents retrieved in the Bavarian Foreign Office.

Eisner's possibly well-intentioned but *de facto* pandering move elicited an uproar of indignation from the still patriotically sensitive masses, whom he was thus beginning to alienate.

The frenzied march of the Munich Council proceeded nevertheless; in late November, at the cry of *'Los von Berlin!'* ('Away from Berlin!') the Bavarian Republic broke off relations with Berlin's Foreign Ministry.

The middle class grew restive, and a White repression was feared. The Bavarians voted on January 15, 1919. In all 32 districts in which he had presented his candidacy, Eisner was beaten – his affiliated party fringe garnered about 2 percent of the vote. His career was finished.

On February 21, as he rehearsed the farewell speech on his way to the Landtag,[*] Count Anton von Arco-Valley, a youth of 24, emptied his revolver at Eisner, who, hit repeatedly in the head, sank down in a pool of blood.

---

[*]   The building of the State Assembly.

Arco-Valley was knocked senseless with a crowbar by Eisner's bodyguard and surrendered to the authorities, to which he confessed that he had committed the crime to prove his mettle to the recruiters of a secret lodge, a certain Thule Society, which had refused him admission on account of his racial 'impurity' – his mother was Jewish. Another useful idiot? Most likely.

Possibly, the Thulists, by inspiring Arco with the 'pledge,' sought to cause a Red (Bolshevik) takeover of the Councils, and thereby elicit the retaliation of White forces, to which they were providing a logistical base of sorts.[26]

After the assassination, the Central Committee of Munich's Councils imposed a curfew and declared a general strike all across Bavaria. In March, the legacy of Eisner was disputed by two hostile factions: the Socialists under the local leader Hoffman, and the anarcho-Communist revolutionaries. In a five-day interlude – from April 7, the day of the official proclamation of the first Munich *Räterepublik*, through to April 12, 1919 – during which the Hoffman Cabinet, overwhelmed by the conjoint revolutionary action of the Councils of several neighboring cities, retreated to the nearby city of Bamberg, the anarchist harlequins staged a fanfare against boredom in the newly proclaimed Bavarian Soviet. The programmatic highlights of their sideshow were state-mandated proficiency in the poetry of Walt Whitman for all pupils by the age of ten along with the abolition of history classes, and issues of a special money stamped with an expiration date.[27]

In a still mysterious succession of maneuvers, a triumvirate of Russian Social Revolutionaries* – Levien, Léviné, and Axelrod – allegedly operating without any sort of mandate from Moscow,[28] supplanted the incumbent rebels and managed to establish itself at the head of what would be the second and final Conciliar experiment in Munich on April 12, 1919. The anarchists scampered at once from the political scene,

'...vivas to those who have failed...' (Walt Whitman)[29]

while the three 'Russians,' as the revolutionary agents came to be referred to, nurtured with the help of the local Red Army a recrudescence of terror and debauchery.

Their tenure was not bound to last longer than a fortnight, however, for the White guards of Noske, previously summoned by the Hoffman government exiled in Franconia, were about to encircle Munich. In the

---

\*    One of the competing revolutionary factions of Russia, which in principle, and unlike Bolshevism, stood for the peasantry but which ultimately, before it was wiped out by Lenin and his associates, afforded many a nest to an inchoate and perplexing pack of political assassins.

last scramble before the White wrath descended upon the Bavarian capital, Levien and Léviné, reviled as 'Jewish instigators of the working masses,' were expelled from the Councils' Congress, though their connection to the Red Army remained strong.

Determined to suppress the source of anti-Semitic instigation, which, so they held, had turned popular sentiment against them, the 'Russians' ordered the liquidation of the Thule Society, whose authorship and diffusion of an endless stream of Jew-baiting pamphlets had been identified without difficulty.[30] Two hundred of its affiliates were wanted; by the end of April, seven of them – men and women of high 'lineage' – were apprehended and sequestered in a public gymnasium. Before the Whites entered the city, they were put against the wall and executed – the martyrs of Thule.

The White retribution for the Red anarchy, and its crazed Russian coda, was bloodier than Berlin's. The White 'liberators' of Munich featured among others a Captain Ernst Röhm, as the chief of munitions in von Epp's brigade, and Thulist war veteran Rudolf Hess, a new recruit in the Regensburg Freikorps.

By May, order had been re-established in Bavaria.

### Inducting Hitler into the mother lodge

Such was the world Hitler found upon returning to Munich as a convalescing soldier in December 1918. Allegedly, his first political duty – an appointment to distribute 'educational' material to the troops – took place under the revolutionary administration of the Workers' and Soldiers' Councils (from late February to April, 1919), and was thus carried out under Socialist auspices.

Of this chapter of his life the Führer was reticent.* Upon leaving the hospital Hitler did not join a Freikorps to fight Left-wing radicalism; he steered clear of the bloody street-fighting of the spring.[31] Ever since Nazi hierarchs had wondered, 'What the hell was Adolf doing in Munich in March–April of 1919?'[32]

Hitler was waiting to be molded.

When in May discipline was instituted anew in the ranks of the army, Hitler was exposed to a program of anti-Bolshevik propaganda coordinated

---

* Indeed, this early account of Hitler's activities has saddled him with the additional charge – surely a trifle, if weighed against the Führer's load of sins – of political incoherence and opportunism. Yet the inconsistency is more apparent than real: for instance, Hitler's avowed anti-monarchism, like that of the *Geächteten,* would remain one of his abiding traits, as much as his attraction to corporatist economics – both of which were two defining features the Right shared with Left. This embarrassing falter in the Führer's evolution strengthens the contention that Hitler in 1919 was in fact far more a *creation* than a creator: a pupil seeking a master, and not vice versa.

by a Captain Mayr, who, after the liquidation of the Red Army, had been in search of capable proselytizers in uniform. Mayr would serve as Hitler's first political 'midwife.'

After attending a series of courses at Munich University in politics and economics, the latter taught by Gottfried Feder, an engineer by profession, it was not long before Hitler discovered the prodigious effects of his own oratorical gifts. By August, in the capacity of *Bildungsoffizier* ('instruction officer'), he was already entrusted with a jam-packed lecturing assignment, which he fulfilled with enthusiasm, drawing increasing numbers of soldiers and listeners, who recognized him as Mayr's most talented propagandist.

In early autumn, he was dispatched as an informant to spy on the several political formations that were mushrooming all over Germany in these times of political upheaval.

On Friday, September 12, 1919, he was sent to report on a meeting of the German Workers' Party (Deutsche Arbeiterpartei, DAP). As he walked into a squalid tavern attended by a meager scatter of listless hangers-on, Gottfried Feder was delivering a tirade on usury, which Hitler had already heard. As he prepared to leave, a Professor Baumann stepped up to perorate the merits of separatism – France was indeed conspiring at this time with whatever natives it could bribe to sever from the Fatherland as large as piece of southwestern territory as it could to create a buffer zone between herself and Germany.

Suddenly, Hitler lunged for the lectern, and in a bout of possessed nationalist eloquence, drove Baumann out of the locale. Anton Drexler, a railroad locksmith and chairman of the Party, did little to conceal his exhilaration at such a display of rhetorical virtuosity; he pushed on Hitler a pamphlet of his composition and invited him to return, forthwith. He immediately confided to the others: 'He's got guts, we can use him.'[33]

A few days later Hitler received in the mail an unsolicited membership card of the DAP bearing the number 555.[34] He did return.

On October 16, 1919, in a crammed basement hall of one of Munich's large drinking saloons, the Hofbräukeller,[35] which was hosting the DAP's first public appearance, Hitler provided a torrential diatribe to an audience of 111 individuals, including a young Balt sociology student, Alfred Rosenberg, and his master, Dietrich Eckart.

Upon inhaling the fluid, the two, who had of late been vainly scouting the Bavarian waste for a suitable 'drummer,' tapped each other with sideglances of gleeful shock: 'He's come.'[36]

Once in every generation a spiritual epidemic spreads like lightning... attacking the souls of the living for some purpose which is hidden from us and causing a kind of mirage in the shape of some being characteristic of the place that, perhaps, lived here hundreds years ago and still yearns for physical form...You can't hear the note from a vibrating tuning fork until it touches wood and sets it resonating. Perhaps it is simply a spiritual growth without any inherent consciousness, a structure that develops like a crystal out of formless chaos according to a constant law.[37]

For a time Hitler drew two stipends, as an army informant, and party speaker. On March 31, 1920, the date of his official discharge, Hitler committed to a life of political activism.

At the behest of an occultist by the name of von Sebottendorff, Karl Harrer, a sports journalist, together with Anton Drexler, had in October 1918 founded a 'Political Workers Circle' with a view to constituting a front for the Thule Society. The Thule Gesellschaft was incorporated in August of 1918 by Sebottendorff, as a branch of 'a much more important secret society known as the *Germanenorden*—Germanic Order'[38] – which in turn had been founded in 1912, and whose role in the counter-revolutionary movement in Munich has been mentioned above.[*]

The creation in January 1919 of the DAP, a political unit in full trim that would have relayed the 'masses to the nationalist Right,' achieved this purpose.[39] From the Germanic Order, Thule inherited the symbolic insignia of the swastika,[40] the eagle and the dagger, and a racial gnosis insisting on the purity of the affiliate's blood.

The *Hakenkreuz* or gamma cross is a solar emblem and a polar sign: 'it evokes a circular movement around an axis or a fixed point...it is always suggestive of movement, dynamism, unlike the cross.'[41] According to the Germanic mythology of the *Germanenorden*, the swastika rotated around a polar axis planted in the Hyperborean (northernmost) sacred island of Thule, the cradle of a white race of ancestors.

When order begins to totter, particularly during the caesura between two historical epochs, [peculiar] forces rise from their subterranean and angular lairs, or even from the zone of their private dissoluteness. Their end is despotism, more or less intelligent, but always shaped after the model of the animal kingdom. Therefore, even in their speeches and writings, they are wont to attribute beastly traits to the victims they strive to annihilate.[42]

*   See pp. 56–7.

In June 1918 von Sebottendorff had boosted the nascent organization with the acquisition of a newspaper, the *Völkischer Beobachter*. Poet and freelance writer Dietrich Eckart, one of the Society's 'luminaries' that attended the October 16 gathering, would later provide the sum with which the Nazi party acquired the paper as its official press organ in December 1920.[43]

Eckart had continuously made use of his own periodical, *Auf gut deutsch* (*In Plain German*) – a forum for conservative-revolutionary *literati* – to inveigh against 'Jewishness,' which, he averred, consisted at heart of a form of earthly, materialist, worship. To such adamant 'affirmation of life' on the part of Jews, he added, must be opposed a peculiar feeling for immortality, which was through and through a Teutonic sentiment – a notion of eternal regeneration through unrelenting death and sacrifice. Something which Ernst Jünger, a bard whose visions were not too remote from the lore of the Thulists, would describe as 'the double-entry of life' – *die doppelte Buchführung des Lebens*.[44]

Eckart's meditation ended in a somber tone, brooding over the forthcoming irreconcilable yet necessary coexistence of Jews and Germans, the former acting upon the latter as a formication of vital 'bacteria' within an organism, the German nation, yearning for eschatological deliverance at the end of time.[45]

From the columns of the *Völkischer Beobachter*, von Sebottendorff had similarly intimated on November 9, 1918, the day of the Revolution, that 'the whole living realm is doomed to extinction, so as to make everything else live; even we must be prepared to suffer death in order to let our children and the children of our children live. The humiliated anguish of Germany is the threshold beyond which life renews itself.'[46]

Following his induction into the Society as an honorary member by way of the DAP,[47] Hitler underwent the proper initiation into mysteries of the mother lodge.[48]

Other members of the Thule Gesellschaft that would bear upon the vicissitudes of Nazism were, among others, Hitler's economics teacher Gottfried Feder; Hans Frank, the governor of occupied Poland during World War II; the future Deputy Führer, Rudolf Hess, and the Third Reich's ideologue of the race, Alfred Rosenberg.

There develop in the great Orders secret and subterranean channels in which the historian is lost.[49]

## The Allied betrayal of the Russian Whites

But in Russia the fratricide was going to be something else.

Many critics of contemporary historiography have demanded that the Russian chapter in modern primers be rewritten; and rightly so. What ought to be spelt out in simple words is that the 'Bolshevik menace from the East' was from beginning to end a fake specter animated by the lies of the Western apparatuses. The Communist presence in Eurasia added yet another degree of complexity to the 'strategy of tension' in the West: in fact, it allowed to keep Eurasia in check, and the world poised on the brink of an ever pending ideological, or rather imaginary, conflict – a conflict with the faceless, despotic, 'asiatic enemy'. How Western Russia had been consigned to Lenin and his acolytes has been recounted in Chapter 1. Thereafter, the Allies had to shield their 'revolutionary assets' and see to it that these consolidated their hold over the entire landmass, from Moscow to Vladivostok. To effect this, the White counter-revolutionary armies of the generals loyal to the Czar had to be wiped out – and Britain had to come up with a peculiar plan. Peculiar, because the scenario was rather awkward: the Reds, who with the support of foreign capital, had been gradually erecting from Moscow a despotic bureaucracy since late 1917, were surrounded by the White czarists in the north (Murmansk), the south (the Caucasus), and the east (Siberia). The Whites, dynastic and traditionalists, professed themselves as friends of the Allies – and they were sincere – whereas the Communist Reds employed only the foulest language when speaking of the American and European 'Liberal democracies': in words, and in words only, their ideological hatred for Western capitalism knew no bounds. Now the catch of such a scenario was that the West had to behave in such a way as to fool both its public and the Whites into believing that it was supporting the latter, when in fact the Anglo-Americans were looking forward to the complete physical elimination of the White czarists – their allies, on paper. And all of this had to be done to fulfill the aim of setting up a Communist enemy in the East, against whom, in time, the 'new reactionary' Germany would have risen.[*]
So the problem which faced the British clubs was how to make a clean job of backstabbing the Whites, after these had repeatedly called upon Britain and her allies to help them defeat the 'Red, blasphemous monsters.' What Britain would do, with the help of America and the most heinous complicity of France and Japan, who should have had no part in this anti-European plot, was to engage in a mock fight on the side of the Whites versus the Reds, committing very limited resources and men. Thus what was in fact an operation of sabotage by neglect – a pretense to fight – was masked as a pro-White intervention, whose surreptitious objective was to instigate

---

[*] The dynamics of this part of the plot are discussed in the final sections of this chapter.

the Whites to combat under unfavorable conditions, deceitfully hamper their advances, prepare the terrain for their rout, and finally evacuate the Allied contingent by blaming the defeat on the putative inefficiency of the Whites. This would have turned out to be yet another indescribable disaster engineered by the western elites, not only for the terrible loss of Russian life it would have entailed, but especially for the murderous mendacity and duplicity displayed by the Western governments in provoking it, and subsequently justifying it to their electorates.

As had been the wish of the Sea Powers, the Bolsheviks were now in command of a region corresponding to the heart of the 'land-mass,' that is, western Russia, with its 70 million people, half of the country's population. Now one had to monitor and steer the next steps of this infant power. As promised, Lenin signed the peace with Germany (the Treaty of Brest of March 1918), and the truce on the Eastern Front brought the complexities of the 'game' into relief.

1. Germany, as seen, was 'at peace' with Bolshevik Russia in March 1918; she could now shift her eastern divisions to the Western Front. To parry this eventuality, Britain involved the United States in the war, and thus propped up the Western Front with massive American reinforcements.

2. In June 1918, the fear of the Allies, according to a US State Department memorandum, was that Germany might at any time violate the Treaty of Brest, turn against the detested Bolsheviks, and ally herself with the former inimical yet kindred White czarist generals to build a counter-revolutionary White International across the Eurasian landmass. The Germans had indeed begun to move in this direction in early 1918 by dispatching forces in Finland, the Baltic states, and the Ukraine to support White against Red troops.[50]

3. It was going to take pains to convince the public of the Allied Liberal democracies, whose raison d'être was the sacred defense of property, that Bolshevism, which lived to abolish it, was 'the lesser evil' between Red and White rule. This was done by resorting to the bogey of 'White autocracy' – a diversionary exercise that had been conjured with success during the deposition of Czar Nicholas in March 1917.* It was hoped that the average Westerner would come to fear in his dreams the traditional bugaboo of the ferocious Boyar far more than the thoroughly unfamiliar figure of the 'collectivizing commissar.'

---

* See Chapter 1, p. 29.

4. The Sea Powers in effect looked forward to the strengthening of Lenin's regime, and to its eventual unbridgeable opposition to any form of German influence.
5. To counteract point (2), namely, Germany's advance into Russia, a makeshift Eastern Front had to be recreated immediately.
6. *The Whites had to be lured into the Allied camp, away from any tempting alliance with the Germans, and, by a savvy and systematic policy of multiple sabotage by neglect, be thrown to the Reds to die a slow death in a civil war.* In other words, what was required was an Allied scheme that could afford a light military intervention in the cardinal apices of the landmass. From such a fanned vantage point, the Allied outposts would have sentried the conduct of the Whites.
7. If the Whites, the better soldiers, could not be so debilitated as to lose the Civil War against the Reds; if the Whites, that is, should have won the Civil War, the Allied vanguards in Russia were to encourage at once the fragmentation of the heartland into as a many competing fiefdoms as there were White commanders.[51]

The plan was difficult, but feasible.

A sizable portion thereof had already been completed during the 1917 intrigues, which had dealt the rival factions highly uneven hands. In the fall of 1919, when the decisive battles of the Civil War took place, the Red Army had 3 million men under arms, who would become 5 million by the spring of 1920,[52] whereas the combined effectives of the White Armies never exceeded 250,000.[53] While the Reds could tap a population of 70 million, altogether the Whites could never rely on more than 9 million individuals. Though they were the superior fighters, they could be strangled with moderate ease. It was going to be a game of debilitation and patience.

Before signing the peace with Germany, Lenin and Trotsky had already declared themselves amenable to take 'potatoes and ammunition from the Anglo-French imperialist robbers'; now, they wondered naively what prevented all the imperialist powers, including Germany, from burying their past grudges and ganging up against their Communist foe;[54] and while they mused, the Allies set out to implement the second phase of the plan.

*Far eastern Russia.* As their 'eastern sentinel,' in February 1918 Japan, France and Britain hired Semenov, the notorious Cossack chief of a gang of torturers, rapists and assassins,[55] and enjoined him *not* to extend his radius of terror beyond his remote base at the confines of Mongolia.[56] On the surface Semenov passed for a White, but he was merely a pawn. In April 1918, with a nod from Washington, Tokyo debarked the first squadron of reconnoitering officers in eastern Siberia to keep an eye on the Whites from Manchuria, whose western periphery would be guarded by the Cossack satraps.

*Northwestern Russia.* Simultaneously, a British corps was landed in northern Russia – in the Murmansk region, neighboring Finland. The official mission of such a corps was to rally the local forces against German meddling in Finland. In this northern corner of the heartland, and in open defiance of Moscow's anti-imperialist directives, the Soviet of Murmansk would work hand in glove with the Allies to repel the Finnish White Guards, and thwart the German scheme of establishing a submarine base in the White Sea. By November 11, 1918, the day of the armistice, these goals were accomplished.[57]

*Siberia and The Urals.* In May 1918, there were 40,000 native Czech soldiers strewn in several trains along the Trans-Siberian railroad, bound for Vladivostok – Russia's far eastern port on the Pacific Ocean. Thence, this corps of Legionnaires recruited in Ukraine before the war and once loyal to the Czar was to be conveyed halfway across the world to the Western Front as reinforcement to the Allies. France had an idea: responding to the Sea Powers' urge to recreate an Eastern Front, she took the fate of the Czechs under her own wing, and instigated her new protégés to cause an incident with the Reds whereby hostilities might be opened. Easily effected: when the Soviet authorities demanded that the Czechs surrendered their weapons, the Legionnaires refused. The tension degenerated into conflict. On May 25, the Czechs overpowered the Red garrison at Chelyabinsk in the Urals. A month thereafter they would have occupied several other Siberian centers, and overseen therein the constitution of Councils by the local bourgeoisie. Playing cat's paw for France and her seafaring Allies, the Czechs had thus erected a new front in the east. Then, upon orders from France, they were ordered to dig in into the heart of Eurasia and stake another vantage point from which the Allies might survey the Russian evolution.

In July the Legion seized the city of Ekaterinburg: the bodies of the imperial family were found littering the cellar of a merchant's villa, in which they had been sequestered by the Soviets. Before the Czechs entered the city, the Bolsheviks had murdered all the Romanovs at close range to eliminate the possibility of their restoration to the throne: in 1917, the Kerensky government had entreated Britain to offer asylum to the Czar and his family, but not to mar the sensitivities of the Labour Party, the British, always the foes of 'autocracy,' had declined.[58] Apparently, Britain hadn't been able to forgive the Czar for attempting to betray her in 1916.

With the momentary Czech capture of Kazan on the Volga, in August 1918, the treasure trove of the Red government – the former gold hoard of the Czar – fell into the possession of the Allied camp.

Moved by the cavalier actions of the Czechs, on July 17, 1918, President Wilson drafted his controversial *Aide Memoir*, in which he gauged America's military intervention in the Russian quagmire admissible 'only to help the Czechoslovaks consolidate their forces...'[59] America's standby operation – entrusted in late August to US General William Graves, who, before taking his leave was admonished by the President to 'watch his step'[60] – was not orchestrated to engage Bolshevism, but, again, to observe the steps of the Whites. Finally, in August, 1918, the expeditionary corps of all three Sea Powers, Britain, America, and Japan, and of their French minion were landed in Vladivostok. Upon being deployed, all four powers publicly announced to Russia that they had come in peace, 'as friends' to save them 'from dismemberment and destruction at the hands of Germany.'[61] But no one in Siberia ever caught sight of German troops intent on harassing either the native peoples or the Czechs. The Allies were not speaking a word of truth. By autumn, the Japanese contingent numbered 72,000 men – ten times larger than the American one.[62]

By mid-1918, Siberia demanded a White commander.

Before the local orientation could identify a chief, the British rushed to slip a straw man in the cockpit. For the role British intelligence cast a former czarist admiral, Aleksandr Kolchak, who had been on its payroll since November 1917.

Flanked and directed by General Knox, Britain's intelligence officer in the Siberia, Kolchak, with the cooperation of the Siberian Whites, and the discreet assent of the Czechs, usurped command of the Siberian counter-revolutionary outpost a week after the armistice in the West, on November 18, 1918, and made Omsk the capital of his dictatorship. His was also the gold taken at Kazan, for the time being. News of the riches at the disposal of the Supreme Ruler were then flashed around the world.[63]

*Prague.* As a thank you to the Czechs for their rumble in the Urals, on October 28, 1918, from the fragmentation of Austria-Hungary, the Allies reinvented Bohemia as the brand new Czechoslovak Republic, and, duly, France was the first to give it official recognition on October 15, 1919; the others followed suit.

*London.* At the end of the war, everyone was betting on a surefire victory of the Whites over the Reds.[64] In January 1919, on Churchill's map in Whitehall, the situation looked desperate for the Reds.[65]

*Paris*. In the same month, the Great Powers had convened at Versailles[*] for the Peace Conference that would redraw the world map after the Great War. Russia's absence from the proceedings was conspicuous: the country had in fact no legitimate representation, riven as it was by the contest yet unsettled between Whites and Reds. The time had come for the Allies to tilt the scales in favor of their Red creature. Against the czarists, they elaborated a sophisticated tactic of debilitation by tarry and deceit, whereby the designated White victim, while cordoned off and 'outgunned,'[66] *would be goaded by the slowly evanescing presence of the Allied instigators to engage the far more numerous Reds along a vast, fissured front, which the Whites could not control.*

The first step in this terrible Anglo-American ploy was to isolate progressively the Whites with a diplomatic discourtesy: from Versailles, with studied aloofness towards their White 'ally,' and tacit encouragement for their Bolshevik work-horse, the Allies invited the two factions to meet in Turkey with a view to negotiate. In Paris, and elsewhere, the Whites felt outrageously offended: this, they railed, amounted to granting the Bolsheviks official status and treating them like equals! Though the Reds said yes, the Whites would not deal with the godless impostors.

In the West the public, ever confused, did not quite understand why their governments were so slow in doing away with this nasty Bolshevik variable – Whites aside. Were not the Reds a plague on the capitalist West, they asked?

Ever mendacious, the Elder Statesmen of the West adduced the customary pretexts: a blockade round Russia, they responded, would be cruel, and a serious intervention would have required no fewer than 400,000 men – an absolute luxury, exclaimed the British Prime Minister, Lloyd George, who, like his American counterpart, agreed instead to a 'plan of limited intervention' – by now, a code-name for the Allied standby operation of anti-White sabotage.[67]

In fact, no restraint – ethical or otherwise – had prevented the British (1) from killing by means of the 1914–19 blockade approximately 800,000 innocent Germans,[68] and (2) from fitting an army of 900,000 for their Middle-Eastern expedition in World War I: cruelty and expense had hardly ever detracted Britain from pursuing a vital imperial goal. Clearly the Western spokesmen were yet again peddling lies, and the public never seemed to possess sufficient imagination to conceive that its very leaders

[*]   See the following section.

Map by Sergei Domashenko and Jessica Graybill

*Figure 2.1*  White nests in the Russian Civil War

had not only installed the Bolsheviks in power, but were presently scheming to hand them over the whole of Eurasia.

*Southwestern Russia.* In the South, White General Denikin was the master of a sector projecting from the northern shores of the Black and Caspian seas (see Figure 2.1).[69] Britain and France would see to it that Denikin's muster for 'Russia, One and Indivisible' went to the devil.

Since November 1918, Britain had intrigued with as many satellites as she could bribe abaft the Whites' enclave: that is, beyond the Caspian Sea in Transcaspia, where she struck several oil deals, and in Transcaucasia – Azerbaijan and Georgia – from which she killed two birds with one stone by securing imports of cotton and *opposing every effort of Denikin's to restore the Caspian fleet*.[70] Likewise, France, whom czarist Russia had saved from defeat in the summer of 1914 by attacking the Reich, declared, most ungratefully, that she did 'not believe in White Russia.' Nor did she profess to have any liking for the Red Kremlin either – so what would she do? She would 'concentrate on separating Russia from Germany by means of a "barbed wired fence" of friendly states anchored in Poland.'[71] And Britain could not be more approving.

> The British Establishment had, as usual, inveigled the French politicians into their Russian occupation scheme. [Prime Minister] Clémenceau was invited to sign, in the utmost secrecy, a convention whereby the British would cut the French in on some of Southern Russia's choicest real estate. On December 23, 1917, two months after Lenin's coup, the treaty was signed by Clémenceau and the British. French divisions would be sent to occupy Ukraine, in exchange for which Clémenceau would receive concessions in Bessarabia and the Crimea, as well as in Ukraine – an area larger than France herself. The British Establishment had conceived this munificent scheme in order to divert attention from their own monopolization of petroleum in the Caucasus and the Persian Gulf.[72]

So in December 1918, escorted by a regiment of Greeks and Poles, the French wetted the anchor at Odessa in Crimea. But after being severely thrashed by a corps of Ukrainian irregulars, the French disengaged in April 1919, though not before destroying the entire Russian Black Sea Fleet – 'to leave nothing for the Bolsheviks,' so they claimed – [73] and laying open thereby the whole of Denikin's left flank.[74]

Throughout this distressing intermission, hamstrung in the rear by France on the Black, and Britain on the Caspian Sea, General Denikin sent repeated requests for aid to representatives of those self-same powers, who took no time to respond 'absorbed' as they were in the intricacies of the Peace Conference.[75] Yet in spite of the crippling, Denikin's recruiting élan in the South grew in June, so much so that he pledged allegiance to Kolchak in a drive to unite Russia that moved the admiral to tears.

*White Siberia.* Presently, the focus shifted to Kolchak. By May of 1919, his western advance across the Urals was nearly triumphant.

The Whites, enthusiastic, kept pressuring the Anglo-Americans for official recognition. The latter, hard pressed to mask their dissatisfaction, had to resort to some other charade to gain precious time: raising their brows like distrustful schoolmasters, they conditioned diplomatic recognition upon the establishment in White Siberia of a Liberal democratic order à la Kerensky. In other words, to obtain London's seal of approval the Whites were warned that they had better introduce reform in land tenure, suffrage, and so on – the usual institutional package containing all that is fit, according to Britain.[76] Kolchak naturally assented, and the Allies curtly replied that 'they would consider': naturally, the recognition would never be granted.

But Kolchak could not be sacrificed just yet: *his gold chest exceeded by 52.7 percent the entire gold reserve of the Bank of England.*[77] In the summer of 1919, over a third of this treasure was dispatched by train to Vladivostok, where no less than 18 foreign banks, eager for a share of the Russian business, had established branches. Thereafter the gold was either sold on the international market in exchange for foreign cash, or was swallowed in the vaults of banks in Yokohama, Osaka, Shanghai, Honk Kong, and San Francisco as security for loans.[78]

Though Kolchak splurged like a king, the Siberian tangle was such as to make his task 'almost impossible.'[79] How?

1. The Cossaks to the Far East had been planted in his side by the Japanese to strangle the vital flow of provisions traveling on the Trans-Siberian railway from Vladivostok to Omsk.
2. Immediately after Kolchak's *coup*, the Czechs suddenly made a public display of their fatigue and confessed the desire to withdraw from the fray. Directed by General Janin, specially expedited from France to engineer the Czech backstab of Kolchak's White armies, the Legion left the Ural front en masse, receding towards Japan's westernmost outpost. Presently, the Czechs abstained vigorously from all participation in Russian central affairs, exasperating Kolchak 'to the point of madness.'[80]
3. As for US General William Graves, the gossip in Siberia was that by not supporting Kolchak he was in fact giving aid to the Bolsheviks.[81] Which was the truth. Likewise, the British did nothing.

By August, Kolchak was losing.

Thereafter, the stories of White discomfiture were all the same: they began with smashing offensives that brought the Whites to over-extend themselves, until they were systematically routed by the Red Army, whose far superior numbers always allowed it to regroup and drive back the White assault. Numbers and numbers alone settled this matter.

By November Kolchak was finished; he had lasted but a year.

In a two-month epic exodus along the Trans-Siberian railroad, Kolchak hitched his six convoys to a locomotive bound to Vladivostok to escape from the creeping Red hordes – in one such convoy was the gold. Traveling in the front cars of the caravan were the French General Janin and the Czechs, who so relented the pace of the advance as to allow the Reds to overtake the tail of the train. In the long 1,500-mile trek, 1 million men, women, and children would perish.

In January 1920, the British War Office was proud to report that Kolchak had ceased to be a factor in Russian military affairs.[82] The mission was accomplished: American and British troops evacuated Siberia. On January 31, two Czech officers boarded Kolchak's car and informed the commander that he would be surrendered to the local authorities. 'So the Allies have betrayed me?' the White admiral calmly enquired. In February 1920, while facing interrogation by the Reds, Kolchak, this sad king of all dupes, would avow in a moment of placated distress: 'the meaning and essence of this [Allied] intervention remains quite obscure to me.'[83] He was shot and dumped under the icy crust of the Ushakovka river soon thereafter. Along with the head of Kolchak, the Bolsheviks were served two-thirds of the Czar's gold, the remainder having previously been deposited in the safes of the West.

The only losses suffered by the Allies were incurred in the North. There, owing to the ragged countenance of the White resistance, the Allies, commanded by Anglo-American forces, were reluctantly called upon from backstage to engage the Reds in a series of broken *escaramouches*, which enabled them to temporize and hold the position in a stratagem of wait-and-see staked on the fortune of Kolchak. Demobilization began in March, and was completed by the end of 1919, when the admiral was lost. After relinquishing some war *matériel*, the Allies left the White generals behind to grapple with their (bleak) destiny. Upon seizing Archangel'sk in February 1920, the Bolsheviks immediately butchered 500 White officers.

In Russia, the Anglo-American death toll for what had been in essence a game of make-believe tallied up to approximately 500 lives out of a force of 18,000 men – in the West, instead, the United States had promptly expended 114,000 lives of the 2 million troops sent to France, in a deployment costing

$36.2 billion.[84] When it came to killing the Germans, America had been ready to see 2 million of its soldiers die. But when the time had arrived to fight the 3–5 million 'evil Communists,' London and Washington committed together approximately 1 percent of the American contingent in France. And of their men, sent to overview the end of the Whites, the Anglo-Americans had even been willing to sacrifice a handful, just in order to keep up appearances – to 'show' that, because a few of theirs had been cut down by Red fire, Britain and America had indeed come to 'help the Whites.' Which was the opposite of the truth. Siding 'officially' with the Whites, 500 Anglo-Americans soldiers were killed by the Reds in a tussle in the polar north, which was part of an extraordinary double-cross of the White generals staged by the Anglo-American clubs for the benefit of the Reds themselves: such was the twisted beauty of imperial scheming.

In the Baltic, the recurrent pattern was slightly altered by the paradoxical presence of German regulars and Freikorps, commanded by General von Goltz. A clause of the armistice tolerated their incumbency in Courland* 'as a stopgap measure,'[85] to oppose the Red invasion of the Baltic seaboard, which the Allies sought to retain as an independent buffer between Germany and Russia.

As Goltz's armies prepared in June 1919 to give White commander Yudenitch *main forte* to launch a wide offensive against St. Petersburg, they were recalled by the German government under the peremptory injunction of the Allies, disbanded and repatriated forthwith. Embittered, Goltz would later remember how Yudenitch's Northern Army of unkempt beggars was massacred after having been 'egged on in the most unscrupulous manner [by] the British.'[86]

In the South, France cut the Bolsheviks further slack by encouraging its other great protégé in the East, Poland, with whom the Reds had locked horns over territorial disputes, to sign two successive truces with the Russians. Thereupon the Red Army, commanded by the dashing young General Mikahil Tukhachevsky, shifted massive reinforcements to the south to defeat Denikin in the fall of 1919, and Wrangel, the second-in-command, the following year, thus suppressing once and for all the southern hotbed of anti-Bolshevik resistance. As the White squadron chiefs were hurriedly evacuated aboard Allied vessels, their horses, forsaken on the surf of Crimea, thrust themselves in the water chasing after their riders.[87]

Japan, the sole Sea Power with a contingent of 70,000 men that could have struck the Reds and never did,[88] finally retired in 1922 after having

---

* The ancient region lying astride Latvia and Lithuania.

lamed Kolchak, vouched for the indescribable violence of the Cossack cutthroats, and corroborated its hold over Manchuria. In 1922, the czarist empire became the USSR, the Union of Soviet Socialist Republics. The great 'imaginary foe' of the West had at long last been conjured.[89]

US President Wilson was satisfied that it had been left to the Russians 'to fight it out amongst themselves.'[90] And Secretary of State Lansing, officially America's most vehement anti-Bolshevik, resignedly declared in early 1920: 'We simply did the best we could in an impossible situation, which resulted from Kolchak's inability to create an efficient army.'[91]

On the surface, the Sea Powers seemed to have been moonstruck by an odd sort of geopolitical geometry, whereby the prospect of facing a viscerally anti-Western Communist dictatorship ruling over a surface 60 times greater than the German Reich roused far less concern than the Germans' appetite for Middle Europe. Indeed, Lloyd George assured his Cabinet in December 1918 that a Bolshevized Russia was by no means 'such a danger [to England] as the old Russian Empire, with all its aggressive officials and million troops,'[92] and a year later he candidly reiterated, shattering therewith the hopes of the last fighting Whites, that Kolchak's and Denikin's Russia, 'One and Indivisible,' was not in Britain's 'best interests.'[93]

Nor could they be blamed of cynical indifference, the Allies pleaded, for they had extended aid to the Whites to the extent of tons of war *matériel* and provided millions of dollars worth of assistance, although Churchill himself admittedly found such a claim 'to be vastly exaggerated on the grounds that British aid consisted largely of WWI surplus that was of no further use to Britain and had little monetary value.'[94]

Presumably, the actual beneficiaries of Allied aid, as many had suspected, were not the Whites, but, contrary to all preconceptions except those of geopolitics, the Reds themselves.

The magnitude of Western assistance to the Bolsheviks is not known, though in early 1918, for instance, it was a matter of some notoriety that the United States was conveying funds to Bolshevik Russia for purchases of weaponry and munitions via Wall Street operator Raymond Robins, for whom Trotsky was 'the greatest Jew since Jesus.'[95]

The significant number of contracts, concessions, and licenses subsequently released by Lenin's empire to American firms during the Civil War, and in its immediate aftermath, formed something of a smoking gun of Bolshevism's early Allied sponsorship: $25 million of Soviet commissions for US manufactures between July 1919 and January 1920,[96] not to mention Lenin's concession for the extraction of asbestos to Armand Hammer in

1921,[97] and the 60-year lease granted in 1920 to Frank Vanderlip's* US consortium formed to exploit the coal, petroleum and fisheries of a North Siberian region covering 600,000 square kilometers (*Frankfurter Zeitung,* November 20, 1920).[98]

Finally, in 1933, the Soviet government, upon perusal of 'official American documentation,' would waive 'any and all claims...for the damages allegedly caused by the United States in the Soviet Union through its participation in the [Siberian] intervention':[99] for nebulous reasons, it would take the Reds 13 years to acknowledge officially that General Graves had come to Siberia to help, not to thwart them.

> Never, surely, have countries continued to show themselves so much at their worst as did the Allies in Russia from 1917 to 1920. Among other things, their efforts served everywhere to compromise the enemies of Bolshevism and to strengthen the Communist themselves. So important was this factor that I think it may well be questioned whether Bolshevism would ever have prevailed throughout Russia had the Western governments not aided its progress to power by this ill-conceived interference...These expeditions were little side-shows of policy, complicated and obscure in origin...embracing in their motivation many considerations having nothing to do with a desire to overthrow Soviet power for ideological reasons.[100]

American historian and diplomat George F. Kennan had, like many of his compatriots, been somewhat at a loss to plumb what had been a contrived method of solving the first equation of Eurasia's system: that is, by raising a phantom regime in Russia hostile to Germany. Contemporaries had failed to appreciate that the White elephants were naturally foredoomed – the breaking of the Eurasian embrace demanded it, and all such Allied 'sideshows' were but sequences of premeditated butchery. Feigning a cautious policy of intervention, the governments of Britain, France and the United States misled their public into believing that they indeed requited the hatred of the Communists by 'siding' with their enemies' enemies (the Whites), when in fact they had been double-crossing these Whites all along. Hence the reproach that the Allies had shown themselves 'at their worst,' translated by and large into an ungracious refusal to tribute the due credit to what amounted to a perfectly executed maneuver, costing a collateral loss of but 500 lives, to rid the landmass of the bulk of the Junkers' potential Russian allies beyond the Eurasian fault line. Save for the

---

*   The chairman of the National City Bank in New York.

distasteful bickering of Russia's fratricidal war, whose loss of life amounted to around 10 million souls, the operation had been a complete success – this was rather the Allied West 'at its best.'

## The peace treaty that was too harsh

Woodrow Wilson's Fourteen Points, issued during the terminal phase of the war, in January 1918, as the tentative charter of the world's post-war community, had merely contemplated the 'restoration' of invaded territories, and assured the fighting parties that there would be 'no annexations, no contributions, no punitive damages.'

On November 5, the American position was further clarified by the note of the US Secretary of State, Lansing, to Germany, according to which the latter would 'make compensation for all damage done to the civilian population of the Allied...Powers and to their property...by such an aggression by land, by sea, and from the air.'[101] Upon these premises the Germans signed the Armistice.

Meanwhile, on February 6, 1919, the National Assembly convened in Weimar, away from the provisional disorders of Berlin, and five days later republican Germany was given her first president: the Socialist Friedrich Ebert.

Soon it was the 'reparations' that they all began to argue about. If by 'damage' only wreckage of property had been intended, France, upon whose soil the devastation had been wrought, would have claimed the bulk of the indemnities. To tilt the scales somewhat more in Britain's favor, Jan Smuts, an affiliate of Milner's Kindergarten* as well as South Africa's negotiator in Paris, found a loophole in the Lansing Note: citing the wording of the clause, according to which Germany 'was liable for all damage done to civilians,' he cunningly bent Wilson into including in the reparation bill allowances for soldiers' families, as well as pensions for widows and orphans.

Economist John Maynard Keynes, representing the British Treasury at Versailles, reckoned that not only did such allowances violate Wilson's negotiatory Points, but they also amounted to a figure two and half times the total bill for the war damages inflicted on the Western Front. Adding to a preliminary remittance in cash of $5 million, expected by May 1921, the allowances (25 billion dollars), and the compensation for war ravages (10 billion dollars), Keynes assessed the reparation load at 40 million dollars: a figure equal to three times the Reich's pre-war income, which,

---

\*   See above, p. 39.

he affirmed, was beyond the paying capacity of vanquished Germany.[102] He was indignant – the envisaged sums appeared patently absurd.

But the victorious public was fed expectations of another species: the British adumbrated a request of $120 billion; the French a fantastic toll of $220 billion.[103] With such a heated audience thirsting for extravagantly vindictive tributes, Lloyd George and the French Prime Minister, Clémenceau, Britain's and France's chief negotiators, could scarcely afford to parade on the home front a loot of 'merely' $40 million without risking a political lynching. Then Lloyd George chanced upon the clever device of leaving the final figure unnamed, deputizing the task to a commission of experts, which was scheduled to deliver an estimate in two years – by May 1921. The explosive mixture was skillfully inoculated in the text of the Treaty by John Foster Dulles – a New York lawyer connected in high places – in the form of the infamous Article 231, which had gone down in history as the 'war guilt clause' (*Kriegsschuldfrage*). By this Article Germany was coerced to accept the responsibility, and thus sign a 'blank check,' 'for causing all the loss and damage to which the Allied…and their nationals have been subjected as a consequence of the war imposed upon them by the aggression of Germany.'

The apportionment of the prospective German spoils was thus tentatively arranged by the victors: 50 per cent to France, 30 percent to Britain and the remaining 20 percent divided up amongst the lesser allies.[104]

Having served its purpose, the decoy of the Fourteen Points was torn up and tossed in the trashcan. Its mouthpiece, Wilson, like a dollar watch wound too tight and then discarded, ticked into malfunction and finally broke down: in Paris the President fell seriously ill. He had sworn for no annexations, yet he acquiesced in Allied occupation; he had promised no indemnities, but he agreed to unilateral reparations. He had vowed to uproot 'secret diplomacy' and watched his allies make it the very clay wherewith the Treaty was being fashioned: when the German delegation arrived in Paris in late April to receive the contents of the Treaty on May 7, 1919, Lloyd George stuttered as he read a document that neither he nor any other Allied plenipotentiary had seen in its completed form.[105] They had all haggled furiously, but the hand that had drafted the achieved compact had remained hidden.

When the Germans were apprised of the Treaty's nature, they sat back dumbstruck. Then, recomposing themselves somewhat, they invited their leader, Foreign Minister Count Ulrich von Brockdorff-Rantzau – the very man whom Parvus Helphand had gulled in 1917* – to deliver the legation's

---

* See Chapter 1, pp. 31–2.

remonstrance: in a long speech, Brockdorff lamented the violation of the 'pre-armistice commitments. As a deliberate insult to his listeners, he spoke from a seated position.'[106]

In Berlin, the Reichstag (the parliament) excoriated the Treaty with an uproar of abuse. At Versailles the German legation counter-proposed: in a masterful 443-page response redacted in keeping with the original Wilsonian pact, the Treaty's Articles were rebuffed one by one: Germany offered $25 billion dollars, and 'most territorial changes were rejected except where they could be shown to be based on self-determination (thus adopting Wilson's point of view)'.[107] Even the doyen of sociology, Max Weber, was dragged by Germany into the foray to protest, as Lenin had done years previously, that the war had been *every power's* sin.[108]

But the Allies were irremovable: Germany, the sole culprit of the war's atrocities, was given a five-day ultimatum to accept the Treaty on pain of military invasion. Not to affix its signature to such a *Schandfrieden* (shameful peace), Weimar's first government under the Socialist Scheidemann resigned in concert after only four months. In a desparate act of wounded patriotism, on June 21 the crews of the German fleet impounded at Scapa Flow in the Orkney Isles scuttled 400,000 tons of expensive shipping, and lost ten sailors to British gunfire in the undertaking.[109] In Berlin it was Matthias Erzberger, once again, who bent over to take the brunt of unpopular decisions: in November he had signed the humiliating armistice, now, as Finance Minister of the new Cabinet, he took it upon himself to inflict upon this whole affair the last turn of the screw. He challenged the parliament's diehard opponents of ratification to lead, as men of their word, a government that would face renewed hostilities. While these immediately recoiled from the prospective engagement, General Groener assured Reich President Ebert that he would placate the (infuriated) army. By a parliamentary maneuver designed to save the honor of the 'patriots' as well as to enable the pragmatists to ratify it, the Treaty was accepted on June 23, and Germany was spared Allied occupation.[110]

As to the territorial alterations, the Treaty carried two significant dispositions. The first was the Polish Corridor: France had wanted to give east Prussia to Poland, but the drafters of the Treaty conceived a far more sophisticated arrangement whereby east Prussia was to be traversed by a corridor connecting Poland to the North Sea by way of the free city of Danzig, a full-fledged German enclave to be placed under international tutelage. This corridor thus severed a sizable block of eastern Germany from the body of the Fatherland. As a contraption for sparking eventual ethnic, territorial, and political incendiary dispute, it was bound to be efficacious: in fact, it was the trigger set up for the next war.[*]

The second territorial provision was the Rhineland settlement: the Rhineland and a zone 50 kilometers wide along the right bank were to be permanently demilitarized and any violation of the clause could be regarded as a hostile act by the signatories of the Treaty. The condition implied that any German troops or fortifications were excluded from this area forever. 'This was the most important disposition of the Treaty of Versailles, as it exposed the economic backbone of Germany's ability to wage warfare to a quick French military thrust.'[111] French troops were granted the right to occupy such a zone for 15 years.

Bearing down 'like two jailers' upon the flanks of 'the chained giant,'[112] Versailles' novel creations, Poland and Czechoslovakia, kept a careful watch over Germany, who thus found herself stripped of her armed forces, which were reduced to a professional contingent of 100,000 men. The country was deprived of many of her mines; reduced in population by 6.5 million citizens (10 percent of the total)[113] and 2.4 million souls lost at war; bereft of her merchant navy, her colonies, and 13 percent of her territory; depleted of 75 percent of her iron ore reserves, 26 percent of her coal production, as well as 44 percent and 38 percent of her pig iron and steel production respectively;[114] and 'obliged to devote part of [her] industrial might to building ships for the Allies and to provide coal to France.'[115]

By the time the Germans assented to ratify the Treaty, Keynes had already abandoned the Conference in high dudgeon, chagrined by the pensions clause – 'one of the most serious acts of political unwisdom,' he wailed, 'for which our statesmen have ever been responsible.'[116] A clause whose provenance, however, he could not afford to divulge because it was the ruse of his good friend Smuts.[117]

When the final bill was issued in May 1921, Germany would be asked to pay, in 37 yearly installments, $34 billion: two and half times her 1913 annual income and ten times the tribute she had imposed upon France in 1871. Keynes had decried the pretension that such a sum could have been remitted through trade surpluses by a much weakened Reich in a competitive environment. After much diligent accounting of Germany's assets, he had suggested a reparation tribute of $10 billion dollars (that is, 75 percent of Germany's 1913 net product), to be amortized over several decades.[118]

With the blockade the Allies had already murdered 800,000 Germans and 1 million of their productive animals; blackmailing Weimar to kill more,

---

* See Chapter 5, p. 242–3.

Britain had her way, and brought Germany to sign the humiliating compact. On June 28, 1919, exactly five years after Gavrilo Princip's assassination of Archduke Ferdinand, as Dr. Johannes Bell, Minister of Transportation in Weimar's second Cabinet, accompanied to Versailles by Foreign Minister Müller, stooped to sign the Treaty, the pen's ink, like the blood in Faustus's arm, congealed: the pen would not work. Edward House, America's secretive negotiator, who stood by, leaned forward to offer his.[119]

Only then was the blockade lifted; only then did the Allies allow ships carrying food to dock at German ports.

Though his virtuosity and 'good heart' might have all been expended for naught, Keynes was yet determined not to begrudge his bourgeois aficionados another 'classic' inspired by the recent Parisian events, which he drafted hastily in the winter of 1919; he entitled it *The Economic Consequences of the Peace*. The book, which sold 100,000 copies instantly, and was translated into eleven languages, featured an unrelenting and self-satisfied indulgence in technical detail, mingled with occasional psychologistic portraiture, which alternatively dwelt on the buckle of Clémenceau's shoe, Wilson's neck muscles, and Lloyd George's goat-footed purposelessness. The Treaty, Keynes sentenced, was harsh and unjust, and it would fuel terrible resentment.

The book was the sort of Christmas buy that the educated middle classes could never forbear in their periodical and conscientious drive to keep abreast of international affairs. And it was the kind of book, too, that whispered the things these educated and yet perennially baffled readers wished to hear: little tales about the regrettable myopia, benighted judgment and malicious blunders of senescent fighters called upon tasks greater than they; little tales whose moral is that bad deeds always happen by pernicious mistake. Needless to say, Keynes's opus, like all expressions of so-called 'enlightened conservatism,' did not challenge the current state of affairs: the best solution, he concluded, was to stand behind the Weimar Republic, which was after all the creature of Versailles. He invited the various parties to moderation. So he played it safe and took the 'the middle road,' enumerating in his valediction the alternatives to Versailles, which were made to appear invariably worse than the status quo. Interestingly, this 'appeasing' excerpt foreshadowed the taste of the game that Britain would play in the 1930s versus the rest of the international community to push Hitler to war.* A game featuring Soviet Russia as the proverbial 'subversive enemy in the East,' against whom Britain would pit a Germany

---

*    See Chapter 5.

dumbfounded, and perennially jostled by her fear of Communist Russia, on one hand, and her no less intense contempt for the European neighbors, on the other.

> The present Government of Germany stands for German unity more perhaps than for anything else…A victory of [Communism] in Germany might well be the prelude to revolution everywhere; it…would precipitate the dreaded union of Germany and Russia; it would certainly put an end to any expectation which have been built on the financial and economic clauses of the Treaty of Peace…But, on the other hand, a victory of reaction in Germany…from the ashes of cosmopolitan militarism… would be regarded by everyone as a threat to the security of Europe, and as endangering the fruits of victory on the basis of the Peace…Let us encourage and assist Germany to take up again her place in Europe as a creator and organizer of wealth…[120]

Overall the Germans relished the book.

The seemingly honest and straightforward self-denunciation coming from a prestigious exponent of the British camp could not fail to soothe somewhat Germany's wounded honor, and much hope was thus staked on the book's cheering exhortation to set in motion 'those forces of imagination' necessary to overcome this 'dead season of [the West's] fortunes.'[121]

'Dead season', indeed, which did not, however, prevent Keynes from engaging immediately thereafter in happy-go-lucky speculation against the Reichsmark of poor, 'ruined' Germany: he sold it short, while buying dollars, making a killing. But in May 1920 the fall of the German currency momentarily halted: Keynes went under by £13,000. The book's royalties and a further advance from Macmillan, the publisher, of £1500 were not sufficient to plug the gamble loss: pawning his good name, Keynes was afforded a credit reprieve by his bank's director, who knew him as a famous man.[122]

The ball was now in the court of the United States, which was entitled vis-à-vis the Allies to approximately $10 billion worth of credits, over 40 percent of which from the British. Britain was a net war creditor as well, but the bulk of her loans to France, Russia, and Italy (roughly 90 percent) was of poor quality; understandably, Keynes had suggested as the chief remedy to the financial deadlock of the Peace Conference the cancellation of Allied inter-indebtedness.[123] But America, still holding on to her legitimate claims, withdrew from the European swamp. With two successive votes (November 1919 and March 1920) the American Senate, in a sudden plot led by Republican Senator Henry Cabot Lodge, defeated the Treaty, and left it to France and Britain to deal directly with their German neighbor. The United States would seal a separate peace with Germany in Berlin, on August 25, 1921, whereby the reparation dues indirectly owed to the United States were safeguarded.

By killing the Treaty, America not only yielded purposely to Britain and France the delicate management of the reparations, of which she ultimately held the strings, she also voided, no less designedly, a triangle of military assistance, contracted separately in 1919, between America, Britain, and France, aimed at protecting the latter '*in the event of any unprovoked aggression by Germany.*'[124]

Wilson, the rusted air pipe of much empty promise who had sworn to keep America out of the war in 1916, succumbed to thrombosis in a campaigning *tour de force* across the American heartland from Kansas City to Tacoma, which he had undertaken in early 1920 as a last measure to garner votes in favor of active American participation in the post-war administration of Europe. He was voted out of office in 1921. In Omaha Wilson, like many other 'moderates,' saw in the Parisian Treaty the seed of 'another and far more disastrous war.'[125]

But his Fourteen Points had baited the Germans into surrender – it had not all been in vain.

### Dreaming of Hitler and deciphering Versailles

Thorstein Veblen (1857–1929), more than a social scientist (the West's greatest), was a sea captain.

Shortly before the new century, he embarked on an evolutionary expedition to scrutinize human anthills with the cool meticulousness of an entomologist. But humans being in some critical respects different from insects, he soon ran into methodological difficulties: how was he to account for society's several forms of aggregate motion? Like various arthropods, men might practise deception, wage war, toil for the sustentation of the 'home,' and minister to an awesome 'queen' – thus far the zoological similitude might impose itself with cogency. But there were things that men did which the ants did not: for instance, *they prayed and they dissipated*. Why?

Veblen recognized that there was an entire range of human activities that were afforded no representation in the animal kingdom, which was broadly delimited by survival, cunning, and organization. And these activities were too singular and too strikingly human not to be accounted for in some form. What of, say, witch hunts, religious worship, mass sacrifice, or imperial pageantry? Who thought them first, and why? The origin of all such collective rites, Veblen reasoned, had to be lurking in a remoter lagoon he was yet to find. And while in the solitude of the cabin he engraved with neat calligraphy his travelogue in violet ink, his drifting ship kept gliding along. Until the bowsprit struck upon something. He had reached the reefs of 'occult agencies'. He never would or could steer his vessel through such a cruising ground, but he circumnavigated it, closely, and almost obsessively, alone, for over two decades – too frightened to penetrate it, too enthralled to lose sight of it.

> There is no call to undervalue occult agencies [such as manifest destiny, national genius, or Providential guidance]...but granting that these and their like are the hidden springs, it is also to be called to mind that it is their nature to remain hidden, and that the tangible agencies through which these presumed hidden prime movers work must therefore be sufficient for the work without recourse to the hidden springs; which can have an effect only by force of a magical efficacy.[126]

In 1915, Veblen returned from a long, virtual exploration of the German anthill. The famed culture of the Fatherland, whose language he read with facility, was far from foreign to him. Though a hyphenate creature of three worlds – the heart in Norway, the mind in America and the spirit at sea – by style, school, method, and erudition, Veblen was a 'German' institutionalist scholar himself.

But the re-emergence in the late Wilhelmine empire of the 'feudalistic ideal,' the 'overbearing magniloquence,' and the 'predaceous rule of the Teutonic invaders,' gripped him with a discomfort so acute that by the end of the investigation it had matured into full-blown revulsion.[127] As emphasized earlier, Veblen believed that the commonwealths of the West should have had much to fear from Germany's peculiar blend of 'warlike swagger' and technological sophistication.[128] But beyond this central political preoccupation, Veblen had discovered in the folds of German society, underneath the thin cloak of Prussianism, the presence of a deeper spring of collective motion. Something whose alien drift, under particular circumstances and through the agency of 'gifted personalities,' might have carried sufficient force to envelop the whole of Germany's social aggregate and transform it into an entity altogether diverse. Possibly inspired by recollections of Anabaptist furor, the captain gave the following description of the singular categories of 'gifted' types and of their potential doings under the influence of this hidden source:

In the successful departures in the domain of faith...it will be seen that any such novel or aberrant scheme of habits of thought touching the supernatural uniformly takes its rise as an affection of a certain small number of individuals, who, it may be presumed, have been thrown into a frame of mind propitious to this new fashion of thinking by some line of discipline, physical and spiritual, or rather both, that is not congruous with the previously accepted views on these matters. It will ordinarily be admitted by all but the converts that such pioneers in the domain of the supernatural are exceptional or erratic individuals, specially gifted personalities, perhaps even affected with pathological idiosyncrasies or subject to præternatural influences...The resulting variant of the cult will then presently find a wider acceptance, in case the discipline exercised by current conditions is such as to bend the habits of thought of some appreciable number of persons with a bias that conforms to this novel drift of religious conceit. And if the new variant of the faith is fortunate enough to coincide passably with the current drift of workday habituation, the band of proselytes will presently multiply into such a formidable popular religious movement as will acquire general credibility and become an authentic formulation of the faith. *Quid ab omnibus, quid unique creditur, credendum est.* Many will so come into line with the new religious conceit who could not conceivably have spun the same yarn out of their own wool under any provocation; and the variant may then even come to supplant the parent type of the cult from which it sprang.[129]

Veblen would not conclude his report without a physiognomic sketch of this German aberrant type that periodically heralded such religious awakenings 'from the deep.'

Temperamentally erratic individuals..., and such as are schooled by special class traditions or predisposed by special class interest, will readily see the merits of warlike enterprise and keep alive the tradition of national animosity. Patriotism, piracy, and prerogative converge to a common issue. Where it happens that ***an individual gifted with an extravagant congenital basis of this character is at the same time exposed to circumstances favorable to the development of truculent megalomania*** and is placed in such a position of irresponsible authority and authentic prerogative as will lend countenance to his idiosyncrasies, his bent may easily gather vogue, become fashionable, and with due persistence and shrewd management come so ubiquitously into habitual acceptance as in effect to throw the population at large into an enthusiastically bellicose frame of mind.[130]

The year was 1915. Veblen had dreamt of the Freikorps, Jünger, and beyond.

A convinced pacifist before 1914, he turned his coat to the disbelief of his colleagues and friends in 1917, when America entered the war. Shielding his approval of the US Administration's military effort behind a wall of silence and impenetrable reserve,[131] he advanced a proposal for securing lasting peace in the terminal chapters of his 1917 opus *The Nature of Peace and the Terms of its Perpetuation.*

For Veblen, the Great War offered the opportunity to rid the West of its chief ill: the dynastic spirit, of which, he claimed, Germany was imbued to a pathological degree.

Veblen insisted that with Germany's dynastic spirit, whose proneness to mischief was compounded by its extreme and unpredictable fanatical excrescences, no compromise was possible. It had to be extirpated, root and branch. The German people, he added, was no less susceptible to kindness than its European neighbors, but prolonged and unfortunate habituation to received schemes of feudalistic servility had molded its mind into a ferocious patriotic bent, which was 'not of the essence of human life.'[132] Germany, after the fire, would have to *unlearn* such archaic preconceptions. The remedy he envisaged for cementing a peaceful alliance of the West was what he termed 'coalescence by neutralization.' This meant forming a League of Nations, which would be led pedagogically by Britain and America – Veblen recognized these two countries *for the time being* as the pacific pillars of the world comity, despite the grave shortcomings of their inequitable monetary systems. Admitted within the League 'on a footing of formal equality,' Germany was to divest herself of her monarchy and shape her citizens into 'ungraded and masterless men before the law.'[133]

Veblen admonished the Western statesmen, were they to win the war, not to impose on Germany a trade boycott – a traditional trigger of national jealousy: 'the people underlying the defeated governments,' he wrote, 'are not to be dealt with as vanquished enemies but as fellows in undeserved misfortune brought on by their culpable masters.'[134] There followed a list of categorical directives applicable in the eventuality of Germany's defeat: (1) elimination of the imperial establishment, (2) removal of all warlike equipment, (3) cancellation of the German public debt, (4) assumption by the League of all debts incurred and equal distribution of the obligations assumed impartially among the members of the League, victors and vanquished alike, and (5) a single indemnification for all civilians in the invaded territories. He trusted that Britain, in whose hands the naval control would 'best be left,'[135] and America, 'about whom the pacific nations are to cluster as some sort of queen-bee,'[136] would implement them faultlessly. In 1917 Veblen appeared to confide in the good faith and missionary calling of the Sea Powers.

But the latter draft, in spite of the impeccable mechanics, was more the fruit of wish than of dispassionate reflection.

Veblen detested the Anglo-Saxon captains of finance and the inequality they congenitally thrived upon not much less than he despised the Junkers, the German absentees. And when the Russian Communists stormed the Winter Palace in St. Petersburg, his heart caught fire—he hurrahed the Bolshevik takeover of November 1917.

It thus seemed that in Lenin's Russia, the aspirations of Veblen might have found their definitive countenance: a promised land without landlords and corporate officers, where machines would be allowed to whir at capacity under the expert watch of disarticulated 'Soviets of engineers.'[137] Eden, perhaps. And though he was an assiduous traveler, he never visited the Soviet utopia, but rather contented himself with reading the extraordinary tales of early Red enthusiasts, who marveled over the thousand wonders of this mythical Eurasian realm of social emancipation.

'Bolshevism,' he wrote in 1919,

is revolutionary. It aims to carry democracy and majority rule over into the domain of industry. Therefore it is a menace to the established order. It is charged with being a menace to private property, to business, to industry, to state and church, to law and morals, to civilization, and to mankind at large.[138]

Enough, that was, to throw a heretic and master of iconoclasm of his caliber squarely into the Red camp. By the end of the war he had taken sides, he had chosen his colors.

And then in 1920 he was asked to review for the *Political Science Quarterly* what had already become the Liberals' new bible: Keynes' bestseller on the Peace Conference.

Hardly anyone noticed, but on this occasion, the captain sculpted Political Economy's most beautiful piece.

Sparing formalities, Veblen moved to demolish Keynes's tract *in toto*. The book's 'wide vogue,' he wrote, was in fact the commercial echo of the prevailing attitude of thoughtful men toward the same range of questions. It is the attitude of men accustomed to take political *documents at face value*...Keynes accepts the Treaty as...a conclusive settlement rather than a strategic point of departure for further negotiations and a continuation of warlike enterprise.[139]

It was rather unforgivable, Veblen suggested, for an expert 'so advantageously placed' as Keynes to fail so sonorously to discern the obvious nature of the pantomime orchestrated at Versailles. Behind a 'screen of diplomatic verbiage,' the Elder Statesmen were pursuing a precise design, whose main points Keynes, above all desirous like any other publicist of repute to reflect 'the commonplace attitude of thoughtful citizens,' successfully avoided.

The main argument, which Veblen was presently ready to unfold, was comprised of three propositions: (1) the thesis, (2) the prophecy, (3) the clue.

*1. Veblen's thesis.* 'The central and most binding provision of the Treaty is an unrecorded clause by which the governments of the Great Powers are banded together for the suppression of Soviet Russia...It may be said to have been the parchment upon which the Treaty was written.'[140] Veblen presently broke his brief intellectual truce with the Western establishment and resumed his inveterate opposition to capitalist oligarchism, determined this last time to fight till the end. Still riding on the wave of his starry-eyed tryst with Bolshevism, he reiterated that Communist Russia was a menace to absentee ownership, that is, a threat to a system predicated on the abolition of the disproportionate rents afforded by property and finance. Therefore, he continued, only the complete and swift annihilation of Bolshevism might be counted on to guarantee the peace of the business democracies of the West.

*2. The prophecy.* The pessimism, shock, and moral indignation at the Treaty's provisions, which ever since Keynes are still a must for anyone eager to strike the 'Liberal pose,' footed up to much unwarranted affectation, said Veblen, for 'the stipulations touching the German indemnity' rather betrayed 'a notable leniency, amounting to something like collusive remissness.' In other words, all the reparations garble was truly 'a diplomatic bluff, designed to gain time, divert attention, and keep the various claimants in a reasonably patient frame of mind during the period of rehabilitation to reinstate the reactionary regime in Germany and erect it as a bulwark against Bolshevism.'[141] The contrivance thought out by the British delegates in Versailles not to fix the terms of the German tribute sought to flush a torrent of 'bargaining, counter-chaffering and indefinite further adjustments,' in the swirl of which 'Germany must not be crippled in such a degree as would leave the imperial establishment materially weakened in its campaign against Bolshevism abroad and radicalism at home.'[142] So the Treaty was in essence an articulate trap by which the German upper class – the custodians of Reaction – were to be left untouched, and thus uncured of the feudal disease, while the grief and resentment of the underclass – the proximate victims of the reparations' bloodletting – was counted on to provide as much fodder for 'radicalism' as the sheltered Junkers required to re-establish a reactionary, anti-Bolshevik regime.

3. *The Clue.* What gave the Allied plot away? On the basis of his 1917 recommendations, Veblen observed that 'The provisions of the Treaty shrewdly avoid any measures that would involve confiscation of property.' 'There is no reason, other than the reason of absentee ownership', he continued,

> why the Treaty should not have provided for a comprehensive repudiation of the *German war debt*, imperial, state, and municipal, with a view to diverting that much of German income to the benefit of those who suffered from German aggression. So also no other reason stood in the way of a comprehensive confiscation of German wealth, so far as that wealth is covered by securities and is therefore held by absentee owners, and there is no question as to the war guilt of these owners.[143]

The levers of command of a modern democracy are not operated from its ministries, but from its financial network. *The financial strength of a capitalist regime is crushed the moment its portfolios of securities – bonds, stocks, debentures, and cash and all like titles of ownership – are passed into foreign hands. Such critical confiscation, which would have sapped the tenure of the German absentee owners, was never effected under the terms of the Treaty, and deliberately so.* Thus the nature of Versailles' diplomatic contrivances revealed that 'the statesmen of the victorious Powers have taken sides with the war-guilty absentee owners of Germany against their underlying population.'[144]

From this it followed that *all dispositions touching disarmament and indemnification* were to be sabotaged behind a hustle and bustle of diplomatic trucking so prolonged and muddled as to disaffect the participation of the unknowing public. Hereafter it will be seen how[*] Germany would begin to rearm in earnest with the secret cooperation of Russia as early as 1920, while, as a whole, her burden of reparations would have been, by 1932,

---

[*]   See Chapters 3 and 4.

*'very slight.'*[145] 'Indeed,' Veblen concluded, 'the measures hitherto taken in the execution of this Peace Treaty's provisional terms throw something of an air if fantasy over Mr. Keynes's apprehensions on this head.'[146]

In sum, Veblen's thesis was, of course, wrong: one thing of which the Liberal regimes of the West were *never* afraid was precisely Bolshevism, which they secretly nurtured since it took its baby steps in the spring of 1917. Veblen remained convinced to the last of Germany's war-guilt, when in fact, as argued in the previous chapter, the Prussian Reich had been but the drunken victim of an extraordinary siege entirely orchestrated by England.

As to the clue, the fate of Germany's financial wealth, whose complicated shuffle in the international system would indeed set off the disastrous hyperinflation of 1923,[†] followed a path more tortuous than Veblen could have foreseen in 1920, though his inference was on the mark.

But as far as the conspiratorial dynamics of the Treaty was concerned, Veblen was clairvoyant; he had made three considerations: (1) Germany was spiritually prone to a cyclical recrudescence of eerie fanaticism; (2) the sham of the reparations was designed to cause distress only among ordinary Germans; (3) the German dynastic absentees, that is, the true rulers, had been spared by the Allies any sort of punitive sanction. Therefore Veblen could deduce that the Treaty concealed a complex manipulation of the German situation – a manipulation whereby a movement animated by 'truculent megalomania' could be expected (1) to exploit popular dissatisfaction by fomenting radicalism at home, and (2) eventually come to an understanding with the propertied and military elites under the sign of war. The attack would be suitably directed against the enemy of choice: Bolshevism. In brief, with the terminology of hindsight, Veblen's review divined the advent of Nazism as the conjured champion of the disgraced German masses, and as Europe's contrived anti-Communist bastion. Versailles was an indescribable fabrication.

Thus Veblen prophesied no less than: (1) the religious nature of Nazism (2) the reactionary coming of the Hitlerites, and (3) Operation Barbarossa, Germany's invasion of Russia of June 22, 1941 (in his words: 'suppression of Soviet Russia,' 'Germany...as a bulwark against Bolshevism'), *more than 20 years prior to the events.*

The Treaty was no lamentable fumble, or, say, 'a disaster of the first rank,'[147] as all Keynesian fans have always been itching to believe; it was *not* the accidental prelude to World War II, but rather its conscious blueprint.

Had Veblen not invited all those Bolshevik romances to cloud his gaze, this gentle Quixote of the deep north would have seen that Versailles was

---

[†]   See Chapter 3, p. 121ff.

not aimed at Moscow, but at Germany herself; aimed, that is, at a colossal conflagration by which Germany, caught again between two fronts, could at long last be razed to the ground and *sundered in two,* right along the fault line – as she would be after World War II.

# 3 The Meltdown and the Geopolitical Correctness of *Mein Kampf*

## Between the Kapp and the Beerhall Putsch, 1920–23

Barbarians since time immemorial, rendered ever more barbarous by diligence, science and even by religion…This is a harsh thing to say, yet I must, because it is true: I cannot imagine a people that is more torn than the Germans. You see craftsmen, but no human beings, thinkers, but no human beings, priests, but no human beings, masters and servants, young ones and settled families but no human beings – is this not like a battlefield, where hands, arms and limbs lie scattered helter-skelter, while gushes of lifeblood sink through the sand?…

Friedrich Hölderlin, Hyperion[1]

Yet I long for Kaukasos!…I was told long ago that our forefathers, the German tribe quietly coasted down the Danube of a summer's day and reached the Black Sea, meeting with the children of the Sun seeking shade…For a while they stood in silence, then offered their hands in friendship.

Friedrich Hölderlin, *The Migration*[2]

### Erzberger: one man alone against the inflation

After the Treaty of Versailles was ratified, the incubation of Nazism began. Underneath the republican pretense of Weimar, the reactionary Right slowly reorganized itself: it spoke through the Nationalist press, and intimidated the Leftist opposition by unleashing against it the rage of jobless hooligans, whom the Conservatives shielded and patronized. Mistaking the Weimar regime, which was but the sham government imposed by the Allies, for a workable political experiment, the Catholic politician Matthias Erzberger treated the phoney Republic as a frail outfit which he trusted he might heal, without suspecting the perilous nature of the task. As he proceeded in the guise of Finance Minister to tax the elite heavily (1919), hoping thereby to defuse the risk of an inflationary implosion that loomed in the massive public debt amassed by Germany to fund the war, Erzberger was slandered, warned, and finally killed (1921). The incubation of Hitlerism, however, was from the first threatened by stalwarts of the old order – army generals and erstwhile high-ranking stewards of the Reich – that were seeking to enliven a monarchical league across Central Europe and Russia (1920). Nazism was still in its embryonic stage, and would have not survived such a change: the disgruntled royalists within the army wanted to go back to the old days; they shared a vision that had virtually nothing in common with that of the Nazis. England signed on Ignatz Trebitsch-Lincoln, an agent steeped in counter-insurgency tactics and disinformation, to thwart, expose, and burn all the monarchists conspiring against the Weimar Republic. The powerful industrialist Walter Rathenau, who threw himself actively into the politics of Weimar in 1921, likewise had ideas about taxing the rich into oblivion and therefore elude the provisions of the Versailles Treaty, but he too was defamed at home, and manipulated abroad into ratifying a 'secret' and, at first glance, strange pact of Russo-German collaboration (1922), through which the two 'European outcasts' would engage in full military cooperation before worrying at each other's throats in 1941. Before Matthias Erzberger might even begin to tap the financial holdings of the German absentee owners, these cashed in their War Loan certificates, and exported abroad the wealth of the country. As the rich redeemed their Treasury Bills and the government bought foreign exchange with which to pay reparations, the Reichsmark lost value fast: thus the so-called 'external depreciation' of the German currency was caused. Thence the Reich, in order to sustain the payments system, began to indebt itself at an accelerating pace by selling a swelling mass of government bonds (1921). The Reich's short-term indebtedness soared until it literally 'exploded' in 1923 under the pressure of non-renewal and massive redemption on the part of the former subscribers, both of which contingencies obligated the central bank to transform the bonds into a sea of (worthless) paper notes. The year 1923 marked the near disintegration of the German community: in its calamitous course, the infant Nazi Party made its first attempt at seizing power with the Beerhall putsch in early November. The putsch failed, but the Nazi creature, though immature, held remarkable promise: marked by a fervent Anglophilism and a fanatical, unbounded hatred for the USSR, which Hitler perceived as an expression of Judaic subversion, a new movement had emerged that might very well be none other than Britain's reactionary candidate for the forthcoming Russo-German conflict, as predicted by Veblen in 1920.

The story of Matthias Erzberger may best be understood if it is borne in mind that the Treaty of Versailles was never meant to weaken the elites of Germany, although the diplomatic and official rhetoric of the time gave credence to the contrary. As one historian put it, the Germany of the Second Reich was made of a Quartet and a head. The head of the quadruped was the monarchy, the administrative front legs were the bureaucracy and the army, whereas the agrarians and the industry formed the hind legs – the rest was cartilage and sinew. 'The essence of German history from 1918 to 1933 can be found in the statement *There was no revolution in 1918*...The only visible change was [the monarchy's] decapitation in November.'[3] What this signified was that any politician that would attempt to effect any sort of reform in the name of democracy with the newly available tools of a parliamentary system, would in fact be confronted by the opposing strength of the old order, which presently stood behind Nationalist parties set up ad hoc, with its industrial and financial might literally undiminished. That being so, any attack leveled at the upper class would be counteracted by a barrage of threats and abuse from the press, physical intimidation by thugs secretly protected by the elite, hostility from the judicial courts, and, last but not least, by the utter impassibility of Britain and the Allies, who would look on, surveying these savage fights with attentive detachment, like spectators in an amphitheater.

\* \* \*

Ever since its unreal conclusion, it has often been the vogue among historians to look upon Weimar as an era of missed opportunities.

> There were really two Germanies...Germany had tried the way of Bismarck...now it was ready to try the way of Goethe...The Republic was born in defeat, lived in turmoil, and died in disaster...Still, the choice of Weimar was neither quixotic, nor arbitrary; for a time the Republic had a real chance.[4]

It *never* did.

The Republic was, as Veblen understood, damned from the start. The salient developments of Weimar's 15-year run-up to the Third Reich were but the pangs of Nazism's gestation. The interminable parliamentary jockeying; the failures of 32 parties, 20 Cabinets and 9 elections; the 224,900 suicides[5] and 300 political assassinations;[6] the relentless shuffling of numberless economic proposals with no future; the two financial shock therapies (1923 and 1931); the literal inexistence of the republic's statesmanship and the puppeteering of the Anglo-American clubs; the violence; the allegedly impotent cynicism of the Allies; the population's leaden pessimism; the 'hairsplittings and tortured compromises over [the reparations' imaginary] millions and billions, [which] all seem scarcely worth studying today';[7] all these are pieces of a chronicle captioning the rise of Hitlerism.

The life-cycle of Germany's sham republic may be divided into three periods:[8]

1. a period of turmoil, 1918–23
2. a period of fulfillment, 1924–30
3. a period of disintegration, 1930–33.[*]

The Weimar republic was a laboratory for a social experiment: with the clauses of Versailles, Britain was waiting to resurrect from the rubble of the Wilhelmine Reich a political manifestation not unlike Prussian militarized conservatism, yet far more 'pure' in its hostility: a German reactionary movement, without the cloying accoutrements of regality. That the operation was going to yield the hordes of the swastika, might not, possibly, have been forecast by the majority of the Elder Statesmen of the West. But the expectation of witnessing in post-war Germany the rebirth of a grassroots front, wrathful and vengeful, was hotly entertained from the outset. The Veblenian prophecy is proof of such anticipation. The Allies were playing a most dangerous game.

In the helter-skelter aftermath of the failed revolution, the Germans, already sundered by the failure of all those policies of social insurance that Bismarck had introduced three decades earlier to pacify the proletarians, began to cannibalize one another immediately. 'November 1918' proved that Germany was incapable of revolution: *the turmoil did not produce a single charismatic leader of the working masses.*[9] After the generals were given *carte blanche* by the Socialist leaders to suppress the haphazard and hardly menacing riots of 1919, few doubted that the warriors would wait long before turning against the republic itself.

No sooner did the war end than the forces of reaction fomented at home a clime of acrimonious antagonism. After the war, General Malcolm, head of the British Mission in Germany, paid a visit to General Ludendorff – the reckless soldier who had come to govern Germany during the last three years of the war in the company of his elderly duumvir, General

---

[*]   The second and third periods will be dealt with in Chapter 4.

Hindenburg, until he had been sacked by the Kaiser shortly before the surrender.* And as they sipped tea, the German tried to convey to his guest how deeply betrayed the General Staff had felt in 1918 by the weakness of the domestic front and the sailors' mutinies; Malcolm, seeking clarification, queried the ex-Quartermaster: 'Are you trying to tell me, General, that you were stabbed in the back?' 'Ludendorff's prominent blue eyes lit up at the phrase, "That's it!" he shouted triumphantly. "They stabbed me in the back! They stabbed me in the back!"'[10]

During his testimony to the constitutional assembly's investigative committee on the war in November 1919, the other half of Germany's former military tandem, General Hindenburg, the hero of the East that had smashed the Russian armies on the Masurian Lakes,† would have coined this construction into the abiding slogan of Reaction: '[because of] *the intentional mutilation of the fleet and the army*...our operation necessarily miscarried; the *collapse* was inevitable...An English general said with justice: "The German army was stabbed in the back".'[11]

A 'stab in the back': it seemed plausible at the time – after all, the German army had not suffered a crushing rout. The Red agitation had been real enough; the republic was Wilson's idea, and the Treaty of Versailles was to all Germans a revolting disgrace. Therefore, many reasoned, Weimar was but a travesty, and an odious one to boot, regarded with indifference, at best, or contempt; Weimar could ask nothing else of Germany. The republic became a politicians' affair – gray, tedious, and purposeless. Weimar's interminable list of stewards was a triumph of anonymity – all obliterated figures, middling *brasseurs d'affaires* who took brief turns at the helm of a sinking ship swayed by external currents, which they could never resist. History, however, remembers two names: Matthias Erzberger and Walter Rathenau.

Both men, though starkly different, were extraordinary expressions of the *possible*: protean creatures of such skill and flexibility – intellectual and worldly – as to believe by an enormous sin of vanity that they could bend the world in whichever direction they listed. Each thought himself capable of altering the course of Germany's tragic destiny, and more concretely, of outwitting Britain at her own game *by making Weimar a workable proposition*: that is why history should remember them. Theirs was a gratuitous sacrifice, yet a revealing one as far as the Nazi gestation was concerned.

Matthias Erzberger, a parliamentarian for the Catholic *Zentrum* of indomitable energy, began his career in the first decade of the twentieth

---

* Chapter 2, p. 47.
† Chapter 1, p. 26.

century by investigating aggressively the scandals of the empire's colonial policies (embezzlement, mistreatment of natives, inflated bills for government orders, and so on): his revelations in 1906 brought about the downfall of the director of the colonial administration, and of his young secretary, Karl Helfferich, who nonetheless would rise to great heights in German political life, and subsequently swear undying hatred for Erzberger.[12] Like most of his contemporaries, Erzberger appeared to be an embodiment of Germany's jarring duality, which Veblen unveiled at the time, namely the commixture of chauvinism and progressive aspirations. In the name of the 'possible' Erzberger resigned himself to the impossibility of winning the war: in 1914 he had clamored for conflict and demanded annexations; two years later he found himself seconding most actively by innumerable missions abroad a peace proposal initiated by the Vatican. When all efforts failed, undeterred, ever the partisan of feasibility, he lent himself to the scapegoating tactic of the generals, and brokered, as mentioned previously, both the Armistice (November 1918), and the ratification of the Versailles Treaty (June 1919). The conservatives had so far turned Erzberger's vanity to account by making use of his prodigious art of the palliative, yet at heart they utterly despised his evolving appetite for practicable solutions, especially as these were now encroaching upon the 'national honor.' Thus, of the so-called 'November criminals' whom German reactionaries accused of having stabbed the nation in the back, Erzberger, blind to the consequences, had willingly and disingenuously become the symbol. After Versailles, a Democrat warned him: 'Today we still need you, but in a few months...we will get rid of you.'[13] This was an omen, but Erzberger confidently flouted it.

Since June 1919 Erzberger was aboard Weimar's second Cabinet as Finance Minister. In his first speech delivered the following month at the National Assembly in that capacity, he outlined Germany's present financial burden. By the end of the war, Germany had expended over 160 billion marks; this sum amounted roughly to twice her annual income at the end of 1918. The expense had been covered with long-term debentures to the extent of over 98 billion marks – this was the hard core of the country's debt, the war loan (*die Kriegsanleihe*) – and 47 billion marks of short-term government bills, the paltry remainder having been paid for with taxes.[14]

A war debt was a fair instance of the insanity of modern monetary systems: in this case, the German public was indebted 'to itself' for an amount twice as large as its income, expended on resources entirely dissipated. Individuals held portfolios of financial titles corresponding to property pulverized in a lost engagement, and they called it *wealth* – they expected to receive interest on it for many years to come.

As to who owed what to whom, Erzberger provided the details. Over 90 percent of all subscriptions to the war loan* were for modest amounts; this was the investment of the 'small people': they stood behind a quarter of the Loan. This implied that the remaining 10 percent of the subscribers (4 million out of 39 million investors), that is, the rich and super-rich, accounted for the 75 million marks left over – not to mention their quota of the short-term portion.[15] Of these 4 million affluent investors, about half possessed another quarter of the *Kriegsanleihe*. Finally, this breakdown led to the individuation of Germany's richest, the absentee owners: 5 percent of the total claiming *half the entire sum of the Loan*. Thus, sampling the war debt confirmed that *there existed before and after the war an elite numbering roughly 3 million individuals that commanded over half the country's resources.*[16] This was Germany's top out-of-sight class, which the architects of Versailles had taken pains to shield, and expected therefrom, in time, the financial encouragement of an anti-Bolshevik movement.

In defense of the petty investors, Erzberger vowed a financial crusade aimed at safeguarding the regular remittance of interest, that is, the income of the securities, to their legitimate owners. In sum, there were 160 billion marks worth of securities, yielding a yearly burden of 10 billion marks per annum weighing on the state's budget. Now, the question was, 'Who's going to pay the interest?' As it customarily happened, it was out of the wages of the laborers and, to a degree, of the middle class that the government levied the taxes with which the country's rentiers – the coupon-clippers – obtained their free stream of unearned income, what was otherwise called 'rent' (that is, something for nothing).[†] The pernicious repercussions of such a toll upon the German underclass prompted Veblen to recommend the unconditional repudiation of the war debt in its entirety, so as to curtail the sustenance of the German elite, and channel the amounts saved thereby to the reconstruction of the war-devastated areas.

But the Allies, *deliberately*, would not touch the war loan, and Erzberger had an unconventional idea. He declared his intention to overhaul drastically the incumbent fiscal system, centralize it, and instead of sweating the underclass for the benefit of the upper class, he left the underclass where it stood, and guaranteed the *Mittelstand* (the middle class) its flow of rents, at the expense of the absentees, *which he proposed to tax incisively*. His plan was, in fact, simple: single-handedly, he would have raised dramatically the

---

* The subscribers to the loan numbered 39 million individuals.
† Today, the system remains the same.

tax bill of the wealthy, and invited them to discharge their obligations by paying, if they so wished, with the war loan certificates themselves. Once in its hands, the Reich would have proceeded to destroy them instantly. It was a roundabout scheme to force the absentees to surrender their paper certificates almost for free. Thus Erzberger thought he could gradually deflate the public debt – take the water out of the jar, so to speak, before it flooded the markets...

In those days, neither such a paragon of the attainable as Erzberger, nor anyone else had sufficient imagination to contrive ways with which Weimar could service a debt of 160 billion marks, as well as transfer the forthcoming reparations installments and pay for the republic's new social commitments.

From Berlin's Finance Ministry, the apex of a swiftly renovated and most efficient reticulation of fiscal collection, Erzberger fired an arsenal of newfangled levies at the elite. The absentees were now the target of five different types of exaction: a two-pronged war profit tax on property and income, a hefty inheritance tax, a luxury tax on consumption, and to crown it all, a capital levy – the infamous *Reichsnotopfer*, 'Sacrifice to the Reich in its hour of need.' The new directives were buttressed by additional regulations designed to block capital flight, and the modern innovation of tax 'payment from the source by deduction from wages.'[17] The Finance Minister proclaimed then 'that in the future Germany the rich should be no more.'[18] In short, Erzberger had committed political suicide.

The tax-gathering had merely begun, when Karl Helfferich, conservative stalwart, former imperial Vice-Chancellor and Finance Minister during the war – indeed, the artificer of the giant war debt bubble – launched a libelous campaign against his arch-enemy Erzberger charging the latter of corruption, mendacity, and unlawful meddling in politics and personal business. While the Right-wing press supported the scourging passionately, and the Center-Left kept suspiciously mum, Helfferich bound his stack of tirades in a pamphlet titled '*Fort mit Erzberger!*' ('Let's get rid of Erzberger!'). Erzberger bit the bait and sued for libel. He was forsaken, and fought alone. The trial began in January 1920. It nearly came to a premature end when a 21-year-old 'half-crazed demobilized officer candidate,' Oltwig von Hirschfeld, attempted to assassinate Erzberger as he was leaving the court a mere week after the beginning of the proceedings. The first bullet pierced the minister's shoulder, whereas the second, the lethal one fired at the lungs, was deflected by the chain of his gold watch. After a few days, Erzberger was ready to resume the suit. Hirschfeld would claim in court that 'Germany was injured every day that Erzberger continued in power.' He expressed no regret, but, yielding to counsel, he pleaded that his intent was to wound, not kill, the politician. The female audience was charmed, and the useful idiot was 'sentenced to a grand total of eighteen months.'[19] In the meantime the Right did not spare itself in kindling the slander against Erzberger, including the fledgling Nazis, who, within the great choir of reaction, squealed from the nook of their taverns that the 'fat' Erzberger was a traitor for selling out the country to the victors at Compiègne in November, and foisting the Treaty upon the people. Yet no one dared to interject that both acts had been prompted by the military. Hugenberg, former director at Krupp, Germany's steel temple, and presently leader of the Nationalists and of a powerful media consortium, moved in, too, to pillory 'Erzberger the traitor' and decry the minister's 'socialization measures,' such as the 'expropriation,' he clamored, 'of the *middle class...*'[20] The denunciation did not lack in effect, though Hugenberg made his tongue slip in uttering it, for the class Erzberger was seeking to expropriate was not the middle, but the upper one.

In fact, the absentees scented the brew of trouble and started to export hurriedly their liquid balances denominated in marks, which they converted, beyond the border, into foreign currencies. At the end of 1919, the *Neue Zürcher Zeitung* published the news that by June 35 billion marks had already fled the country.[21] Between 1914 and 1918, because of the large injections of paper money devoted to financing the war virtually without taxes, the mark had lost half its purchasing power: so the inflation had already begun, *but by early 1920 it was accelerating.* Erzberger's hope to defuse inflationary outbursts turned out to be 'a poor prophecy.' Not only did the *Reichsnotopfer* fail to stem the mounting inflation, but it actually stimulated it.[22]

The trial was stacked, yet the prosecution could not even pin a crumb of malfeasant evidence on Erzberger. He was clean. His opponent, the tool of the elites, Helfferich, was found 'guilty of both libel and making false accusations' and ordered to pay the allegedly high cost of the trial,[23] and a ludicrous fee, whose paucity the judge justified 'by the fact that Helfferich had proved the substantial accuracy of his charges.'[24] In other words, the calumnies of Helfferich were not judged unfounded, but merely fulsome. The plaintiff paid the symbolic charge and carried the day. The tribunal's deliberation ended the political career of the defendant: Erzberger had defied the absentees, and, by plowing ever creative avenues of political understanding between the Socialists and Germany's progressive bourgeoisie, he had striven, in Weimar, for the achievable.[25] And thus, like Weimar, he was condemned. After the trial Erzberger resigned from his ministerial post, vowing to make a comeback as soon as the storm cleared up.

The court delivered its verdict on March 12, 1920. The following day, the republic experienced its first praetorian coup: the so-called Kapp-Lüttwitz putsch.

## Hiring Trebitsch-Lincoln to foil the Kapp Putsch

After the stipulation of the peace, the supreme command of the German army – the Hindenburg-Groener duo – stepped down. With the lapse of the link connecting the army to the government, the troops found themselves effectively without command from June to November 1919.

In the vacuum, the parties of Reaction, displaying uncommon resilience, joined forces at once to recapture what they perceived legitimately as theirs.[26] Naturally, Britain had contemplated such an eventuality. What the British were observing in 1919, as they and their Allies waged the invisible war against the Russian Whites, was a counter-movement of sizable chunks of the German army seeking to reorganize themselves to reclaim their Middle-European tenure. This somewhat confused but menacing stirring among the German warriors assumed unmistakable shape and color in eastern Prussia and portions of the Baltic states, where, many a month after the war's end, a farrago of Freikorps and uniformed renegades had stubbornly entrenched itself, fighting the Poles on one front and the Bolsheviks on the other, while fraternizing with Russian White chiefs.

The post-war situation stabilized after the lines of demarcation between Germany and Russia were made to encompass a cordon of brand new buffer states – from Czechoslovakia to Estonia by way of Poland – which were designed to keep the two states separated during the Versailles experiment. Then, at the insistent request of the Allies, the recalcitrant German generals were repatriated. Von der Goltz, the hero of the Latvian campaign,* and a solid anti-Bolshevik, returned in August 1919, while his troops for the most part stayed behind to rally round a White adventurer, Avalov-Bermondt. Funded by Germany's heavy industry to spearhead the overthrow of the Reds, Avalov's vanguard was on standby, serving through the winter of 1919 as a bridgehead to penetrate Russia's markets.[27] Over the ridge, Avalov and the German divisions expected to make contact with Kolchak, Denikin, Wrangel, and the other White chieftains.

From Tilsit in Eastern Prussia,† on December 9, 1919, the British representative of an international commission set up to deal with this mutiny, General Turner, reported:

---

* Chapter 2, p. 71.
† Now Sovetsk in the Kaliningrad area – Russia's carved-out dock on the Baltic Sea.

Eastern Prussia does seem not aware that Germany has lost the war. The military party is omnipotent and militarism flourishes in all its forms. Personally I have no doubt that a plot is being hatched to overthrow the government at this time, nor do I doubt that the army has sufficient force to carry it out.[28]

From his temporary exile in Sweden, Ludendorff regained Germany in February 1919. In October he patronized the Nationale Vereinigung (National Association), which garnered the cream of reactionary Germany: officers, bureaucrats, and industrialists, who since the Conciliar uprising and its bloody suppression in the spring of 1919, were bent on wrecking Weimar.

Indeed, the Germans had not been routed: they could still count, adding to the army a vast constellation of subterranean paramilitary groupings, on a fully-equipped strike force of approximately 2 million men.[29] If their coup succeeded, with the Russian panorama still in a state of flux, the Sea Powers' strategy of protracted encirclement would have suffered a disastrous setback. If the coup succeeded, and likely it would, a consolidated front of Whites – Germans, Russians, and Hungarians – jutting out into European Russia, would have undermined, if not wiped out Russia's Bolshevik rule, which was an Allied asset; and constituted the kernel of a Eurasian partnership, which in turn would have immediately led to Germany's repudiation of Versailles and afforded her immunity from a British blockade. The men of the *Nationale Vereinigung*, monarchist Prussians of the old school, no less anti-Bolshevik than Anglophobic, posed a clear threat to Britain's plans, and therefore they had to be stopped. Or better, *burnt*.

How Britain effectively deepsixed the forthcoming coup of the German Whites – another glorious masterpiece of intrigue of the history of the twentieth century – remains something of a mystery to this day. But a string of elements gleaned from the known chronicles may afford a partial threading through this affair.

On July 5, 1919, Ludendorff sent his former aide-de-camp Colonel Bauer to sound the British. Bauer, seemingly, laid out his cards on the table and queried the chief of staff of the British military government in Köln, Colonel Ryan, whether Britain would welcome a 'stronger' German government. Not a dictatorship, Bauer specified, but a resolute republic, which would brook no Socialist unrest, make the country 'work,' and thus honor its international obligations with punctuality and thoroughness. A republic, he concluded with a wink, which would find its most harmonious resolution in a constitutional monarchy, British-style.[30]

Ryan sensed the bluff; he merely had to take Bauer for what he was: the emissary of a faction of staunch monarchists, who did not harbor the least inclination to bow to Versailles, and who had sworn revenge against Britain by seeking some form of entente with White Russia.[31] But Ryan played the game and invited Bauer to pursue his project; he guaranteed the Allied blessing to the endeavor, provided that Bauer's boss, the conspicuous Ludendorff, whom the Franco-British public still looked upon as a 'war criminal,' confined himself to the background.[32]

On the same day, 'a leading light' of the reactionary cabal, Wolfgang Kapp, a former east Prussian officer in charge of agricultural affairs, and at the time an exponent of the Nationalists,[33] felt the pulse of the *Armeekommando Nord* (northern detachment of the Reichswehr), and ran by its chief, General von Seeckt, the idea of tearing up the Treaty of Versailles, and expelling by force the Poles from the Posen enclave.* Seeckt was no friend of Poland, but he had no desire to plot, rashly, against the British. Kapp was temporarily rebuffed.[34]

Meantime, in August, 1919, officially discharged from a British prison a month previously, Trebistch-Lincoln arrived in Berlin.

If there are, indeed, more things in heaven and earth than are dreamt of in our sorry materialist philosophy, Ignatz Trebitsch-Lincoln is assuredly one of them. Hungarian by birth, in 1879 in Paks on the Danube, he watched his father, a petty merchant, go bankrupt at the end of the century.[35] He then stole a gold watch, and fled family and jailers by seeking shelter in the Barbican mission for Jewish converts in London. There he pilfered the gold watch of his Anglican protector and returned to Hungary, which he abandoned immediately, and forever, as he found he was still wanted for the first theft. He was 19.

He then reached, by the skin of his teeth, Hamburg, where he converted to Christianity (Presbyterian). Disliking the stern life of the seminary, and finding no employ there, he embarked, with a German wife, en route to the Jewish mission in Montreal. In Canada, he passed to the Anglican camp, did not convert a soul, but was ordained a deacon nonetheless. To anglicize his surname, he appended 'Lincoln' thereto. After two years, monetary strictures forced him back to Europe: to London, via Hamburg. In 1903, he found employment as a curate in Appledore, Kent, though he failed to become a priest. Lloyd George was allegedly seen attending a few of his sermons.[36]

When Trebistch's father-in-law died, leaving the couple a small fortune, he forsook his clerical post at once and hunted for an aperture into politics.

---

* One of the portions of Germany ceded at Versailles to the new state of Poland.

Interviewed for a propagandist position in the temperance movement (anti-alcohol campaign), he was turned down, but on the occasion he stumbled upon the Cocoa King, chocolate entrepreneur Benjamin Rowntree, who was charmed by Trebitsch and offered him employment as a private secretary. From 1909 to 1916, as Rowntree's retainer, he conducted social empirical research on the rural conditions of northern Europe. Possibly, he joined a lodge at this time.[37] Boosted presumably by Lloyd George,[38] he then ran as the Liberal nominee for the district of Darlington in York; Winston Churchill, by letter, wished him success, so did Lloyd George. His frequent travels to the Balkan area attracted the curiosity of consuls and attachés of the Foreign Office. On a free trade platform, Trebitsch won, sensationally, by 30 votes over the incumbent conservative opponent. The improbable MP did not last beyond two speeches, as shady business left him insolvent and without the Liberals' endorsement.

Like Parvus Helphand a decade earlier, he descended to the Balkans in search of easy money: he promoted oil undertakings fitted with expensive American equipment acquired heaven-knows-how, but unlike his brother in conspiracy, Helphand, Trebistch failed his hand at business. At the outbreak of World War I, he was back in London and offered to spy for British intelligence 'as a censor of Hungarian and Rumanian correspondence at the War Office and Post Office.'[39] At this juncture the record becomes misty: it bifurcates into cautious yet terse archival collages on the one hand, and the vibrant narratives of dazzled raconteurs on the other, which the scribes of the former school dismiss altogether as 'entertaining absurdities.'[40]

Between December 1914 and January 1915, Trebitsch was in Rotterdam, the war's torrid crucible of espionage. What he cooked therein for a fortnight was left unsaid. The masters of embroidery swore he was working as a double agent, passing on to British intelligence information on the positions of the German troops on the one hand, while studying with the German Services, on the other, a plan to block the Suez Canal – England's gate to India – by sinking in its midst one or two ocean liners replete with cement.[41] Upon his return to London, he tendered to the intelligence officers an envelope containing the Germans' draft of unrestricted submarine warfare and the secret codes of Germany's intelligence in America.[42] A gift, he said. His case was then referred to Captain Reginald Hall, Director of Naval Intelligence, who gave him three days to disappear: it was unclear whether the British services were allowing Trebitsch to pay his way out of a death sentence for treason with the documents or setting him up for an assignment elsewhere.

In February he reached New York where he peddled sensationalist articles on his espionage activity between Britain and Holland. At the instigation of the British consul, he was arrested on charges of fraud: before the war, in the dire straits of insolvency, Trebitsch had falsified Rowntree's signature on a series of promissory notes. While waiting for Scotland Yard to dock in New York and extradite him to Britain, Trebitsch gained some reprieve by offering the FBI his services as a decipherer of intricate German cables. The Bureau accepted. Trebitsch was thereby granted a regime of semi-liberty, which he escaped altogether by running to a farm in New Jersey, where he would be finally apprehended and shipped back to Britain to stand trial. In July 1916 he was 'sentenced to three years' penal servitude' in a British penitentiary.[43] In other words, he vanished from the official record for three years – it is hard to believe that he stayed behind bars for so long.[44] Some claim that in the interim he even sojourned in Russia.[45]

On August 11, 1919, from Britain he sailed off to Holland. From Holland he crossed over into Germany.

'Stalking the pavements of Berlin...unemployed, friendless and starved... a penniless refugee,'[46] 'foreign-born, Jewish-born, ex-jailbird,'[47] Trebitsch, a mere fortnight after his arrival, managed to hook up with journalists gravitating in Right-wing circles and publish in their tendentious rags anti-British articles of the genre he had hawked in Manhattan in 1915.

By mid September he had so comfortably penetrated the inner core of Ludendorff's Nationale Vereinigung that he was ready to *lead a mission to Holland to harness no less than the ex-Kaiser to the forthcoming coup.*

The cool-headed biographers of Trebitsch, anxious to discount any 'conspiratorial fancies' that could arise from musing over such outlandish happenings, are unsparing in their efforts to characterize Trebitsch's trajectory merely as 'the empty pyrotechnic display...of a manic-depressive scoundrel,'[48] which, patently, is the most entertaining of all absurdities on this count.

Neither a spy[49] nor an impostor, Trebitsch in all likelihood was, like Parvus, one of those 'specialists' fluent in the art of subversion, who were part of a wider network of mercenaries fascinated in one form or another by the ways of *power*.

In 1919, so it appeared, Trebitsch, after being cooped up for a time, ransomed his freedom from Britain by carrying out one last assignment for the Crown. From the outset, isolated voices within Germany's Right cried wolf, denouncing Trebitsch as an agent provocateur of Britain, dispatched to Berlin to sink the anti-republican enterprise. For instance, Helfferich, Erzberger's foe, and allegedly former admiral Tirpitz, the father of the submarine sink-at-sight program, walked out of the game as soon as they were apprised of Trebitsch's involvement.[50] Yet by October, Trebitsch had Colonel Bauer completely in his grasp, and would work thenceforth as his closest collaborator.

The mission in Holland to lure the ex-Kaiser and the Crown Prince failed: Wilhelm and his son, possibly advised by their residential councilors, refused, so as not to compromise themselves more than they already had, to see this strange adventurer who was inviting them to march at the front of a monarchist coup. Apparently, they wanted no more truck with power.

Spun by the undaunted Trebitsch, the intrigues suddenly took a swerving turn towards the East: *Soviet Russia became involved*. The adventurer from Paks seemed to have talked the German conspirators into trucking with the Bolsheviks, as an insurance policy in view of an eventual defeat of the Russian Whites.

In November 1919, the Soviets had *de facto* two representatives in Berlin. One was Karl Radek, former Polish Socialist and talented publicist, who had thrown in his lot with the Bolsheviks, and had been thereafter selected as one of the privileged few that had accompanied Lenin in the journey through Germany scheduled by Parvus in April 1917. On December 8, 1919, Bauer met Radek.[51]

Before Radek, Bauer adumbrated the possibility of an understanding between officers and workers: he asked Radek whether Moscow could placate the laborers via their German mouthpiece, the KPD, and thus prevent them from striking and thus disrupting the smooth development of the impending coup. Radek, non-committal, replied that such a decision rested with Moscow.[52]

The other Soviet official presence in Berlin, was that of Vigdor Kopp, ambassador of sorts since November 1919, who, according to the memoirs of Trebitsch, encountered Bauer several times. Again, Bauer asked Kopp to exert pressure on the KPD not to hamper the coup with the proclamation of a strike.[53] But while these fantastic negotiations were being woven, the German monarchists secretly printed counterfeit money for the White Army of Avalov.[54]

In 1920 the pace of events accelerated. On January 10 the Versailles Treaty went in force. The Allied note demanding that Germany hand over the 'war criminals' (Articles 227–30 of the Peace Treaty) exploded 'like a bomb' on February 3; it was accompanied by a list of 900 names, including those of Kaiser Wilhelm, Ludendorff, Tirpitz (who pioneered the use of poison gas on the Western Front) and Helfferich. Though France was not feigning, Britain, of course, was: she had no desire to see Kaiser Wilhelm, one of

Victoria's grandchildren, hang, but the news had sufficiently envenomed the public spirit: the Reichswehr generals were ready to resume the war.[55] The German government tarried, and nothing would come of the Allied requests – no 'patriot' would ever be surrendered.

On March 8, Colonel Bauer called on the British once again, but this time, General Malcolm, Chief of the British Mission in Germany, responded with a clear rebuff. 'The Entente,' he sentenced, 'refuses categorically any counter-revolutionary coup.'[56] Such an action, Malcolm added, was 'sheer madness.'[57]

On March 10, the commander of the Berlin detachment of the Reichswehr, General von Lüttwitz, refusing to comply with the injunction to reduce the army by 200,000 by April 10, 'aggressed' the Cabinet enjoining it to resign, revoke the disbandment order, call for new elections, and allow the formation of a cabinet of non-partisan technocrats. His demands were rejected; President Ebert ordered Lüttwitz to give way and go into retirement at once.

On March 12, Erzberger was politically finished, and on March 13, the Ehrhardtbrigade, the jewel in the crown of the Freikorps, marched into Berlin – the coup had begun. It would last exactly 100 hours, from March 13 to March 17, 1920.

The ex-bureaucrat Wolfgang Kapp and the dastardly von Lüttwitz fronted the putsch. *Trebitsch had taken over the post of Press Chief.* All the while, the meanest of the mean poured through the *schick* arteries of the capital: Freikorps troops mingled with the *Baltikums* – the veterans of the Baltic fights, identifiable by the white gamma cross adorning their helmet. They could be heard singing: '*Hakenkreuz am stahlhelm, schwarz weiss rotes Band, die Brigade Ehrhardt werden wir gennant*' ('Swastika on helmet, black, white, and red brassard, the Ehrhardt brigade is what we are called').[58]

> They are young, green young for the most part. They display the grimy countenance of men who have long campaigned. They are swift and supple, drilled. Beautiful soldiers...They examine the riches and occasionally the landmarks of the great city with a curiosity laced with savage covetousness...The Gauls must have been like this on the first hours of the conquest of Rome.[59]

Germany was torn: East and North were with Kapp, whereas the South and West, excepting Bavaria, seemed loyal to the republic, or resolved to stay neutral. The army, however, was silent and on the lookout: von Seeckt, since November 1919 Chief of the Army Command – the reconstituted and much reduced replica of the General Staff of yore – pressured by the Cabinet, refused to intervene against Lüttwitz: 'the army would sit on a fence until the issue of this trial of strength could more clearly be discerned; it would then descend...on the side of the winner...Whatever the outcome,...the army would retain its position as the ultimate source of sovereign power.'[60] Which is to say that the success of the coup would *not* hinge on the will of the army, no matter how favorable it was to the putsch.

In principle, three were the parties whose endorsement the putsch needed to succeed: the army, labor, and banking. The first, as proven by Seeckt's temporizing, had been virtually won over. The second, in spite of Colonel Bauer's anxiety, was in fact irrelevant.

It has often been claimed that the Kapp putsch was muffled in the general paralysis created by the unions' courageous call to strike in Berlin. But that was not the case. The strike was set in train haltingly, as the coup was struck on a Saturday. It was *not* proclaimed by the Cabinet exiled in Stuttgart,[61] but triggered by the Socialist unions, initially *without* the accolade of the KPD's leadership, which, instead, diffused an appeal on the 13th not 'to lift a single finger for a government engulfed in the shame of the murderers of Karl Liebknecht and Rosa Luxemburg.'[62] Rhetorical reference was here being made to the responsibility of the Socialist Minister Noske, who had bargained with the Freikorps for suppressing the Berlin Council in January 1919.* This instance was of singular importance, for it proved that the Russian representatives (Radek and Kopp) had kept their word, at least for a day, and that the German Communist Party (the KPD) was indeed being instructed by Moscow to refrain from thwarting the praetorians' putsch.

Only on the following day would the KPD join the strike, pulled by the fervor of the rank and file eager to lend a hand to 'their trade-union comrades.'[63] The initial abstention of the KPD was all the more striking as the officer directly responsible for the assassination of Liebknecht and Luxemburg in 1919, Captain Waldemar Pabst, *was himself one of Kapp's putschists*.

The strike gathered steam only after March 15, on Monday, *when the coup had already failed*. In fact, the true protagonists of the putsch, the soldiers, did not in the least suffer from the faltering interruption of public services: shops and telephone lines were unaffected, while the strike was indeed in risk of misfiring as distress was mostly felt in the working-class neighborhoods, which could not avail themselves of any kind of technical assistance.[64]

* See Chapter 2, p. 53.

General van der Goltz, in putschist outfit, ordered to shoot at the picketers, but his order was disobeyed for the match had been settled elsewhere, and it was now over.

The fate of the putsch was decided in the halls of the Reichsbank. On Sunday, March 14, Rudolf Havenstein, the governor of the central bank, received emissaries of the putschists, who addressed him with a request for money with which to pay the troops drafted on a mere piece of paper undersigned by Kapp. Havenstein with protocolar punctiliousness responded that withdrawals could only be effected by means of special checks, which were in possession of the Chancellery. And, almost derisively, the governor added that the bank did no business on Sundays...The envoys politely retired, and reappeared the next morning with the checks regularly signed by Kapp; the banker, cool as ever, replied that he knew of no Kapp. The scene repeated itself the following day, as Havenstein refused to honor a few more checks signed this time by Lüttwitz. On the brink of desperation, the cabal summoned Ehrhardt, the *Kapitän* himself, to seize by force the reserves of the Reichsbank. Ehrhardt retorted that he was an officer, not a safe-cracker. The *Kapitän* must have understood that cash could only tide the coup over for a week, as banks were not chests bursting with shimmering tokens, but *lenders of 'keys'* – keys to their network, which in common parlance were referred to as 'lines of credit.' And the lines of credit, that is, the money, had been denied; the jig was up.

By the 17th, all had fled: Kapp had taken a plane to Sweden; Lüttwitz had gone into hiding in Hungary; Ehrhardt, Ludendorff, and several other Freikorps commanders had run south, to Munich; Trebitsch was 'among the last of the conspirators to leave the Reich Chancellery building.'[65]

On March 17, an old war plane flown out of Munich by the former ace Greim had just landed on a Berlin airfield, carrying Dietrich Eckart and his assistant Adolf Hitler, who had been sent by Captain Mayr 'to instruct Wolfgang Kapp on the situation in Bavaria.'[66] As Hitler alighted, a man rushed in his direction and shouted at him: 'Beat it! Lüttwitz is finished, the Reds have taken over the city!'[67] Allegedly, the man was Trebitsch. According to another source, in the disarray of the last hours, Eckart and Hitler reached the Chancellery, where they caught a glimpse of Trebistch climbing up the stairs. Eckart was supposed to have said: 'Come on, Adolf, we have no further business here.'[68]

With false identification supplied by the legate of the Soviet embassy, Vigdor Kopp, Trebitsch and Bauer abandoned Berlin.[69] The insurrections sparked by the general strike across Germany (especially in the Ruhr), and subsequently repressed by the Reichswehr battalions all through the spring, caused about 3,000 deaths, and proved once again that proletarian uprisings in Germany, however truculent, never posed a serious threat.

In Bavaria events had taken the opposite course. The local Reichswehr commander, von Möhl, 'without supporting Kapp directly,' had taken the 'opportunity to remove the Hoffman (Social-Democratic) government from office at to install Gustav von Kahr, a senior official with conservative-monarchist leanings, as commissioner.'[70] Thus in Munich, unlike in Berlin, the officers had managed *not to alienate* the party of finance and industry. Had the Kappists proceeded likewise in Berlin, so thought historian Arthur Rosenberg, the coup would have succeeded.[71] The British press representative in Germany, Lord Riddell, confided to his diary in March 1920 that a successful royalist coup might 'change everything.'[72]

What was Trebitsch attempting to achieve through this enterprise? After the conspirators' escape from Berlin, rumors circulated in the press to the effect that the coup 'could be blamed on a certain British agent – Trebitsch-Lincoln, [who] had started the *putsch* and then had caused it to fail, "with the object of winning the confidence of credulous officers and politicians, and of keeping the British Government informed – naturally by indirect channels – and receiving its instructions for every step".'[73] This surmise of an 'imaginative journalist from Berlin,' otherwise discarded by Lincoln's biographers as yet another 'absurd conjecture,' held, however, more promise than the opposite contention, namely that Trebitsch had thrown himself body and soul in the coup for the sake of his putative megalomaniacal thirst.

Though we may reasonably assume that Trebitsch was indeed hired to make the putsch fail, we do not know exactly *how* he did it:[74] the documentary evidence is too thin, although there is every warrant in the presumption that the true paralysis created at the center of the Reich in mid March 1920 issued not from the strikers, but from Trebitsch's improvised Press Office. He disseminated, solo or in concert is impossible to tell, an avalanche of false, incendiary, and contradictory information in a cross-pattern of unfathomable complexity. At least three of such key messages seemed to originate from him:

1. To the political Left. On April 18, 1920, the press organ of the KPD (*Die rote Fahne*, the *Red Flag*) revealed that the adventurer Trebitsch-Lincoln, 'the true political mind of the Ludendorff-Bauer consortium,' had declared to a 'trustworthy source' that the Kappists were looking forward to provoking the working classes to launch a putsch of their own, which would be 'drowned in blood.'[75]

2. To the bourgeoisie. Starting on March 17, the *Frankfurter Zeitung,* the voice of finance and heavy industry, which for the past three days had in an odd turn of phrase called for open resistance against Kapp and 'foreign imperialism'[76] (who was the foreigner?), diffused a series of communiqués, according to which von Lüttwitz himself, Colonel Bauer, and Captain Pabst had conducted negotiations with the Independent Socialists aimed at guaranteeing the *Baltikums' support to the Communists for the establishment of a Councils' Republic.*[77]

3. 'To the British.' At the putsch's inception Trebitsch told 'the foreign correspondents that he had spoken with General Malcolm, who assured him that the British government favored the new regime.'[78] The British Mission denied the canard so vehemently as to incommode Brockdorff-Rantzau, Germany's former Foreign Secretary, beseeching him to disabuse the Kappists of such dangerous fancies. Thereupon the diplomat stormed into the Chancellery to inform the putschists Kapp and Ludendorff, who swore to the friendship of the British, that the claim was a *sacré mensonge* ('a bloody lie'). 'That got the two gentlemen.'[79] The collapse ensued.

Two additional clues:

1. When one of Russia's chief envoys to Germany, the journalist Radek, returned to Moscow in February 1920, he drafted a report for the People's Commissars, in which he opposed the project of a military league with Germany; the Soviets decided neither to accept or refuse. On March 3, however, Radek was heard on the radio conciliating: 'We think that now capitalist countries can exist alongside a proletarian state.'[80] And on March 14, the second day of the Kapp putsch, he wrote in the mouthpiece of the Soviet regime, *Isvestia*: 'The military coup in Germany is an event of world significance…By ousting Noske, General Lüttwitz has torn that rag called the Treaty of Versailles…As long as this regime lasts we are ready to live in peace with it, though we expect its imminent end…'[81]

   This was the identical line recited by the German KPD in summoning the workers *not* to join the anti-Kapp strikes.

2. Trebitsch disclosed to the correspondent of the *Daily News* 'that his party had the support of Winston Churchill, received through Cologne.' In this regard, Britain's chief military representative in Germany, General Malcolm, annotated in his diary on April 15, 1920, '*Except in so far as Winston Churchill is concerned there is just the shadow of truth in it,* and this, no doubt is the foundation of all the stories of British support.'[82]

'Rumors of British involvement persisted for several weeks in spite of further denials...by Malcolm, and even by Prime Minister Lloyd George, in a statement at the House of Commons.'[83]

So the chief of the British Mission in Germany did confirm that Winston Churchill had indeed granted some sort of recommendation to Trebitsch. This was an extraordinary confession. A confession that enables one to guess with some ease the nature of the operation.

The Trebitsch mission filled a twofold role. First, it was a plan to flush from the brush the German White guards and prevent them from consolidating their not insignificant influence within industry and finance, by dragging them to center stage in a premature coup that could only abort.

Trebitsch *must* have presented exceptional credentials to the generals for being taken in so fast and so deeply within the conspiracy: amongst these a 'solid connection' to the British – *this was the link to Churchill, which Malcolm authenticated*, and which explained the stubborn conviction of Kapp, Bauer, and Ludendorff that their position was always secure from that angle. At this time, Churchill served officially as Air Minister, though he acted, thought, and breathed for Britain's Secret Intelligence, with which since 1909 he had sealed an indissoluble bond that would govern the rest of his life.[84]

The other, indispensable ace was, as previously emphasized, *the connivance of Soviet Russia*, who pretended from the start to flirt with the German generals, knowing as well as the British, whom the Russians informed of every move,[85] that Ludendorff and company were bent on overthrowing them: everyone was aware that it was with the Russian Whites, not the Reds, that the German generals wanted to consort. When the putsch began, the KPD stayed put. Soviet Russia's fake-up allowed Trebistch to conjure a specter of enormous proportions, which would have appalled the bourgeoisie and kept newspapers of all colors abuzz with speculation for a long time thereafter: *namely the fantastic bogus of a so-called 'National-Bolshevik conspiracy'*; that is, the rumored entente between German officers and working-class leaders – *which was an impossibility*.[86]

In the KPD's *rote Fahne*, Trebitsch would be depicted as the 'deus ex machina of National-Bolshevism.' General Ludendorff's right-hand man, Colonel Bauer, and a handful of officers were indeed seen in Berlin confabulating with trade union leaders but not one of these showed any desire to cooperate. The depth of the mystification was such that a paper as informed as the *Frankfurter Zeitung* went as far as to contend,[*] absurdly,

---

[*]  See above, p. 108.

that Freikorps commanders like, say, Pabst and Ehrhardt, who had truly drowned in blood the Workers' Councils of Berlin and Munich in 1919, were actually partaking in a National-Bolshevik coup seeking to resurrect those very same Councils (!). These were all falsehoods manufactured and artfully diffused by Trebitsch, thanks to the excellent and complicit stage acting of Britain and the USSR.

Trebitsch played his cards all at once: (1) he foxed the generals with the trump of his 'British connection'; (2) he terrified the Socialists and led them to strike by fabricating the rumor that the Freikorps had come to provoke, and thence terminate violently, a rebellion of the workers; (3) and he estranged the parties of finance and industry with the bogey of the resurrected Councils.

Second, the miscarriage of the Kapp putsch was a spectacular dress rehearsal of the scheme performed 20 years later to deceive Hitler prior to the attack against Russia,* which consisted in splitting the British power base into two virtually opposed factions (that is, Churchill versus Malcolm), and employing some means – in this case Trebitsch – to make the opponent believe that the faction allegedly supporting him was the stronger one.

After the storm, Berlin's chief of police, Richter, was at a loss to read the conspirators' mind: 'either they belong to the asylum,' he reflected, 'or they have been deceived deceivers.'[87]

But the European adventure of Trebitsch was not yet over. Undeterred, the putsch survivors gathered in Munich to revive a drawn-out scheme 'for monarchical *coups* in Austria, Hungary, Czechoslovakia and Germany, and for a subsequent march on Russia by forces of these countries assisted by White Russians and former prisoners of war.'[88] By mid 1920, the rout of the White Russians was all but complete, and such conspiracies had grown somewhat threadbare, but Trebitsch's task was not accomplished – not until, that is, Middle Europe was rinsed clean of all Whites.

Of the inner clique of plotters, only Major Franz von Stephani, another Freikorps chief, suspected the truth, and without mincing words he proposed to Bauer and fellow Freikorps commander Ehrhardt to dispatch Trebitsch on the spot. Bauer paid no heed to the murderous purposes of Stephani. But Trebitsch found out. The juncture was propitious for exploding the so-called 'White International,' once and for all.

Disguising it as the panicked counter-move of a man fearing for his life, Trebitsch spirited a thick folder of the Whites' late conspiratorial designs, which he sold to the Czechs in Vienna, who in turn handed it over to the French and the British: as a result several secret military organizations

*    See Chapter 5.

were disarmed and most Middle European White conspirators exposed and burnt. Then, armed with six passports, Trebitsch disappeared in the Far East. 'Nothing more is heard of him until September 4th, 1922, when he called upon the United States Embassy in Tokyo. One report, never verified, stated that at the time he carried a Soviet Russian passport,...and that he was on his way to Tibet to help German officers organize an attack on India'. Trebitsch would resurface in Shanghai as a Buddhist monk named Chao-Kung ('Light on the Expanse').[89]

'A royalist coup,' as the British put it, would indeed have 'changed everything.' Had the coup succeeded, the Versailles Treaty might have all been for naught. True, Kolchak was already finished when the Kappists invaded Berlin: thus a White, full-fledged Russo-German alliance could hardly have come into being at the time of the putsch, but a revived dynastic Reich, propped by a few satellites in Central Europe, would have certainly conspired, and successfully so, to loosen completely the unsteady grip of Bolshevism over Eurasia in the medium term by bolstering the armies of the other Russian Whites – Denikin, Yudenitch, and the survivors of the Siberian debacle. Second, though the sparse presence among the Kapp conspirators of the *Baltikums*, with their be-swastikaed helmets and chilling chants, might have made the putsch look like a precursor of Nazi awakening, to interpret it as such would be a great mistake: this coup was a royalist, not a Nazi, uprising. Kapp, Ludendorff, and associates had nothing to share with the resurfaced racialist cult of underground Germany, which would later rally round the 'gifted personality' of Hitler – the eventuality that Veblen had scented in 1915. Had the generals had their way in 1920, they would have re-established a pale copy of the Wilhelmine order, and this would have thrown a wrench in the British works; it would have thrown the Nazi incubation out of kilter. Thus, all in all, Trebitsch fulfilled his assignment splendidly: he burnt the European Whites at the a critical time when these could have helped to reverse the fate of the Russian civil war, and repudiated Weimar, with its mock parliamentarism, reparations, chronic social strife, and built-in devices for incubating 'the enemy of tomorrow.'

Trebitsch had been a midwife to Nazism.

On March 31, 1920, virtually on the morrow of the Kapp putsch, Hitler was officially discharged from the army, and would from then on devote himself exclusively to politics. He set out to rebuild the party, which was so broke that it did not even have a rubber stamp,[90] by changing its name to the 'National Socialist Workers' Party of Germany' (NSDAP).[*]

---

[*]  Nationalsozialistische deutsche Arbeiterpartei.

By February of the following year he had eclipsed all other personalities within his burgeoning movement, and risen as its leader and unchallenged propagandist. In August 1921, preparing for the clash against Communist and Socialist militias, he assembled the nucleus of the SA (Sturm Abteilung: 'shock division,' also known as the 'Brownshirts'), which he disguised under the charter of an athletic association.

While the SA were being fitted, Matthias Erzberger spent a holiday in the Black Forest of Baden before his return to politics, which he had announced in June at a meeting of his party – the Catholic Center-party, the Zentrum. He intimately trusted that he would become Chancellor soon.

On his walk up to the Kneiben mountain on August 26, 1921, accompanied by a friend, he was accosted by two youths, who crippled him with bullets and finished him off at close range as he crawled to seek shelter behind a pine tree.

The police had warned him repeatedly of a possible attack. No tears were shed. The conservative press wrote that: 'A man like Erzberger…was a standing menace so long as he was alive.'[91] The killers, two young officers by the names of Heinrich Tillesen and Heinrich Schultz, fled to Hungary, aided by certain nationalist elements within the Bavarian police.

Hitler's shock troops were put to the test in November 1921 in the first of a lengthy sequence of bloody tavern brawls with Socialist and Communist workers: SA commander Rudolf Hess proved his mettle.

In May 1921, the London schedule for the war reparations was finally disclosed. Germany presently owed the Allies a total sum of 132 billion marks ($34 billion). The Germans were, unsurprisingly, outraged.

In June, the country went to the election booths, and the vote swung unmistakably to the Right – no less unsurprisingly, the SPD, and with it the republic, had pleased no one. Now the leadership was made of a coalition of the Center with the Democratic Party. There began the so-called *Erfüllungspolitik* (the 'policy of fulfillment'): the government declared that Germany would do its best to comply with Allied demands.

## Walter Rathenau, the reluctant victim of the Russo-German pact

Walter Rathenau was, despite the progressive if not revolutionary nature of his late social visions, one of those diehards of yesterday's world – a late captain of industry longing to become a utopian king. He came to symbolize the spiritual disarray of Germany: a country unhinged by the war, and incapable of mastering the consequences. Resolved after the defeat to commit seriously to politics, Rathenau, as Reich Minister, would try to reason with the Allies on the subject of reparations and foreign policy – the keystones of the British conspiracy. Though honest and well intentioned, he, like Erzberger before him, would do so with a conceit and presumption such that all he would be able to procure for Germany and himself was a death sentence from the Right-wing clans. His was but one of many remarkable German tragedies of the era: an exceptionally gifted individual who refused to acknowledge the devilish entrapment into which the British had fitted Germany after the war; he refused to own that he was in fact attempting to do politics 'in a cage,' and that no amount of maneuvering, however brilliantly conceived, could dissolve those constraints. Not even a man of his stature, in fact, would be able to achieve a single task of all those he had set out to accomplish; and his conspicuous political impotence culminated in the reluctant acquiescence to the 1922 deal between Russia and Germany: a semi-secret military cooperation that would pave the way for Germany's martial rehabilitation, and would last, unbelievably, *two decades* – until the very last days preceding Barbarossa, in June 1941.

By May 1921, Germany paid only 40 percent of the preliminary $5 million slice it owed according to the Treaty of Versailles. When the final bill was issued the grand bluff of the reparations reached a climax amidst a welter of conferences, experts' opinions, and infinite accounting cryptograms filling the pages of Europe's financial papers that rendered the matter all the more impenetrable: of the $132 billion, $82 billion was packaged as bond issues to be honored in the foreseeable future, which is to say that they were set aside and forgotten – the extra ciphers had been thrown in for mere sensational display.

That meant that Germany was to pay the other $50 billion at a rate of $2.5 billion a year in interest and $0.5 billion a year to reduce the total debt.[92] An annual tranche of the debt amounted to around 5.8 percent of Germany's 1921 GDP, or about 40 percent of the country's foreign obligations per annum:[93] to remit that much in gold or foreign exchange seemed unthinkable.[94]

Could Germany pay? She could if (1) the Reich scored a perennial budget surplus, or (2) if she sold abroad more than she bought from foreigners: a surplus on the foreign accounts would afford pools of foreign currencies, which would be then remitted to the enemies of yesterday. The scheme would in fact amount to sending gifts abroad: exporting gratis. Because of her immense war debt, and because of the Allies' steely resolve to impede Germany's competing on the world markets, neither condition was satisfied.[95] As proven by the murder of Erzberger, German absentees resisted taxation; and the French, themselves indebted to Britain and America, refused to be paid the reparations in the only form in which they could have been remitted: that is, through acceptance of German goods and services. To cap it all, Britain placed a 26 percent tax on all imports from Germany. Thus everybody knew, as Veblen had presumed, that *Germany could not, and thus would not pay.*

So, Germany found herself beholden to France (and Britain), France to Britain, and Britain to America: the United States was therefore saddled with the unattractive role of the soulless financial taskmaster. Not a single encounter at the top on the subject of reparations would end without a choral entreaty to the American representatives to cancel the inter-Allied debt. And not one would end without their 'sadistic' refusal.[96]

As all blamed the Americans for the deadlock, the latter bounced the issue back to the British, who blamed the French, who again blamed the Germans. And so on. In this unique script of the *théâtre de l'absurde*, Germany, as Minister for Reconstruction Walther Rathenau saw it, played the part 'of a sane man taken and confined against his will in an insane asylum during a long period with the result that he gradually assimilates the mental traits of his associates.'[97] Menaced in the distance by America, harassed by a hysterical France, listened to but profoundly deceived by the British hypocrite and her pet Soviet sphinx, Germany did go insane.

In such an atmosphere, Walther Rathenau made himself the victim of hopeless candor when, in March 1921, he approached the US negotiators to suggest that Germany could perhaps put an end to the charade by cutting the Gordian knot: she could shoulder the Allied debts in bulk, by offering to pay America $11 billion in 41 installments of $1.95 million each.[98] Thereby she would indebt herself directly to the United States, set the Allies free, and deflate at once the bulging load of European grievances. Upon hearing the proposition, Washington hissed, and the British Foreign Office rebuked: 'no such compromises would be tolerated.' A recent study found Rathenau's proposal 'bizarre': thus, even to this day, Rathenau has not been pardoned for partially discerning in a moment of stillness the purposeful perfidy of the reparations.[99]

Diplomats...handled the important but alien field of economics with the circumspection of men charged with the care of an unpredictable elephant, while [Rathenau] treated it with the nonchalance of the native speaker.[100]

And though he grasped the technical details of the matter at hand, Rathenau yielded to vanity: like Erzberger, this other Demiurge of the 'possible' belittled the chauvinistic hostility of the German environment, and thought himself fully capable, alone, to redress the fate of Germany and shape her in his image.

On August 31, 1921, Germany paid her first billion gold marks of reparations. The transfer was a veritable ordeal: the money was raised by pawning with the international banking network thousands of tons of silver and gold, which were conveyed by caravans of railroad boxcars to Switzerland, Denmark and Holland, and by a fleet of steamers to the United States – a treasure trove epic from the Dark Ages.[101] This first remittance caused an immediate drop of the mark vis-à-vis the dollar, from 60 to 100 (marks per dollar).[102] As Germany suffered the hemorrhage of gold, which by law had to cover every paper note in a ratio of 1 to 3, the market predicted a fall in the 'value' of the paper mark. Indeed, in May 1921, the German central bank had suspended the gold convertibility: in other words, it had proclaimed that its notes were no longer 'as good as gold' – the hyperinflation was approaching.

Walther Rathenau was the crown heir of an economic empire inherited from his father, Emil, who had built it with the sweat of his brow. With a patent purchased from Edison, Rathenau senior founded AEG (Allgemeine Elektrizitäts Gesellschaft, the 'General Electric' of Germany), which illuminated Berlin and Germany, and through interlocking stakes in a galaxy of local companies and foreign banks, brightened Madrid, Lisbon, Genoa, Naples, Christiania, Mexico City, Rio de Janeiro, Irkutsk, and Moscow.[103] A brilliant scion of a great corporate dynasty, Walther was groomed, schooled and raised like a prince; he juggled with polyvalent facility business intricacies and technological detail, which he seasoned with Talmudic lore and classical erudition. 'He talks about love and economics, chemistry and trips in kayaks; he is a scholar, a landowner and a stockbroker, in short, what the rest of us are separately, he is rolled into one.'[104]

Rathenau's first political assignment, like Erzberger's, concerned the colonies of the empire: in 1907 he had accompanied the colonial secretary Dernburg on an inspection in Africa. During the war, Rathenau helped to organize the home front by designing the mechanics of an imposing system of resource mobilization (the so-called *Kriegswirtschaftsgesellschaften*),* which, via requisitions, foreign purchases, and the procurement of ersatz materials (substitutes), fed the hungry war machine[105] – a tradition that would be

---

*  Consortium for the War Economy.

resurrected in Göring's Four-Year Plan in preparation for World War II.[*]
Then, sensing 'change' in the air, as the war had unleashed new spiritual
flows, he etched out a blueprint for tomorrow's society in a bestseller that
consecrated him as one of Germany's most popular authors.

Society, he averred without blushing, was governed by '300 individuals'
who knew one another, an odious oligarchy, 'arrogant in its wealth,'
exercising 'both secret and open influence,' which was trailed by a 'decaying
middle-class...[endeavoring] to save itself from being pushed down into
the proletariat,' all the while 'the real proletariat...silent, stands beneath;
a nation by itself, a dark sea.'[106] In *Von kommenden Dingen* (*In Days to
Come*), written in 1916, Rathenau prophesied that 'a will surging from the
depths of the folk soul' was bound to destroy capitalism; 'a responsible
lordship' made of 'intelligent dynasts' would cleanse Germany of the
encumbrances and injustices of inheritance rights and forever impeach
free trade in capital, so that the community's wealth might be shielded
and its lifeblood conserved. In October 1918, he could not bring himself to
digest the surrender of the Reich; from the columns of the *Vossische Zeitung*,
he summoned the German soldiers to put up a dogged resistance, while
haranguing the citizenry at the same time to take to the streets in a *levée
en masse*. Then, in 1921–22, he contributed the fruits of this kaleidoscopic
experience to the *Erfüllungspolitik* – he too was now a modern champion
of the possible, as well as a compromised creature of the old order.

In April 1922, as Weimar's Foreign Minister (since October 1921), Rathenau,
despite himself, became at last the unwitting prey of the 'asylum tactics'
played against Germany on the international scene. The occasion was the
Genoa conference, which for the first time since Versailles, gathered 'both the
Russians and the Germans – the two bad boys of the European family.'[107]

At Genoa, the customary comedy was re-enacted: Britain encouraged
France by inviting it to draft, jointly, a memorandum on reparations, in
which emphasis was laid on Article 116 of the Treaty. Article 116 provided
that Russia could, whenever she wanted, be cut in on the German
reparations.[108] The gambit whetted France's appetite in that she believed
that she was offered yet another weapon with which Germany might be
further excruciated: and that was by offering Russia an economic partnership
to be funded not by France herself, but by an additional amputation of
Germany's wealth. The Soviets were then instructed to exploit this threat by
luring the Germans, who were fearful of Article 116, into ratifying a secret
alliance with them. The stratagem was orchestrated from Lloyd George's

---

[*] See Chapter 5, p. 227.

residence, the Villa Alberti, where British, French, and Russian diplomats held negotiations behind closed doors, while the Germans were left outside to consume themselves with anxiety. Three times Rathenau demanded to be received by the British Prime Minister while the *pourparlers* were under way; three times he was ignored. Historians have lamented ever since Lloyd George's 'discourtesy,' but the 'impoliteness' was merely the final ruse in a critical sub-game of Versailles' ploy. Late in the evening of April 14, the Russians sought out the Germans, and proposed to retreat like elopers to the nearby resort of Rapallo where they would conclude a friendly compact. The German diplomats held a session in their pajamas, and after much deliberation, agreed – it was 'Rathenau who held out the longest.'[109] The Treaty of Rapallo was signed on April 16, 1922. Rathenau signed somewhat against his will.[110] He was attracted to the Bolshevik idea, but he then confided to his entourage that he wished he could have undertaken such a step with the official accolade of the Allies: he was not comprehending the game in the least; he had lost all touch with political reality.

The treaty with the Russians acknowledged the intention of both countries to resume commercial intercourse, and nullified any financial cross-claims that existed before the war: in other words, Russia would not claim any moneys from Germany. This move seemed a tiny step in the direction of the Eurasian embrace. But was it? Did Britain appear worried? Hardly. Naturally France screamed with disappointment, but Maltzan, the German diplomat in charge of Russian affairs, was seen dancing at the conference's ball with Mrs. Lloyd George, whose husband entertained no doubt that Rapallo signified first and foremost a pact of military cooperation between Russia and Germany. Not only did the British Prime Minister not disapprove of the treaty, but he also justified it conveniently and diplomatically as a beneficent counterweight to France's bullheaded pressure to extend the French border to the Rhine and thus dissolve German national unity: *British 'appeasement' towards Germany had already begun.*[111] Thus Britain had altered her tactics somewhat: now she openly declared that a rehabilitation of Germany was necessary to counteract French arrogance; but behind this ploy lay Britain's ultimate goal, and that was the gradual rearmament of Germany. Here we may observe another standard British routine at work: Britain used French hostility as a pretext to shield Germany, and relied on the assistance of Russia to achieve the objective.

Twice so far the expectant recruits of the Freikorps had been let down: after the liquidation of the Councils, and with the cacophonic coda to the Kapp putsch. In the seedy rentals of Berlin, they talked politics, plotted, and drew up lists. Lists filled with names of *Erfüllung* politicians, artificers of the possible that were trying their best, by nurturing Weimar, to impede the exhalation of 'mystical forces which the mind, with all its patterns, cannot get to know.'[112] Weimar's new 'outlaws' – Cadets, Freikorps veterans, and demobilized soldiers, the young crop of Germany's Conservative Revolutionaries – were on the hunt: men like Rathenau stifled them – he was on the list.

'One can't breathe!' panged ex-Naval officer of the Ehrhardtbrigade, Erwin Kern, 24, as he painted his despair to his comrades Ernst von Salomon and Hermann Fischer. 'We've got to pierce the crust to let in some air in our cramped German spaces!'[113] Von Salomon would live to tell the tales of these *Geächteten* (the Banished Ones) in a book by the same title that would become one of the 'sacred texts' of Germany's New Right. 'On November 9,' Kern cried, 'I shot a bullet through my head...I am dead...the force demands destruction, and I destroy...I have no choice but to devote myself to my beautiful, implacable destiny.'[114] Rathenau?

Rathenau had begun an 'active policy' of fulfillment; he was 'a bridge': a bridge between Jewry, which Rathenau depicted as 'the dark, pusillanimous cerebral breed' of his ancestors,[115] and the blond heroic, mindless Aryans, whom he adored; he was a corporate scion wishing for capital taxation and the abolition of bequeaths; an economist yearning for theocracy, a technician dreaming of the commune. Rathenau, von Salomon complained, was too much, and too little, 'all rolled into one,' like his book, *Of Days to Come*, which all the *Geächteten* had read and thought it lacked 'dynamite': to them, he was attempting to lock Germany on a path that was not her own.[116]

The assassination was scheduled for June 24, 1922.

Von Salomon, not selected to turn the heat on Rathenau because of his 19 years of age, asked Kern what to tell the police if the rest of the commandos were arrested. 'Say whatever you will,' he replied, 'say that Rathenau was one of the Elders of Zion, or some such idiocy...They will never understand what moves us.'[117]

Meanwhile, on the political stage, Rathenau, like Erzberger, was thrown to the wrath of the Right. The Nationalist partisan Helfferich, again, not content with having driven Erzberger to his death, resumed the invectives of yesteryear to lash out at Rathenau in the same fashion.

As the pan-Serbs did with Ferdinand, the Outlaws ambushed their victim's limousine. As the car came into view, Kern sallied forth and squeezed on Rathenau 'a nine-bullet burst point blank.' Fischer lobbed a grenade. Rathenau was seen being catapulted in the air. His chauffeur sped him home, where a doctor pronounced him dead.[118]

The mark began to plummet: from 370 in June it fell to 1175 to the dollar in August, 1922.

Barricaded, after a mad chase, in the top floor of the ramshackle castle of Saaleck, the two young assassins, Kern and Fischer, made a last stand against the siege of the police. In the ensuing shoot-out Kern was killed by a bullet through the temple. Fischer laid his companion on a stretcher, shouted out the window a last 'Hoch!' for his leader Ehrhardt, and blew his brains out.[119] At the trial, Kern's accomplices perfunctorily rehashed as the motive for their crime the 'idiocy' that Rathenau was indeed one of the 300 Elders of Zion conspiring to dominate the world.

All these murderous youths were armed and financed, and all recent political killings, including Erzberger's and Rathenau's, were systematically traced back to the conspiratorial panel of an unidentified OC (*Organization Consul*, Ehrhardt's informal crew of bodyguards). Speculation was rife, but proof was scant; Freikorps commander Ehrhardt, for instance, denied that his boys had anything to do with Erzberger's death, though he did not entirely disown the kids that participated in the assassination of Rathenau.

Yet forensic certitude was never of the essence: everyone intuited that the 'boys' were simply the *longa manus* of Germany's reactionary Right: Erzberger, Rathenau, and many others, were but the collateral damage of this horrid fratricidal feud, which Britain had caused by shoehorning the dynastic Reich into a sham republic. She made the Germans play the parliamentary game, while waiting for the Reaction to make a comeback at the opportune time: these deaths, like the rest of the innumerable catastrophes that would beset Germany throughout the interwar period, were the effect of this perverse plan.

[Writer Ernst Jünger] asked [von Salomon] in his drawling Lower Saxon accent: 'Why didn't you have enough courage just to say that Rathenau was killed because he was a Jew?'...[von Salomon] answered: 'Because it wasn't so.'[120]

Hitler, however, disapproved of the Outlaws' terroristic tactics: 'It is laughably illogical to kill some [isolated] fellow,' he commented, 'while nearby sit dogs who have two million dead on their conscience. [What we need is] 100,000 fanatical fighters for our way of life.'[121]

The Treaty of Rapallo was the formal ratification of an entente that dated back to late 1920, when the envoys of the *Truppenamt** chief, General von

---

* 'A camouflage for the General Staff, which Germany was forbidden, by the Versailles Treaty, to maintain' (Carr, *Bolshevik Revolution*, p. 319).

Seeckt, had established contact with Trotsky, Radek, and the commanders of the Red Army for laying the groundwork of both countries' rearmament.[122] Already by January 1920, *even before the Kapp putsch*, Seeckt had accepted 'a future political and economic agreement with soviet Russia as "an irreversible purpose of our policy", while at the same time proclaiming that "we are ready to form a wall against Bolshevism".'[123] Putatively, the cornerstone of the new alliance was the destruction of Poland, their common enemy, yet Poland for the time being was left alone while military collaboration on the other hand was sizably scaled up. Facilitated since 1921 by the Soviet factotum in Berlin, Vigdor Kopp, with the approval of Trostky, and the full intelligence of the French, British, and Polish services, the promotion on Russian soil of German drilling stations and factories of poison gas, planes, and tanks, and an intense traffic of officers in both directions proceeded most smoothly.[124] For the purpose 'General Kurt von Schleicher created within the Defense Ministry the "Special Branch R", which in 1922 sent the first officers to be trained in Russia…A number of Russian officers, among them the future Chief of Staff of the Red Army, Tukhachevsky…came to Berlin to study the way of the Truppenamt trained aspiring officers.'[125] Further plants for military production were built in Turkey, Sweden, the Netherlands, and Switzerland.[126]

> The telegraph wires remained hot with news of German arms sales to Russia, [and] German officers serving in the Russian army…Foreign Office officials noted these violations of articles 170 and 179 of the treaty of Versailles*, but nothing happened. At no time did the Foreign Office visibly react to the incoming information. In reply to a parliamentary question concerning German-Russian negotiations [Secretary] Curzon simply evaded the issue by stating that His Majesty's Government had no *official* information about the talks.[127]

And so, if Germany had to rearm, she had to do it in a 'presentable' fashion: namely by hiding the process behind a pact of outcasts, as it were, sealed with the Soviets, which were engaged from the start in a double deception: passing off as capitalism's enemy and Germany's friend. As for France, Britain would never let her perform as anything other than the perennial thorn in Germany's side.

With or without Seeckt, who resigned in 1926, or Rathenau, the so-called Abmachungen – the 'special operations' of the Reichswehr in Russia

---

* Article 170 forbade in Germany the production, import and export of 'war material,' whereas Article 179 prohibited the promotion of German foreign military missions and exchanges.

– would continue until March 1935, when Hitler abrogated the Treaty of Versailles.[128]

Indeed, the only stable feature of the Weimar regime was the tenure of Defense Minister Gessler, the army's nexus to the government, who would hold on to his ministerial saddle through 13 Cabinets, from 1920 to 1928. The constancy denoted the permanence of the Reichswehr as 'a state within the State,' provisioned by a special budget out of the purview of the Reichstag, which cascaded in a myriad of secret slush funds untraceable even by the most seasoned of parliamentarians.

> Since 1920, the German Republic always had a double government: that of the Chancellor of the Reich with his ministers and that of the generals. Whenever a disagreement arose, the army always won. All of this was called 'German democracy.'[129]

### The hyperinflationary purge of 1923

The collapse of the German currency in the winter of 1923 is one of the most famous economic disasters of the twentieth century. The great German inflation concluded Weimar's preliminary period of turmoil; and it was of tremendous significance for it projected the Nazis to the forefront of international news. This episode was a spectacular illustration of the way in which financial earthquakes might give birth to peculiar political developments. There is no basis for claiming that the plotters of Versailles could have aimed at provoking a Nazi coup by engineering a financial landslide. But there remains the incriminating clue that the British deliberately abstained from sequestering at Versailles the certificates of the German war loan from their wealthy subscribers, who held the bulk of such securities. Now, when the victors of World War I imposed the payment of vast sums in foreign cash to Germany, whose debt bubble was twice the size of her income, it is somewhat difficult to believe that they could be unaware of the serious repercussions of such a set-up. Therefore, considering how deeply proficient the British stewards were in the matters of finance, we may confidently assume that London fully anticipated a short-term financial calamity in Germany. What Britain most likely sought to obtain therefrom was a 'purge' of the Reich's accounts: as a gargantuan inflation has the effect of annulling the government's debt, the Allies were possibly counting on turning Germany into a *tabula rasa* for a massive foreign investment campaign, which would indeed be organized from London with American money in 1924 (see Chapter 4). In addition to this immediate and crucial economic result, the annihilation of the country's currency, clearly, might also be expected to destabilize the nation greatly; and at the paroxysm of Germany's monetary dissolution (November 1923), finally, the Nazi movement irrupted onto center stage. It attempted, and bungled, a rash coup in Munich, which recycled even a few Kappists. But, most important, it introduced to the great audiences the 'gifted,' 'erratic' drummer of the movement: the 34-year-old Führer, Adolf Hitler.

Thus evolved the exchange rate of the paper mark to the dollar according to the official statistics of the Reichsbank and the quotes of the Berlin Exchange between 1918 and 1923 (Table 3.1):[130]

*Table 3.1*   Paper mark – dollar exchange rates, 1918–23

|  | Exchange rate |
| --- | --- |
| 1 October 1918 | 4.00 |
| 1 October 1919 | 31.28 |
| 1 March 1920 | 100.00 |
| 1 June 1920 | 44.87 |
| 2 January 1921 | 74.40 |
| 1 July 1921 | 75.00 |
| 2 January 1922 | 186.75 |
| 1 July 1922 | 401.49 |
| 2 January 1923 | 7260.00 |
| 1 July 1923 | 160,000.00 |
| 1 August 1923 | 1,100,000.00 |
| 4 September 1923 | 13,000,000.00 |
| 1 October 1923 | 242,000,000.00 |
| 1 November 1923 | 130,000,000,000.00 |
| 30 November 1923 | 4,200,000,000,000,000.00 |

In this interval, the German currency traversed four phases.[131] In 1919, with the lifting of the blockade, as imports of necessities far exceed exports, the government relied on its depreciated currency to stimulate international commerce. Foreign investors banked on it too, and from July to November 1920 the mark experienced a short spell of 'good health': unemployment was virtually null and trade, domestic and foreign, was brisk (second phase). Then, from May to November 1921 (third phase), when the London schedule of reparations began to bite into the foreign reserves of Weimar, the upswing of 1920 betrayed its artificial nature, and the public alienated itself from the mark progressively: in other words, people started to get rid of their marks either by jettisoning them on the exchanges or spending them on tangible goods *(Sachwerte)*. From late 1921, and especially since the assassination of Rathenau (June 1922) until the end of the 1923, Germany was in the clutches of hyperinflation – that regime of currency depreciation whereby prices rise by a monthly rate greater than 50 percent.[132]

Exasperated by America's veto to the cancellation of the inter-Allied debt, France, in a fit of fury far exceeding the expectations of Britain, decided to improvise: on January 9, 1923, she accused Germany of defaulting on her obligations. Two days later, 17,000 French and Belgian troops, accompanied by a corps of professional engineers, marched in the Ruhr – West Germany's coal-rich industrial basin – to commandeer the deliveries of coal, which, by the letter of the Treaty, were their due. Alluding to the intransigence of a number of Midwestern congressmen behind the American veto to European debt remission, a British journalist sneered: 'The secret of the Ruhr must be sought into the Mississippi Valley.'[133]

Britain publicly condemned the invasion, yet she did not budge to hinder it. The area occupied was no more than 60 miles long by 30 miles wide, but contained 10 percent of Germany's population and produced 80 percent of Germany's coal, iron, and steel; its railway system was the most complex in the world.[134]

The 'policy of fulfillment' died with Rathenau: the Wirth Cabinet fell in November 1922, to be replaced by Weimar's first uniform 'capitalist government,'[135] headed by the director of a prominent shipping company, Wilhelm Cuno. When the French invaded, Cuno proclaimed Weimar's new course, 'passive resistance' it was called: a general summons to resist Allied prevarication by refusing to comply. The French raped, provoked, and bullied. Special money was printed by the state to sustain the striking miners. In 1923 an egg came to cost 8 million marks, and pasteboard shells were substituted for wooden coffins.[136] Unemployment trebled, prostitution was rampant, and malnutrition in the slums led to malformation: working-class children, according to zealous Reich inquests, formed a miserable lot in these days. The Nationalists were ablaze. For the first time since 1919, the people rallied solidly behind the Republic, though Hitler and the Nazis roused them to boycott the general strike: 'Weimar is the proximate enemy,' Hitler raged, 'not France!' All the while, countless acts of sabotage by isolated and despaired patriots – 400 of whom would be executed, 300 by Germans – hardly made a dent in France's requisitions: the Ruhr industrialists themselves, for fear of losing market share, guaranteed the supply. At dawn the workers rose to extract the coal; they heaped it into towering piles, which at dusk the invaders carted off to France. So much for 'passive resistance,' which, with the complete collapse of the mark in late 1923, marked the catastrophic conclusion of Cuno's Cabinet and of Weimar's convulsed preamble.[137]

How could a single dollar reach a quotation of 4.2 trillion marks by November 1923? Two broad explanations have since been advanced: an inculpatory and an exculpatory one. The Anglo-American inculpatory thesis held in brief that the Germans cheated their way out of the reparations burden by printing money recklessly; whereas according to the German exculpatory thesis, the reparations toll imposed at Versailles had sent the Reich authorities scrambling for foreign cash, which they could only obtain by depleting part of the country's stock of precious metals, and by selling marks ever more cheaply. Such a drop of the Reichsmark abroad, so went the German thesis, rendered imports more expensive, and therefore caused a general rise in price levels: the general price increase spread to wages and salaries, and forced the government to accommodate, by running an exploding short-term debt, the growing requests for more means of payment. In the words of Reichsbank governor Havenstein:

> The fundamental cause...is the boundless growth of the floating [short-term] debt and its transformation into the means of payment through the discounting of the Reich Treasury bills and the Reichsbank. *The root of this growth, the enormous burden of reparations on the one hand, the lack of sufficient sources of income for the ordinary budget of the Reich, on the other, are known*...For the Reich must live, and real renunciation of discounting in the face of the tasks set by the budget...would have led to chaos.[138]

The British thesis, more specifically, ascribed every surge in domestic prices and the international fall of the mark to the steadily swelling short-term indebtedness of the Reich, which, indeed, as shown by the record, suffered an irresistible expansion throughout the triennium 1920–23. What additional money the public was not eager to lend to the state, the latter procured from the central bank, which 'discounted,' that is, advanced cash against the Treasury bills: to every such advance corresponded a net injection of liquidity into the economy. Every time the central bank bought government bonds, it 'transformed' these bonds into 'money': partly in check money, which traveled on checking accounts, and partly in cash – bills and coins, which the state printed and minted upon orders from the central bank. Up until mid 1922, the public and the Reichsbank each covered half the Reich's expenditures.

This was how the British ambassador in Berlin, Lord d'Abernon, characterized the Reichsbank policy:

[Reichsbank governor] Havenstein...although honest and straightforward, is ignorant and obstinate...*Havenstein apparently considers that the fall in German exchange is quite unconnected with the gigantic increases of German note issues*, and he goes on merely turning the handle of the printing press, completely unconscious of its disastrous effect.[139]

Despite the state of disrepair that still characterizes the debate on the German hyperinflation, the British thesis seems to have won the day and acquired in time the veneer of dogma: in fact, it is simple, plausible, self-righteous and, despite d'Abernon, *completely false*, whereas the German argument, instead, is ashamedly elliptical, and thus only half true.

German wealth was rated at 300 billion marks in 1913.[140] Approximately a third of this wealth had been shot into the air during the war, which left Matthias Erzberger in 1919 with the implausible task of taxing, especially by means of his capital levy, about half the country's patrimony to redeem the 98 billion marks of the war loan: he failed, and paid with his life for having tried.

But Erzberger's attempt triggered a fundamental reaction that has been egregiously undocumented by the Reich statistics and the vast literature on the subject: capital flight. In the absence of reliable figures, many a 'scholar'[141] has hastened to belittle the significance of the capital escapades through the 'the hole in the West' (*das Loch im Westen*), that is, all those avenues afforded by complacent banks for the export of capital out of Germany and into the marketplaces of the West. Yet there is no ground to impeach the supposition that after 1919 the net transfer of German wealth abroad was immense. In 1923, the *New York Times*, in an attempt to assess the magnitude of German deposits in the United States, arrived by guesswork at a figure of nearly $2 billion,[142] that is, approximately a quarter of Germany's GDP in 1923: that in the United States alone.[143] But the largest recipient of Germany's capital flight was reputedly Holland, though Switzerland, Norway, Sweden, Denmark, and Spain were the repositories of much additional fleeing money. Innumerable steel and industrial potentates literally dismantled the factories at home and re-erected them across the border. From the Netherlands, the re-established corporations proceeded by mergers to acquire in Germany insolvent concerns, which were used to camouflage profitable ventures abroad: these German branches supplied the holding company headquartered in Holland for amounts denominated in paper marks, and well below the true value of the consignments to defraud the German fisc, while the mother firm stored abroad the precious foreign exchange earned through her international sales.[144]

After 1923 the [Dutch] economy began to grow at an unprecedented rate...The large deficits on the balance of trade disappeared...Shipment of goods through Dutch harbors that were dominated by transit trade with the German hinterland grew at the staggering rate of 16% p.a. between 1920 and 1929...The Dutch economy had never seen anything like this before, and these rates still compare favorably with the 1950s and 1960s.[145]

Goodwill. Holland would not show herself an ingrate 20 years later: in the first months of World War II, when fighting in France was still in progress, Dutch arms manufacturers already accepted German orders, and the railway system was put at the disposal of the German authorities so that trains could run directly to the French border.[146]

Large patrimonial possessions in Germany were seldom caught in the nets of the fiscal authorities, which unavoidably ended up collecting (depreciated) money mostly from the middle class: Erzberger's financial crusade, run aground by the inflation, boomeranged and ended up harming his very protégés. By 1921, the Right would have wrecked in the Reichstag every project designed to confiscate the money of the wealthy investors.[147]

So capital flight, as mentioned earlier, was already in motion by the end of 1919; what quota of Germany's wealth the absentees managed to lay away in foreign countries is unknown. *The transfer of such funds in marks, and their subsequent conversion into other currencies, exerted a tremendous pressure on the exchange value of the mark, and on the Reich's budget, which was deprived to a large extent of its taxable base.*

Contra the British thesis, the advocates of the German explanation have repeatedly and justifiably called attention to the Reich statistics, which reveal: (1) that the public debt rose as the inflation regressed, and vice versa (lack of systematic correlation); (2) that the drop in the exchange value of the mark was always far steeper than the increase in paper money circulation;[148] and (3) that the so-called 'external' depreciation of the mark always *preceded* the domestic rise in prices, the 'internal' depreciation:[149] that is, it was *only after* the mark lost points abroad that the currency's growing weakness was revealed at home by rising prices – which led Havenstein to arraign the reparations payments for such a loss and its pernicious consequences. But the (external) depreciation was truly driven by the capital flight, and only at a second remove by the tribute of Versailles.

The fact that in 1920 the fall of the mark was not as dramatic as a massive outflow of capital would cause it to be was due to a counterbalancing of foreign capital, which began earnestly in 1920. *Between 1919 and 1921, foreigners acquired more than 40 percent of all German liquid balances* (that is, cash and checking accounts). Theirs was a purely speculative bet: as soon as Germany began to disappoint the investors' gluttonous anticipation, a scramble to convert these balances should have followed.[150] Thus what the German absentees withdrew, the rich 'tourists' – British, American and French – provisionally and partly poured back in the course of an unedifying razzia, whereby they also looted with their 'strong' currencies Germany's 'dirt-cheap' property, goods, and services.

The German thesis provided only a partial explanation of the phenomenon; aside from glossing over capital flight, it made no mention of the kernel round which the hyperinflation snowballed.

The seed of the meltdown lay, quite naturally, in the war loan.[151] In this connection, British press representative Lord Riddell noted in his diary during his stay at Versailles:

We talked of the indemnity. [Lloyd George] read me [a] memorandum suggesting seizure of the German War Loan, which would place the Allies in possession of eight million pounds. I said: 'That is a ridiculous scheme. It begs the whole question.' Lloyd George: 'Yes. A pretentious foolish proposal.'[152]

It is not at all clear why Lloyd George should have thought that the seizure of the German war loan for the purpose of indemnification was a 'pretentious, foolish proposal.' In fact, the opposite was true: it did not 'beg the question,' it would have actually solved it, provided 'the question' remained indeed how to exact from the Germans a tribute with which the devastated areas could have been rebuilt.* Therefore the only remaining explanation accounting for the astounding 'negligence' on the part of the British was that they intentionally left the bomb ticking. The ultimate objective being, as mentioned above, to purge the Reich of its war debt, and proceed to bail Germany out with foreign capital in the second half of the 1920s (see the following chapter).

Simple ratios afford some interesting considerations: *between 1919 and 1920, the money allotted to pay interest on the war loan and redeem (in cash) the certificates not renewed by the subscribers amounted approximately to 30 percent*

---

* Which could have been effected by seizing the War Loan, freezing the principal, reducing the amount of the annual interest payment, extending the diminished payments over two or three decades, and allowing Germany at all times to discharge her obligation by paying in kind. But in the light of the game that was being played by Britain, which was to impoverish the ordinary people and strengthen the German elite, these considerations are by the way.

*of the Reich's comprehensive expenditure – that is, a figure roughly equivalent to 60 percent of all money (cash and check money) created in Germany during that biennium.*[153]

In fact, as they exported the country's wealth abroad while the mark depreciated, the wealthy Germans also cashed in their war loan certificates: between 1920 and early 1922, 50 percent of the war debt had been refunded by the state. The other half stayed in the hands of the petty investors, who clung to their certificates till the end, when they would be worth nothing.

*The interest payments, on short- and long-term state bonds, plus the redemption of the war loan certificates into cash, contributed a net addition of monetary signs on the markets, with no physical counterpart whatsoever:* it was pure 'air,' pure inflation.

The public conveyed this net shot of liquidity along two avenues. They converted them either into foreign currencies or tangible goods, and thus depressed the mark further. Alternatively, or in conjunction, they reinvested them in short-term Reich bills, which were, until late 1921, still considered 'safe': needless to say, such recycling imposed an ever growing layer of interest dues on the books of the Reich.

It was this second channel that precipitated the herd movement in late 1922. In 1920 the foreigners followed suit and bought the Reich's bills: the meltdown was briefly postponed. The decline of the mark was irreversible, however: after Rathenau was killed, and the Ruhr invaded, *the debacle triggered a stampede of conversions of Reich bills into cash,* which led to the frantic issues of late 1923, when the state, impotent before the innumerable requests for redemption, activated the country's provincial mints to print notes around the clock. Such was the meltdown: a wholesale conversion of government bonds into paper money.

Havenstein was not 'playing the victim' when he lamented that 'his hands were tied.' 'The quantity of notes issued every year...depended exclusively (then as much as today) on the number of Treasury bills that the public was willing to renew, subscribe, or not renew.'[154] Thus Hitler, in a private conversation, condensed in 1941 the other half of the work of inflationary dynamics – to which, in spite of all, he owed his grand debut on the political stage:

The inflation could have been overcome. The decisive thing was a home war-debt: in other words, the yearly payments of 10,000 millions in interest a year on a debt of 166 thousand millions...To pay the interest the people were compelled to walk the plank with paper money – hence the depreciation of the currency. The just thing would have been...to suspend payment of interest on the debt...I'd have forced the war-profiteers to buy, with good...coin of the realm, various securities which I would have frozen for a period of twenty, thirty or forty years...Inflation is not caused by increasing the fiduciary circulation. It begins on the day when the purchaser is obligated to pay, for the same goods, a higher sum than asked the day before.[155]

In sum, the causal sequence: (1) to pay interest on the enormous war loan, the Reich commissioned to the Reichsbank a vast amount of cash and check money, which was shot in the system, causing domestic prices to climb steadily; (2) when the rich perceived that the inflation was eroding their wealth and fearing Erzberger's draconian tax reform, they began to cash in their war loan certificates and send their capital abroad; (3) the evaded capital denominated in marks was converted beyond the border into dollars, guilders, pounds and francs: thus the mark depreciated steeply against these (the 'external depreciation'); (4) the tax shortfall at home forced the Reich to run further into short-term debt: it printed more bonds, half of which until 1922 were converted into cash by the central bank, the other half being bought by private savers; (5) to pay for reparations, Germany purchased foreign cash, pawning gold and spending marks, and thus weakened even more the Reichsmark vis-à-vis the other currencies; (6) this reinforced external depreciation affected the price of imports, which in turn affected the cost of living, and so prices kept soaring; (7) the Reich sank ever more deeply into debt, but for about two years (1920–22) the foreign and domestic subscriptions of government bonds prevented the inflation from detonating the meltdown; (8) after the invasion of the Ruhr in early 1923, the final repudiation of the floating (short-term) debt left the government and the Reichsbank no choice but to reimburse in cash, mark for mark, all the certificates that the investors, foreign and otherwise, were no longer willing to renew; from then on all new bond issues, which the Reich emitted to pay for its expenditures, were shouldered by the central bank alone: it sucked in all the bonds and converted them into (by now worthless) bank notes – the mark accordingly plunged.

In the avalanche, the Reichsbank suffered the drain of half of its gold, and Governor Havenstein died of a heart attack in November 1923. The farmers weathered the storm and kept their granaries bursting while the people went hungry, the proletarians had nothing to lose, and the absentee owners, their wealth being sheltered abroad, were better off than they were at the end of the war. But the petty bourgeoisie *(die Kleinbürgertum)*, which lived and saved off a *fixed* income, was literally wiped out. The hyperinflation effaced the savings of the middle class: from the mid 1920s this pauperized cohort would merge into the Nazi mass following.

The Weimar hyperinflation was a story of foreign conspiracy and domestic betrayal, hence the dishonesty of the British thesis and the contrite incompleteness of the German apologia: contrary to what the German defense held, the reparations did *not* set off the meltdown; they merely speeded it up. Between 1919 and 1922, Germany would surrender under that head around 10 percent of her income,[156] *this was all Germany would ever pay as war tribute to the Allies until the advent of Hitler.*[157]

Within the 'cage' of Weimar, the German elite savaged the mark by exporting to nearby fiscal havens a considerable, though never assessed, portion of the wealth of the country. The Reich palliated by running a massive floating debt, which by 1923 had been all but redeemed in an ocean of paper. It was rather the German absentees that had relentlessly stabbed their own country in the back, allowing thereafter, unconcerned, the bitterly resentful middle class to fall prey to the slogans of the Nazis, who would frequently speak of the merits of *Radikalisierung*. Such was precisely the development that Veblen foresaw when he uncannily presaged that the reparations would foment 'radicalism at home.'[*]

In the end, the Reich was 'purged' of the war loan. Germany's entire war debt, which had amounted to over a third of the entire wealth of the Kaiserland at its apogee, was worth $1.23 (almost nothing) in November 1923.

Now that Germany was cleansed of her imperial debt, America suddenly manifested the desire to reappear on European shores to meddle directly in the monetary overhauling of her former enemy: Weimar was at the threshold of her 'golden' quinquennium (1924–29).

## The maiden storm of the Nazi fundamentalists

Right when the Reichsmark was about to hit bottom, they finally arrived, the Nazis. At first, no one but a fistful of Bavarians showed any awareness of this splinter group. They seemed to cut the figure of yet another bunch of rowdy homeboys wanting to go back to the pre-war days of national glory. But the Nazis, as the Germans would come to learn in time, formed something altogether alien to the general patriotic nostalgia, which was presently putting up a truculent resistance to the Weimar republic. Whereas most veterans' and Nationalists' associations fluttered a variety of insignia borrowed from their recent imperial past – eagles, crosses, and the black,

[*]    See Chapter 2, p. 86.

white, and red of the Prussian Reich – it was only the swastika that defined the Nazis; it was as though the Hitlerites, riding German nationalism like a Trojan horse, had come to diffuse a foreign creed in a common language – the reactionary idiom understandable by the disheartened folk. The particular cosmology symbolized by the dextrogyrate* swastika – all that lore treasured behind the closed doors of the Thule lodge† – never figured, not even allusively in the speeches of Hitler and his followers; that was the exclusive privilege of the initiates. Unlike the Nationalists of the old guard, the Nazis were, instead, a religious sect fronted by a political outfit, the NSDAP, and shielded by a private militia, the SA (later reinforced by the praetorian squad of the SS). For the time being, however, with the conspicuous exception of their emblem, the Nazis deported themselves like the vast majority of Right-wing reactionaries: they fought their political battle against Weimar with invectives, obstructionism, rabble-rousing, and continual clashes against the 'proletarian battalions' of the regimented Left.

For the USSR, whose every move towards Germany seemed to complement perfectly Britain's agenda, the disaster of the inflation presented a unique opportunity to taunt the German Right with political subversion: on the one hand the Soviets helped the Reichswehr rearm (as officially sanctioned by the Treaty of Rapallo), while on the other they purposely enflamed the Nationalists. As later revealed in the memoirs of Krivitsky, the Soviet intelligence chief in charge of German destabilization at this time, acts of terror, sabotage and violence designed to spread fear in the German community were carried out by Bolshevik agents through secrets cells, called 'T-units.' These were funded and trained by Moscow 'to demoralize the Reichswehr and the police [especially by means of] assassinations.'[158] The Red Terror was not intended to have durable effects, but sought only to shock the country and provoke riots by instigating cohorts of patsies, young German Communists for the most part, in gratuitous deeds of defiance: tavern and street brawls, strikes, intimidation, and so on. It was on such Soviet-inspired 'insurrections' that the Right-wing activists, and the Nazis, would feed. *Everything seemed to conspire in favor of the Hitlerites: they could count on London for the political and financial strangulation of the German people, and they could thank Moscow for causing all this Communist inferno, which made them stand tall as the Fatherland's defenders.*

It was thus hardly a shock to see the Hitlerites mature into political adolescence in the fall of 1923, when Germany came to be torn by a mayhem of strikes, street battles, and runaway inflation. During the Franco-

---

* Spinning to the right.
† Chapter 2, pp. 59–60.

Belgian invasion of the Ruhr, Hitler cried 'Let us have misery!' from the columns of the Nazi organ, the *Völkischer Beobachter*.[159]

Disgraced by the hyperinflation, the Cuno Cabinet fell in August 1923 and was replaced by a new one, led by the bourgeois Stresemann, which featured the heartily unwelcome reappearance of Socialist ministers.

On September 25, owing to Nazism's rising popularity, Hitler was nominated political chief of the *Kampfbund*, the encompassing 'Fighting League' of the southern Right. But on September 26, 1923, the Bavarian government, hell-bent on opposing the re-emergence of Socialist politics and Hitler's takeover as Reaction's populist leader, declared a state of emergency and delegated dictatorial powers to the former Bavarian Premier von Kahr.* In Berlin, as a sensational counter-measure, the new Chancellor Stresemann devolved power to the chief of the army, von Seeckt. The head of the Bavarian Reichswehr, General von Lossow, resolved not to pledge allegiance to his chief in Berlin von Seeckt, and put his armies at the disposal of the seditious von Kahr. There ensued between Munich and Berlin a confrontation that might have ushered in civil war.

In October, two states (Saxony and Thuringia) swept a coalition of Communists and Socialists into power. Again, the German Right shuddered with horror.

Attentively, Hitler studied the standoff between the Bavarian Nationalists and the Berlin central. He understood that the forces of Reaction centered in Munich were gearing up to replay a royalist putsch à la Kapp: this junta of army generals and colluded administrators was ready to conquer Munich, restore the Bavarian king to his throne, march against these newly elected Red constituencies in Saxony and Thuringia, topple them, and eventually storm Berlin. If this plan got off the ground, the royalists would be strong enough to rally all Reactionary protesters to their banner and muffle in the process the slightly discordant voice of the Nazis.

The Hitlerites had to act fast, and insinuate themselves onto the monarchist bandwagon, so as to impede the latter to mastermind entirely the forthcoming 'National Revolution.' Hitler chose the anniversary of the Revolution, November 9, to stage an uprising, but upon being informed that von Kahr was scheduled to address on the 8 a crowd at a large beerhall, the Bügerbräukeller, by a day he shortened the wait. To snatch the revolution from the royalists, the Nazis irrupted in the tavern. Hitler, interrupting von Kahr, hopped on a table, unsheathed a gun and fired a shot at the ceiling. He proclaimed the National Revolution and received an ovation.

---

* Von Kahr, who had risen to power on the occasion of the Kapp putsch, stepped down in 1921.

The monarchist triumvirate – Kahr, Lossow, and the commander of the Bavarian state police, Seisser, present at the occasion under duress, vowed its support.

But as soon as Hitler and his boyish neo-pagans turned their backs to let Kahr go home, the latter proceeded to cross them at once by signing with the approval of the army a decree promulgating the disbanding of the NSDAP. When Hitler and his troopers discovered the treachery the following morning, accompanied by Ludendorff, they improvised a desperate cortege through the streets of downtown Munich, until they reached the Odeonplatz, where files of policemen were waiting for them, poised to take aim. The Nazis marched on. Fourteen were shot dead – the first martyrs of Nazism. Hitler was thrust to the floor by a wounded companion, and bruised his shoulder.

In fact, the previous night, Bavaria and Berlin had already made peace behind the back of the Nazis: to pacify Munich's royalists, the armies of General von Seeckt had marched from Berlin to overthrow the Leftist governments of Saxony and Thuringia; afterwards, the Bavarians had given up their plans for revolt. The Beerhall putsch was finished before it began. Again, Seeckt's army prevailed: the General would rather see Germany the captive of Weimar than surrendering her 'to those sinister forces which the distracted masses had produced and which were aiming at power'.[160]

The recidivist General Ludendorff, who had taken part in this putsch as well, strode past the bullets with frosty indifference; he was taken in by the police and promptly released. Hitler was arrested; he was arraigned for high treason and turned his defense into a mesmerizing ventriloquy of the nation's lament: his time was yet to come, but the turbulence of the hyperinflation had made a German sensation out of him. Hitler stated: 'You may pronounce us guilty a thousand times, but the Goddess who presides over the Eternal Court of History...acquits us.'[161] He was sentenced to five years' imprisonment in the state prison of Landsberg. The detention would be commuted to nine months. Hitler's teacher, Dietrich Eckart, the guru of the Thule lodge that had pulled a few strings in this putsch, was also incarcerated; the shock of detainment rattled his heart, which failed shortly after his acquittance.

In Landsberg, with the ghost-hand of his faithful Hess, Hitler composed *Mein Kampf* (*My Struggle*). To his master, the recently defunct Dietrich Eckart, 'who devoted his life to the awakening of his...people,'[162] he dedicated the opus. The first volume would be published in July 1925, the second in December 1926.

*Mein Kampf* was the exploded scheme for the creation of an Aztec-like empire in the plains of Central Asia. As a political program, whose dispositions the Third Reich would enact with unfaltering rigor, *Mein Kampf* was a fusion of Gnosticism with a compatible strategic appendage. As hinted in an earlier section, the religious fervor of the movement fed off the lore of the Thule society. According to this peculiar cosmology, 'the body of light', that is, the German people as a *collective* 'folk spirit', was encrusted in the corrupting darkness of matter, whose 'affirmers' were believed to issue from the antagonistic clan of the Jews. Salvation for the Germans could only be achieved by *separation* – separation from the fetters of materiality. For the Germans, existence perforce signified struggle – the two were inseparable.[163] The missionary elan was coupled with the political imperative, as Bolshevism and Judaism were made to coincide. The enemy – a Soviet International fraught with Jewish leaders – had nested in Russia.

'Germany awake!': such was the last verse of a strophe reworked by Eckart in 1922, which his pupil Alfred Rosenberg, the future race ideologue of the Third Reich, selected as the motto underlining the swastika on the red standards of Nazism.[164]

> *Sturm, Sturm, Sturm!*
> *Läutet die Glocken von Turm zu Turm!...*
> *Judas erscheint, das Reich zu gewinnen,*
> *Läutet, daß blutig die Seile sich röten...*
> *Wehe dem Volk, das heute noch träumt,*
> *Deutschland erwache!*
>
> [Storm, Storm, Storm!
> Toll the bells from tower to tower!...
> Judas has come to conquer the Reich,
> So may the bell ropes be crimsoned with blood...
> Woe to those that are still adream,
> Germany awake!]

In Chapters IV, XIII and XIV of *Mein Kampf*, Hitler detailed the geopolitics of Nazism. *Overpopulation*, always an oligarchic byword veiling genocidal intent, marked the point of departure of the Hitlerite discourse. There are four ways, he wrote, to tackle the hypothetical strain of human reproduction upon Nature's powers of sustenance: (1) artificial reduction of births, (2) internal colonization, that is, increase the yield of domestic acreage, (3) acquisition of new soil, (4) engage in active world trade to procure vital imports.

To limit birth, Hitler contended, was to shield at all costs the life one saved: it was thus the avowed fostering of weaklings, who would enfeeble the hardy fiber of the race. To colonize internally was but a prorogation of the problem, and a disastrous one at that, as it afforded rival races a decisive territorial advantage in the struggle for life. To acquire protectorates and play the colonial game versus Britain, as the Second Reich had foolishly done, had borne the catastrophic fruits now before the eyes of the world. Therefore, the Führer concluded, the only workable alternative was the third one: conquest.

Where?

If land was desired in Europe, it could be obtained by and large only at the expense of Russia...*For such a policy there was but one ally: England*...No sacrifice should have been too great for winning England's willingness...Only an absolutely clear orientation could lead to such a goal: renunciation of world trade and colonies...Concentration of all the State's instruments of power on the land army.[165]

This was in synthesis the foreign policy of Nazism; nothing more and nothing less than a profession of passionate admiration for Britain, whose folklore and tradition Hitler revered,[166] and whose partnership he desired above all else; a passion for Britain and a promised carnage in the East to create the great Nazi empire of the *Herrenvolk* – the Chosen Race.

The heedlessness of the testament of Mackinder was all the more astonishing as Hitler was on several occasions during the reclusion at Landsberg, mentored by an expert strategist, by no less a figure than the founder of the German school of *Geopolitik*, General Karl Haushofer, who was fluently conversant with these themes. As the derivation of Hitler's anti-Semitism was easily traceable to Eckart, the formation of the Führer's geopolitical outlook was, instead, hazy. Hitler's 1920 allocutions made no room for the staples of his mature oratory, namely the preoccupation with overpopulation and the emphasis upon the notion of *Lebensraum* ('living space'). Indeed, in August 1920, he jotted 'among the notes of one of his speeches "brotherhood toward the East (*Verbrüderung nach Osten*),"'[167] which attested to the shapelessness of his politics at the beginning of his career. However, by 1922 Hitler was growing increasingly deaf to any score of Eurasian harmony: conservative ideologue Moeller van den Bruck, who longed to witness a blending of the Occident with 'the great human poetry of the Orient',[168] encountered the Nazi leader and engaged him in a long discussion, at the end of which, exhausted, he confided to a friend: 'The fellow never comprehends.'[169] Ernst Hanfstaengl, a sophisticated art dealer and early *haut-bourgeois* maecenas of the gruff lance corporal, remembered Hitler rehearsing in early 1923 one of his customary lines: 'The most important thing in the next war will be to make sure we control the grain and food supply of Western Russia.'[170] Hanfstaengl chalked up Hitler's anti-Slav fixation to the influence of Alfred Rosenberg, who, indeed, envisioned the reconfiguration of the Eurasian living spaces under the joint rule of Germany, and her Nordic racial sisterhood: Balts, Scandinavians, and *Britons*.[171]

The point has been disputed,[172] yet there should be no reason to doubt that Hitler perfected his geopolitical outlook with the mysterious Haushofer, who was also Rudolf Hess's Professor of geopolitics at the University of Munich, as well as an initiate into many secrets of the Orient. While it is true that Haushofer did not voice in his voluminous scholarly production a radical opposition to Soviet Russia, he nonetheless left the choice open between 'the pan-Asiatic movement of the Soviets' and 'the pan-Pacific alliance of the Anglo-Americans,' on the one hand,[173] and encouraged an active geopolitical partnership with Britain, on the other.[174] Such a position hardly entailed a choice, in fact; it was very much in keeping with late Nazi diplomacy, which planned to sign a truce with Russia, only to smash her later with the hopeful support of Britain.*

In the concluding section of the book, the geopolitical agenda of the Third Reich was clearly exposed: 'The aim of German foreign policy,' announced Hitler, 'must be the preparation for the reconquest of freedom for tomorrow.'[175] Britain, indeed, was bent upon 'world dominion,' but she had no further interest, he added, 'in the complete effacement of Germany,' which would bring about 'French hegemony on the continent.' Therefore, he concluded, since: (1) 'Britain's desire is and remains the prevention of the rise of a continental power to political importance'; (2) 'French diplomacy will always stand in conflict with...British statesmanship'; and (3) 'the inexorable mortal enemy of the German people is and remains France'; the initial conclusion was reaffirmed: *Germany's priority was an alliance with Britain*.[176] The foregoing argument, which failed to consider that the first proposition best applied to Germany, was a reiteration of the fallacious hope that Britain could be lured with such a shoddy bait as the hostility towards France, when in fact the fate of the British empire had always been

---

* See Chapter 5.

staked on the prevention of the Eurasian embrace. No amount of coaxing could induce Britain to conceive her dominion otherwise.

During World War I, Hitler conceded, 'we could have propped ourselves on Russia and turned against Britain.' But 'today conditions are different.'[177] Today, 'Fate itself,' insisted the Führer, 'seems desirous to give us a sign': *Fate had handed Russia to Bolshevism.* Germany would march to the East, and in the East loomed the true, archetypal, enemy. To dispel the doubts of his British readership, Hitler envisioned for an instant the possible consequences of a German alliance with Russia: if it were consummated, he averred, France and Britain would pounce upon Germany 'with the speed of light.' The conflict upon German soil would degenerate into a catastrophic devastation, against which the irremediably retarded industrial base of Russia would afford no defense worth the name. Hitler's simulation of the embrace with Russia was a mere abstraction, however, as no alliance whatever was possible with the Bolsheviks, the 'scum of humanity,' for whom Germany was 'the next great war aim.'[178] Thus the embrace was being contemplated, analysed, and unconditionally rejected.

A final admonishment from the 'Political Testament of the German Nation' achieved the Nazi manifesto:

Never suffer the rise of two continental powers in Europe. Never forget that the most sacred right on this earth is a man's right to till with his own hands, and the most sacred sacrifice the blood that a man sheds for this earth.[179]

So here was a German 'drummer,' a hater of Weimar, a herald of bloody crusades in the East, enamored of Britain, and haunted by nightmares of breeds exceeding the 'natural limits'; a veteran of the Great War turned hierofant of a cult disguised as a political party; and a charmer of Germany's patriotic elite, who was also prone to crush France.

Admittedly for Britain, here was a dark horse that was truly worth playing.

# 4 'Death on the Installment Plan'

## Whereby Governor Norman Came to Pace the Damnation of Europe, 1924–33

'Twas I did not yet know men. Never more will I believe what they say, what they think. It is of men and of men alone that one must be afraid, always.

How long will it take for their delirium to end, how long before they just stop exhausted at last, these monsters?

Louis-Ferdinand Céline, *Voyage au bout de la nuit*[1]

They gorge on God and the world. They do not sow. They just reap. They are the sorcerers in the flesh [who] make gold over the phone...

Erich Kästner, *Hymn to the Bankers*[2]

'I was sitting in a great waiting-room and its name was Europe. The train was due to leave in a week. I knew that. But no one could tell me where it was going or what would become of me. And now we are again seated in the waiting-room, and again its name is Europe! And again we do not know what will happen! We live provisionally, the crisis goes on without end!'

Erich Kästner, *Fabian*[3]

### The banking 'grid' and the rules of the gold game

Germany had to be resurrected, that is, rearmed and renovated: the Veblenian prophecy had foretold this much. As seen in the previous chapter, the date marking Germany's military reawakening was April 1922, when the Treaty of Rapallo sealed that seemingly bizarre entente between the generals behind Weimar and Russia's Red Army. Then one had to see to it that the industrial basis of Germany was restructured as well. Before the German economy might be overhauled, the drafters of Versailles waited until the hyperinflation annihilated the old mark. That crash had been a facile presumption on the part of the British experts: forcing the German government, which was mired in a (war) debt that was twice as large as the country's income, to pay reparations (in foreign cash or gold) without confiscating that debt, had driven the Reich into a corner. In the strictures of that corner – capital flight, depreciation of the mark, and tax evasion – the standard action of the Reich–Reichsbank duo could not but lead to an inflationary meltdown; there had been no mystery to it, no mistake about it. The only uncertainty had lain in assessing the time lag required for the completion of this financial burnout. It would have taken roughly three years to wipe Weimar clean of the old debt incurred to fight the Great War: that is, from 1920 to 1923.

In the meantime, the Bank of England found a suitable Governor possessing the ability to direct the forthcoming German bailout from London with American cash. A most strange and intriguing character by the name of Montagu Norman was the chosen custodian: Norman would be Governor for the extraordinary duration of 24 years (1920–44); a case unique in the entire history of the Bank. During the last stages of the German inflation, Norman initiated the process that would re-anchor Britain and most industrialized countries to the so-called gold exchange standard. This operation – grossly misunderstood by contemporary scholarship – was by no means a sorry attempt bungled by a few nostalgic gentlemen of leisure to resuscitate the monetary system of yore (pre-World War I). Rather, it was the peculiar creation of the Governor, whereby he enveloped, so to speak, for the length of six years (1925–1931) the banking networks of the West into a single, highly leveraged and palpably unstable web of payments, which was in fact designed to self-disintegrate. This too was a game, in which all participating central banks 'chipped in' a given quota in gold. To amass and protect the gold base of his bank, Montagu Norman in 1920 tested two fundamental techniques, which he would employ a decade later to achieve the Empire's objectives: (1) the pauperization of India by restricting her money supply (that is, deliberate deflation) with a view to attracting Indian gold hoards to London, and (2) the encouragement of massive monetary expansion (that is, inflation) in America as a means to lure gold away from New York, and convey it to sustain a steady flow of investment in Europe. By the mid 1920s, Austria (1922) and Germany (1924) were the first countries bailed out in this fashion, and the infrastructure of the latter was turned into a technological jewel. The modernization of Germany was consummated by unleashing speculative fury in America, whose public rushed to subscribe en masse reams of German securities between 1924 and 1929. Norman interrupted this speculative frenzy with the Great Crash of October 1929 to retain control of the last stages of the German incubation and the anticipated agony of Weimar. When, in March 1931, Austria and Germany announced their common desire to form a customs union, and thereby a political condominium of sorts which *de facto* attempted to overcome the overall state of provisional fragmentation established at Versailles, Norman's new Gold Standard suddenly imploded. By having prearranged in the late 1920s the constitution of a so-called 'sterling block,' in which London would have drawn the colonies closer to itself to trade in a compact, self-sufficient core, the Governor readied Britain and her Dominions in the summer of 1931 to sever themselves financially from the rest of the world. Following a monumental charade, during which the Bank of England feigned to be the victim of endemic financial fragility, Britain abandoned the Gold Standard in September 1931; thus she deliberately wrecked the international system of payments, and financial oxygen was definitively cut off from the Weimar Republic. Thereafter, while the republic was easily torn apart by mounting unemployment, street violence, and social dissolution, the British clubs awaited the tempestuous rise of Germany's reactionary and radicalized movement: this was National Socialism, whose leaders had indeed begun since the fall of 1931 to circle around the president of the Reich, Hindenburg, bidding for power. But the civil and humanist forcers of Germany resisted, and refused to give Hitler an electoral majority for the length of two additional years, at the cost of unspeakable suffering, until, on January 4, 1933, the London–New York axis of high finance, abetted by (1) the duplicitous yet cryptically pro-British posturing and meddling of the USSR, (2) the ignoble panic of the Vatican, and (3) the blind numbness of the SPD (German Social Democrats), cut to the chase by coming out into the open to pay for Hitler's accession to the Chancellery of the Reich.

1924–33: this period witnessed the transition of Nazism from a state of quasi-irrelevance to that of champion of the long awaited German Recovery. Until 1929 it seemed that Veblen's forecast was given the lie, and then, suddenly, the dark horse of *Mein Kampf* was thrown onto the main stage – thanks to social disorder.

And there is the difficulty. In standard textbooks, the economics behind the rise of Nazism suffers a dreadful treatment at best, or, most often, is not treated at all, and the reader is customarily defrauded by being hastily assured that Hitler came 'because of the crisis,' no further explanation being forthcoming. What of the crisis? Unless an effort is made to unveil the mechanics of this spectral collapse, Hitler remains an effect of chance, the social by-product of a silly financial season gone awry. And such a view is absurd.

For the student, these are difficult years since the phenomenology of this peculiar phase, which encompasses first and foremost the complexities of (1) the Wall Street Crash, (2) the banking crises of Austria, Germany, and

Britain, (3) the severance from gold of the British pound, or (4) the open intervention of Anglo-American finance to bring Hitler to power on January 4, 1933, has been meagerly documented, and the chain of co-responsibility among the political and economic circles involved in these events has remained in most instances most carefully hidden to this day. Nonetheless, the known facts are by themselves amply sufficient to incorporate seamlessly into the main narrative of the Nazi incubation a reinterpretation of the disquieting intermission of 1930–32. A reinterpretation that still points to the direct and conscious manipulation of financial aggregates on the part of Britain to obtain specific results in Europe, and especially in Germany.

From 1924 until 1933, British financiers led by the Bank of England became the absolute protagonists of the incubation. Diplomacy took the back seat, and banking artistry came in to play the lead in an astonishing performance begun in an atmosphere of deluded hopefulness (1924–25) and ended in utter catastrophe (1930–33). Montagu Norman was the soloist of this complex and crucial interlude.

Without properly comprehending the functioning of traditional banking systems and the nature of money, the key to Hitler's rise to power may never be held. And it is the lack of such comprehension that is chiefly to blame for discarding the decisive passage in the promotion of Nazism as the fruit of bad luck in times of crisis. Yet in history there is no such thing as luck – good or bad – and 'the crisis' does not belong to the order of natural catastrophes, but is the mere trough of a cyclical pattern that is generated by the relatively simple dynamics of money. And to this essential problem we now turn. What follows is here presented as a necessary introduction to the policies and monetary vicissitudes that stand in the background of Hitler's accession to power.

\* \* \*

The world is divided between those that create money and those that don't.

It all began with gold. Precious metals have a virtue, a property above all others, and that is their *imperishability*.[4] So the blond metal became a medium of exchange, recognized by all – a token for transactions, which could also be hoarded in uncertain times, and promptly regain the markets as soon as the skies cleared. A disc of metal that was a barter unit and means of saving at the same time. Because men would not trust other men, gold they resolved to call money: it allowed them to petrify wealth into a ware that transcended the bonds of their community, which they felt was always prone to collapse. They could bury the coins in the yard.

Then a group of individuals gradually came to be entrusted with the deposit of such gold stashes and the bankers were born; these realized that the owners of the gold stashes would claim for their weekly business only a small fraction of the amounts deposited, which fact enabled the bankers to loan the gold to others, while their legitimate proprietors assumed it still rested in the vaults of the banks. And soon the bankers distributed notes instead of shifting the cumbrous metal, and the concept of *cover* emerged: so much gold for so much more bank paper; in other words, the gold on deposit at the bank would always be a fraction of the paper notes distributed – the smaller the proportion of gold to the notes, the riskier the banking policy. Against gold the bank would offer its clients drafts and checkbooks with which to purchase goods and services. The banker that lent improvidently would suffer the infamous 'run' when rumors about his insolvency spread amongst the depositors: these would all rush to the bank to withdraw their moneys in gold, because it was always suspected that the bank never had sufficient cash at hand to pay everyone. All of this was known: it was known that traditional banking was erected upon an enormous fraud. For bankers, the trick was (1) to make people accept the bank notes as if they were gold, (2) to possess the metal itself, (3) to hide it in vaults, and (4) to withdraw it gradually from circulation.

But banking was never reformed, nor were traditional banks shut down. Instead they ramified, fast. And it could not have been otherwise, for once money was turned into a ware, that is, gold, and was *appropriated*, it was capable of wielding an archetypal force, unlike any other, which found its immediate manifestation in *the rate of interest*.

This mere percent, which came to rule the lives of empires – what is it? An insurance fee, a commission? Neither: both of these the banks are wont to charge their customers separately. The rate of interest is the story itself. It is the price of the gold money, it is the expression of that particular virtue which gold possesses and which its owner, as a rule, employs to embarrass others. *It is the power of those (the bankers) that 'sell' a medium that does not perish (money) to take advantage of the rest of economy, which is made of producers eager to offer for sale goods that decay* – from vegetables to housing, and machinery.

Thereafter, the name of the game was to corner the supply of gold and monopolize the circulation of money. He who controlled the money, controlled the system itself: its activity, its politics, its arts, and its sciences. Everything. And so the race began, a fierce one, which coincided with the constitution of the 'Grid', the banking network. The Grid came to be made of a series of nodes located in the heart of economic activity, where the accounts were managed by their secretive custodians, the bankers, and linked by couriers.

Gold, for the most part, disappeared from circulation: it was hidden in the underground cellars of reserve banks, which gave the economy their paper instead. And so it was done: the gold had been relegated to whence it came, beneath the earth, and money assumed the form it should always have taken, that bespeaking its nature: *an intangible symbol.* Money began to travel in the form of ciphers through numbered accounts, while the gold, dense and cumbersome, was duly stowed underground. But this money, these balances on numbered bank accounts, was never public money. The money was *owned* from the start. One could look at it as from behind a screen: but to lay hold of the cash the banker's permission was required. If granted, one could employ those filigreed checkbooks as special passes for navigating what had by the nineteenth century become an extraordinary tangle of commercial relationships. Therefore, the rate of interest was (and still is) the price paid (1) for employing a means that was imperishable, when money, like everything else, should have an expiry date, and (2) for gaining access to the proprietary Grid of the bankers.

This was merely the beginning. Then the bankers proceeded to amass the gold, expand paper notes bearing their name by a multiple of the gold hoard, charge usurious rates thereon, and impose their private, corporate monopoly to the national constituencies.

How did the Grid interact with the economic organism? The underlying principle was simple: whoever wished to gain access to the Grid – that is, whoever needed cash – presented the banker with a *promise, a piece of paper*, that is, an IOU upon which he signed his freedom away to the extent of the amount of dollars requested plus the interest. These were the producers' (commercial) 'bills,' debts secured on the producer's capital (house, tools, land, future income...), or even the state's Treasury bills, debts based on its power to tax the citizens – for the collectivity as a whole was the Grid's client; both citizens and state had to pay if they demanded money for daily exchanges. The banker put money into the economy by mortgaging the life and goods of the economy – it was as if the banks, by dint of their control of a scarce, imperishable medium of exchange, were the pawnbrokers of citizens and state.

The promises (IOUs, debts) of parties, public and private, whose credentials and name passed muster were then ranged carefully in a large portfolio, which held the bank's assets. The banker's operation was called *discount*: he took a debt worth 100, discounted it by, say, 10 (interest), and surrendered 90 in cash. *The money market was nothing but the sum total of the Grid's appetite for the economy's paper*: domestic or national stocks, short-term or long-term bonds, public and private debentures of the most diverse sorts. The more paper-promises the banks purchased from the people and the municipalities by discount, the more sanguine their expectations of the economy's vigor, and the more cheaply they sold their money: *the interest rates decreased.*

Decreasing rates, coupled with steady injections of bank cash, set off the boom, and a boom was accompanied by rising prices: this was a *credit inflation.* If the boom was strong, the going rate of interest would climb to match the price rise – this was the phenomenon of the *hausse*: it was an automatic mechanism implemented by banks for sharing in the windfall profits of abundant money, and for keeping the price rise under relative control; it also boiled down to rationing credit away from the least profitable concerns.[5] The boom lasted until the earning capacity of the borrowers covered the interest; but when, owing to abundance, *prices after a while began to decrease,* this differential (rate of profit minus rate of interest) shrank rapidly. Suddenly the economy recalled that the money it had been given stemmed from debts.

When producers could no longer pay interest, it was the end: the banks said 'enough,' they recalled the loan, the concerns went bankrupt, workers worked no more, and the cash retreated in canals of the Grid. The crisis, the misery, the strangulation of society.

This sort of pervasive paralysis had become a defining trait of modern financial systems after the several banking oligarchies, each in control of its particular node along the network, had been prompted to erect a representative body – the central bank – to watch the gold and to fix the rate of interest (that is, the price of money); in such a bank the private concerns partook through shareholding, and to its Court or Directorate they would send a councilor in order to handle the delicate interaction between the Grid, the state, and the underlying economy.

And the great societies of the West fell one by one: by the end of the nineteenth century, each country suffered a Grid of her own, which culminated in a central organ presiding over a credit structure arranged like an inverted pyramid, the inverted summit being its hoarded gold. Upon this hoard (that is, the 'gold cover'), along with the mortgaged property of the world, were piled the reserves of the member banks held on deposit at the mother institute, and upon this cover the member banks carried on their extortionary business. The money of the big banks itself furnished a cover to lesser banks until such leveraged expansion of check money reached the peripheral banking branches, which delimited the base of the pyramid whereon the economy itself was perched most precariously.

A vein of ochre metal thus led to the creation of a monumental structure.

By the second half of the nineteenth century, under the famed 'Gold Standard,' all industrialized powers had a currency expressed in gold – a mark, a franc, or a pound was decreed to be worth so many grams of gold, and notes were declared by law to be convertible into gold at the given ratio, called the *parity*. National currencies were anchored to gold, and the parity linked the several currencies in a grid of cross-exchange rates. For instance, in Britain, under the regime of the Gold Standard, which prevailed before the Great War, 77s. 10½d equaled a standard ounce ($11^{11}$ 12 pure gold),[*] whereas in the United States, \$20.67 equaled a fine ounce ($12^{12}$ 12 pure gold), so that the exchange rate between the two currencies pegged to gold was £1= \$4.86. We shall bear this particular 'parity' in mind.

To compete in this game, governments, supported by their central banks, had to manage their commercial affairs and financial ventures with a view to protecting, if not steadily augmenting, their gold stock, which to a degree was a fair indicator of a power's mercantile accomplishment. The valve which regulated a country's inflows and outflows of gold was her *balance of payments*.

A balance of payments was a compound prospectus, which comprised a current account and a capital balance. The current account was a synopsis of the country's overall trade achievements; it looked into the mismatch, if any, between imports and exports of tangible merchandise (that is, the *trade balance*), and of the so-called '*invisibles*': shipping leases, insurance premiums, and interest payments. Indeed, the invisibles had always been the British empire's forte. The capital balance, instead, measured the difference between the influx and efflux of funds into and out of the nation's financial center. *The chief instrument for the regulation of such flows of money was the bank rate*. The bank might raise it significantly and thus *attract* foreign moneys to her banks; 7–10 percent, they said, could 'pull money out of the moon.' Conversely, low rates at home would prompt domestic gold-owners to seek higher returns on their idle funds abroad.

The obvious drawback of a policy of 'high rates' at home, however, was that it strangled the domestic economy: it might bring plentiful financial gains to the financial firms, the banking grid and the absentee owners, but it harmed everyone else. And therefore as a policy tool it was safe to use it only sparingly, and never for prolonged intervals. When money was dear, investment was costly, and thus work was scarce.

[*]   That is, 77s 10½d, which was equivalent to £3 (20 shillings in a pound) and 17s 10½d.

As far as the movement of gold was concerned, the action on the bank rate was the one relied upon to bring about the desired effects in the most rapid manner. It was invoked, unfailingly, as the capital principle of 'sound finance' in times of crisis, that is, when a central bank's cover was imperiled because herds of speculators sought to jettison the domestic currency and exchange it for gold: a 'run' on the bank's reserves.

If a currency fell, and monetary authorities remained passive, speculators were inclined to borrow additional amounts of that currency, convert it into gold, wait for the currency to fall further, reconvert the gold in that currency, and gain from the extent of the fall. And so on. A most pronounced raise (for example, from 3 to 8 percent) of the interest rate by the bank could be counted on to inhibit such a practice (by making the speculators' loans much more expensive), and, most importantly, it functioned as an instantaneous summons for additional funds from external investors, with which to replenish the bank's reserves and for which the bank stood ready to pay 'extra', that is, the rate differential (5 percent in the above example).

When a country ran a deficit on her balance of payments vis-à-vis another, either because she was buying from abroad far more than she was selling, or because capital had been fleeing for some time, or both, she had to settle the balance in gold with her trading partner. When a country lost gold, the 'cover' of the central bank was accordingly diminished: she would thus have to restrict the amount of credit money in circulation in order to maintain a given, workable ratio (of gold to bank money). And what did she do? She raised the rate to signal that cash availability was reduced, because of the gold hemorrhage. As a result, the exporters of capitals – all those absentees that had been investing against the national currency by converting it into gold, and shipping the gold wherever it might found a more remunerative yield – were discouraged, while foreign investors found renewed interest in the domestic capital market in light of the heightened interest. Thus gold could be expected to flow back home, and equilibrium could be re-established.[6] Conversely, a country that found herself fattened by an excessive inflow of gold, which had been streaming in on the wake of a persistent surplus on her balance of payments (owing to successful exports of goods, and/or to the offer of enticing investing opportunities), could afford to lower her rate and be expected to trigger a massive expansion of liquidity on her markets as a consequence of a swelling base of gold. This is what America would do in the 1920s. An important consideration.

These were the so-called 'rules of the game' of the pre-war Gold Standard.

With the outbreak of World War I, all players, with the exception of the United States, abandoned the gold anchor. When the European governments resolved upon waging war, they pressed the Grid for permission to print much paper money with which they might outbid all the required resources away from their former employment, and devote them to the war effort. In view of such massive inflation, which would have made gold convertibility impossible, the gold figment was given up, but the privilege of the Grid to sell cash and checks to the war ministries certainly was not. And thus the patriotic communities of the world came in for another historical round of that prodigious swindle known as 'public finance': the Treasury of each fighting nation printed many a bond, the Grid discounted them against the provision of credit lines for the purchase of munitions, the public debt billowed, and the commoners paid taxes to the warring states, which in turn employed these funds to pay the interest to the absentee clients and proprietors of the Grid that had loaned them the bank money in the first place.

On the vestiges of this awesomely savage cult Britain terminated the incubation of Nazism.

## Montagu Norman and the 'nationalization of the bank'

Montagu Collet Norman was born in 1871 to a family of bankers. His father, Frederick, was a barrister in a banking house of the City. His paternal grandfather had long sat on the Court of directors of the Bank of England, and cunningly avoided the promotion to Governor for the sake of aristocratic phlegm, whereas his maternal grandfather, Sir Mark Collet, had accepted the same post (1887–89), and earned a modicum of glory in the process. Montagu was sent to Eton, whose regimen he came to dislike much. And when he reached Cambridge, he found himself out of sorts, and dropped out of school, not knowing whither to turn. The young man needed advice. Grandfather Collet was happy to oblige, and directed him at once to his own parish, the respectable acceptance house of Brown Shipley. Brown Shipley was the London Branch of the prestigious American bank, Brown Brothers & Co., which had carried on its ships 'fully 75 percent of the slave cotton from the American South over to British mill owners.'[7]

Thus in 1895 Montagu Norman was inducted into the banking brethren of the Grid. The rest followed: he was brought up to love imperial Britain, and her bard, Kipling, whose *Soldiers Three* he knew by rote. But the family soon discovered that there was something wrong with him. Something that had to do with his nerves. Norman would frequently be preyed upon by sudden fits of harrowing melancholy, seizures of despondency so unbearable that his nerves would snap and his delicate frame would swoosh to the floor like ballast from a shredded pouch. In the darkness of interminable convalescences he would nurse his nerves and a 'raging head'[8] back to life, and resume his activities thereafter. Often, hapless physicians would send him on exotic cruises to the sunny areas of the world. And these recurrent fugues from madness to faraway havens would from early on punctuate his tireless ministry for half a century.

At Brown Shipley he cut the figure of a 'lonely queer man'; he was unhappy there.[9] He found the atmosphere slow and fusty, and disagreement with the partners over the firm's management often led to nasty altercations, for which he soon ceased to be forgiven. Clearly, he had been conceiving a vision of some sort, and whatever it was, Brown Shipley was too tight an outfit for giving it expression. In 1913, for desperate lack of a manageable diagnosis, he paid C. G. Jung a visit and offered the illustrious psychiatrist his 'raging head' for observation. The diagnosis was issued, and it was so terrible that Norman would never confide it to anyone. To his acquaintances he delivered the version that 'his brain had been found to "work wrong in a mechanical way" and that there was "an erratic corner in it in which it makes all the trouble".'[10]

By 1915, he had spent 20 years with Brown Shipley, cut his teeth with the company, learned about the Grid – its labyrinthine sub-alleys, its keys, and its many doors and traps – everything there was to learn, and felt, at 44, over-ripe for taking his leave. And the partners, who could no longer tolerate his presence, somewhat hastened Norman's departure in a mood of relieved expectancy. If finally came. The war raged then, in earnest.

By that time, some of his distinguishing traits were fully formed and appreciable to an outsider: a 'restless energy,'[11] a 'secretiveness, sometime of a quite absurd kind,'[12] 'a formidable memory, for places, names and facts,'[13] 'a knack for dissimulation and acting,'[14] 'a tendency to over-dramatize... beguile, and bamboozle the whole world,'[15] which he could commingle with a fair dose of effusive charm that most could not resist; and a patent, if intermittent, insanity.

For a time he took almost every job that offered; he consulted and advised in matters related to postal censorship and aircraft insurance, until Brian Cockayne, Deputy Governor of the Bank of England, took pity and brought him to the Court as some kind of posh secretary without official status. Cockayne lost no time in disabusing Norman of any hope the latter might have placed on such an invitation, which 'would not in any way imply that [he] would be nominated as the next Deputy Governor.'[16]

How the majority of the directors of the Bank of England really come to be on the Court...must, except to a few, remain a mystery...There is an inner cabinet called the Treasury Committee which deals with general policy and the Bank's relations with the Government. It is this Committee which really governs the Bank. It consists of the Governor, Deputy-Governor, and seven other directors. Who those other directors are is not disclosed. The Bank is really directed by a Secret Council.[17]

But then it is not known precisely how – possibly owing to his keen understanding of the American financial realities, which the war had brought on a path naturally convergent to Britain's interests – Norman so put his knowledge and experience to good use that he managed to make himself 'indispensable.' The custom at the Bank was to select among the directors a Deputy Governor for two years and then to elect him Governor for the ensuing two years. The circumstances of the Great War caused an exception to be made and Walter Cunliffe, who was Governor when the war broke out, retained that office for five years, from 1913 to 1918.[18] And when Cunliffe bowed out, Cockayne succeeded him, with Norman as his Deputy in 1918. Cunliffe, a difficult man who had by no means left amongst the colleagues a pleasant memory of his tenure, began nonetheless to voice to close relations a deep fear of his that had taken on the guise of an obsession.

'Montagu Norman' he said, 'is far and away the best person they have at the Bank. He'll be the next Governor. There's nobody else in sight. But his brilliant neurotic personality is certain to cause trouble. I feel my responsibility now for having put him and the Bank in a very dangerous position'...'He *needs* the power just to keep going and he won't give up until it's too late...What I'm really afraid of is that the Bank of England will be nationalised in Norman's lifetime, and my only consolation is that I shan't be here to see it.'[19]

Virtually nothing is known of the important dialogue that must have intensified among the bank, the clubs and the Foreign Office at the war's end, especially in view of the financial action that needed to be taken in post-war Europe. Considering the monetary complexity of the process that had been set afoot at Versailles, it could have no longer been a matter of semi-indifference to the empire what sort of professional the banking dynasty of London was going to crown Governor. Cunliffe had spoken intriguing words. He had confusedly sensed that what he and most of his predecessors had always viewed as the representative collegium of an exclusive guild could, in the capable hands of another banking priest, more imaginative than they, be imperceptibly rearranged so as to fulfill aims and duties, which were not going to be those selectively dictated by the inner circle of such a guild. Not only was the empire, because of the war, enjoining the bank to stand firm behind it, but it also seemed to look favorably upon the selection of a Governor who could successfully harness the banking network of the commonwealth to Britain's new, far more intrusive imperial directives, without bringing excessive disruption to the daily business of the banking community. This was most probably what Cunliffe intended by 'nationalization.'

On March 31, 1920, what Cunliffe dreaded came to pass: Montagu Norman was elected Governor of the Bank of England. 'For no more than two years,' they immediately captioned, 'just as prescribed by the old statute.'

With sufficiency, the doges of the Court had let him in from the back door. And he stayed on. In five years he was consecrated pontiff of the Bank. And acclaimed, biennium after biennium, he would perform his duties as Governor for the length of 24 years. The oak had found its druid, and vice versa.

And though, at first, he was resisted – certain quarters of the City complained that they 'didn't know the man'[20] – he proceeded without wasting an instant to refit the ship in keeping with the exigencies of the post-war era.

Allies: above all Norman cultivated the connection to the mandarinate of the American Grid: J. P. Morgan & Co. Of that clan, first and foremost of his trumps was the Governor of the Federal Reserve Bank of New York (FRBNY), Benjamin Strong, whom Norman had come to know and like in the last two years of the war.[21] Strong, who became Governor in 1914 'as the joint nominee of J. P. Morgan and Kuhn, Loeb and Company,'[22] was allegedly the first of a long series of preys that surrendered to the charisma of Norman, so much so that the American banker would later be accused by US President Herbert Hoover of being a 'mental annex' of Europe and Norman.

Style and mystique:

The reputation for mysterious god-like aloofness and for tantalizing omniscience, which transformed the name of Montagu Norman into a legend well before the end of the nineteen-twenties, was one which the Governor deliberately and carefully sought...Open conflicts...even private disagreements, were crude methods which he abhorred...Norman developed refined techniques of his own to impose on the City of London, [which] as a whole quickly succumbed to the almost superstitious awe inspired by the uncanny reputation he acquired for simultaneously knowing his own mind and everyone else's intentions. His first and greatest talent lay in bending to his own ideas and purposes those friends and colleagues who had already fallen under the spell of his personal charm...*Like a human spider, he chose to spin a finely meshed web of private contacts radiating from his office into every nook and cranny of the City...* Nothing new or significant could happen without Norman's coming to hear of it at once...He would then...approve or disapprove,...support or condemn. His sources of information were unrivalled and usually accurate. He was...astoundingly well-informed.

And with a remarkable display of condescending apologia, Norman's biographer achieved this esquisse of the 'human spider' with a bold reflection, which is a fair instance of a long 'scholarly' tradition of omission and complicit muddling surrounding the record of Norman and the Bank of England in the interwar period:

And what was Norman if not a long-frustrated understudy destined at last to play a major part in the drama of public life? Sure enough of his lines, he was less sure of the plot.[23]

One may wonder: how can a consummate arch-priest of the Grid endure a 24-year long pontificate as the treasurer of the world's empire, which coincided with the most critical juncture of Western history, without being 'sure of the plot?'

The plot, in fact, had begun to unfold at Versailles, and Veblen's prophecy concluded the first act. The second act, set in Germany, was a crescendo of putschist shenanigans that culminated through the apotheosis of national bankruptcy in Hitler's Beerhall coup. Presently the action had shifted to the world markets, while the German experiment was left to simmer in a pool of unknowns. And the Bank of England had not lain idle in the meanwhile. Norman had watched everything studiously, and paid especial heed for some time to the deeds of his friend Ben Strong across the Atlantic.

Right at the time of Versailles, in June 1919, the United States was experiencing her first post-war boom, an extraordinary credit inflation that had been sparked throughout the world conflict by the massive orders for foodstuffs and supplies on the part of the Allies. Given a plentiful gold reserve, a swelling credit base, surging prices, and low unemployment,

America's additional credit-money had set off a feverish stock exchange and real estate speculation, which reached its height in November 1919.[24] The gambling mania on the exchanges drove the rates for 'money on call'* to phenomenal heights – 20 percent and higher. In London, as in other financial centers, no sooner were such quotes available than balances were drawn from the City, and conveyed along the banking network to Wall Street, to fetch the higher rates. In other words, capital was exported at once, and as the transfer persisted (British investors selling pounds to purchase dollars), the pound sterling weakened vis-à-vis the dollar, which was the only currency anchored to gold in 1919: to lose versus the dollar was to lose versus gold.

Considering that the chief objective of Britain after the 'return to normalcy' was indeed to re-anchor her currency to gold, such an escape of capital and the consequential drop of the exchange posed a serious problem. Why was it imperative to re-anchor the currency to gold? 'Prestige!,' replied the constables. But that was a lie, and a big one.

The bank was in fact readying herself to plan a game of strategy so complex and potentially so dangerous that it required the greatest prudence on the part of the clubs privy to its nature. And these knew what mien to deport when it came to avoiding impudent enquiries from the public into their activities: they simply would 'never explain, never excuse.' A maxim of which 'Norman was inordinately fond.'[25]

To go back on gold, Britain gave herself five years – till the end of 1925.[26] But first, she had to tackle a few problems in her colonies.

India, whose Grid was rather rudimentary, had a proverbial hunger for noble metals, with which debts were settled on an ordinary basis. Her contribution to Britain's war exertion had been such that, from September 1919 to February 1920, she demanded to be satisfied in gold for her conspicuous trade surplus vis-à-vis the imperial center, thus bringing tremendous pressure to bear upon London. And that, what with the pull from the speculative craze in Wall Street, further enfeebled sterling. India had tried to secure gold during the war, but had been sourly rebuffed. She thus had to content herself with either silver or sterling balances.[27] Of the latter India wanted no more, and so since gold could not be had from London, she drew on her sterling balances in London to purchase silver from the Americans. But that too, lamented the British Treasury, weakened the pound (versus the dollar). It was time for the financial stewards of the empire to intervene; and here is what they did.

* Loans repayable at the option of the lender or the borrower with 24 hours' notice.

They conducted a two-pronged maneuver against their Indian colony. First they struck at the silver market. They unilaterally decreed in 1920 that the silver coinage of Britain was going to be reduced from a standard of 0.925 fine to a basic fineness of 0.500, which is to say that the alloy content of each silver coin was about to become double what it used to be. 'Australia, New Zealand and later most of the principal countries of Europe and South America followed suit.'[28] So Britain withdrew her good (fine) silver coins from circulation and sold them on the markets at the stellar quotes of 1920. The movement brought about immediately a precipitous fall in the price of silver. Thus the steep depreciation of the white metal alleviated the strain exerted on sterling,[*] and in the long run would altogether dispose of one channel through which India imperiled Britain's restocking of gold.

Simultaneously the stewards assailed the gold front. On February 1920, they decreed unilaterally that the rupee was to be pegged at 2s, two gold shillings. In other words, the British financial officers rendered the rupee enormously expensive in terms of gold, deliberately. The semi-coercive measure was introduced by blandishing India with the deceptive prospect of her buying silver, or anything else she wished around the world, at bargain prices. And so Indian imports, boosted by an artificially strong currency, did boom, while naturally her exports suffered a disastrous decline, which abruptly reversed the trade balance with Britain.[29] Farmers dependent upon exports suffered as they witnessed their prices plummet to match the world level, and as a consequence their income sagged. The final blow was struck by way of the capital account: those absentees in India who could afford to do so, realizing the blatant overvaluation of the rupee and its inevitable fall, moved at once to convert their rupees into pounds, and then convert the pounds into gold. Such capital flight (towards Britain to buy gold) automatically diminished the Gold Standard reserve, which the Indian government maintained in London. To restore this reserve, sterling securities (the standard form of banking collateral), which formed the 'cover' of the Indian paper money circulation, had to be withdrawn from Bombay and remitted to London, and thus, to compensate for the transfer, credit in India had to be restricted.[30]

Smitten once with an overvalued currency, which by depressing prices struck at their livelihood, and smitten twice with a credit crunch, Indians were at last bereft of any means wherewith to demand gold. Not only that: the empire's stewards were also shockingly pleased to notice that their scheme had prodded a vast segment of the colony's population to

---

[*]  For far fewer pounds were now needed to purchase silver with dollars on the American market; thus sterling was relieved.

unearth its silver and gold hoards to pay for a debt burden exacerbated by the artificial dearness of the rupee. Indeed, it had caused some gold to come out of the Indian soil, reach the government offices, and ultimately find its way to London in repayment of the adverse balance of payments.[31] By October 1920, India emerged as a net exporter of gold and remained one until the last quarter of 1921. It has been lamented that the government of India 'was, at best, a mute witness in this sordid affair.'[32]

Rather devilish than sordid, the tactic succeeded splendidly. The solution was yet provisional, and Norman had had no central part in it, though he must have known every inside detail of the operation, which had begun shortly before he took over at the bank, and of which, given that India was one of his 'most important financial interests,'[33] he impressed a capillary image in his vast memory. Norman certainly had a part, however, and the chief one at that, in the resolution of the first post-war American boom, which truly marked the beginning of his financial regency and stood as the initial, crucial instance of the stratagems he would employ a decade later to achieve his and the Empire's far-reaching goals.

From Figure 4.1, which depicts the evolution of the cost of money in Britain and the United States, it can be seen that as soon as Norman was elected Governor, the rate in London jumped from a high level of 6 percent to a heady 7 percent – one full point above New York. This was the gambit of a policy coordinated in tandem with the Federal Reserve in New York, which would be replicated in 1929.

When Norman smothered Britain with a rate of 7 percent, 'sending unemployment above the one million mark,'[34] Strong followed suit, and the rates were kept at that level for an entire year, so that by the spring of 1921 both countries had come to live through one of their all-time severest depressions: in the 1920–21 biennium, unemployment in the United States increased by 6.5 percent; industrial production, agricultural production, and GNP decreased respectively by 19.3, 6.1, and 2.3 percent,[35] while a vertiginous drop in prices of 44 percent inscribed itself as the sharpest price decline in the entire history of the country.

Norman justified his move by stating in his first official speech of 15 July, 1920: 'We are striving to return to...the gold standard. A debtor nation cannot expect lower rates than those of a creditor nation, and our rates are now below those in America.'[36] So, the swiftest means by which gold might be recaptured and preserved was to up a bank rate that was already high above the rate prevailing in the 'competing' marketplace of New York. 'The unemployed,' Norman would argue in general, 'were

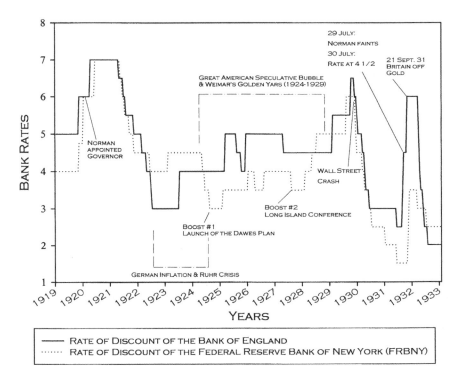

*Figure 4.1*   The London/New York tandem discount policy, 1919–32

unemployable.'[37] In Britain, under Norman, one out of ten workers would remain idle throughout the interwar years.[38]

Norman always affirmed quite rightly that joblessness was not his affair, but that of the government; his task was to attend to the financial welfare of the empire, and he did: with the collusion of Strong, he killed the stock market boom in Wall Street, shattered America's real estate prices and bankrupted her farmsteads, and all that, indeed, to check the dispersion of British money to Wall Street. The important question that remained was why would the American banking elite go along with this British policy of economic strangulation?

When the two governors met in December, 1920, they were pleased to concur that the policy of making money dearer, though somewhat precipitate, had been 'wonderfully successful.'[39] What they meant by 'successful' can be seen in Figure 4.2, which portrays the rate of exchange between sterling and dollar. It is clearly visible that since the accession of Norman (March 1920), Britain was attempting tenaciously to regain the

Gold Standard at the old pre-war parity of $4.86 to the pound. Governor Strong at the Federal Reserve was not only looking forward to that event, but he was also satisfied to have terminated the abnormal growth of the US money supply, which had been increasing since June 1919 and had been allowed in 1920 to reach unprecedented levels.[40] Many have wondered why the Federal Reserve, which had been incorporated at the end of 1913 with the avowed goal to dampen the wild fluctuations of the cycle and prevent a generalized state of insolvency of the domestic economy, failed so miserably its first serious test as America's financial watchdog in the aftermath of the war: the 1920–21 recession appeared abrupt, brutal, inexplicable. Again, why had the rate been kept so high, so long? In 1920 as well as in 1929, and indeed throughout the interwar years, American monetary policy is incomprehensible if taken out of the context of European politics, and specifically of Britain's agenda.

*The truth was that after 1920, Strong, the American Governor, consciously restricted credit at home to reduce significantly the volume of cheap credit to Europe.* Indeed, the stewards at the Fed coordinated with London a rate increase to 7 percent, which allowed both countries to pile up gold: it was in fact between 1921 and 1924 that America underwent one of its great

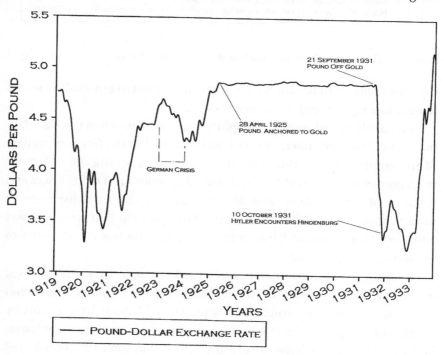

*Figure 4.2* Sterling–dollar exchange rate, 1919–33

waves of gold accumulation, and of all European nations Britain was the only one that accumulated gold after 1920.[41] So then, why did the Federal Reserve decide to store up gold at this time? What was it anticipating?

For years it had been a commonplace of monetary discussion in the United States that the gold which came in just after the war would return to Europe when it was again needed to support gold-standard currencies in Europe...[42]

*The interest rate hike in the US was a clear indication that the time to invest in Germany and surrounding states had not yet arrived and had thus been postponed.* Norman and Strong were preparing the terrain for the great German bailout, and the concurrent return to gold by Britain, which were going to take a few years to engineer. Figure 4.1 illustrates this pantomimed chase of the rates, in which each governor feigned in public to saddle on the other the responsibility for the tightening. And whatever the bankers did, which the public never comprehended, these punctually justified their actions by blaming 'the fear of inflation': oracular nonsense that was seldom, if ever questioned. And so it went: Norman upped the rate in April 1920, Strong followed in May, and after a year of 'wonderful success' in attracting gold to their respective cellars, Norman again took the lead in 'easing the markets' by pulling the cost of money downwards, and New York followed.

Thus far the experience of Norman had been to relive one of the fundamental teachings of the old Gold Standard, namely, that Britain always had to strengthen herself to govern between India and the United States,[43] her two gold-hungry 'colonies'; *and that, when it came to protecting and adding to the gold treasure of the Bank of England, the most incisive impact might be achieved by causing 'money famine' in India (deflation), and monetary abundance in the United States (inflation):*[44] *that is, by forcing the ryots to unload their gold, and encouraging a boom in America while keeping London's rate above New York's.*

When Germany was cleared of her war debt, this policy would be implemented to the full as London would succeed in staying above New York for a protracted period of time (that is, the duration of the five-year bailout; see Figure 4.1).

Thus, between 1919 and 1920, the Bank of England managed to shield the sterling exchange rate and increase her gold stocks by £50 million, reaching a total figure of £128 million (around 865 metric tons).[45] This amount was slightly less than what would become the statutory cover of the bank upon her return to gold in April 1925: £150 million (8 percent of the total world reserves).[46] In short, by late 1920 Britain's gold hoard had been reconstituted. Where were these additional ingots, presently in Norman's vaults, being shipped from? Stenographic sources mentioned South Africa, and *Russia*.[47] Were they then a chunk of Kolchak's treasure trove?

From this time on, the markets expected the pound sterling to become convertible into gold. The anticipation is discernible in the ascending path of the sterling/dollar exchange, whose initial point (the first quarter of 1920), coincides with Norman's appointment to the governorship (Figure 4.2). The ascent of the pound was interrupted three times: in the second half of 1920, in mid 1921, and throughout the controversy on reparations and the Ruhr crisis, from the summer of 1922 till the end of 1923. The war between Russia and Poland, and a sizable reparations payment remitted in dollars through London, accounted for the first two troughs in the curve,[48] thereafter the fate of the pound appeared to hinge on that of Germany: unless the latter was cleansed of her war debt, Britain's plan could not be set in train.

Therefore, between 1922 and 1924, the Bank of England adopted a 'policy of waiting':[49] trade was stagnant, and hiding behind a bank rate of 3 percent – up to 1½ percentage points below New York (Figure 4.1) – which did not rock the British economy, Norman kept an eye on the Reich. He let America swallow more gold, confident that in time he would be able to lure the Americans into expanding credit, lowering their rates, and therefore relinquishing some of their copious gold. Because in these years, though Norman's grip on Strong was potent, the latter, acting as the Anglophile mediator between Britain's imperatives and Wall Street, had been incapable of prodding US bankers to launch another inflationary boom for the sake of 'international cooperation':[50] at this time the American financiers failed to see what they would stand to gain from pumping in new money to invest in Europe's uncertain environment.

Germany, as Norman well knew, was the key with which he would unlock the stalemate.

So, in the meantime, while in 1922 the American Grid momentarily recoiled, Norman, the 'human spider,' ventured in a peripheral experiment around the German unknown: using all his persuasiveness on Dutch, Swiss, and American bankers, he secured a jumbo loan for Austria. Thanks to this, inflation was halted, the currency stabilized, and the economy of a former enemy country was restored with exemplary rapidity.

The Chancellor of Austria...dropped a remark, which reached his ears in due course: 'I'd like to erect a statue of gold to the remarkable Mr. Norman.'[51]

Norman thus established a precedent that he would later apply to the pièce de résistance of the plan: Germany.

By the end of 1923, three of Britain's chief financial stratagems had been rewardingly rehearsed under Norman's direction: (1) a concerted (with the FRBNY), stepwise tightening of bank rates to deflate a speculative bubble and swallow gold, followed by acute depression; (2) the overvaluation of the rupee coupled with mass sales of silver, by means of which the scourging of Indian peasant-farmers might be relied upon to suck into London their gold hoards; (3) a small-scale bailout, with which a former hostile country, Austria, was shored up with foreign credits, and was thus rendered prone to crashing violently upon the withdrawal of such Allied financial props.

In November 1923, the Reich was being purged of its debt; diplomatic prisoner, cosmopolitan whorehouse, financial hostage, and Nazi hothouse, the Weimar Republic was presently scheduled for a great jamboree, a five-year blowout at the American manger, catered by the Governor of the Bank of England. This would be the most spectacular bailout of the twentieth century, followed by the bitterest harvest of history: the Dawes Plan of 1924 – generally recognized as Montagu Norman's 'masterpiece.'[52]

Credits lines would be shot out from the Allied Grid to hook onto Germany's brand new monetary network like grappling irons. And before the transfusion might begin, a native adjutant issued from the great banking brethren would be specially ordained to oversee the plan.

### The Dawes bailout and the Hierodule Schacht

Hjalmar Horace Greeley Schacht was born in 1877 in Schleswig-Holstein. His father William harbored a passion for America. One year before Hjalmar was born, William Schacht had returned from Manhattan to Schleswig-Holstein with a basket of failures, a membership to a Masonic Lodge and the acquaintance of the *New York Tribune*'s powerful editor, whom he revered, Horace Greeley – a vocal anti-slavery advocate in Lincoln's era. Of these three meager spoils, Hjalmar bore the mark of the third (in his name), inherited the seed of the second (freemasonry), and would want to have nothing of the first (failures).

As a youth Hjalmar felt called on to 'great things' and his attraction to the mysteries of the Grid, which in Germany had developed by the late nineteenth century into a voluptuous embrace between heavy industry and cosmopolitan merchant banking, was immediate and intense. His apprenticeship, which lasted 13 years (1903–15), was completed within the halls of the Dresdner Bank, one of the great Berlin banks, where, like Norman at Brown Shipley, he acquainted himself with every aspect of the business. Then the war came, and he served briefly (October 1914-July 1915) as a steward of the banking administration in occupied Belgium.[53]

The problem he was hired to solve was how to induce the Belgians to remit the occupation costs in cash.[54] The method Schacht applied in Belgium was a standard banking routine, which he would systematically perform in the course of his professional career, in Weimar as well as under the Third Reich, to squeeze money out of the Grid.

Schacht suggested using a *loan*. He proposed that the Belgian municipalities issued bonds. Bonds which would be purchased by the wealthy Belgians. The cash thus collected would go to the German soldiers via the occupied municipalities, and the Belgian people would be counted on to 'sell' goods to the German armies and pay taxes with which the Belgian authorities were to repay the Belgian rich. The scheme, which was clever, would not work, however, because the Prussian generals, rapacious as ever, had no patience, and decided to print money instead, crassly. The Belgian stint did not have a graceful ending for Schacht: upon his return to Berlin, the banker was accused of favoritism and embezzlement for having provided his employer, the Dresdner Bank, with a great deal of those 'Belgian notes of occupation' at a significant discount. He defended himself, lying his way out of the snag, with the complicity of many highly-placed others. Case closed: '*à la guerre comme à la guerre.*'

At the war's end, along with Rathenau, he was one of the founders of the German Democratic Party, but unlike Rathenau, he was not too discriminating in finding the proper vehicle for his inhuman pride – provided it was the winning number, anything would do, be it Weimar's, the Allies' or, later, the Nazis' bandwagon.

And so, under Weimar, he discreetly added to his 'interests' that of 'a minor official of the Allied-created German banking authority.'[55] On 22 March 1922, he submitted a memorandum to John Foster Dulles, the resourceful lawyer of the Wall Street firm Sullivan & Cromwell that had fashioned at Versailles the cavil thanks to which the cost for defraying Allied war pensions had been most dishonorably added to the final reparations bill. A midwife of the German 'reawakening' all along, Dulles presently oversaw in Berlin, among many other things, the overhaul of the German Grid.

In his proposal, Schacht envisaged 'a solution of the reparations problem' – a visionary draft whereby the Allies, rather than loaning money to the profligate ministries of Weimar, would extend it to a cluster of giant conglomerates specially created for the purpose. Schacht contemplated the formation of giant industrial cartels, which would become the recipients of American cash credits, as well as of special exporting licenses from the

Weimar authorities that would enable them in, say, a decade to repay the original loan, and relaunch the German economy.

It was science fiction: a plausible scenario (the cartels) constructed on unripe fantasies (the concreteness of the reparations). And it made Dulles jubilant: it seemed as if the Anglo-American clubs had finally found 'their man.' Dulles forwarded the memo instantly to Thomas Lamont, a top fiduciary of J. P. Morgan & Co. with his plaudits: 'Dr. Schacht is one of the ablest and most progressive of the young German bankers, and it seems to me that *his plan may contain some thoughts which may have some merit.*' And two weeks later Dulles responded enthusiastically to Schacht's proposal: 'If a period of political stability could be assured, I have no doubt that bonds issued by such monopolistic corporations as you mention would command the confidence of the investing public.'[56]

Now that Germany had blasted her currency, Schacht might be brought in to lead the 'reconstruction.' Out of thin air and five days after Hitler's putsch, on November 13, 1923, he was catapulted on the public stage as Germany's new Commissioner for the National Currency. His task was to bridge Weimar over the transition from the old, murdered Reichmark to the new, captive one.

Sitting behind a bare desk with only a telephone, he called around his brethren of the Grid day and night for a week. Finally, by refusing to grant credits to speculators in a provisional currency devised for the transition, he signed the death certificate of the old mark, fixing its final purchase price at 4.2 trillion for a dollar. Thus the mark came to be stabilized at that fateful gold peg, $1 = 4.2 gold marks, with a net erasure of twelve zeroes. 'The 20th of November,' said Schacht, 'contributed a milestone in the history of the stabilization of the mark...'[57]

On that very day Reichsbank president Rudolf Havenstein, the governor that had spurned the Kappists, lost half the bank's gold to inflation and succumbed miserably before the rout of his currency, died of a heart attack. Norman had met him earlier that year, when the German Governor had come crawling to him for compassion, and the human spider had found him 'a very attractive man: but so sad.'[58]

But the directorate of the Reichsbank, an inbred and 'malicious fronde of moth-eaten pashas,'[59] were hardly bedazzled by Schacht's financial hokey-pokey, and had taken no liking to him. They wanted good old Helfferich, the Nationalist stalwart, former Imperial Vice-Chancellor and Finance Minister, and chief Reichstag slanderer of Erzberger and Rathenau: a true, perfidiously impenitent column of the old order. Yet in Weimar it was not the Germans that decided but the Anglo-American clubs. Dulles recommended Schacht to Morgan & Co., Morgan & Co. to Norman, and Norman to Weimar's incumbent figureheads. 'During the summer and autumn of [1923, Norman] had first heard of Dr. Hjalmar Schacht as a rising German financier with a paradoxical mind and a will of his own.'[60]

On December 22, 1923, Hjalmar Schacht was elected governor of Germany's Central Bank. And Helfferich had, by the bye, only a handful of moons left to enjoy: he would die in a train crash in April of the following year. Decidedly, even the gods were for Dr. Schacht. Norman could not wait to meet him; he confided to his entourage: 'I *want* to get on well with him.'[61] So well, that on New Year's Eve, 1923, he summoned the German without ado to call at his office in the bank on the following day, at 11:00 am; 'I hope we shall be friends,' he told Schacht before hanging up.[62] They met and became more than friends; they became and came to be referred to as 'twins.'

> ...Schacht was only a useful instrument, the means to a greater end, yet one so necessary that Norman went out of his way to cultivate him for the good points he might possess.[63]

The November 1923 stabilization at 4.2 was merely the preface to the great Weimar bailout that would bestow upon German five years of 'synthetic prosperity,'[64] her so-called 'Golden Years' (1924–29). John Foster Dulles had mentioned in 1922 the need for 'political stability.' And that presently signified putting an end to 'French madness', for that was how Norman viewed the French occupation of the Ruhr.[65]

In March 1924, the clubs, via Morgan & Co., launched a massive speculative attack against the French currency. The clubs' agents, posted in the several nodes of the European Grid, gathered francs and, coordinating the tempo with one another, dumped them on the exchanges.[66] The franc plummeted; the Bank of France found herself impotent before the raid: she did not possess sufficient means (foreign cash) with which to absorb the dumped francs and prop up their value. After having dealt the blow, Morgan & Co. came forth with the medicament: they offered France a $100 million credit for six months gauged on the French gold. In late April, the US Ambassador to Berlin, Alanson Houghton, wrote in his diary: 'England and America have the franc in their control and can probably do with it what they want.'[67]

On April 9 the Dawes Plan was announced. It bore the name of yet another one of those American 'great nobodies' of the Morgan era: replaceable, mediocre souls with average talents and a hard frame, itching to give history a nervous bite. Banker, Comptroller of the Currency under President McKinley, and former chief intendant of the American Expeditionary forces during World War I (a post he owed to his old-time buddy, Commander-in-Chief General John J. Pershing), Charles G. Dawes offered, in the capacity of American representative of the Reparations Commission, a foretaste of what was coming on January 15, 1924, at a meeting in Paris.

> The first step which we should take, it seems to me, is to devise a system for stabilizing Germany's currency, so that we can get some water to run through the budget's mill. Let us build the mill after we find the stream to turn its wheels.[68]

It bore Dawes' name, but it wasn't *his* plan – it actually 'made him sick,' out of modesty, to hear it said afterwards that he did it alone.[69] No, in fact, the Dawes Plan was 'largely a J. P. Morgan production,'[70] *directed by Norman*, who proceeded at this critical stage, by the proxy of his American colleagues, to blackmail the French. If the French wished to see their $100 million loan renewed, Morgan & Co. warned them, they had better adopt a 'peaceful foreign policy' peremptorily. Which meant that France had to accede to: (1) the hollowing out of the Reparations Commissions of any power; (2) the transfer of all such power to a special Reparations Agent, a role soon to be assumed by S. Parker Gilbert, a graying bureaucrat parked at the US Treasury, subsequently risen to better fortune under the wing of Morgan & Co.; and (3) the immediate evacuation of the Ruhr.[71]

In spite of its gratuitous brutality, the French impromptu in the Ruhr would be Europe's last semiconscious revolt against the encirclement by the Sea Powers. When in 1924, France gave in, it was definitively over for Europe: Britain finally held the continent solidly in her grip.[72]

As to the 'building of the mill,' the 'new' Reichsbank was entrusted to a General Council of 14 members, half of whom were drawn from Allied countries. And by limiting, statutorily, the bank's advances to the Reich to 100 million marks,* the mechanism for transforming the state's bills into worthless cash was dismantled.[73] Next time, if fall she would, Germany was bound to suffer the penury, rather than the depreciation of money – which was even worse.

The gold hoard. Norman's cherished hope was to fill the German cash box with pounds sterling, which would afford him the complete and exclusive control of the country, but the Americans demurred: this was

---

*  Raised by law to 400 million marks in 1926.

*their* 'deal.' And Norman acquiesced benevolently; he would explain in a letter to his mother:

The Dawes machine, while nominally international, is in practice dominated by Americans. This suits me well...Europe is the 'promised land' to America; to be possessed even without competition![74]

In the end, it was agreed, Schacht's hoard would consist of a loan of $190 million; half to be floated in New York, the other half, for the most part, in London. For that, Germany agreed to pay 7.75 percent – two points above the world average. Of the Wall Street syndicate appointed to float the American tranche of the Dawes loan, Morgan & Co. realized $865,000 in mere commissions (53 percent of the total).[75] A quarter of the money thus raised was distilled into pounds sterling, and gold for the remaining three-quarters, that is, US dollars, thus reflecting the financial power ratio between the two powers in control of the German prey. This borrowed money would 'cover' the forthcoming issues of new, post-inflation marks to the extent of 40 percent. In August 1924, the old mark was replaced by the new Reichsmark, 2,790 of which might buy 1 kg of fine gold – this was the old parity – and all capital controls were removed.[76]

The United States, who had not even signed the Treaty of Versailles, then unleashed packs of accountants to appraise the value of the creeks, industries, forests, and meadows of Germany before mortgaging the whole country: all her bounties had at last become collateral for the jumbo Morgan loan.[77]

And the reparations. The keystone of the Dawes bailout, ratified on August 30, 1924, was the new agreement on the reparation payments. The plan lightened considerably the obligations of Germany. Without determining their number, the annuities were established as moderate in the beginning and becoming fixed, in 1928–29, at a figure that was susceptible to increase later, according to a certain indicator of prosperity.[78] This plan did not supersede the German reparation obligations as established in 1921, and the difference between the Dawes payments and the payments due on the London schedule were added to the total reparations debt. Thus Germany would pay reparations for five years (1924–29), ending up owing more at the end than she did at the beginning.[79]

The pivot of the entire contraption was the role of the Agent General, who could at all times invoke from Berlin the so-called 'transfer clause,' *whereby the annual reparation installment might be suspended if the strain against the mark should become too strong.* The clause thus worked as a 'breaker switch,'[80] which was designed to protect a steady flow of foreign investment into Germany from any interference that might be caused by the cash transfers of the reparations. If the Agent deemed that any such transfer might have weakened the mark, he might stop the payment: clearly, the clubs had engineered a system which minimized the risk of capital flight internally, and thus ensured for a number of years the remittance of the American funds earmarked for Germany's preliminary rearmament and industrial renovation.

The final touch. To crown it all, 25 percent of Germany's public employees were sacked in 1924 (the number unemployed would reach 2 million in 1926), the absentees were invited with little success to repatriate their exported capitals, and the rest of the economy was inevitably subjected to a *Kreditstopp*.

The truth was that $190 million scarcely sufficed to jump-start the German economy; ten years earlier, in 1913, the gold reserves of the Reichsbank had amounted to $280 million. On April 7, 1924, not to endanger his hoard and the 'cover,' Schacht had no choice but to turn off the taps. He wished he could have raised the rate of discount, but having the latter being put out of commission because of the hyperinflation – it stood at 100 percent – he could only distribute the new bank notes by rationing them on a discretionary basis. So he gave them to the sound concerns and let the unsound ones, along with a hefty slice of the population, go bankrupt: in the spring of 1924, business failures increased by 450 percent.[81] But the stringency was not imposed for the sake of harshness: there just was not enough borrowed money to re-start the economy. So, where was the rest going to come from? The *Kreditstopp* was indeed decisive for it opened 'the door to the internationalization of the German monetary supply': whatever was not provided in the first installment would come by way of additional foreign loans.[82] Not a single drop of Germany's circulatory system was to be hers; throughout the 'golden bailout' she would breathe on borrowed blood. Now that the mill was achieved, Germany would live off *'the stream,'* as Dawes had metaphorized in his Parisian allocution.

In 1925, as a token of gratitude for his financial embassy, the clubs elected Charles Gates Dawes Vice President of the United States.

### I. G. Farben and Germany's first Five-Year Plan

And then the American blood came gushing in.

The experts found the ship itself to be quite sound, and so reported. All that was necessary was to float it again on a tide of confidence. Once afloat it could bear a reparations debt burden of $625 million a year...That was the Dawes Plan, and on the undertaking to make it work the German government borrowed $200 million gold from Great Britain, France and the United States to begin a policy of fulfillment.[83]

Swarms of brokers, soliciting on behalf of the American banks, were suddenly seen buzzing in every nook of the German establishment. Rates in Berlin were high – 9 percent on average throughout the 'golden years'; Morgan & Co. with their mouth watering, packed bundles of German bonds with a view to selling them to the 'American public.' And these cohorts of middle-class gulls, avidly wishing to see their money 'work for them' in the bank, parted with their savings to buy the German paper-promises.

It was to the American public that the bulk of the German reparations were to be sold, and to accomplish this purpose a systematic falsification of historical, financial, and economic fact was necessary in order to create in America a state of mind that would make the sale of the bonds successful.[84]

Up until 1930, some $28 billion flowed into Germany, 50 percent as short-term credits; the Unites States accounted for half the total. Only $10.3 billion was used for reparations; the rest went into many different, and interesting, directions. *Which is to say that after 1923 Germany never paid a cent for reparations out of her own pocket.*[85]

Finally, when Germany resumed paying France the reparations, pacifying her, as it were, with an American-bred bone to gnaw at, the Franco-Belgian troops abandoned the Ruhr.[*] This initiated Weimar's absurd cycle of the 'golden years': the gold that Germany had paid as tribute after the war, sold, pawned, and lost during the inflation to the United States, was sent in the form of Dawes loans back to Germany, who then remitted it to France and Britain, who shipped it as payment for the war debts to the United States, who channeled it once again, burdened with an additional layer of interest, to Germany, and so on.[86]

In Germany, everyone and everything borrowed: the Reich, banks, municipalities, counties, businesses, and households. The money was spent on housing, industrial machines, and public works. Weimar erected cathedrals of steel and glass, planetariums, stadiums, velodromes, fancy aerodromes, amusement parks, modernistic morgues, skyscrapers, titanic swimming pools, and suspended bridges. Yet the world, and even the

---

[*]   The last troops left in July 1925.

lenders at home, enquired of their politicians: 'Why is Germany being boosted thus?' 'She is our ally against Communism,' they replied, and the Weimar clerks hastened to toe the party line.[87] It is difficult to guess who must have been more nauseated by the telling of this lie, whether the Allies, or the Germans themselves. Be all this as it may, the money kept pouring in, and no one anywhere did anything to stop it. Germany was being turned into a veritable colony of Wall Street.[88]

It did not take much to realize that the arrangement was a house of cards: the moment Wall Street decided to recall its loans, Germany would plunge into complete, irremediable bankruptcy. What next? Nobody wished to give the prospect a careful thought. Only the fall was certain. It was just a matter of time.

> The whole country, politically and economically is falling more and more into the hands of foreigners...A pin prick and the whole thing will blow up. If once the money is recalled in large quantities, we shall go broke – the banks, the municipalities, the joint-stock companies, and the Reich.[89]

But there was no tomorrow in 'Golden Weimar': as it gave bread and work, money was good, wherever it came from; the SPD and the trade unions, all led by solid Marxists, were enthusiastic supporters of the Dawes loans.[90]

As for the 'interesting' uses of the foreign money, a substantial quantum of it was sold by the Reichsbank in exchange for gold to the Russian Communists themselves, with whom the secret rearmament plans were proceeding apace, thus affording the Soviets access to the Western market for purchases.[91]

But far more significant at this time was the reorganization of the I. G. Farben concern into one of those giant conglomerates imagined by Schacht in his draft to John Foster Dulles in 1922.

The story of I. G. had begun, in the early 1900s, with colors (*Farben*, in German). The dyestuff industry had consisted then of a nucleus of venturesome combines that had invested heavily in the quest for color and pigment. BASF, the boldest of the group, and 'a trademark surrounded by awe in the corporate realm, mastered early on reds and yellows. But unlocking the secret of synthetic blues was more troublesome.'[92] Eventually, after the mystery of synthetic indigoes had been solved, and added to a long list of ground-breaking discoveries, the so-called Big Three, BASF, Bayer, and Hoechst, joined by a few other satellites of Germany's intimidating chemical pole, had merged into a cartel in 1916. They had formed thus a loose but sweeping amalgamation congruent with Rathenau's office for war resources, from which it drew its leading assistants.[93] 'The structure came to be known simply as I. G.': *Interessen Gemeinschaft* (community of interests).[94] It stood as 'an industrial colossus...that dominated the chemical business of the world...Few universities could match the profusion of Nobel Prizes earned by its scientists.'[95]

At the war's end the drafters of Versailles had instructed the Allied inspectors to leave I. G. in peace.

> Unlike the French, the Americans and the British were careful not unduly to upset the I. G. officials. Assurances were given that the investigators would not 'pry into the secrets of commercial value in times of peace'. No technology would have to be revealed nor questions answered unless they concerned weapons or military applications. 'This reassurance', reported a U. S. Chemical Warfare Service officer, 'established a more or less cordial relationship between us'.[96]

Indeed, when the questions touched on military patents, not only did the Anglo-Americans not reveal anything either, but they even actively collaborated with the German princes of alchemy.

Thanks to the bailout and the 'capital liberalization' of the Dawes intermission, the six concerns of the I. G. cartel, desirous to increase world market share, finally resolved to coalesce into a single pool of know-how and financial might. 'The fusion took place on December 9, 1925. The companies were merged to become Internationale Gesellschaft Farbenindustrie A. G. – or I. G. Farben, for short.'[97] The monstrous consolidation followed from the dream of its leader, Carl Bosch, to liberate Germany from depending on foreign oil wells.

Were these not the days when the great cannon-maker, Krupp, whose assembly lines in the Urals and near Leningrad were clangoring at full throttle, discreetly rented a suite in Berlin around the corner from the Defense Ministry? A suite where his best engineers might design in tranquility the weapons of mass destruction of the future, while the top brass living next door drafted mobilization plans that called for a 63-division army?[98] It was thus a certainty: 'in the mechanized war of the future the need for liquid fuel was going to be astronomical.'[99]

For the purpose, the alchemists of I. G. concocted a marvelous process called hydrogenation, whereby coal, of which Germany held abundant supplies, might be mutated into oil. At that time BASF has performed the transformation up to half the weight in coal. Therefor Bosch would be awarded the Nobel Prize, 'the first engineer so honored.'[100]

The only way to make the dream come true, Bosch reasoned, was to draw America's top petroleum trust, Standard Oil, into some type of alliance, with which the great corporation from New Jersey might be made to shoulder the cost of Farben's research and development of synthetic fuel. After years of mutually fascinated cooperation, especially on the part of the Americans, the accord with Standard Oil was sealed in 1929. In exchange for the world rights for the hydrogenation process, with the exception of Germany, Standard transferred to I. G. $35 billion in Standard Oil stock. December 1929 witnessed the creation of a joint venture subscribed by I. G. and Standard Oil, for the mutual exploitation of precious patents and the manufacture of synthetic oil, named American I. G. Company, on whose board sat a few of America's great captains of industry and business: Edsel Ford of Ford Motor Company; Walter Teagle, head of Standard, and Director of the FRBNY; C. E. Mitchell, chief of National City Bank, and Director of the FRBNY; and Paul Warburg, first member and creator of the Federal Reserve Board, and Chairman of Manhattan Bank.[101]

'The full story of I. G. Farben and its world-wide activities before World War II can never be known, as key German records were destroyed in anticipation of Allied victory,'[102] but there are sufficient testimonies to suggest that German-American technical and military collaboration, shielded by complex corporate contracts, hosted in the 'neutral' nodes of the Grid (such as Holland and Switzerland), went on throughout the 1930s and well into the duration of the second world conflict:

Standard Oil [will keep] its cartel with I. G. Farben alive, war or no war...A Standard official said:..."Technology has to carry on..."[103]

During World War II, I. G. would provision and supply the Nazi regime with the bulk, if not the entirety, of the following essential staples: synthetic rubber (100 percent), dyestuffs (100 percent), poison gas (95 percent), plastics (90 percent), explosives (84 percent), gunpowder (70 percent), aviation gasoline (46 percent), synthetic gasoline (33 percent), not to mention the manufacture of Zyklon B, the canned cyanide employed to annihilate the inmates of concentration camps, which was produced by I. G. Leverkusen and sold from the Bayer sales office through an outfit called Degesch.[104]

An American post-war committee, drawn from the Senate and chaired by Harley M. Kilgore, a Democrat from West Virginia, after gaining a fairly deep insight into the ramifications of American collusion with the enemy, and not without edulcorating to the point of distortion the obscenities found therein, framed its conclusion according to what has since Versailles become the customary apologetic template of the Allies:

> The United States *accidentally* played an *important* role in the technical arming of Germany...Neither the military economists nor the corporations *seem to have realized* to the full extent what that meant...Germans were brought to Detroit to learn the techniques of specialized production of components...The techniques learned in Detroit were eventually used to construct the dive-bombing Stukas...[105]

Thus the meager evidence accessible suggests by itself that the American collaboration with the German military-industrial complex, through Weimar and the Nazi regime, was indeed intense and pervasive. The 'Dawes machine' inaugurated this determining phase of the incubation, in 1924, when the dynasts of the American Grid, egged on by Norman, set out to divide amongst themselves in a rational fashion the bond sales of Germany's giant industrial axes.

Morgan & Co. and Rockefeller, via Chase National, promoted I. G. Farben and the German chemicals on Wall Street. Dillon & Read placed $70 million worth of debentures on behalf of the coal and steel concerns, such as Alfred Thyssen's Vereinigte Stahlwerke, which would serve as a Nazi slush fund,* and one of the prime founts of pig iron and heavy plate for the Third Reich. V. A. Harriman & Co., which merged with Brown Brothers in 1931, sponsored the electro-technical conglomerates.[106] As shall be seen, the revision of the Dawes Plan, the so-called Young Plan of 1929, would be named after a General Electric Co. officer, Owen Young. Young would be appointed thereafter as one of AEG's foreign directors. AEG, Germany's General Electric, the great *Konzern* founded by Rathenau's father, received under the Dawes Plan at least $35 million worth of loans. By 1933, at which time there was irrefutable evidence that it financed Hitler, AEG was owned by its American counterpart GE to the tune of 30 percent.[107]

No accident: Germany was being gradually, but steadily, rearmed, in keeping with the dictates of Versailles. Since 1924, the Anglo-Americans equipped what would become Hitler's war machine through well over 150 foreign long-term loans contracted in less than seven years:[108] the more thorough and elaborate the fitting, the more devastating the German army, the bloodier the war, the more resounding the foregone victory of the Allies (and the defeat of Germans, who were being set up), and the more sweeping

---

*   See below, p. 198.

and permanent the Anglo-American conquest. There was neither greed nor treason behind the Dawes bailout, but solely the long-term objective of fitting a prospective enemy with a view to bringing him down in a fiery confrontation – a confrontation to be orchestrated at a later stage.

> With these American loans Germany was able to rebuild her industrial system to make it the second best in the world by a wide margin...and to pay reparations without either a balanced budget or a favorable balance of trade.[109]

> The great German machine, having been raised on borrowed capital to be the most powerful and the most efficient in Europe, was running on borrowed gas...Why were the Germans putting their own gas out of Germany for safe-keeping, in the banks of foreign countries?[110]

The Dawes bailout was in fact Germany's first Five-Year Plan (1924–29) in view of the forthcoming world war.

Throughout this critical quinquennium, Norman had been busily at work: to sustain at such a pace the flux of American money into Weimar had required of the Bank of England such financial acrobatics that only he, in the world, could have performed. For Norman brought the foreign money in, and, when it was time to alter the political physiognomy of Germany, he took it out.

### Britain's grand charade to crash the new Gold Standard

Much underwater paddling had gone into opening the gates of the American feeder to Germany, and most of it conceived, organized, and effected by Montagu Norman. The succession of his maneuvers punctuated each salient date of the interwar period: he was the uncontested and unrivaled architect of Europe's downfall; the priest that expedited and turned to account the obscene degeneration of European civilization. With World War II, the Anglo-Americans came, saw, and conquered, but before they did all that, Montagu Norman schemed – and *his* peculiar doings, unjustly misreckoned, remained so far the most astonishing feat of the great Anglo-American siege of the landmass, which had begun with World War I.

As Germany underwent the Dawes transfusion, the path for the Allies was cleared: the mark was being made fully convertible into gold, and sterling might presently resume its ascent towards the old parity of $4.86.

So in April 1924, the Dawes Plan, which in fact postponed the gravamen of the reparations transfers for some years, was announced, and from that moment onward, the pound rose without ever wavering again (Figure 4.2). In May, J. P. Morgan & Co. and the FRBNY communicated to Norman and associates that they were ready to grant their British counterpart generous lines of credit for defending the gold convertibility of sterling when it came, which, they all anticipated, would be in early 1925. The British Treasury haggled a bit, and in the end they all agreed, reassured and confident. And then the Norman/Strong tandem resumed its favorite game, that of the bank rates.

In July 1923 Norman had raised his rate from 3 to 4 percent, thus sending the signal to New York that London was ready – ready to pull gold (Figure 4.1). It took some time to allow the German debacle to run its course and set up Schacht for the bailout, but finally New York responded by lowering its rate by three half-point reductions from 4.5 percent in May 1924 to 3 percent in August. The positions were inverted; New York was then below London. The plan, of course, was to attract lenders in London, the expensive money market, and borrowers in New York, the affordable one. The switch was of decisive importance. New York initiated thereby a policy of 'easy money': she swallowed at once conspicuous amounts of private and public paper-promises and injected cash into the economy, which was magnified by the lax credit routine of the commercial banks.[111] America was flush with cash, and London, the tighter market, pulled gold like a magnet. *Thus America's phenomenal stock exchange mania of the Roaring Twenties was sparked: it started in the late summer of 1924 to give Norman a hand in attracting gold to London.*[112]

But it was not until the great Dawes loan was floated in October that sterling began its final and decisive convergence to parity. The unbroken improvement from October (4.43 dollars to the pound) to April (4.86) was made 'in the face of formidable adverse conditions': buttressed by the American Grid, the pound reached the yearned gold parity on 28 April 1925, even with a 'strongly negative merchandise balance.' It was in fact the *invisible balance* (capital imports) that did all the work in lifting the pound to the gold plateau.[113] Norman had had his way; there were no 'rules of the game' other than the particular ways of bending the Grid.

And so it was finally done: Britain returned to gold, at £1 = $4.86. Over 30 countries followed her example; the City of London was once more the clearing center of the world.

Upon closer inspection, however, a few attentive scholars came to notice that Britain's new 'Gold Standard' was rather peculiar. First of all, gold virtually disappeared from circulation:[114]: the note-holder *could not* under the terms of the new act convert his Bank of England note into gold at the bank. And the latter was obliged to sell gold only in amounts of 400 fine ounces, that is, 'for...not less than $8268 worth at a time':[115] gold was quietly dropped out from the public traffic, and confined to a special inner circuit accessible only to 'the big players.' What was Norman after? By excluding the possibility for the economy to transact in gold, and, most importantly, hoard it in times of crisis, he was removing from the system a buffer, which could have rendered its actions and reactions much more sluggish. Norman was calibrating the system to play a fast game.

Second, he leveraged this new gold circuit greatly by imposing upon all central banks presently tied to it to keep part of their reserves in pounds sterling, which was presently anchored to gold, and which London would proceed to invest on their behalf.[116]

On the one hand, this device of the gold exchange diluted enormously the 'cover' for the standard as a whole, and thus predisposed the world system to an unprecedented inflationary swelling; and on the other, it preset the game for a catastrophic chain reaction, which should have started as soon as either of the two gold currencies, the pound or the dollar, should have suffered a run for having been overextended: if, for instance, London were to lose much gold, the pound would collapse, and if the pound collapsed, as most satellites were forced to hold large amounts of sterling as 'cover,' the entire circuit would disintegrate.

Norman was playing for high stakes: he demanded a swift and momentous response from the set-up; he was literally assembling a time bomb, and the world, unawares, looked distractedly the other way.

> The banking structure of the modern world with its huge pyramid of deposits nominally convertible into gold on demand, and actually represented by assets that cannot be liquidated, *is full of dynamite*.[117]

Third, the parity itself. No doubt, the pound at $4.86 was expensive. And Norman knew that well. Sterling at such a level was obviously not likely to pull British exports through, though it might certainly be counted on to strengthen Britain's vital produce imports and, far more important, her invisibles: overseas investment, shipping freight, and financial services, all of which were denominated in sterling. Having conquered anew the position of world clearing center, London and the empire might confidently expect to derive a rich source of revenue from the forthcoming magnified flux of foreign moneys in search of high interest – hence the importance of keeping the interest rate in London above that of New York.

At last, in 1925, after a full decade in the temple, Norman was on top of his game; most of the industrialized world was on gold now, and the great financial carousel, strapped with dynamite, might be spun in motion. Truly, Norman had impressed the world; building against all odds this new, formidable machine that seemed to have brought the chances for world prosperity and cooperation to levels hitherto unimaginable. And he was feared.

His persona, as the events, corridor rumors, and legends had come by this time to incise it in the public fantasy, was a fair match to the enigma of his nature. Completely wedded to the empire and the adored bank – 'his sole mistress,' as he said – [118] he led a veritable monastic life, without company and friends worthy of the name.

> He had some fundamental dislikes...The French, Roman Catholics, Jews... An innate ruler with a profound distaste for so-called democracy...[119]

> Norman was a strange man whose mental look was one of suppressed hysteria... When he rebuilt the Bank of England, he constructed it as a fortress prepared to defend itself against popular revolt, with the sacred gold reserves hidden in deep vaults below the level of underground waters which could be released to cover them by pressing a button on the governor's desk. For much of his life Norma rushed around the world in steamship, covering thousands of miles each years traveling incognito... under the assumed name of 'Professor Skinner'...[120]

This was the individual that the French had to reckon with in 1926. Because he had laid eyes on them. Presently, the achievement of his plans had to pass through the French tangle. France was, in fact, the last of the big players, and was still not hooked onto the newly assembled Gold Standard.

Like Germany, France after the war was shaken by a violent inflation and an extraordinary flight of capital. In the early 1920s, because of the perennial uncertainty surrounding the German reparations, and the organized speculation against the franc at the time of the Ruhr invasion, the French absentees exported en masse a fabulous treasure, which they remitted for custody to New York, and especially London. Statistics measuring the magnitude of the outflow are as usual unavailable, but what seemed a certitude among bankers in the know, was that it was far more significant than the German export of capital had been a few years previously.[121] Now, realizing what fugitive wealth had done to Germany in 1923, a few experts, lucid enough to appraise the situation for what it was, took fright and found the time to fire warnings to the outside world. On September 10, 1926, one of such dispirited omen-mongers, Swiss banker Felix Somary, put two and two together in a public lecture hosted by the University of Vienna.

We now find ourselves at a provisional state of rest. Yet this is the calm before the tempest. How can we Europeans cope with a power such as the United States, who wields a surplus both on her trade and capital account? The only way out is for America to keep on extending short-term-credits. Never has an economic cycle initiated under such hazardous conditions as the bailouts of Austria and Germany. Beware, America is the strongest protectionist of the world. She will bolt her door when Europe will come knocking with her wares for export. And if today the United States must lend to keep the system afloat, this cheap money policy cannot but usher in a Gargantuan stock exchange bubble. What if all the French refugee capital, which is now being invested from New York by its American custodians, is suddenly repatriated? That will set off the collapse. Therefore, only the immediate withdrawal of French funds from their foreign shelters and the peremptory abolition of the new gold standard can prevent a stock exchange boom from developing. For if both movements were to unravel during an upswing, or in the midst of an American crisis, the dimension of the catastrophe that would befall Europe would be unimaginable.[122]

The great 1929 Wall Street Crash was thus fully anticipated by a common practitioner of the Grid in 1926. Which is to say that Norman could by no means have failed to envision the eventuality himself, especially in the light of the 1920 crunch, which *he* had wrought.

As for the French expatriated capitals, timing, as Somary intuited, was of the essence. Norman, who was keenly alert to the potential of such funds, could scarcely afford to yield to France any form of control, albeit a tangential one, over the fate of Germany, which was now fed vital money from America. A mass recall of French gold from London and New York, on terms other than Norman's, might indeed have wrecked the new Gold Standard and swept the momentum from under the Wall Street lending bonanza. So the money had to be repatriated to France immediately, *but through London*, and in ways congruent with the Governor's plans.

At once, in the summer of 1926, the empire dispatched its human spiders to spin the web round France.

On July 29, 1926, at 11:00 am sharp, Norman crept in the Banque de France to face his opposite, Emile Moreau. The Frenchman was somewhat uneasy; he had been told that Norman was *'très dur en affaires et très rusé'*: Moreau knew he was coming face to face with the 'best governor in the world.'[123]

Not before speaking ill of the Jews, yet passionately of his bank and Great Britain, to whom he wished the domination of the world, Norman urged Moreau to join the 'Bankers' club' by readying himself as quickly as possible to convert the franc at a fixed rate under the new Gold Standard.[124]

A few weeks later, in August, the Agent General for the reparations, Parker Gilbert, met the French President, Raymond Poincaré, and the two cut a deal. For the first three years, the installments which France owed to America for the war credits would be subtracted from the larger Dawes payments which Germany presently owed to France. Britain and America nodded. On the sly, the three parties had thus revised the Dawes Plan *to link war debts and reparations.*[125] Poincaré was triumphant – the accord would keep him in power: he had made France safe for the investors again.[126] The Banque de France was advised to prepare itself for a major absorption of francs from abroad.

All of a sudden, in the second half of 1926, a wave of capital returned to the French motherland. The Banque de France swallowed these foreign moneys and printed francs galore, in exchange. Its foreign reserves swelled to extraordinary heights. The franc left the doldrums behind, appreciated rapidly, and became the object of a frantic, international speculation, which was systematically organized from London. The latest rumor was that 'speculators from Berlin' borrowed pounds in London, and sold the pounds in Paris for francs. Paris deposited these pounds in London, where they were lent anew, and so on.[127] But the truth was that the chief speculators on the franc were British financiers.[128] Which leads one to infer that Norman, 'the trusted confidant of the whole City,'[129] was, in fact, allowing the London market to feed the French with oodles of sterling...Feeding the French, until in May 1927, with their mouths full, and fearing a disruptive appreciation of their currency, *they demanded to convert some of their enormous sterling reserves in gold.* And that was exactly what Norman was waiting for.

Though his biographers were always fond of recounting that there was 'calculation in the face...[this] character with a thousand and one disguises...chose to wear,'[130] the reader, however, is never told on which occasions Norman was supposed to have performed these extraordinary theatrical shows. There is reason to surmise that May 1927 was one such remarkable instance.

Feigning unspeakable distress at the French conversion of £1.5 million into gold on 19 May, 1927, Norman rushed a week later to Paris with an adjutant to confront Moreau. The latter rehashed peevishly his argument against speculation, and defiantly dug his heels in by telling Norman that France was playing by the book, and that such a conversion (of sterling into gold) was the least Britain should expect since her imperial return to gold two years ago: London, sentenced Moreau, should now raise its rate to defend its gold. Norman retorted that there would be a public outcry if he did that.[131] The British Governor then proceeded to explain that London's monetary market was a high precision mechanism, perfectly gauged to lubricate the British economy; any abnormal tampering with this device would be insufferable; an unwarranted and disproportionate withdrawal of gold from London would topple the entire system. Moreover, Norman went on, it was impossible to spot the source of the speculation; speculators were faceless: Paris had power over London, Norman declared, but London had none over third parties. Finally, with such high rates in Paris and the continual allurement of an appreciating franc, capital affluence to France was simply unstoppable. Paris, Norman concluded, should lower her rate.[132]

Framed to inflate the French Governor's self-importance and corroborate France's newfound feeling of financial allure, the lines of Norman were cleverly crafted and effective. He had told Moreau that Britain was at France's mercy. Which was not true; nor was a single word of his entire act.

Officially France and Britain had reached a stalemate in May; neither party agreed to alter its rate, though they signed a truce of sorts whereby Moreau, sufficiently cajoled, forbore for the time being from withdrawing more gold from London, and directed his requirements to New York, whereas Norman willingly tweaked upwards by an eighth of a percentage point some rather insignificant short-term rate in London: 'I shouldn't want to throw the pound sterling in the dirt,' Moreau signed off on his diary, gloating and diligent, 'that would earn us the justified reproach of Ben Strong and the Americans.'[133] He had been completely fooled.

From the start, Norman operated deliberately with a 'very slender gold reserve', that is, with a cover rarely larger than 2–3 percent of the country's total money supply.[134] With a gold base spread so thin, any incoming monetary mass of substantial magnitude, such as the repatriation of French capitals, likely to be satisfied, at least in part, in gold might be assuredly counted on to rattle the system. Which was precisely the effect Norman sought from the sudden reversal of French money transiting in London. *He* was the one encouraging the speculation against the franc; besides, he felt neither awkwardness in cohabiting with 1.2 million unemployed, nor inhibition in raising the rate to 7 percent when necessary: he was afraid of no riot. All of which bespoke, instead, his intention to obtain something altogether different from this maneuver.

> He somehow managed to get a great number and a great variety of people to do just what he wanted them to do, although very often they did not want to do it...He could mobilise, in effect, an army out of the ground, and he did so, time and again.[135]

And that was to persuade his companion Benjamin Strong in New York to postpone the tightening that was in the offing, the measure being necessary in the United States to cool the bustling activity on the stock exchange, which of late had become too audacious. Norman presented the stalemate with Paris as a question of life and death for the new Gold Standard, and begged Strong to come to his aid. A conference was immediately arranged in July 1927 in Long Island; Norman, Schacht, Strong, and Charles Rist, former law professor and second-in-command at the Banque de France, attended. The result was, at first glance, a rather inconspicuous dip in the Federal Reserve's rate from 4 to 3.5 percent in August of 1927. New York was one full point below London (Figure 4.1).

But this apparently innocuous cheapening of money in New York, coupled with more paper-swallowing on the part of the Federal Reserve, was the turning point of the interwar period. This second boost, compounded with the much ampler and still effective inflationary push of late 1924,[136] would trigger Wall Street's infamous wild ride to the Faustian heights of September 1929. Thus 'the Federal Reserve Board permitted a speculative spree, which was already out of hand by August 1928, to grow progressively worse until July 1929.'[137]

To help Britain temporarily 'survive' the contrived 'French shock,' America, through cash injections and the mechanism of the interest differential, released excess gold reserves (overall around 17 percent) from her enormous coffers once more.

> In the first half of 1925 [the United States] lost 140 million dollars worth of gold, and in the 14 months which ended in May 1928, lost nearly 540 million dollars. The first outflow furnished much of the basis for the new gold currency of Germany and the second for that of France.[138]

The aim of this British game of ricochet was always the same: namely, to keep the 'Dawes machine' running. The American policy of cheap money renewed in August 1927 went in fact to sustain the continuous flotation of German securities in New York, and thereby strengthen the Reichsmark in terms of the dollar.[139] Another brilliant move deftly executed.

And so the Anglo-Americans replayed what they had done in 1924: the borrowers borrowed money in New York, the cheaper market, and wired the proceeds to London to earn the higher rate. US private short-term funds moved to London in considerable volume. Norman's gold reserves were plenteous again, and until June 1928, the sterling–dollar exchange averaged the highest for any of the years 1924–31.[140] American gold had started to flow in since the previous December. And certain interests in the United States, including the Federal Reserve Bank of Chicago, protested: they did not understand why New York had to overheat the American economy for the sake of Norman – for no amount of mystification, anywhere, succeeded in convincing anyone that it was otherwise.[141] It was at this time that Benjamin Strong earned that semi-insult of being the 'mental annex' of the British Governor.[142] Yet for all of the hue and cry, the step was not reversed.

The relief brought to London, however, was merely temporary. Already in July the tide began to turn. It so happened that, because of the revamped speculation, short-time money on Wall Street was shooting to levels so recklessly high (20 percent) that the funds that had hitherto been flowing from New York to London and the rest of Europe, were being recalled in New York by the fatter baits. And the dismal news for Norman was that money was therefore being pulled out of Germany as well.

In brief, the world economy was back to the late 1919 scenario, yet encumbered by a mass of credit several orders of magnitude greater; it barreled along like a file of overloaded wagons, pulled by the Anglo-American locomotive along a roller-coaster without any safeguards.

The Federal Reserve had a mind to kill the euphoria softly, by accompanying it, as it were. The American bankers set out to ration credit gradually, hoping that the bubble would eventually run out of steam. Thus, in July, the Federal Reserve in New York raised the rate to 5 percent, half a point above London, but well below the market rates prevailing on Wall Street. With this move, the game changed radically; the June 1924 switch between London and New York was reversed (Figure 4.1). As in 1920, this was for Norman the summons to intervene peremptorily: the crash had to come as soon as possible, or else sterling, and the empire's policies, would be weakened to the point of impotence: Norman could not watch Wall

Street send Britain into a spin by sucking out of her all the gold amassed previously in London.

At this time, in late 1928, things worsened for Britain; she kept losing gold to Wall Street, and, again, to France. Norman wrote to Schacht: 'The Jews continue day by day to take away our gold.'[143] As if it hadn't been enough, his partner Strong died in October of tuberculosis.

It took Norman little time to win over George Harrison, Strong's successor. Not long after the replacement, Harrison's fellow directors could already be heard saying that the new boss 'lived and breathed for Norman.'[144] The British Governor courted his new prey immediately, entreating him to engage without delay in that chase of the rates that Norman and the former Fed Governor had run in 1920: that is, to prick the bubble for the sake of Britain's gold. And as proof of his resolve, Norman took the plunge and raised the bank rate on February 7, 1929, by a full point to 5.5 percent (Figure 4.1), awaiting immediate reaction in New York.

But New York lingered. There was a communication breakdown within the American Grid; Harrison and the Anglophiles in New York wanted to play the game and step the rate up forthwith to 6 percent, but the seven-member Federal Board, a separate supervisory board presiding in Washington, seemed to have lost all sense of New York's doings and intentions. Ten consecutive times between February and August 1929, fearful of affecting business unfavorably, the Board denied New York's request for raising the rate to 6 percent.[145] Finally, on August 9, 1929, in a delirious convergence of policy inspired by diametrically opposed objectives – the Board interpreting the measure as an expansive and accommodating gesture towards the market, and New York willing it instead as the coveted, and restrictive response to an anxious Norman – the Federal Reserve finally set its rate at 6 percent.

At last, with the green light from New York, on September 26, 1929, a week after the all-time peak for share prices,[146] Norman raised his rate to 6.5 percent and yanked the air out of the bubble. 'Then, suddenly,' wrote the Financial Editor of the New York Times, Alexander Dana Noyes, 'the great decline began...No one seemed able to explain the source of the huge selling orders which poured in...Possibly London...started indiscriminate foreign selling.'[147] London sold and gold flowed back to Britain.

> It is certain that...the raise of the London bank Rate to 6½ percent... hastened the downfall of speculation in the United States...[and] precipitated the stock exchange crisis and slump of October.[148]

It was done: Norman arrested America's long season of profits, 1914–29, 15 years of avid dreams and opulence, suggested by Britain, and inspired by the ravage of Europe. Afterwards the rates of London and New York, like twined serpents in a caduceus of folly, came rolling down as well (Figure 4.1): the world economy was crippled by debt contracted during the boom at exorbitant rates, and the central banks' crunch had so depressed prices as to send the money scampering underground: it was locked up in the vaults – the rates decreased, banks lent no more, the Grid closed. A crisis the likes of which no one had ever experienced had begun. Begun as a mere repetition of the Norman/Strong sabotage of 1920.

The ratio of gold to total credit in America had sunk to less than 7 percent in April 1929, the lowest point in her history; when the crash hit the US the paralysis was extensive:[149] through bank failures the American elite had burnt a third of her Grid to play this British game. It would take the United States ten years to come out of the Depression. The Dawes bailout, barring a momentary lending spurt to a comatose Germany in 1930, was *finished*: Americans wanted their money back. *Suddenly and completely they ceased to buy German securities.*[150]

Thereafter, Norman waited. It was a slow process of suffocation that he observed at home, and especially in Germany. There, the clutches of the Dawes machine, without the 'stream,' had brought political despair to such a pitch that in March 1931, Germany and Austria, Norman's two bailed-out creatures, announced their intention to unite into a customs union (*Zollverein*) as a means to overcome the commercial drought of Middle-Europe. But on May 11, Austria's leading bank, the Creditanstalt, suffered a run and, with it, the whole Austrian banking system collapsed. How it collapsed remains a mystery to this day. The documents available mention some obscure and 'intricate system of cross-deposits between [the Austrian Grid] and a number of American and British banks' which had been set up in 1929 – 'tainted money,' in the words of Norman. What the role of such a system might have been in this connection is still unknown.[151] Three weeks later, the rupture spread to Germany. The Reichsbank accused foreigners of an external run, while the Federal Reserve laid the blame on the Germans for exporting their money. Either way, the money fled, and Norman knew that Britain was next.

He had been planning and preparing for this fateful juncture a long time since – at least for the six years that it had taken him to assemble his new Gold Standard. For indeed it had been constructed for self-disintegration; the aggregate of his bank's policies throughout this period proved it irrefutably.

Whenever he had lost gold, Norman was the first to violate the 'rules of the game' by expanding the money supply instead of restricting it:[152] between 1924 and 1929, a significant percentage of the foreign moneys that Norman had attracted with the trick of the interest differential between London and New York was taken in by the London joint stock banks and relent to Germany continually in excess of their resources, with the full knowledge of the Governor.[153] In the process, the London banks relaxed their cover and made it twice as thin as customary. An inquiry into such inexplicable 'oversights' was solicited after the 1931 rout, but nothing came of it.[154]

Shortly after Germany's complete financial collapse, in mid-July, a run was launched against sterling.

On July 13 an ad hoc committee set up to report on the health of British banking completed its work: the Macmillan Report, which bared the lewd foreign indebtedness of British banks, was released with suspiciously good timing and no explanation whatever of the 'large figures' published therein.[155] Alarmed by the report and the crisis in Berlin, between July 16 and 29 the central banks of France, Holland, Switzerland, and Belgium liquidated a small part of their bulky sterling balances in London, and took away with them £32 million in gold – about 20 percent of Norman's stock. What followed from that moment on was a tale from an alien realm.

Harrison cabled Norman immediately; 'Can you throw light on this?' he asked. 'I cannot explain this drop…,' answered Norman.[156] The situation, to say the least, was serious, and it called for drastic measures. Such as tightening the rate to 7 or 8 percent, as Norman conceded on July 23, when speaking again with Harrison over the phone.[157] So what did the Bank of England finally opt for? *On July 29 it raised its rate from 3.5 to 4.5 percent, when 10 could have 'pulled money from the moon'…A meager point,* as if it were bandaging a hemorrhage with a gossamer gauze. Bankers round the world were flabbergasted by London's reaction: unforgivably inane, they thought.

On the same day, Norman, 'feeling queer,' eventually collapsed during a meeting at the Treasury.[158] He abandoned the helm at the bank. Adducing health complications, and without allowing his name to appear on the passenger list,[159] he boarded a fast liner to Quebec on August 15. His Deputy, Ernest Harvey, was now in charge, and *duly instructed*. Washington and Paris immediately came forth with offers of help. Harvey floated the decoy of Britain's government deficit: 'that,' he averred, 'is the source of our trouble, and it really can't be helped.' No one believed him, and fellow international bankers insisted on assisting the Old Lady of Threadneedle

Street.* On July 31, Paris and New York extended credits to London to defend sterling, to use it as ammunition, as it were, with which the Bank of England might repurchase the pounds that speculation was dumping in London. On August 5, the pound kept skidding, and more gold was forfeited, but Harvey did not draw on the new Franco-American credits. The French wondered what on earth he was doing; Harvey replied that he had let the gold go to teach his colleagues at the Treasury a lesson; to prod them to balance the budget. Moret, the new French Governor, could not believe his ears, 'he was appalled.'[160]

Harvey, undaunted, and slathering falsehood upon falsehood, professed further that the source of the run remained inexplicable, and that British citizens were only marginally involved in it, when in truth suspicion ran high in the banking community that the British financiers of the City were the chief speculators against their own currency.[161] The pound continued to sag, and eventually the Franco-American credits were blown away in a matter of days. The French and the Americans, not daring to doubt the good faith of Britain, persisted and in late August offered two additional lines of credit, in dollars and francs, for a last-ditch defense of the pound. The Bank of England, instead of keeping the new ammunition close at hand and firing it from its own defense lines, dispatched it to two minor forts, the British Overseas Bank and the Anglo-International Bank; and these two banks, by the frequency and magnitude of their purchases of pounds, revealed to the speculation what never ought to have been revealed: that is, the amount of the reserves themselves.[162] Everyone guessed that the money was on tap, so to speak, and that it wouldn't last long – and so it was wasted in little time.

Mid-September dealt sterling the *coup de grace*: no one knows for sure, but the last fatal withdrawal appears to come by way of the Netherlands,[163] though not on official account:[164] the central bankers stayed put. France had nothing to do with this last raid. Given the size of her sterling account, she stood only to lose tremendously from a depreciation of the British currency; she actually bought sterling at this time. The same applied to the Dutch central bank. So who really mugged the Old Lady?

The evidence is 'scanty,' regret the historians.[165]

Therefore, this had to have been the work of that gray blob conveniently referred to as 'speculation' or 'the market' – ghost privateers, who in September ransacked the cellars of the bank some more, thus bringing the

---

*  The moniker of the Bank of England.

total loss in the final two months to £200 million in gold and deposits.[166] But it was known that

> In its operations with...foreign exchanges balances, the Bank of England was continuously preoccupied by the need for secrecy and discretion. That its efforts in this respect were generally successful...is beyond doubt, as the paucity of press, and even Treasury, guesses as to the extent of its activities indicates...Public knowledge of the fact that the Bank held hidden reserves, at times as large as its published, would have made execution of its...policy impossible...In its market operations, [the Bank] deliberately disguised itself. Through a number of accounts at the Federal Reserve Bank of New York, it prevented banks paying in funds or receiving them from knowing their ultimate destination or origin.[167]

As these were the methods of the Old Lady, the temptation to conclude that it was the bank itself that led the speculation from under the cover of its secret foreign accounts by way of short sales and like operations, with a view to igniting a herd movement, which it then deviously lured into its own gold sanctum through 'the line of least resistance' – that is, an absurdly low rate of discount at 4.5 and the weak defense of the two small banks in September, is rather irresistible.

Then, on September 15, 500 sailors mutinied at Invergordon, Scotland, because of a pay cut. The meretricious press jumped at the story and blared out in the open that the Royal Navy was in disarray. The organs of the empire were now diffusing the psychosis that Britain was on the verge of a precipice. From Nova Scotia, Norman acted with Harvey to draw up the draft bill that would abrogate the 1925 Gold Act. On September 18 the defense of sterling was given up. A day out from Quebec, on the homeward voyage, Norman received a cable from his men at the bank: 'Old Lady goes off on Monday.'

On Monday, September 21, before a speechless world, Britain suspended gold payments.

Within four weeks 18 countries would depart from the Gold Standard. To disperse the loitering speculation, the bank hiked up the rate to 6 percent, where it would stay for the next four months (Figure 4.1).

At first it seemed one of those incomprehensible losses which the British didn't quite know whether they were to hail or mourn. Though soon 'the politicians, the press, and the public seemed to arrive at the belief that those who...had driven Britain off gold had forced a *blessing* upon her government against her will.'[168]

But it wasn't over: the empire's stewards, to make it perfect, achieved this *pièce extraordinaire* with a solemn finale. Snowden, the chief of the Treasury and 'Norman's devoted slave,'[169] in officiating over the funeral of the Gold Standard in the House of Commons, appealed with maudlin majesty 'to everyone not to use words...at this moment, which will make things more difficult.' The few skeptics in the House, lest they should crack 'a joke in the cathedral' if they spoke up, kept their mouths shut.[170]

On September 23, Norman docked in Liverpool; on the 28 he was back at the bank. Allegedly, 'he was utterly bowled over on discovering of the terrible truth.'[171] Clearly, Harvey and the others 'had lost their heads.'[172]

So here was Montagu Norman, a controversial and patently ill man in charge of the financial arm of the world's empire until late July 1931 – *nine years* past the customary term – who relinquished the command at the most critical juncture of Britain's recent financial history, and in his absence deputized his most delicate duties to a team of semi-incompetents. As a result, the empire's currency fell so steeply as to sever the connection to the gold anchor and hurl the world economy down a spiral slide into hell. The Navy mutinied, and upon his return the Governor was pilloried like a monumental loser by a wolfish mob of cartoonists. The pound depreciated by 30 percent, and the losses of the French and Dutch central banks realized on their sterling balances numbered in the billions of dollars. The outrage of the Hollanders at the double-cross was such that they contemplated a legal suit versus the Bank of England; the Dutch Governor, Vissering, was fired on the spot.

What did the empire do? Did it fire Norman? Clément Moret, the French Governor, for having held on to his pounds, 'was decorated as a Knight of the British Empire in October.'[173] *And Norman was confirmed governor for the first of 13 additional years.*

What of prices and gold? Did prices in Britain, as all feared, shoot up because of sterling's fall? No; Britain, most seemed to have forgotten, did not suffer the imposition of world prices, *but dictated them herself*: copper, freights, wheat, cotton, fats, jute, rubber, and tin were all quoted on the empire's markets. It was the others that would have to adjust.[174]

And gold? Table 4.1 shows the evolution of the bank's stocks of the metal between 1925 and 1935.[175]

By late 1932, not only was the gold hoard refurbished, but it had even increased. How? Why, by crushing the Indian serf, of course, with the exact same device employed ten years before. Between 1928 and 1930, the Indian government was ordered to dump a third of its surplus stocks of silver (90 million ounces), thus causing a decrease in the price of the

*Table 4.1*    Bank of England gold reserves, 1925–35

| Year | Gold reserves ($ millions at 1929 level) |
|------|------------------------------------------|
| 1925 | 695 |
| 1926 | 729 |
| 1927 | 737 |
| 1928 | 748 |
| 1929 | 710 |
| 1930 | 718 |
| 1931 | 588 |
| 1932 | 583 |
| 1933 | 928 |
| 1934 | 935 |
| 1935 | 973 |

metal of 50 percent.[176] In 1931, India's Imperial Bank, besieged by the furious protests of India's farmers and merchants, was enjoined to peg the rate at 6 percent; and even the Bank's director, hand-picked by Norman, remonstrated. The monetary stringency was coupled with a rupee whose artificial expensiveness in terms of gold was kept maddeningly high, all of which conspired, in keeping with Norman's expressed wish, to depress local prices and cause a devastating 'money famine.'[177] Despite the turmoil and the fiery indignation of Gandhi, Indians had no alternative but to discharge their debts with the empire by exhuming their stashes of metal.[178] Which: gold, *sona*, or silver, *chandi*? Since *chandi* had been rendered nearly worthless, they could only pay Britain with *sona*. 'Distress sales,' they were called. After September 1931, and for the rest of the decade, a torrent of gold welled out of India to irrigate the coffers of the City – the flow was steady and intense. Viceroy Willingdon, ecstatic, reported from the Raj: 'Indians are disgorging gold...'[179]

September 1931 was indeed 'the watershed of the interwar period.' The British betrayal signaled the 'end of the international financial system established in the 1920s and contributed substantially to the disruption of the international economy.'[180]

While he had been setting up the Gold Standard, Norman, in view of its forthcoming breakdown, had pulled the sub-Grid of the British empire together: South Africa, Canada, India, New Zealand, and Australia were financially re-engineered, either with the creation of a central bank or the modernization of the existing one. September 1931 thus found the empire financially compact and self-sufficient, with a vast, closed market sheltered by imperial preference and soon to be walled by a 20 percent tariff (October 1932).

In October 1933, at a dinner hosted by the Lord Mayor at the Mansion House, Winston Churchill lifted a glass to the health of the Governor: 'British banks,' he orated, 'have shown themselves capable of a...resourcefulness which has been a definite contributory factor in the strength of the country [Cheers].' Norman capped it off with an Arab proverb: 'The dogs may bark but the caravan moves on.'[181]

## The last scheme of Kurt von Schleicher and the end of Weimar

In December 1924 Hitler was amnestied. He had been in prison since November 12, 1923 – 13 months of detention in all. He told the faithful Hess that it would take him five years to resume control of the party.[182] He was provident: five years that coincided with the course of the Dawes bailout. There was no more question of coups and the like; this time, he swore, he would gain power by 'legal means.' Röhm, the SA commander, had no patience for such dilatory tactics: he gave up and shipped to Bolivia to train the local army. Meanwhile, the Anglo-American secret services had been watching Hitler with interest since 1922.[183]

Ebert, Weimar's first president, died in 1925, and in March new presidential elections were scheduled. The Nazis threw their slender weight behind the chief strategist of World War I, General Ludendorff, who found himself competing against his former other half: Field Marshal Hindenburg. Hindenburg carried the day with nearly 15 million votes, and his alter ego, Ludendorff, the reckless gambler to whom Hindenburg truly owed his fame, garnered a humiliating 1 percent of the people's sympathy: he was finished, and Hitler, deep down, was quite satisfied to be rid of this cumbrous, antiquated piece of furniture.

But the measure of the electoral rout gave a fair idea of the Nazis' overall prostration. Until 1927, Hitler suffered moreover from the handicap that the Bavarian government had barred him from making public speeches; Prussia would hold out until 1928. The 'golden years' had shut 'the drummer' up. So, unable to speak, he delegated the organization of the party to the zealous Left wing of the northwest, which was led by the capable organizers Gregor and Otto Strasser. Veterans of the Great War and Freikorps volunteers, the Strasser brothers incarnated the anti-capitalist current of Germany's petty bourgeoisie, a movement that hearkened back to late-Renaissance German utopianism, for which land was conceived as inalienable and protected by a 'peasant aristocracy,' industry segmented into guilds, and national union achieved by a federation of self-governed cantons. *A federated Germany, in the view of the Strassers, meant a federated Europe, and an anti-British alliance of free workers across Eurasia.* There was no trace of the religious racialism of the Hitlerites in the Strassers' outlook.

In 1926, on the occasion of the *Fürstenenteignung,* a motion introduced by the Communists to demand the immediate expropriation of princely estates for public redistribution, Hitler and Strasser clashed for the first time. The latter, who wanted to second the Communists, was also campaigning for an alliance with the East, and widespread socialization at home: the very antipodes of the Hitlerite strategy. Hitler called a meeting in Bamberg on February 14, 1926, and lambasted Strasser before the party's vanguard, deriding, moreover, the Strasser line as '*Spielerei*' ('pie in the sky').[184] Strasser was no match for the Führer; even Strasser's young assistant, Josef Goebbels, who had been full of pugnacious hope about the confrontation, was dismayed by his boss's performance. In fact, he was bewitched by Hitler, the halo, the bodyguards, and the caravan of expensive limousines that motored him around. The club-footed Goebbels jumped the fence to rejoin Hitler, who dispatched him to Berlin as the NSDAP's new *Gauleiter* (district leader), with the composite task of smashing the Reds, luring the working class to Nazism, and ousting the Strasserites from the capital. Gregor Strasser hung his head and fell back within the ranks, while Otto remained defiant. It was just a matter of time before Hitler would sacrifice the Left wing entirely; it was altogether a foreign body within the party, which might have mobilized dissent but was not committed to waging a European war. A war, which, for Hitler, was the *sine qua non* for fashioning the empire of the swastika. And to fight the war the princely estates, the Grid, absentee power, and heavy industry, for the time being should have stayed right where they were. On this occasion, because the German Democratic Party had also ranged itself temporarily 'against the protection of private property,' Governor Schacht gave up his party membership in a huff.[185] The Führer and the banker drew a small step closer to each other. The motion of the Communists was defeated.

The Litmus test of Gregor Strasser's recruiting effort came with the national elections of 1928, in which the NSDAP scored a miserable 2.6 percent of the vote, 809,000 voices. The marginalization of the movement might have been suitably blamed on Strasser by Hitler and his Munich retinue, but selling Nazism ever as the receptacle of brutal malcontent, especially during the fat years of the American lending feast, could not but yield null results. And the Hitlerites were aware of it. It was misery they needed, as in 1923, and Montagu Norman would not tarry long before setting them loose upon the Fatherland.

When in 1928 Prussia lifted its ban on the public appearance of the Nazi leader, whom Weimar no longer seemed to fear, Wall Street happened to be slowly withdrawing its credits from Germany; Hitler was about to be summoned to the stage once more – five years after his release, five years since the foreign overhaul of the German economy.

Firmly moved forward by the strange certainty of its *Führer* Adolf Hitler that the decisive breakthrough was near, the NSDAP had meanwhile completed its organisational battle preparations, as if it had prior information about the impending crisis.[186]

In all, and without counting the abominable Zeitgeist of the Modern Era, three clans contributed to the Nazi seizure of power: Anglo-American finance, the USSR, and the Vatican – the first two designedly, the third less so.

With the Wall Street Crash of October 1929, something the Nazi organ, the *Völkischer Beobachter*, did not even bother to mention,[187] and the severance of the pound from gold in September 1931, Anglo-American finance interrupted the monetary transfusion to Germany, causing automatically, as shall be seen, the electoral success of the Nazis. In the same interval of time, as if faithfully aiding the plots of London, the Russian Soviets engineered within Germany a civil war to 'baptize' the freshly elected Hitlerite contingent.

The 1923–24 biennium was indeed an historical divide: key personages that had accompanied the first phase of the German incubation in one capacity or another had all departed: Havenstein (November 1923), Parvus Helphand (December 1924), Helfferich (April 1924), Wilson (February 1924), and the cardinal of all professional revolutionaries, Lenin (January 1924). In the five years that followed the death of Lenin, Stalin purged the Soviet Union of its 'true believers.' There was a group belonging to the old Leninist guard that still clung fanatically to the notion of 'permanent revolution.' Drunk with the blood and success achieved thus far upon the land that was once the Czar's, men like Trotsky, in 1924, were still convinced of the world's imminent revolution in the industrialized West: from Germany to America, via France. Trotsky was evidently drifting in an illusory world of his own, and this would not have been a complication for his rival Stalin, had it not been that the former was still one of the symbols of the USSR, and far more worrisome, an exponent and leader of that group within the Soviets that was seeking a peaceful entente with the Socialist forces of Germany.[188]

In 1927, after three years of demoniac intrigues, back-stabbing, orchestral maneuvers, and Siberian confinement for his men, Trotsky was expelled from the Politburo – he delivered his last speech parrying with a forearm a hail of inkwells, tumblers, books, and insults.[189] He went into exile in 1929.

Meanwhile, Stalin prepared his part of the German ambush, for the ultimate benefit of the Nazi gestation, during the Sixth Congress of the Communist International in Moscow, in 1928.

Already in 1925–26, the Russians had demanded the expulsion of all those leaders of the German Communist Party (KDP) that had put their independence of thought above everything else. Afterwards Moscow had submitted the rest of the KPD to the 'leadership' of its tool, Ernst Thälmann: Stalin had no wish to see the German Communists prosper. From the 1925 purge onwards, he fielded Thälmann and the street fighters of the Red Front as a special shock troop of Soviet foils with which to intensify the clash with the SA. At the same time, the German Red jackals, upon orders from the Russian central, were instructed to fragment the German Left. By painting in its official rhetoric the drowsy Socialists of the German Socialist Party (SPD) as 'Social Fascists,' that is, as an enemy, Moscow sought to confuse the electorate of the Left and prevent the formation of a solid proletarian dam – approximately 40 percent of the vote between the SPD and the KPD – to the forthcoming Nazi onrush.[190]

> Throughout the ensuing years, down to and even after the Nazi take-over, [the line laid down in 1928 at the Comintern Congress] was never altered…Throughout this period, as the shadow of Nazi brutality and intimidation fell deeper and deeper over German political life, the attitude of the Communists toward the moderate opponents of Hitler remained undeviatingly hostile and destructive. It was clear that this aided the Nazis…Less than three months before Hitler's take-over, the Social Democrats in their despair…appealed repeatedly to the Soviet embassy in Berlin to induce the German Communists to give them help against the Nazis…The blunt answer was given by the secretary of the embassy: 'Moscow was convinced that the road to a Soviet Germany lay through Hitler'.[191]

And then there were the Catholics – a whole third of the German population under Weimar. Hitler could not afford the luxury of alienating the absentee owners, nor could he repel outright the adepts of Rome with his racial gnosis, which, in its esoteric details, should only have been shared among the Nazi initiates. In religious matters, the stance advocated by the party was one of neutrality.

In 1928, when the Dawes annuity was increased, Germany protested so violently that a new Committee, chaired this time by the General Electric director, Owen D. Young, was constituted to draw up the revision of the original bailout. Between February and June 1929, the clubs drafted in Paris the final installment of 'the merry-go-round of reparations of debts, the most preposterous episode in modern history':[192] this was the Young Plan. It was a direct sequel to the 1926 business with the French over the link between German payment and war remittances to the Allies. According to its terms, Germany was to pay 59 slightly reduced installments until 1988. Part of the burden was to be securitized, that is, packaged and sold to private investors on the money markets of the West, so as to raise some cash pronto for the ever-thirsty French, who in exchange promised to evacuate the Rhineland in 1930, five years before the original deadline imposed at Versailles. To assist in the task of selling the bonds, a new private bank, the Bank for International Settlements (BIS) was established in Switzerland at Basle. The Agent General was demobilized, and Germany was the mistress of her railroads once again. The Depression would cut short the life of such a plan to a mere year and a half.

As Reichsbank president and financial expert of the German delegation, Schacht signed the Young Plan in June 1929, but then the ebb from New York began to sponge off the money from Germany. Foreseeing what lay ahead, Schacht probably panicked. He had to cut loose from the sinking ship. So in December, in the midst of the final round of negotiations for the new plan, he troubled the waters by circulating an official letter, 'a bomb,' in which he recanted his commitment adducing all manners of diplomatic and financial quibbles. The government, he claimed, had inserted late additions that violated the original document.[193] The effect in the financial community was so distasteful that the Finance Ministry recommended that he should resign, which was precisely the egress Schacht was hoping to fish from his mischief. In March 1930, President Hindenburg, indignant for what seemed to him as a shameful 'mutiny before the enemy,'[194] and not quite capable of fathoming the motives of this petulant Schacht, accepted the banker's resignation disdainfully.

Schacht, it is true, had attempted in vain throughout his tenure as Weimar's Governor (1924–29) to curb the extravagant borrowing of the municipalities, though he had clearly done absolutely nothing to interrupt the giant American transfer, pecuniary and technological, to the great industrial poles of Germany[195] – for good reason: this had been the objective of the prize essay he had submitted to Dulles in 1922. All in all, Norman and the clubs were delighted with him. He had done well. And they all surmised that it was not yet over for this resourceful hierodule of the great Grid, who retired to his estate in Brandenburg to watch from a distance how the story unfolded, while reading *Mein Kampf.*

1930: with high finance wreaking havoc in the background, the Red Front in battle trim, and an open Nazi hand outstretched towards Catholicism, the crisis finally struck Germany with all the violence the savvy of men could muster.

Unemployment began to decimate the country. On paper, there were over 3 million jobless individuals by 1930. Despair would lead to many of them committing suicide.

The republic was finished: in March 1930, unable to force through a hostile House a raise in the unemployment insurance, the last of Weimar's ghost Cabinets fell. A conservative Catholic, Heinrich Brüning, was chosen by president Hindenburg as Weimar's next Chancellor. Brüning was bent on enforcing harsh decrees to balance the budget. Hoping to find some sort of coalition amenable to support his politics, he dissolved the Reichstag in July and called for new elections in September.

Then came the Nazi breakthrough: from 2.6 percent, they jumped to 18.7 percent of the vote – 6.4 million voices. *After the Socialists (24.5 percent), the Nazis ranked as Germany's second political force.* The Catholics wielded 15 percent of the vote; the Communists, 13.5 percent; whereas the Nationalists, the survivors of the Wilhelmine Reich, gradually dissolved themselves into insignificance – as a whole, they had attracted 47 percent in 1924, 39 percent in 1928, 24 percent in 1930, and would fall to 10 percent in 1932.[196] By then the incubation would be complete; the old guard would die giving birth to the Nazi movement. On October 13, 1930, nearly six years after Hitler had been released from prison, 107 Nazi representatives paraded through the Reichstag. Fully obedient to Moscow, armed and trained by agents of the Soviet secret police (the GPU), who filtered through the German borders with false passports, 1 million Red fighters whittled their bludgeons to welcome the new Nazi arrivals. Ready to brawl, Röhm shipped back home from Bolivia in January 1931.

As soon as the 'stream' of foreign money was drained out of Germany, all the trappings of the Allied bailout snapped closed upon her. Since the Reichsbank Law of 1924 forbade the central bank from advancing cash to the Reich above a low statutory level, the federal and regional governments fell back upon the private commercial banks, begging them for money. The banks, lending upon canons of profitability, were not accommodating, and the few that were willing to purchase public bonds reduced proportionately their engagements with the private sectors, exacerbating thus the monetary stringency and unemployment.[197] As in 1923, the German Grid was literally colonized by the Allied investors: *more than 50 percent of all German bank deposits belonged to foreigners in 1930*:[198] this was money that would vaporize at the first sign of distress. And, finally, the unshakable burden of the reparations impeded any freedom of financial initiative on the part of the Reich. The 'Dawes machine' had nailed Germany to the cross, right and proper.

When, in March 1931, Germany and Austria announced their desire to fashion through a customs union what was *de facto* the *Anschluss** – a Greater German-speaking Reich under republican auspices – vital funds were mysteriously withdrawn in sequence from Austria in May and from Germany in June, shortly after the Brüning Cabinet had published a new set of emergency decrees. These contemplated cuts in the salaries of government officials, public expenditure, and war pensions, and an increase in taxation – measures that fell under the caption of 'deflationary policies'. All they effected was to reduce the money supply so as to keep it proportionate to the available hoard of gold and foreign exchange, which, incidentally, foreigners and German absentees, as in 1923, were swiftly exporting out of the country.

A few weeks after the aborted *Anschluss*, the United States, as predicted by Swiss banker Somary in 1926,[†] passed the Hawley-Smoot Tariff Act, which instituted the highest rates in American history, increasing duties on a number of products more than 20 percent.

> After the engagement of the Anschluss, Germany was a city besieged, with the lines of supply all cut, and the resources of the defenders rigidly limited by a watchful foe...Voices raised on every hand celebrated the example of Samson, as indicating the only possible course for a desperate Germany. For deep in the Teutonic soul lies the ineradicable conviction that Germany will not fall alone, nor European civilization long survive her ruin.[199]

On June 20, in the wake of an unsightly hemorrhage of gold out of Germany and the consequent disarray suffered by the leading banking establishments of the West, US President Hoover declared a general moratorium on reparations and debts for a year. The measure was designed

---

* Germany's annexation of Austria.
† See above, p. 175.

to give the German economy some respite and prevent it from collapsing altogether. Four days later, after the entreaties of Chancellor Brüning and Luther, the new Reichsbank Governor, the French, American, and British central banks, in addition to the new Swiss institute, conceded an emergency loan to Germany: crumbs. The Germans begged for more. On July 9, Luther flew to London via Paris to implore the creditors to revive Weimar. Norman shook his head, as he had done eight years previously in the presence of Governor Havenstein; he empathized, but added that there was not much he could do at present. The issue, he concluded regretfully, was political rather than financial. In the meantime, Norman advised Luther to restrict credit further.[200] Evidently, Norman was resolved upon ousting the Brüning-Luther team from power by a maneuver of prolonged financial exhaustion. Already, after the fall of the Creditanstalt, the British Governor had told the media that the Austrian bank needed a 'foreign butcher' and that 'Schacht was the right type of butcher.'[201] Schacht was flattered, but by this time, he was 'taken': in fact, he had liked what he had read in Mein Kampf so much that in January 1931 he had hooked up with the author himself to talk things over. 'It became unmistakably clear that, whereas French policy aimed to perpetuate the status quo, Norman...was working for a *new order*.'[202]

The financial shape of the 'new order' was delineated in the summer of 1931. In July, after the failure of several important banks and their rehabilitation at the public's expense, the most acute phase of the German crisis ended, but there was 'no return to "normal conditions".'[203] Tight exchange controls were introduced, along with the establishment of special banking consortia for rescuing the healthiest part of the starved economy. State control over the economic apparatus was significantly extended. This would be the system that the Nazis would inherit and which would fuel their miraculous recovery. Special Standstill Agreements were reached with the creditors on September 1, which froze within Germany $1.25 billion. Of these frozen credits, 30 percent were British short-term assets; a fortnight thereafter began the final 'run' on sterling. Official unemployment in Germany rose to 5 million.

In October, after the world financial system had been disintegrated, officers of the Royal Air Force escorted Alfred Rosenberg, Hitler's theorist of the race, in a guided tour of the London clubs. Rosenberg encountered, amongst others, the director of *The Times*, Geoffrey Dawson; the editor of the *Daily Express* and Churchill's sidekick, Lord Beaverbrook; the human spider himself, Norman, whom he indulged with anti-Semitic disquisitions; and the future great electors of the Nazis, the directors of the Schröder

Bank.[204] This was a concern towering over a vast network of interests all over the world; its legal office in Wall Street was none other than Sullivan & Cromwell, where the Dulles brothers, John Foster, the lawyer of Versailles and future US Secretary of State, and Allen, the Cold War chief of the CIA, had completed their apprenticeship.[205] Bruno von Schröder, the patriarch, had been one of the founding members in 1905 of the Anglo-German Union Club,[206] and his bank had come to belong to 'that small ring of London finance houses [that had] an acknowledged, if unwritten, claim to be represented...on the Court of the Bank of England.'[207] 'Since the war...Schröders had become the financial agents of Germany in London.'[208] From 1918 to 1945, the fiduciary of Schröders on the Court of the Bank of England was an individual by the name of Frank C. Tiarks. In a variety of posts and assignments, Tiarks had been involved with the 'German experiment' since its inception in 1918.[209]

For a while, the German government paid out the dole, but by the fall of 1931 the jobless were left to fend for themselves. The political troopers of all colors clashed repeatedly on the streets, the blood flowed. In this atmosphere, Hitler, as representative of Germany's novel mass movement, encountered President Hindenburg (see Figure 4.2) on October 10. The timeliness of the encounter was simply extraordinary: *a mere fortnight after the British disruption of the Gold Standard, the Nazis sought an audience with the republic's president to make what was, in fact, their first legitimate bid to power.* And, from the Sea Powers' viewpoint, the preconditions to such an encounter could not have been more favorable: a new, dynamic nationalist leader face to face with the ersatz-Kaiser Hindenburg, a war hero and resplendent symbol of the imperial epoch – 'It is done,' they must have thought.

And yet it wasn't. Hindenburg felt but the most profound revulsion for this 'Bohemian lance corporal'; he received, entertained, and dismissed the latter with iciest coolness. Germany resisted. Hindenburg remained solidly behind his Chancellor, Brüning.

Spited, Hitler joined the great anti-republican manifestation of the Right gathered on October 11 at Bad Harzburg, where the private armies of reaction were seen filing by supportive crowds and a podium of leaders, including Schacht. The latter, in the guise of Hitler's officious economic councilor, could not contain the lust that made him launch into a speech, a vile one, against the pathetic attempts of Luther – Schacht's successor at the Reichsbank – to salvage the situation.

Chancellor Brüning, by now ruled by decrees, invoking the Article 48 of the Weimar Constitution, which enabled him to pass controversial ordinances above the head of the Reichstag: the collegial fashioning of laws in Germany had definitely ceased to function. The vexatious measures Brüning had published in July were enforced on December 8, 1931, through one such decree. The Chancellor took a dangerous gamble: he aimed to disarm emotionally Germany's creditors by making the pain at home ever more excruciating, hoping thence to obtain the cancellation of reparations, and then to launch a program of public works. In fact, he had no choice, much as the foreign creditors had no pity. Like Weimar, Brüning was doomed from the start.

1932, the year of the electoral madness. Having completed his first seven-year term, Hindenburg was up for re-election in March. Hitler, after some hesitation, decided to challenge him. The Nazis spent much money on publicity, as well as on an unprecedented number of plane flights advertised in the press under the slogan of 'Hitler over Germany.'[210] In the first round, Hindenburg polled 49.6 percent, Hitler 30.1 percent of the vote – a disappointment. Hindenburg was re-elected president with the second ballot. Given the violence of the street clashes that accompanied the election campaigns, the Brüning government, for fear of civil war, banned Hitler's paramilitary corps: the SA and the SS were enjoined to disband.

Then Kurt von Schleicher slowly emerged from the mists of the ministerial backwaters. This was the 'field-gray eminence' whose shadow lurked behind every plot that had twisted the uneasy life of this wretched 'republic.'

Schleicher had begun his career of backstage puppeteer in Ludendorff's General Staff during the war by organizing the orderly retreat of the German forces; he had been the one negotiating with Ebert during the sedition of the German Soviets in 1918–19, and a coordinator of their suppression by the White Army; with von Seeckt in 1923 he had planned the state of emergency; and he had been one of the architects of the secret entente with the Trostkyites and the Soviet Army: a sharp brain, a sophisticated officer, enamored of his extraordinary skills. That is all that is known. Schleicher remains the true enigma of Weimar. No one has ever deciphered the man: 'a question mark with the epaulettes of a general,' said Trotsky.[211]

From 1929 on, Schleicher, as head of the political office of the Reichswehr Ministry, had acted as the unofficial liaison between the army and the government.

On April 28, he invited Hitler to initiate a series of secret talks with a view to toppling Brüning, now known as the 'Hunger Chancellor' for having smashed the country and himself into a cul-de-sac. The plan was to lift the ban on the SA and dissolve the Parliament in return for temporary National Socialist tolerance of the new government. As straw-chancellor of the new government, Schleicher had selected a Catholic aristocrat, Franz von Papen, a rather unprepossessing gentleman of leisure, fond of horse riding and intrigue. Papen would lead a Cabinet of barons maneuvered by Schleicher from behind the scenes in the view of the eventual economic rehabilitation of Germany. The 'Old Man' Hindenburg was persuaded, and on May 30, 1932, Brüning fell. 'A hundred meters from the finish line,' the latter would add, sorrowful.

In fact, in June, during the international conference gathered in Lausanne, now that the incubation was finished, the Allies at the suggestion of Britain terminated at long last the reparations scheme by demanding a symbolic lump sum of 3 billion marks, which Germany would never pay – Hitler would repudiate reparations in 1933. And Veblen was vindicated: the Germans had surrendered under that head approximately 10 percent of their income until 1923, and nothing afterwards: all the money for that purpose had been borrowed, and would have never been repaid. The end of reparations ended war debts as well. Between 1918 and 1931, the United States recovered only 20 percent of the total credits extended to the Allies.[212] Thereafter American legislation forbade token payments, and no one insisted on paying anything anymore – this was the last of it. Between German loans and Allied credits, America had so far sunk 20 percent of her 1914 GDP into this European adventure (around $40 billion);[213] she would come collecting in World War II, and make the investment pay off after 1945.

Papen, nominated Chancellor on May 31, 1932, proceded then to dismiss Parliament. Germany geared up for the second electoral joust of the year. This time the Nazis gave their very best. Thousands of speakers rambling across the Fatherland, Hitler's outlandish airplane jaunts from one rostrum to another, radios ablare, vinyl records, marching bands, mounds of merchandise, reels rolling, swastika pins, a state-of-the-art propagandistic film shot by no less than Twentieth Century Fox,[214] towers of pamphlets, oceanic quilts of posters patching the walls of all cities and flags everywhere: a babylonian splash. It was now or never. Also thanks to the strong popular appeal of Gregor Strasser's economic program calling for land-reclaiming projects, rural settlements, and public works to be funded by the somewhat magic suggestion of 'productive credit creation,' which amounted to an insurrectional takeover of the Grid by the communal hordes of Germany's burghers, the NSDAP scored its record poll of 37.3 percent of the votes on July 31, 1932: 13.7 million ballots.[215] This was the maximum Nazism would ever be able to capture by legal means – a significant share, for sure, though far short of the absolute majority. This was no breakthrough.

As soon as the ban on the SA was lifted in June, Reds and Brownshirts tore each other into pieces; more than 100 street killings were counted in a month, with three times as many wounded. Goebbels wrote in his diary: 'We're headed straight for civil war, but the Wilhelmstrasse doesn't seem to notice.'

On August 10, Hitler met Hindenburg again and bid for the chancellorship. Hitler told the president that he was not willing to join the present Cabinet to play second fiddle to Papen, nor did he intend to waste energy searching for a supporting coalition in the Parliament. He too wanted to rule by decrees: all or nothing. Nothing, replied Hindenburg, brusque; he distrusted Hitler completely. Hitler seethed.

At this juncture, the puppet Papen severed the strings from Schleicher and began to conspire on behalf of the Anglo-American cabal against his mastermind.[216] The horse-riding aristocrat expected to bend Hitler into obedience and domesticate him in a baronial Cabinet by strangling his party financially with another election, in which, as Papen correctly intuited, Hitler was most likely to lose seats – by now, the people were weary of electoral campaigns and unfulfilled promises. To carry this out Papen persuaded his absentees friends, bankers, and industrialists to stop their contributions to the Nazis.

Who had been funding them from the beginning? According to one hideously humorous folk tale eagerly circulated, the Nazis financed themselves by way of rallies and contributions, in addition to the storm troopers' late endorsements of razor blades called 'Stürmer' ('Stormer'), and a brand of margarine named 'Kampf' ('Battle').[217] Ten years of political activity all over the nation, and three technologically innovative, mass-publicized elections in a country half-bankrupt, funded by means of tickets, piddling donations, and *margarine*?

A more creditable version exposed by a first-class historian that had access for two years to classified documents alleged that Nazism from 1919 to 1923, the year of the putsch, had been financed by the secret funds of the Reichswehr (the army), and thereafter by German industrialists,[218] such as the steel magnate Fritz Thyssen, who began paying Hitler in 1931 by remitting funds to his deputy, Hess, via an account with a Dutch bank which was interlocked with a Wall Street outfit called Union Banking Corporation. This was a subsidiary of Harriman Brown Bros. that was managed by Prescott Bush.[219] In 1934 the foreign correspondent of the *Manchester Guardian* confirmed the widely diffused rumor that the bulk of Nazi funding was *foreign* in origin:

> Hitler had large funds at his disposal, not obtained entirely from German sources. He got money from certain capitalist interests in foreign countries,

who were attracted by his hostility to Soviet Russia, or by...his policy to increase the demand for armaments...International finance does not seem to be unfavorable to the Nazi regime.[220]

In September, Papen dissolved the Reichstag once more and new elections were scheduled for November 6. His hopes were realized: the Nazis lost 2 million votes – their percentage slid to 33.1. They were bankrupt and losing momentum fast. But Papen himself foundered with the election: the Nationalist block, which he incarnated, suffered a disastrous decline; he and his barons were incapable of taming Germany's riot. The unemployed were now officially 6 million, and adding drifters and the undeclared, the new horde of vagabonds numbered approximately 9 million individuals, that is, about half of Germany's workers.[221] Here was the long-term effect of the 'Dawes machine,' Montagu Norman's masterpiece. Stories of indescribable violence, street clashes, rural incest, and robbery made up the news of an ordinary day.

On November 19, Hitler, who was still in command of Germany's first political force, came knocking on Hindenburg's door to demand once again the president's mandate. And once again he was rebuffed. 'A Cabinet led by you,' Hindenburg told the Führer in all frankness, 'would develop necessarily into a party dictatorship with all the consequences for an extraordinary accentuation of the conflicts in the German people...For that, I cannot answer neither before my oath nor to my own conscience.' This rejection appeared final. In this hour Hitler was afraid – and utterly broke; he confided to Goebbels that if the movement collapsed, it would take him three minutes to blow his brains out, and that would be the end of it.[222]

Now was the time for the serpentine Schleicher to pull the wires of the last, decisive plot: he went to Hindenburg and pleaded with the Old Man to let him, the general, take the matter in his hands. With a shiver of disastrous forebodings, the Old Man consented, and on December 2, he appointed Schleicher Chancellor of the Reich, the last of the Weimar Republic.

On December 15, the general on the radio announced a public program of large-scale work-creating endeavors; he looked to the Left and sought to create a transversal alliance that cut across the Socialist and Catholic unions, the army and the Strasserite wing. It was a superb maneuver, a last sally which Germany conceived through one of her generals to save herself from the abyss, a true fruit of despair. On December 19, Schleicher received Maxim Litvinov, the Russian Foreign Minister, who appeared perfectly cordial.[223] But Litvinov was deceiving the man whom the German reactionary press was presently attacking as the dreaded 'Red General': in the first half of October Litvinov had already told Ivan Maisky, the newly appointed Soviet Ambassador to London, that the Nazis would soon come to power.[224]

In spite of everything, Schleicher set his plan into motion: the post of vice-chancellor he offered to Strasser, and looked forward to tearing away the Left wing onto his camp. And Strasser did not say no...The Parliament he would dissolve and prorogate the elections past the constitutional 60-day limit – he trusted he would sway the old president, Hindenburg, to grant him that much. This would take care of the Nazis, whose ballot-box strength was rapidly waning. And if push came to shove, he would ready the army to engage the Hitlerites in a genuine civil war. Had this maneuver succeeded, by some evasive caprice of fate, Germany would probably have been saved.

To fend off this diversion, on January 4, 1933, Papen summoned Hitler to convene under cover of secrecy at the townhouse of Baron von Schröder. A partner in J. H. Stein of Cologne, the German appendix of Schröders, Kurt von Schröder, along with Schacht and other exponents of German big business, had signed a petition in November 1932 addressed to von Hindenburg, urging the president to appoint Hitler as chancellor.

During the pivotal synod of January 4, Hitler, sobered by the cold shower at the polls, agreed to join a coalition government, which he had until now sternly refused, and to serve as the quartet's spearhead – or rather figurehead, as Papen and friends intended – in overthrowing the republic.[225] From now on, Baron von Schröder and his syndicate of investors stood behind the debts of the party: with the stroke of a pen, the absentees granted the Nazis a new set of keys to the Grid – they granted them unlimited 'credit.'[226] On January 17, Goebbels entered in his diary: 'The financial situation is suddenly improved.'

Simultaneously, asked by an American journalist at his country residence about the permanence of the Schleicher regime, Schacht responded, confident: 'three weeks.'[227]

Schleicher's spies found out about the hidden assembly, and the news of the Papen intrigue was leaked to the press. But everything conspired against the great conspirator. The Junkers and big business, let alone the absentees of the Grid, were all aggressively arrayed against Schleicher's collectivist measures. The Left, devouring herself, still spared some life to worry at his throat, while the Catholics were taking their cues from the ambassador of the Pope, Monsignor Eugenio Pacelli.* As head of the German nunciature for the entire duration of the Weimar regime, Pacelli had expended himself

---

*   The future Pope Pius XII (1939–58).

on a tireless hunt to wrest from each *Land* (German state) a collection of agreements between the Holy See and the *Land*'s secular government, securing rights to a variety of catechumenal trademarks, such as doctrine, education, and worship: the so-called 'concordats.' At this crossroads, in January 1933, jolted by the opportunity offered by the pious von Papen for clinching the much yearned concordat with the Reich, Pacelli prompted the German Catholic leaders to explore 'the possibility of at least a *modus vivendi* with all the Right, including the Nazis, in order to combat the danger from the Left' and the blasphemous Bolsheviks.[228]

Incredible as it all might appear, Weimar's two largest 'democratic' mass parties, the Socialists (the SPD) and the Catholics, who together stood for 35 percent of the electorate, which could have risen to 52 per cent with the added strength of the Communists (a full majority!), feeling more menaced by Schleicher than by Hitler, joined hands to dethrone the Red General.[229]

Indeed, three weeks was what it took the quartet, led by the Papen junta and backed by the conspicuous interference of foreign finance, to buy off, coax, and convert the rest of the establishment, especially its last standing bastion, the old Field Marshal Hindenburg, and obtain thereby the removal of Schleicher. The 'question mark with the epaulettes of a general' faded in less than two months; the president dismissed him on January 28, 1933. Shortly afterwards, Schleicher was seen walking 'in a long oval around his room, whispering to himself, head half bent.'[230]

Ironically, of all the great actors, it was the army of the Reich that was the one least inclined to fight the next war.

On January 30, Hitler was sworn in as Chancellor. Papen was Vice-Chancellor in a Cabinet that numbered only two Nazis, Frick and Göring, the rest of them were blue-blooded aldermen.

Six months later to the day, Montagu Norman, without explaining and without excusing, vouched publicly for the first issue of Nazi debentures to be sold on the markets of London.[231] Three months previously, Schacht had been recalled by the Nazis to resume control of the Reichsbank.

# 5  The Reich on the Marble Cliffs

## Fire, Legerdemain and Mummery All the Way to Barbarossa, 1933–41

Who is inspired and instructed by God, can only do good. Everything that the Englishman does is thereby fundamentally righteous. And even then, if he once does something that is abject according to conventional morality, he so does it as to annihilate the opponent of God, who is in any case unrighteous, and for that all means are sacrosanct.

Reinhold Hoops, *England's Self-Deception*[1]

I regard Halifax as a hypocrite of the worst type and a liar...Churchill is the very type of a corrupt journalist. There is not a worse prostitute in politics. He himself has written that it's unimaginable what can be done in war with the help of lies. He's an utterly amoral, repulsive creature... Stalin is half-beast, half-giant.

Adolf Hitler, *Adolf Hitler's Secret Conversations*[2]

We were entering the Lemur-peopled woods where human justice and man-made laws are unknown; in them there was no fame to be won.

Ernst Jünger, *On the Marble Cliffs*[3]

MEPHISTOPHELES:
To the pressure of our repeated onslaught
Our enemies are forced to yield
And, fighting unsteadily,
They are pushing toward the right
And so confusing the left side
Of their main force in the fight.
The firm head of our phalanx
Is moving toward the right and, like a flash,
They dash into the weak spot. –
Now splashing like storm-tossed
Waves, equal forces are wildly
Raging in the twofold conflict;
A more glorious thing has never been thought up,
This battle has been won for us!

Goethe, *Faust Part Two, Act Four* (10640–10653)[4]

## Nazi Coup d'état

And so in January 1933 Hitler was made Chancellor – which is not to say that he and his associates had truly seized power, yet. In fact they had taken the deal from the barons – Papen, and his patrons – with strings attached. The aristocrats thought that Hitler had been finally 'framed in.' 'Within two months,' Papen smugly told a conservative critic, 'we will have pushed Hitler so far into a corner that he'll squeak.'[5] Including Hitler, there were just three Nazis in the new Cabinet, and at first it seemed indeed that they merely represented the added touch of populist legitimacy to what was by and large a Fascist, elitist remix of the Second Reich. But the Führer had his foot in the door. So now his preoccupation was how to drive the patricians out, let all the other Nazis in, and make himself absolute master of the house. A bankrupt house, that is. All in all there was nothing exceptional in the means he employed to achieve the objective; he resorted to the customary, bloody intrigues of Levantine kingdoms: deceit, backstabbing, physical liquidation and terror. Means so customary, in fact, that one could have almost predicted the Führer's moves from 1933 to 1934 by consulting the second part of Goethe's *Faust* (1831), which tells the story of a monarch who, with the help of the Devil (Mephisto), restores order to his broken-down empire. Acting on Mephisto's counsel, the elite subdues the masses by terrorizing them with one, great sudden fire, and revives the languishing economy by printing special money-bills mortgaged on the imperial right to the land. This late inflationary blaze finds its necessary resolution in a great military campaign against the neighboring 'enemy.'

In broad outlines, the experience of the Third Reich was not much different. Shortly before the March elections of 1933, *from within*, the Hitlerites and the pro-Nazi elements of the establishment launched a *coup d'état*, which was masked by a spectacular act of sabotage: the Reichstag fire. Using this internally manufactured act of terror, the Nazis passed a series of bills limiting civil liberties, and so managed to scare the population as to score, with the additional quota of the traditional conservatives, a narrow electoral majority. Thereafter, on the strength of this emergency legislation, they annihilated the Leftist opposition in a few months. That meant also purging the revolutionaries from within their own ranks, which was done in June 1934 when the question of the succession to the presidency came to the fore: shortly before the death of Hindenburg, Hitler bartered the elimination of the SA hotheads and the surrender of the Brownshirts to the army in exchange for the fealty of the generals.

Then, from 1933 to 1938, the Nazis tackled the gripping economic depression and turned it into an exceptional season of unprecedented growth, which was for the most part characterized by military expenditure. The Nazi Recovery was made possible by the expert coordination of Schacht and his team of specialists operating from the Reichsbank and the Ministry of Economics. To lighten and speed up Germany's industrial revival, the economic stewards of the Third Reich implemented a few modifications in the make-up of the financial apparatus that allowed the preparation for war and the overall performance of the system to proceed untrammeled by cyclical complications. By 1939, Germany had thus completed her second Five-Year Plan, Dawes being the first, and found herself ready to attack.

Now one wonders what the other powers were doing while Hitler was rearming. And the answer is that they – Britain, the USSR, and the United States – did all they could to facilitate his task. They provided the Nazis with resources, military know-how, patents, money, and weapons – in very large quantities. Why? To set the Nazis up, lead them on, and finally destroy them, and take Germany into the bargain at war's end. Throughout the 1930s, the United States acted as a mere supplier to the Nazis in the shadow of Britain, who produced the entire show. This show had to end with Britain's participation in a worldwide conflict as the leader of the coalition of Allied forces against Nazi Germany. But the Hitlerites had to be duped into going to war against Russia with the guarantee that Britain, and thus America, would remain neutral: Hitler would not want to repeat the errors of World War I. Therefore Britain had to 'double' herself, so to speak, into a pro-Nazi and anti-Nazi faction – both of which, of course, were components of one and the same fakery. The complex and rather grotesque whole of Britain's foreign policy in the 1930s was indeed the result of these ghastly theatrical diversions with which the Hitlerites were made to believe that at any time the colorful Nazi-phile camp would overthrow the hawks of the War Party, led by Winston Churchill, and sign a separate peace with the Third Reich. The secret goal of this unbelievable mummery was to drive Hitler away from the Mediterranean in 1941, and into the Soviet marshes, which the British would in fact allow him to 'cleanse' for three years, until the time would arrive to hem the Nazis in and finally crush them.

None of this would have been possible without the unreserved collaboration of Soviet Russia. The Soviets worked in unison with the anti-German directives of Britain as if they were her most faithful ally: they, like Britain, appeased the Führer, and contributed abundantly to the Nazi war machine, shipping carloads of provisions to Germany throughout the entire length of the Nazi rearmament. Furthermore, Russia would take in the brunt of Germany's comprehensive powers of devastation, and absorb it with 20 million dead. After the carnage the Nazis were so exhausted that they fell rather easily when the Allies finally boxed them in, in June 1944. In recompense for such an unspeakable sacrifice, the Anglo-Americans threw half of Europe to their Slav accomplices – their old, grateful beneficiaries of 1917.

*   *   *

The Weimar Republic, Nazism's incubator, was destroyed in five stages:[6] (1) under the Catholic Brüning, the 'Hunger Chancellor' (27 March 1930–30 May 1932), the parliamentary regime was suspended and rule by presidential decree instituted; (2) under von Papen, the petty Catholic aristocrat intriguing on behalf of the absentees, and initially launched as General von Schleicher's figurehead (31 May 1932–17 November 1932), an authoritarian restoration of the old imperial order ('the Cabinet of barons') was briefly attempted, which was marked by the suppression of Leftist opposition and the timid implementation of public works programs; (3) under von Schleicher, the 'Red General' (2 December 1932–28 January 1933), the boldest maneuver took place against the secret built-in provisions of the Treaty of Versailles: a transversal sally led by parts of the army against the agrarians and finance, relying upon the populist support of Socialist trade unions and the Nazi Left wing; (4) under Hitler, a first phase was spent drafting patriotic acts against terrorism (30 January 1933–5 March 1933); (5) under the Nazi *Gleichschaltung* (the 'normalization,' 6 March 1933–2 August 1934), Hitler regimented the whole of Germany in the spirit of his party.

Now that the Nazi creature was formed, it did what had long been expected of it: it broke free of its stifling hothouse and, in time, pushed towards Russia.

On 1 February 1933, 48 hours after taking over, Hitler dissolved the Reichstag. President Hindenburg had needed a little persuasion before granting his new Chancellor the permission to do so – 'Why?,' he asked Hitler, 'I thought you had gathered a working majority...' Hitler's reply was prompt: 'This is time to deal with the Communists and Socialists once and for all.'[7]

New elections were announced for March 5. Yet another electoral round swept the Fatherland. On January 31, Goebbels wrote in his diary: 'The broad outlines of the conflict to be waged against the Red terror have been established in the course of a meeting with Hitler. For the moment we shall abstain from taking countermeasures. Not until the opportune moment when the Communists launch a revolution shall we strike.'[8]

Hitler's electoral calendar, drawn up by Goebbels, was published on February 10: therein no meeting was scheduled for February 25, 26, or 27.[9] On February 26, Berlin's fashionable fortuneteller, a fraudster by the name of Hanussen who had entertained scores of SA leaders in his theatrical venue – a high-class lupanar on the Lietzenburger Strasse – 'predicted' in a publicized seance, that the Communists were about to torch an important governmental building to set off a massive rebellion.[10]

On the night of February 27, 1933, the Reichstag's cupola went up in flames, blazing like a giant piece of charcoal, beckoning the late stragglers of Berlin. The Führer was summoned at once to the site. Upon reaching the smoldering remains of what used to be the Parliament, he exclaimed: 'This is a beacon from heaven...No one can now prevent us from crushing the Communists with a mailed fist.'[11] Even Göring arrived, overexcited – the emotion of both leaders appeared genuine. According to the official version, the Reichstag fire was an 'act of terrorism,' a Communist crime. Yet attempts at sedition were witnessed nowhere round the country. All was silent. Lists of arrests, which had been prepared long before, led to the incarceration of several thousand Communist and Socialist activists – the Gestapo came into being, and the camps received their first inmates. On February 28, the KPD (German Communist Party) was outlawed. Meanwhile, the electoral push was intensified by the squawking of slogans, torch-lit processions, marches and drills.

On March 5, on election day, despite the prodding of the terrorist antics and loads of cash from I. G. Farben,[12] the Nazis were still not capable of reaping a majority: they accumulated 43.9 percent of the ballot, which only with an 8 percent nudge from the moribund Nationalists, allowed them to form a qualified quorum in the House.

In its war against terror, the government issued two ordinances, on February 28 and March 7, respectively, 'for the defense of the people and the state,' which restrained the freedom of the press, individual liberties, and the right of assembly. On March 12, the swastika-crested flag of the party was promoted to National Ensign.

Having the Reichstag burned to the ground, the congress convened in the Kroll Opera House on March 23. No Communists in the House; with the 'suspension' of 30 additional Socialists, the number of representatives had been reduced by 109: the remaining deputies were asked to pass an Enabling Act which would have given the government the right for four years to legislate by decree, without constitutional restrictions. The corollary of such a bill was to reduce the political machine of the country to a one-party decision panel.

The vote: 441 ayes, 94 (Socialist) noes – Hitler was granted full powers. By March 31, the Nazi *Gleichschaltung* was in full swing: a centralized bureaucracy replaced the federal constituency established by Bismarck – all strings were now pulled from Berlin, via the subordinate control of an array of delegates (*Statthalter*) loyal to the Führer.

On April 7, 1933, the bullet-riddled body of the 'clairvoyant' Hanussen was found in the wooded outskirts of Berlin.

In May, the Hitlerites proceeded to dismantle conclusively the party system of Weimar: the SPD leadership was incarcerated wholesale; with one blow an organization commanding 4 million workers, and endowed with a capital of 184 million Reichsmarks, was crumbled into dust. Nowhere was there the slightest reaction. Let alone resistance. The Nationalist veterans' paramilitary formations, like the *Stahlhelm* (the Steel Helmet) were next. Then came the turn of the Catholics: the deal for them was self-dissolution in exchange for a concordat between the Holy See and the Nazi Reich. By the terms of such a pact, the Vatican would have recognized the Nazi state, agreed that the bishops pledge their allegiance to it, and forbidden priests to engage in politics – all this in exchange for a Nazi promise to respect the Church's right to catechesis and its property. The Secretary of State of the Vatican, Eugenio Pacelli, had been swaying the 23 million German Catholics in this direction at least since 1931. Heinrich Brüning, the former unlucky Chancellor, who was now in charge of the Catholic *Zentrum*, pressured from Rome, agreed bitter in his heart on July 4 to dissolve this pillar of German political history – the party that had also been Erzberger's. And to add insult to masochistic injury, the Nazis rejected those members of the Center party that willingly applied to flow into their ranks. The concordat was signed on July 8 and ratified on September 10, 1933.

The concordat broke down almost at once. Within ten days of its signing, Hitler's SA attacked the parades of the Catholic Youth League; the beatings did not cease, they were worsened by the more systematic persecution of active Catholic dissenters, who were interned in the camps and/or bludgeoned to death. Pacelli did not hide from his foreign visitors his disgust at these happenings,[13] but he thought he had no choice, no weapon at this stage other than appeasing the Nazis – things could have always been worse, he sighed: in Germany there could have been Bolshevism, which spared no priest. Veblen had foretold this much: the forthcoming reactionary regime of the Reich would be championed by the Elder Statesmen of the West as the bulwark against the (imaginary) Red menace.

In the span of six months, Hitler and his blackguards had smashed the incubator into pieces – there now remained to consolidate the National-

Socialist Revolution by sealing a twofold pact with the front legs of the quartet: industry/finance and the army.

Meanwhile, September 21, 1933 was the date set for the beginning of the trial of the Reichstag's putative arsonists: a young Dutchman, former Communist sympathizer, by the name of Marinus van der Lubbe, and a handful of Communist leaders, three of whom were Bulgarian Bolshevik agents, all of them suitably trapped in a judicial proceeding that promised to turn into a spellbinding spectacle. The accusations were poorly constructed – too hastily; the case was suspect, the judge was embarrassed, the prosecutors confused. The Communists defended themselves easily, and were forthwith acquitted. There remained van der Lubbe, the inescapable useful idiot of yet another terrorist sham: he *alone*, so claimed the accusation's new theorem, set 11,000 cubic meters of property on fire. During the proceedings, van der Lubbe laughed as he lied – a laugh that was 'strange,' they reported.[14] He driveled; he made no sense. The police had found him meandering in the hall of the Reichstag, haggard, canopied by the long curtains on fire. Commentators at the trial were of one mind: what they observed was 'a human wreck,' an 'unfortunate, doped up...moron.'[15] The world had seen this before: as the next step, the suicidal 'moron' would beg the government's henchmen to finish him off. His plea to the judges: 'I demand that I be punished by imprisonment or death.'[16] The trial ended in December; van der Lubbe was executed on January 10, 1934. Not even at Nuremberg, in 1946, when they could have made the most of it, would the Allied inquisitors be able to shed light on the incident and identify the culprits. So was bestowed on history yet another unsolved act of terror with the usual ingredients: a sacrificial 'moron' without motive, a conspiracy of silence, and a catastrophic sequitur on the high plane of events.

With or without evidence, however, in terror '*is fecit cui prodest*' always: 'the one who did it is the one benefiting from it' – that is, the Nazis themselves. Indeed, not even the evidence was lacking: everyone knew that a group of SA did it, possibly with the connivance of Göring and Goebbels,[17] – a few SA leaders themselves crowed about it in public.[18] In the end it appeared that van der Lubbe was a drifter 'recruited' by Hanussen, the glamorous psychic dispatched in April, as a favor to some SA bigwigs, clients of his.[19] The drifter, whose homosexuality had been exploited by a gang of a dozen Brownshirts,[20] was lured by them into the Reichstag, while they, after igniting the fire in several other spots, had 'left through the secret corridor linking [the Reichstag] to the Residence of Göring, the Reichstag President.'[21] This 'prank' was, in brief, a gift from the SA to their Führer.

And Hitler, indeed, was in dire want of a roaring endorsement from the people; he addressed them on November 12, 1933: 'Men of Germany! Women of Germany! Do you approve the policy of the government? Are you prepared to declare that it expresses your opinion and your own will, and solemnly to make it your own?' This time the plebiscite was in the Führer's favor by over 90 percent of the vote.

But by the spring of 1934, the Nazi tenure was still not petrified: there remained the thorn of Röhm's SA. These troops, now 3 million strong – ten times the size of the official Reichswehr – were demanding the 'Second Revolution.' What this meant from the economic standpoint was unclear: possibly the early socialization schemes of the Nazi party, or a re-edition of Schleicher's programs – in short, naive plans that dreamt of abolishing a most powerful network of interests, those of German business and finance, which Versailles had left, deliberately, untouched. This was the world of the aristocrats and the business moguls – the hated *Bonzen* – who stood 'for law and order, respectability, and philistine values.'[22] And Röhm was no economist, he was the eternal front-line lansquenet; he wanted to absorb the army and not be absorbed by it, to do away with the officer caste and transform Germany into a giant farmstead-economy ruled by a clan of proud Nazi herdsmen (his SA). Hitler tried to reason with him, in vain. To his gang, Röhm vented:

Adolf is rotten. He's betraying all of us. He only goes around with reactionaries. His old comrades aren't good enough for him. So he brings in these East Prussian generals…Adolf knows perfectly what I want…Not a second pot of the Kaiser's army…Are we a revolution or aren't we?…[23]

There began to circulate talk of sedition – plots either to remove Hitler or kill him. Sometimes, the name of the unyielding 'Red General,' von Schleicher, was dropped in this connection, but the conspiracy, if any, was yet fluid. The ground under his feet, Hitler still sensed, was not as firm as he wished it to be. Especially as the Junkers, from their stalls, were showing signs of growing impatience with the factious confusion reigning amongst the Nazis. In Cologne, *chez* von Schröder, on 4 January 1933, it was national cohesiveness upon which Hitler had been sold – the Führer had better keep his end of the bargain with his financial backers.

Looking ahead, in May, it became clear that Hindenburg had not much time left to live. Hitler could not afford to leave the post of Reich president vacant. Meeting with the Defense Minister General von Blomberg aboard the cruiser *Deutschland* he traded the Presidency for the liquidation of the SA.[24]

In June, when the old Field Marshal fell ill, Hitler decided to act. The SA were given a month's furlough, and most of their rebellious chieftains retired, unsuspecting, to the lake resort of Wiessee. On June 30 the purge began. Squads of SS executioners were dispatched to this vacationing retreat to round up Röhm and his clique and shuttle them off to the Stadelheim prison in Munich. One by one, including Röhm, who rejected the offer to die by his own hand, they were shot down by Hitler's praetorian commandos. Loose ends were tied and old scores were settled in the killing. Nine of the ten surviving SA arsonists of the Reichstag disappeared.[25] General von Schleicher, his wife, and Schleicher's assistant General von Bredow, both generals being also adversaries profoundly acquainted with the Reichswehr–Red Army connection, were cut down by volleys of machine-gun fire; Gregor Strasser, the looming wedge of the National Socialist movement, who had retired to private life, was taken to a jail, shot in the neck and left to bleed to death. Funded by a mysterious network, his brother Otto, who had defected from the NSDAP in 1930, would lead, as head of the so-called Black Front, an ineffective propaganda war against Hitler from Czechoslovakia, and then France, before vanishing into Canada at the outbreak of the war.[26] Other Catholic exponents were murdered as well – yet one more warning to Rome. Finally, having not forgotten the double-cross of the 1923 Beerhall putsch, von Kahr, the Bavarian commissioner who dropped Hitler and the putschists to the Weimar police, 'was taken away by SS men and later found hacked to death near Dachau.'[27] In Munich the blasts of gunfire were heard throughout the entire day; then at dusk, silence. The exact figure of victims is not known. Presumably, the purge erased between 300 and 1,200 individuals.[28] The President was alerted; Hitler, strained by tension and exhaustion, reassured the Old Man that a terrible revolt had been headed off. The generals were satisfied.

At the end of July, Hindenburg was on his deathbed; he asked his watchful doctor Sauerbruch, the celebrious surgeon: 'Has Freund Heinz come into the house yet?' 'No,' replied the doctor, 'He is not in the house yet, but he is prowling in the garden.'[29] On August 2, Freund Heinz (that is, death) stole in the house and took the Old Man – he had lived 88 years. For Germany the Field Marshal had done his best, as had Germany during the war, but likewise his best had not been good enough. The following day, on the legal basis of a document drawn up at the Chancellery, with the tacit approval of the army, Hitler announced to the people that he would thenceforth fuse into his hands the titles of Chancellor and President, and assume in their stead the sonorous appellation of Reichsführer. On August 19, 1934, he demanded yet another referendum to be acclaimed as 'the leader,' unique and unchallenged, and thereby to sanction the ultimate effacement of the Weimar Republic. It was 'yes' by 90 percent.

> The pretended Hitlerite revolution was the outcome not of any deep will of the masses but a sort of violent dynamism from which the ruling Right wing expected to profit by canalizing it...It was von Papen who, thanks to his ascendancy over Hindenburg, organized the *coup d'état*. This *coup d'état* was simply a *'Kombination,'* a scheme prepared through fifteen years of diabolical intrigues and spectacular mass demonstrations. It owed its success to terrorism...[30]

## Money magic, work creation, and foreign aid

'There are two great unknowns in the history and politics of the Third Reich: the army and the finances.'[31] Associated with the latter was none other than the 'old wizard' himself, Hjalmar Schacht, the financial druid plugged by Dulles and the Anglo-American cabal in early 1922, and Reichsbank president from 1923 to 1930. François-Poncet, the French ambassador to the Third Reich, remembered him thus:

> Schacht was a cynic, a frantic blusterer, a person possessed of unbridled ambitions. A tall, dry, spare devil of a man, his features might have been hacked out by a bill hook, and his long wrinkled neck was like the neck of a bird of prey.[32]

It must have been harrowing, for such an ambitious creature as he, to sit still away from the levers of power for three interminable and comatose years, 1930–33. Considering his professional origins, sponsors, and character, it was hardly surprising to find him on the Nazi bandwagon at the onset of the Depression. Of the opportunists that swarmed to Nazism after the momentous election of September 1930 – the *Septemberlinge*, as Goebbels contemptuously tagged them – Schacht was the most prestigious by far.[33]

At the time, Schacht told himself that he had to commit; he just could not keep calm at the thought of Germany falling prey, should Hitler have stormed the Chancellery, to all sorts of unsavory monetary cranks, who teemed the back rows of the Nazi apparatus – they had to have professionals there at the top.[34] He had to come back and 'do the trick,' as his by now most intimate friend Montagu Norman, had been taunting him to do, publicly, since 1931. In due time he would have. For the time being, he advised Hitler to be in his speeches as vague and noncommittal as possible in matters relating to the economy.

Notwithstanding the bleak premonitions of the Papen government, Germany experienced in the summer of 1932 a modest economic revival. The truth was that part of the financial network, which was supportive of Papen, put a little faith in him and his barons and loosened the strings of the purse. In fact, lukewarm attempts on the part of the Grid to release some cash in the system had been afoot for over a year.

In the summer of 1931, at the trough of the slump, funds were no longer flowing from abroad. The ailing banks, who had granted credit to businesses for the most part now semi-defunct, rushed to the central institute in hope of selling it their 'frozen notes' (the IOUs of the bankrupt concerns) for a 'sufficient' amount of cash. The Reichsbank, whose discount rate in August was already a steep 10 percent, felt overwhelmed by the request and the tawdry quality of this paper. To pass muster, a bill required three signatures: the drawer's (creditor), the drawee's (debtor), and a guarantor's. Sections of the banking community suggested that the third underwriting come from a specially designed institute, the Akzeptbank, whose capital was promptly subscribed by the corporate leaders of the Grid. When all was done, the price for the rescue added up to 10 percent, plus 2 percent as a commission fee for the middle-role of the Akzeptbank: a net bite of 12 percent in the general tide of insolvency–outrageously expensive.[35]

By mid-1932, the Reichsbank had accumulated a sizable chunk of such 'frozen paper' in its portfolio and made good profits on it. But these advances of cash at such a high cost still amounted to no more than drops in the ocean: joblessness was not relieved in the least. Simply put, the German Grid had no faith whatsoever in the republic.

It was true that the state was bankrupt, but not entirely true that Germany had no money, or no capital. In 1931, the foreigners, indeed, had withdrawn much, as had the expatriate Germans, but the bulk of the foreign exchange sucked in during the great American feast of the 1920s was hoarded underground, and, most important, so was the mass of the nation's aggregate wealth. Such wealth, mostly in the form of securities, represented that sumptuous infrastructure and industrial apparatus – the second largest in the world – erected with the Dawes loans, and which presently lay dormant.

The silent shufflings of these banking consortia between 1930 and 1933 were part of a broader engagement on the part of Germany's financial interests into 'impairing' forms of investment: that is to say that the banks did not employ their funds to create new wealth of productive capital, but…*simply confined themselves to buying capital goods (fixed property, securities, etc.) already in existence.* The savings funds reentered the general circulation of industry and trade not by the act of investment, but by the expenditures of the impoverishing borrowers and sellers, who expended the money to meet their living expenses or their losses in business.[36]

In other words, the banking system and the great industrial conglomerates were making use of their cash literally to buy up the rest of the country by purchasing 'property' (deeds, stocks, mortgages and the like) at slashed prices from insolvent producers and consumers. The modicum of activity registered in 1931 under the auspices of the Reichsbank, the Akzeptbank and their affiliates constituted precisely this redistribution of wealth from the economy to the Grid; redistribution that accentuated, of course, the already skewed concentration of power in the hands of the latter. Between the slump and recovery stood unemployment; meanwhile, the absentees took advantage of the overall cheapness, attracting to their orbit additional titles of ownership. This was also how the central bank came to own, by the end of 1931, conspicuous stakes in several of the great Berlin banks.[37]

In 1932, 'the money,' in the form of cash, stocks, and bonds, was indeed sunk underground in the accounts of Germany's banking network. A succession of ministers pleaded with the bankers, entreated them, while searching for a clever argument that might bring the absentee gentlemen to turn on the money tap. Brüning tried when the match was already lost. Under Papen, because of his connections, the financial interests instead made some room for a trial at reform.

The chief device introduced in the summer of 1932 was the 'tax certificate' (*Steuergutschein*): a variation on a general financing template, which was one of many refined instruments of Germany's national political economy,[38] and which Schacht, as we shall see, would transform for the Nazis into a standardized and swift mechanism.[39]

The idea behind tax certificates was to grant businesses a rebate on their forthcoming tax payments. The authorities would consider the most recent figures of tax yields and multiply these by a percentage (the rebate); the product would then be converted in a number of certificates to be distributed amongst the entrepreneurs, who in turn could use them to remit future tax dues.[40]

The paper bore interest of 4 percent: the intent was to send the recipients of these certificates to knock on the gates of the monetary markets and pressure the banks to discount the paper at their counters – the 4 percent was, again, the lure for the 'investors.' This roundabout device was nothing less than the government's demand on behalf of struggling producers for a cash loan from the powerful investors: the firm would obtain the cash, minus the discount, hopefully thrive thereafter, and the Reich would pay interest on the certificates to the banks with the taxes it expected to levy from a boosted economy. In sum, the scheme comprised a short-term loan from the banks to the Reich, and a favorable (and interest-free) medium-term loan from the Reich to businesses. In the event, the lag would have to be bridged by further long-term borrowing on the part of the government, which, in the light of the anticipated economic improvement, should not have been a problem.[41]

What did the businesses actually do with these certificates? Most spent the cash either to pay their debts or to employ the rebate to cut their prices, thus making things far worse in an environment where falling prices were the crux of the paralysis. The chief objective of the Papen plan was to encourage the use of the certificates as security for credit advances to be devoted to plant expansion and production; and particularly as touched the unemployed masses, the proposal was drafted with an eye only to boosting private consumption.

The whole came far short of the mark: only a very modest contingent of workers was reabsorbed. And when, by mid autumn, the baronial Cabinet of von Papen appeared to be vacillating, the banking Grid recoiled in a heartbeat. 'The market was not prepared to take up the paper as fast as it was offered.'[42] Unemployment, which had decreased until then, started in November to rise once again. And continued to climb under Schleicher, who was dreaded by the financial and aristocratic elites, even though he endorsed the fiscal policy of his predecessor.[*]

Intriguingly, in the dreary days of November 1932, as he cast about for a successor to Papen, the Red General came to consider Schacht himself as a potential candidate for the Chancellery. Not for a moment was the banker

---

[*] At this time, an important think-tank in Berlin (the Institut für Konjunkturforschung) spread the myth that the recession had been overcome in the spring of 1932, and since the end of World War II, the Liberal establishment has repossessed this exaggeration with a view to employing it against the contention that there had been willful action behind the subsequent Nazi boom; no such thing was to be entertained: the boom had thus to be ascribed only to the 'impersonal,' 'unpredictable' swings of the business cycle. We shall briefly show that this was not true. In fact, the alternate vicissitudes of German unemployment in the biennium of 1932–33 may be easily correlated with the political orientation of the said elites: the brief respite registered in the Spring of 1932 was due exclusively to the favor accorded by the German clubs to Papen, whereas the recessionary relapse experienced in late 1932 was but the clubs' manifest sign of hostility towards the Schleicher government.

enticed by the prospect of becoming the puppet of Schleicher. The general seemed to have forgotten that the banker belonged to a wholly different and much more powerful fraternity than his own. Besides, Schacht had already thrown in his lot with Hitler. Nevertheless, morbidly curious, the banker presented himself to the interview to sniff, 'size up' this bothersome, plotting general. Even in his post-war memoirs, in which he spent superhuman energy to depict himself as a paragon of nobility, was Schacht incapable of concealing his clannish, implacable hatred for Schleicher – possibly the only Weimar politician who came close to aborting the Nazi incubation. Schacht reminisced:

> Although I immediately decided to refuse I was interested to discover his political views of the situation. His statements were so colorless that I had time to look around the room. It was every bit as devoid of character as the man's speech – without any personal touch, any sign of individual taste…He pinned his last hope on a split of the National-Socialist Party. When he expressed this hope in my presence I broke in: 'I think, General, that you underrate the iron discipline of the Party so assiduously maintained by Hitler.' On that occasion Schleicher smiled in a superior fashion. Not long afterwards he ceased altogether to smile.[43]

Doubtless, Schacht must not have mourned the Red General the day following the Purge, 30 June 1934. By then, Schacht was solidly enthroned as Hitler's new Reichsbank governor. He also enjoyed the undivided support of the Army and of the organized metallurgy industry, who championed his candidacy for leading an economic dictatorship focused on rearmament. The dream, sketched in the memo that he had forwarded to Dulles more than a decade ago, was about to come true: supreme monetary command over an oligopolized structure. However, Schacht had an adversary in the person of Kurt Schmitt, the Minister of Economics, who favored the development of a domestic consumers' market – Schmitt, moreover, had had the favor of Röhm.[44]

A few days after the Purge, in early July, Minister Schmitt, an asset of the insurance lobby, addressed an assembly of German exporters. No sooner had he opened his allocution, 'What, then, is to be done?' than he fainted dead away, and was hauled off to convalesce in seclusion. Four weeks later, Schacht was summoned by Hitler, who immediately probed him: 'I must find someone else for the post and would like to ask you, Herr Schacht, whether you would be prepared, in addition to your office of President of the Reichsbank to take our Ministry of Economic Affairs?' How could he say 'no'? 'There remained the one and only possibility,' Schacht would recall in his autobiography – the possibility of 'working from within outwards.'[45] In Nuremberg he would confess: 'I'd even join the devil, for a big, strong Germany.'[46]

On July 30, 1934, Schacht officially succeeded Schmitt as Economic Minister; President Hindenburg undersigned the appointment and died three days later.[47] Germany had its new Mephistophelean steward: Schacht was Reichsbank president and newly appointed Economic Minister, vested with the superadded honorific of *Generalbevollmächtigte für die Kriegswirtschaft* (General Plenipotentiary for the War Economy). They now said of him that he was the 'Economic Dictator of Germany.'

July 1934 was but a replay of March 1933. On the 17th of that month, Schacht had been officially recalled at the central bank – to steer the ship he had forsaken three years before. This had been the exchange between Hitler and Schacht:

> [Hitler:] 'Herr Schacht, I am sure we are agreed that at the moment there can be only one urgent duty for the new national Government, and that is to do away with unemployment. For this it will be necessary to find a very large sum of money. Do you see any possibility of raising such a sum – other than through the Reichsbank?'
>
> [Schacht:] I agree with you entirely, Chancellor, that it is essential to wipe out the unemployment figures. But no matter what money can be extorted from other sources, it would still be quite insufficient for the job. You won't be able to avoid recourse to the Reichsbank...
>
> [Hitler:] 'You must be able to say to what extent the Reichsbank can and must – help.'
>
> [Schacht:] 'I am honestly not in a position, Chancellor, to mention any particular sum. My opinion is this: Whatever happens, we must put an end to unemployment and therefore the Reichsbank must furnish whatever will be necessary to take the last unemployed off the streets.'
>
> [Hitler:] 'Would you be prepared to take command of the Reichsbank again?'[48]

Behind Schacht, also known as 'the American,'[49] stood important segments of German absentee ownership and Anglo-Saxon finance. As Hitler recalled, the first allotment earmarked for rearmament purveyed by the Reichsbank to the Hitlerites was of 8 billion marks; of that sum, Schacht and the Reichsbank deducted 500 million marks as interest. Not even the Nazis were spared the payment of interest: – 6.25 percent. And they paid, without protest. They would honor the obligation by availing themselves of the power to tax. The price was high, Hitler fumed, but he kept quiet.

Unlike Röhm, his SA, the Strassers and their Left wing, the Hitlerites had a solid grasp of economic realities. After sacrificing the SA to the army, Hitler now had to play a careful game with the Grid, to which he already owed much, and which he did not underestimate, hence his adulatory conduct while conversing with Schacht. This was his second compromise with the powers that be: like his old comrade Röhm, Hitler hated the bankers ('that other gang...bunch of crooks,' and Schacht, a 'swindler!')[50] no less than he hated the Prussian generals, but he had to accomplish his mission in the East, whatever the cost.

Schacht knew what Hitler wanted from him; now was the time to 'do the trick.' First of all he was expected to ignite that *Initialzuendung*, or 'initial spark,' with which Papen had attempted to shock the German economy in the throes of 1932. The jump-start, all experts agreed, should have come from government expenditure, but, for the rest of the common mortals, the 'big problem remained as it had always been, *where to find the money*,'[51] or, in other words, how to 'make capital appear when seemingly it did not exist.'[52]

As mentioned before, the unemployment condition inherited by the Third Reich was nothing short of catastrophic: 9 million jobless out of a labor force of 20 million – two out of every five Germans employed in 1929 were without work in the winter of 1932–33.[53]

Since 1930, as workers were being laid off and the national income was plummeting, the Grid had made a fortune out of the misery of the Fatherland by buying stacks of securities 'cheap.' This process of financial concentration was achieved in 1933, the year of Hitler. Then, as if materializing out of thin air, a host of 'semi-public' financial institutes appeared that began to issue bills by broadsides of several billion Reichsmarks every year. Bills, which the central bank proceeded to discount, just as it had done in 1931; yet this time neither unsteadily nor with avariciousness, but on a vast scale and at a most generous rate. *Thus began the Nazi economic miracle – the so-called process of 'work creation.'*

In June 1933, the economists of the Third Reich attacked the crisis on the labor front. The operation came to be defined as one of *Vorfinanzierung*: pre-financing.

The financial contrivance the credit institutes employed to stimulate economic activity was a special kind of paper.

After the great inflation, the 1924 statute of the Reichsbank did not allow unrestricted purchases of government paper. The only instrument against which the central institute was permitted to advance cash was the commercial bill, for only this last, at least on a purely formal level, carried the guarantee that tangible wares were indeed being produced.[54] In 1933, by dint of this clause, statutory prohibitions were outflanked* and the legal outfit was at last cleared to accommodate imposing injections of monetary means.

The financing procedure was orchestrated as follows: first of all, the Reich borrowed from the Reichsbank – this was the opening of the Grid propitiated by Schacht. Then the government, via specialized credit agencies, re-loaned such credits to provinces, municipalities, communes, and other local public bodies.

The works were carried out by private entrepreneurs under contracts with the municipalities. The main instrument of financing consisted of so-called 'work-creation bills' (*Arbeitsbeschaffungswechsel*), which were extended to the contractors by the commissioning cities and accepted (discounted) by the banking establishment: at the bank, the bill was immediately transformed into check money (and cash), which was devoted to hiring the jobless and commence the works. If the discounting credit institute was itself in need of cash, it might present these bills for *re-discount* at the mother institute, the Reichsbank (see Figure 5.1).

Of course, the paper bore interest: 4 per cent like the tax certificates – thus these bills were conceived as a perfectly liquid short-term investment medium. Nominally the bills matured in three months, but as a rule they were subject to 20 automatic renewals, which carried the actual maturity of the paper to five years. At maturity the Reich honored the bills with the tax revenues generated by the *Vorfinanzierung*: this obligation represented a long-term liability to the Reich for the amounts originally loaned on short term by the private banking Interests.[55] Stripped of its roundabout features, the procedure of the bills came down to the financing of public spending by central bank credit, with the Reichsbank acting as the credit-generating agent for the Reich. At the beginning of this sudden work-creation campaign, the burden of 'financing' was borne entirely by Schacht's institute.[56]

Simply put, there was money in 1931 which had vanished underground and failed to re-emerge for the length of three long years. Then the Nazis came, and when the banking Grid sent its financial ambassador, Hjalmar Schacht, to the central bank, it thus gave the signal to pour, once again, the monetary base that had vanished back into the main avenues of the

---

\* They would be abrogated the following year in the ambit of the consolidation movement, which is discussed below.

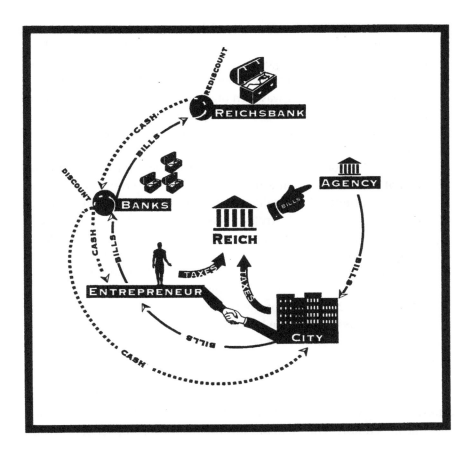

*Figure 5.1*   The cycle of work creation

network. So the big Berlin banks of the Grid returned the money by lending it to the Reich, the Reich lent it to the cities, the cities gave these bills to the people, the people brought them their commercial banks, which changed them into checks, and the system came alive.[*]

The initial monetary injections were allocated for infrastructure. And the bills took on the name of the type of project that they were meant to finance: 'work creation bills,' 'special highway bills,' 'land reclamation bills,' and so on. Entrepreneurs cashed in, had their paper discounted, and paid the workmen. Banks turned to the Reichsbank, which started to print

---

[*]   Technically speaking, the large Berlin banks behind the Reichsbank reinjected the high-powered money in the system, and the commercial banks, on behalf of all the other, lesser absentees, endorsed the bills and magnified the issue through the deposits multiplier: the 4 percent interest on the bills acted as a magnet (of all other hidden deposits) trawled by the Reichsbank in the phase of pre-financing.

paper money; with it banks repaid the debts they couldn't honor during the slump, and fueled the recovery. Men found work again, they did not spend much; what they managed to lay aside was automatically reinvested by the savings banks within the self-same circuit of state expenditure.

Hitler was triumphant; he was seen digging, repeatedly, before delirious crowds: digging the 'first spadefuls' (*erste Spatenstiche*) of the several legs of the *Autobahnen* network that were being laid across the country, the first of which joined Heidelberg and Frankfurt on September 23, 1933.[57]

In August 1933 something decisive came to pass: Schacht encountered the lords of German steel – amongst them the giants Krupp and Siemens. Together they founded the Metallforschungsgesellschaft, or Mefo (Research Corporation of the steel industry) – a fictitious corporation with a meager capital endowment (250,000 marks), against which, from 1934 to 1938, 12 billion Reichsmarks worth of bills were issued for the first war commissions, with the same procedure previously outlined. The Mefo bill was the true spark that triggered the process of rearmament. Although until the outbreak of hostilities only 20 percent of the total rearmament expenditure would be financed in this manner, the Mefo allotment would cover 50 percent of total expenditure on military orders during the initial years. 'The absolute secrecy of this arrangement was preserved until after the war.'[58]

The Mefo bill was peculiar paper: it rested upon virtual treasures – upon titles of ownership which, during the twilight of Weimar, were amassed in the sparse hands of the absentee owners, the new indisputable masters of Germany. The Mefo bill was the fruit of a compact between the economic overlords and a tenebrous knighthood, between the highest German dynasties and the Nazis, who, with the monopoly of violence and the promise of war, fulfilled respectively two fundamental economic prerequisites: they ensured taxation, and warranted the yield promised by the Nazi bill – that 4 percent stamped upon the paper. Namely, the price of gold, of money, which, in a world contorted by vehement protectionism, would hopefully be repaid with the surplus forthcoming from the rapine of war. Hitler confirmed three years into the war:

The payments of debts...presents no problem. In the first place the territories which we have conquered by force of arms represent an increase in national wealth which far exceeds the costs of war; in the second place, the integration of twenty million foreigners at cheap rates into the German industrial system represents a saving which, again, is greatly in excess of the debts contracted by the State.[59]

The obvious legerdemain: there wasn't a gram of gold to back the Nazi bills, just a different set of relationships, which varied by definition with the political humor of the times. Behind the Mefo bill there were but a paltry equity base, a non-existent corporation, the goodwill of German steel lords, the proverbial discipline and industriousness of the Teuton, and the complicity of bankers and high world finance, which, through their own network, managed to convey, as will be detailed hereafter, the raw materials needed to equip with breathtaking rapidity a redoubtable army.

Upon these formidable monetary premises, the economists of the Third Reich redesigned the structure of the capitalist machine. Two were the main difficulties to overcome: (1) to free the economy from disproportionate financial overhead charges; and (2) to find an outlet for the enormous productive potential of modern industrial systems in such a way that remuneration, profit, and interest would not be wholly eroded.

It was up to the Reichsbank to make the opening move if the first objective was to be attained. By rediscounting the bills forwarded to it by credit institutes, the bank of issue ministered the decisive shot of liquidity to the system. Part of this monetary mass went to settle the debts incurred by slump-stricken businesses (banks and firms),[60] part was employed to reanimate the economy. This time Germany had German money, no borrowed cover in gold, pounds, or dollars. In fact, gold reserves officially amounted to 1 percent of note circulation in 1936;[61] in the eyes of the people the seal of the Reich sufficed, the paper was unquestionably taken – it was money all right.

The advent of Nazism coincided with a veritable jubilee: the record shows the virtual annulment of all private debt. Like magic, money became less expensive. At the beginning of 1933, the prime rate of interest was over 8 percent;[62] by 1935, through an intricate reshuffle of a gamut of other variously named bills dealt across Germany's banking network, Schacht compressed it to 2.81 percent.[63] Germany was liquid again.

Then entered the Nazi economic ministries; all their attention was focused upon the industrial sector: first of all, they ordained in July 1933 'compulsory cartels,' that is, a strong concentration of all main concerns; there followed the capital concession: the so-called *Preisfinanzierung* (financing by prices).

The Reich placed the order for goods and construction and agreed to a price that, in addition to entrepreneurial profit, included an accelerated depreciation allowance (that is, a stipulation under the pretense that equipment wore out faster than usual), which was tantamount to the total remission of interest charges, and to the concession of a bonus, which firms would devote to the expansion of plants (self-financing scheme). In 1937 the ratio of interest charges to sales for business bottomed out at 0.40 percent.[64]

Commercial banks were relegated to the mere discounting function: they still held the privileged right to exact interest against the bills tendered by the Reich, yet *they had to forego the far more important prerogative to dictate the nature and direction of all investments*, as well as the copious rents obtainable therefrom.[65] These rents, instead, were appropriated by the Reich, which in turn ceded them to businesses with the *Preisfinanzierung*.

Throughout the cycle (*die Konjunktur*), the level of the workers' wages was pegged at the depression rates of 1932–33, some 21 percent below the prosperity level of 1929.[66] Prices, instead, were capped by decree in November 1936. By thus repressing consumption, the production of weaponry was intensified, and the original loans were transformed from short- to long-term engagements: consolidation was initiated.

Germans were now told that the money they had laid in was being immobilized – maturity dates of Reich securities were gradually postponed (28 years for the initial Reich bond auction of 1935, at 4 percent). War would settle all accounts payable. Meanwhile, the economy pushed on: between 1933 and 1936, German GNP increased by an average annual rate of 9.5 percent, and annual productivity for industry and crafts rose by 17.2 percent. The average annual growth of public consumption during these four years was 18.7 percent, while private consumption increased only by 3.6 percent annually.[67]

In 1935 military expenditure amounted to approximately half of the entire governmental outlay. From then on this share was bound to rise inexorably.

Nazi bills were initially paid off with tax proceeds, but in the course of the consolidation, financial authorities ended up paying only interest on the lengthened loans, putting off the reimbursement of the principal until the end of war. By thus postponing 'the evil day,' observed the specialists of the Bank of England in 1939,[68] the Nazis appeared to have flattened the ups and downs of the cycle for 'ten or perhaps twenty years': *it looked as though the whole endeavor was pervaded with the lightness of a zero-interest loan.*

Hitler had blind faith in his divisions. So did his financial backers, seemingly. In four years, Hitler conscripted these armies, by 1938 erasing 9 million unemployed,[69] redistributing wealth with highly progressive taxation,[70] improving somewhat the quality of life until 1939, and repressing even the least inflationary hiccup.

Finally, the abundance of modern industrial systems, which translated into an overall diminution of the price level, and which failed to comply with the logic of profit. What to do with it? War. Schacht helped Hitler by luring back to the surface those pecuniary hoards that had been concealed for three long years in order to finance the war at 3–4 percent. '[Schacht:] I had to find a way of extracting this fallow capital from the safe deposits and pockets where it…lay, without expecting it to remain absent for long or lose its value.'[71]

Throughout the Nazi boom the money owners had collected interest; they would have to wait for the end of the conflict in the East – such was the understanding – to get their own capital back. They had allowed Hitler to spend over 100 billion marks for the mission.[72] This was no economic recovery but a feverish sweat before the last Herculean labor.

On the international front the affair was no less involved.

Of the 34 vital materials without which a nation cannot live, Germany had only two in ample quantities – potash and coal.[73] For the rest it would have to rely on its chemists and international friends.

Schacht and his associates at the ministry of economies set out on a world tour to conclude general compensation or clearing agreements with whole countries. These agreements were predicated on the creation of a common account into which German importers paid their bills in marks; these same marks could then be drawn by German exporters for their sales to their trading partners. The exchange rates were not allowed to float freely and were often fixed afresh for each major transaction. This system, which ousted all previous methods, became the framework of nearly 65 percent of Germany's foreign trade.[74] Playing (1) on an overvalued clearing rate of the mark and (2) on buying far more from the others than selling to them,[75] Schacht involved over 25 countries into these bilateral waistcoats: Latin America, the Balkans, Greece, Turkey and Eastern Europe – Romania, Bulgaria, Hungary, from which the Germans secured oil-yielding fruits, oilseed, fibers, soya beans, bauxite, oil, against iron and weaponry,[76] mostly for the benefit of the cannon-maker Krupp.[77]

But what of the industrialized West; Anglo-America, for instance?

Britain, of course, now that Nazism had ripened, was particularly scrupulous in grooming it as best as she could. In July 1934, right when Schacht was crowned Economic Dictator, she concluded with Germany the Anglo-German Transfer Agreement, considered one of the 'pillars of British policy towards the Third Reich.'[78] Under its norms, the Third Reich was allowed to accumulate a sizable trade surplus vis-à-vis Britain; the surplus translated into free sterling, which the Nazis could employ to purchase whatever commodities they might need for rearmament on the empire's world markets; rubber and copper being chief amongst these.[79]

*By the end of the decade, Nazi Germany was Britain's principal trading client.* In 1937, for example, she provided a market for more British goods than any other two continents combined and for four times the amount taken by the United States.[80]

Then there was the unending headache of the Dawes loans and of all that money still owed to the City of London, which Germany had captured and was not willing to relinquish. Under the legitimate cloak of the so-called Standstill Agreements, that is, the deal on credits whose principal was frozen in Germany and upon which the debtor was only obliged to pay interest, Britain, despite some top bankers in London who rebuffed the claim as a 'misapprehension,'[81] not only renewed the original 1931 debt standing but also added fresh credit to the original amount at least by a multiple equal to the number of renewals throughout the entire Nazi takeoff (1933–39).[82]

On December 4, 1934, Norman advanced the Nazis a loan of approximately $4 million in order to 'facilitate the mobilization of German commercial credits': that is, new money to pay old debts – or better said, a *gift*.[83] Not yet satisfied, and in direct opposition to that segment of the British interests which keenly insisted on being refunded by Germany, Norman fought nail and tooth against the setting-up of a clearing union between Britain and Germany: in fact, a clearing would have automatically diverted 'free sterling' into debt repayment, and Schacht would therefore have lost his cherished allowance in pounds for international purchases of raw goods and materials.[84]

There were several voices in the City that spoke of further money, outside the Standstill Agreements, being loaned by Britain to German private concerns, such as I. G. Farben. The Bank of England itself instructed its employees not to discuss openly such a matter, which was 'confidential.'[85] The archives of the Bank are indeed mute on this count; these other amicable 'extensions' might very well have been significant.

Of the foreign money she owed in 1932, Germany would repay her creditors less than 10 percent by 1939.[86] Notwithstanding, international business kept on treating Hitler's Germany with *pattes de velours* – especially the arms-makers. In 1935, an Anglo-German Society was founded 'in which Unilever, Dunlop Rubber, the British Steel Export Association, and British Petroleum' all participated.[87] The prestigious British manufacturer of heavy guns, armor plate and warships, Vickers-Armstrong – curiously one of the very few concerns salvaged during the Slump by Montagu Norman himself[88] – had been offering, as early as 1932 in the official publication of the German army, the *Militär-Wochen-Blatt*, tanks and armored cars.[89] At the annual meeting of his company in 1934, Sir Herbert Lawrence, the Chairman of Vickers, was asked to give assurance that the corporation was not being used for the secret rearmament of Germany. This was his reply: 'I cannot give you assurance in definite terms, but I can tell you that nothing is done without the complete sanction and approval of our own government.'[90]

William Dodd, a history professor, served as American ambassador to Berlin from 1933 to 1938. '*Der gute* Dodd,' Hitler would pityingly say of him, 'he can hardly speak German, and made no sense at all.'[91] Dodd might not have spoken good German, but he wrote good enough English to relate the following to his President, Roosevelt, on October 19, 1936:

At the present moment more than a hundred American corporations have subsidiaries here or have cooperative understandings. The Du Pont have three allies: (1) Chief: I. G. Farben Co. (2) Standard Oil has made $500 million a year helping the Germans make Ersatz gas for war purposes; but Standard Oil cannot take any of its earnings out of the country except in goods. They do little of this, report their earnings at home, but do not explain the facts. (3) The International Harvester Company president told me their business here rose 33 per cent a year (arms manufacture, I believe), but they could take nothing out. Even our airplanes people have secret arrangements with Krupp...Why did the Standard Oil Company of New York send $1 million over here in December, 1933, to aid the Germans in making gasoline from soft coal for war emergencies? Why do the International Harvester people continue to manufacture in Germany when their company gets nothing out of the country?[92]

Roosevelt was evasive, but encouraged Dodd to continue his reports. Not satisfied with the official explications (that Germany should have been allowed to rearm in order to regain world status), the candid ambassador had been recording in his diary several suspect transactions since his arrival in Germany: on September 19, 1934, high-class aircraft manufacturers made in the USA were delivered to Germany against $1 million in gold – Dodd confronted Schacht about the sale; the latter tried at first to deny it, but seeing that Dodd was about to brandish a hard copy of the deal, gave in and confirmed. On October 19 of the same year, it was the turn of the British: Vickers had just sold the Nazis a cargo of war matériel, and despite the haggling over the Standstill and the alleged insolvency of Germany, stories of which filled the newspapers daily, the Germans paid for the weapons in cash; with the evidence, Dodd then rushed to the British ambassador, Sir Eric Phipps, who pretended to be surprised.[93]

These were only anecdotal fragments of a deep and intricate intercourse consummated by the Allies with the Nazi regime. The Allies, as is well known, had traded heavily with Hitler; they had traded 'with the enemy.' And it appears, in fact, 'that the *effective* influence of foreign capital, an influence which exerts itself far more with investments than with credits, grew under the Nazi regime.'[94] 'At the time of Pearl Harbor, American investment in Nazi Germany amounted to an estimated total of $475 million. Standard Oil of New Jersey had $120 million invested there; General Motors had $35 million; ITT had $30 million, and Ford had $17.5 million.'[95]

Frank Knox, the US Naval Secretary (1940–44), would admit that in the biennium 1934–35, Hitler received from America hundreds of state-of-the-art airplane engines, and a Senate investigation concluded in 1940 that American industrialists had been freely selling a plethora of military patents to Germany with the consent of the government: Pratt & Whitney, Douglas, Bendix Aviation (controlled by GM, which at the time was controlled by Morgan & Co.), to name but a few, handed over to BMW, Siemens, and others a collection of aviation military secrets,[96] while Stukas bombers, as mentioned earlier, were built with techniques learned in Detroit.

Western pundits have always taken the easy way out, explaining away these treasonous deals as the proverbial misdeeds of a few fat, rotten apples trucking with despots for the sake of 'quick bucks' – the customary litany against 'corporate greed.' That might be the case for the few deals paid in gold – of which the Nazis had virtually none – but certainly not for the colossal Allied investment sunk into Germany without any prospect of retrieving the gains, let alone the original capital on a relatively brief notice: hence the perplexity of Dodd. Many of these 'foreign' installations would be spared the Allied bombs at the end of the war, and one is left to wonder when, in fact, the respective governments of Britain and the United States began to think of Europe as their own private domain – the new western appendix of the empire – and of Hitler and his regime as an obtrusive nuisance to be propped up at first and then annihilated in a prolonged international conflict.

Governor Schacht must also have wondered. For years, almost deaf to Hitler's repeatedly avowed goals of the *Drang nach Osten* (the 'Push to the East'), Schacht preconized, instead, a return to Germany of her former African colonies. He too seemed to envision a Reich that would tower over Middle Europe – the *grossdeutsch* Reich inclusive of Austria and

Czechoslovakia as a minimum – yet one connected to exotic outposts by means of a decent-sized navy. But Hitler had no interest in colonies.

It has been written that by early 1935 two blocs supporting different world views formed inside the Nazi establishment and fought for supremacy: a pro-Anglo-Saxon banking-industrial grouping assembled around 'the American' Schacht versus the party of I. G. Farben/Deutsche Bank, which aimed to decouple Germany from the British-dominated world markets and create a closed Eurasian economic bloc[97] – a self-sufficient fortress stretching from Odessa to Bordeaux.

In August 1936, Hitler drafted a secret memoir which informed the second Four-Year Plan for the rearmament of Nazi Germany. I. G. Farben was indeed the soul of the project, and Göring became its economic supremo. Yet the new Four-Year Plan, which came into force in September, was only a prod to accelerate preparedness for war: home production of foodstuffs, minerals and synthetic ersatz materials,* for which the plan is remembered, were tasks that had been previously coordinated by Schacht – they were merely to be boosted on a much wider scale.[98]

According to the rumor that he himself would spread, Schacht, bitterly and overtly critical of Göring's uneconomic squander of resources and foreign exchange, and fearful of the runaway inflation that might have resulted from turning ever more butter into guns, distanced himself from the Führer and began to lose favor with the Nazi elite.[99] This rumor might have led to the other, according to which the antagonism of Farben would eventually cause the banker's downfall.[100]

As in 1930, Schacht felt the ground quaking, but this time the position of Britain, as will be seen, was so ambivalent that not even the guileful 'American' was quite certain of the posture he should have assumed. That war would come was certain: Schacht himself, with the Mefo bills, had raised the Wehrmacht from the dead – he was no pacifist. But what sort of war? The emergence in Britain of the anti-Nazi War Party led by Churchill was reason enough for him to become apprehensive, and so he receded – a few steps, by arguing in public with Göring. The story of Schacht's protests against the risk of inflation and the uneconomic use of foreign exchange was a fable. In fact, as Hitler would later recall:

[An inflationary] crisis could only have arisen after all the unemployed labour had been absorbed, and this did not happen until late 1937 or early 1938. Up till then the only difficulties we had to face were those

---

* Especially substitutes for rubber and gasoline.

of foreign exchange. Schacht had told me that we had at our disposal a credit of fifteen hundred million marks abroad, and it was on this basis that I planned my Four Year Plan, which never caused me the slightest anxiety...And that is how things are today [August 1942], and we never find ourselves blocked for money.[101]

On November 26, 1936, Schacht was relieved of his post of Minister for Economic Affairs and Plenipotentiary for the War Economy, and confined his duties to governing the Reichsbank.

After *Kristallnacht*, the night of November 9, 1938, during which synagogues all across Germany were desecrated and destroyed, Schacht was offered by Hitler his last opportunity: he was dispatched to propose to influential Jewish captains of Anglo-American finance a plan for the evacuation of Jews from Germany – Montagu Norman would preside. In sum, Schacht's plan sought to impound the wealth of German Jews as collateral, and on that basis issue an international loan at 5 percent to be subscribed by their wealthy co-religionaries: the funds sequestered would go towards the amortization of the loan. A quarter of the dollar proceeds gathered with the subscriptions would then be devoted to paying the prospective evacuees their passage out of the country.[102]

'Not an ideal proposition,' by Schacht's own admission,[103] but better, he reasoned, than leaving the Jews at the mercy of the party. Undoubtedly his plan was larcenous and extortionate; and as such it was scoffed at by Roosevelt in the United Sates and by Chamberlain and Halifax in Britain: between December 14 and 17, emboldened by these politicians' chiding, the Jewish bankers flexed their muscles and sabotaged the conference[104] – no submission to Nazi blackmail, they rebutted.

Schacht had failed, and he was not irreplaceable: on February 21, 1939, he was dismissed from his post of Reichsbanks president. He would retain the honorary title of Minister without Portfolio until January 21, 1943.

## A British masquerade to entrap the Germans anew

'*Nostra maxima culpa*,' 'our gravest fault': so reads the chapter title of one of many books, all alike, devoted by British historians to that disturbing season of their history known as 'appeasement.'[105] '*Culpa*': 'fault,' 'error,' 'regrettable mistake' – for having tried to appease a regime, Hitler's, that would not and could not be pacified by any amount of goodwill, however profligate. A mistake at best, a shameful episode at worst – but a misjudgment in any case.

According to this myth, because her elite unexpectedly found itself deeply torn over foreign policy into several antagonistic currents, Britain well-meaning but short-sighted was incapable of reading Nazism's mind, and ended up as a result bearing some of the guilt for the ensuing disasters. On the surface of Britain's political landscape, it is real factions that we're made to see, headed by real leaders, fighting with vehemence over a range of vital points. Profiting from such political discordance, so goes the apologue, Hitler gave full rein to his mad ambition.

The truth is different. The British establishment was a monolithic structure: the dissension among the stewards, if any, was over policy, never over principles and goals, which were the same for them all. The British were never torn by disagreement as to what ought to be done with Hitler. That much was obvious: destroy him in time, and raze Germany to the ground – imperial logic demanded it. Rather, the point was a pragmatic one: how could the Nazis be most suitably bamboozled into stepping, anew, into a pitfall on two fronts? The answer: by dancing with them. And dance the British would, twirling round the diplomatic ballroom of the 1930s, always leading, and drawing patterns as they spun that followed in fact a predictable trajectory.

The tactic they employed was to animate a variety of political formations, as if laying out tools of differing gauges to be fitted to the task as the opportunity arose.

Since Versailles, the elite fissured into three formations: (1) the anti-Bolsheviks, (2) the Round Table group, and (3) the appeasers (see Figure 5.2). From 1919 to 1926, the first party, which included the leading foreign expert, Sir Eric Simon; the Ambassador to Berlin, D'Abernon; and the South African Imperial Minister, Jan Smuts, dominated the government: in the early 1920s, they posed as the anti-French faction, which gave its blessing to the secret rearmament of Germany with a view to revamping the latter as 'the bulwark' against Communism.[106] It was most probably this gang that Veblen had in mind when in 1920 he alluded to the Elder Statesmen conspiring at Versailles to restore German reaction against Russian Bolshevism. But the plot was thicker than what even Veblen could have imagined.

The true core of the imperial monolith was the Milner group, whose word was printed in the monthly review *The Round Table*.* This party also included Simon and Smuts, as well as the editor of *The Times*, Geoffrey Dawson; two key players of the Foreign Office, Lord Lothian (Philip Kerr) and Lord Halifax (Edward Wood); and Samuel 'Slippery Sam' Hoare, an

---

* See Chapter 1, p. 39.

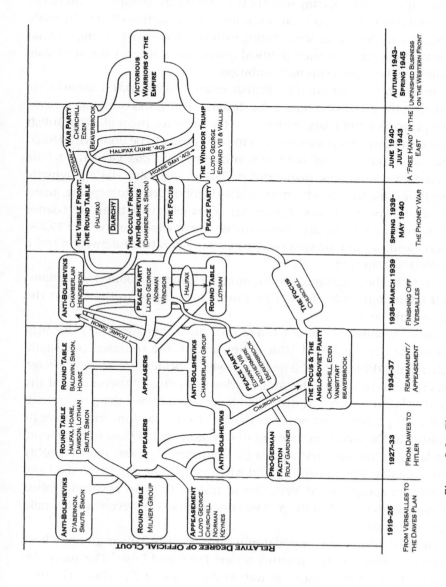

*Figure 5.2* The masquerade of His Majesty's stewards and diplomats

imperial factotum issued from an old banking family, who had spent time in Russia during the war as a member of the British intelligence services – 'he was so expert at his job, the Tsar accused him of foreknowledge of the murder of Rasputin.'[107]

Between 1919 and 1924, this set controlled a fifth of the Cabinet members, a quarter in 1931–35, and a third in 1935–40.[108]

To straddle and wait for events to unfold, The Round Table made a pretense of endorsing as its official policy agenda the utterly spurious scenario of the 'world in three blocs,' whereby a Germany free to roam in Central Europe was to be hedged between the western embankment of France and Britain, and the eastern defense of Russia's 'out-of-the-way… scarcely surveyable' empire.[109]

The Versailles Treaty (1919) and the Dawes Plan (1924), were prevalently the work of these two groups.[110]

Finally, the appeasers included a heterogeneous collection of backbenchers, such as Churchill and Lloyd George, who recommended 'peace with honor,'[111] 'non-partisan' technocrats like Norman, and segments of the intelligentsia – publicists and writers like Keynes. All were keen to show a benevolent face to the enemies of yesterday, and to tie new bonds with them in the name of 'sportsmanship.'

Thus by the middle of the Dawes period, the empire disposed of at least three stock masks: the friendly face of appeasement, the dogged front of anti-Communism, and the placid, middle-of-the-road approach of the Round Table. Towards the end of the Weimar incubation, the anti-Bolsheviks receded in the background, while the appeasers gathered steam – the poker face of the Round Table reigned supreme, and even a pro-German fringe promoted by Rolf Gardiner and similar *ante diem* deep ecologists sensitive to the common heritage of Nordic folklore came into being (Figure 5.2). This was a peripheral movement, however, devoid of popular support and political clout.[112] There was no genuine pro-German feeling in Britain, only a burgeoning jungle of make-believe.

After Hitler's first six months in power the masquerade really began.

On the diplomatic front, the Führer started by signing an alliance with Poland on January 26, 1934: this signaled the end of the old secret policy of the German generals, who during Weimar had rearmed with Russia in view of a joint assault against Poland, their common enemy. Hitler, instead, would have liked to see Poland involved in an anti-Bolshevik campaign spearheaded by Nazi Germany.

On April 9, 1934, Germany publicly announced that she was rearming – against the provisions of Versailles. France worried. Meanwhile, the Germans had guests: Royal Air Force Captain Winterbotham, the spy who had squired Rosenberg during his autumnal tour of the London clubs in 1931,* was presently attended to by his former visitor and the Führer himself: Winterbotham was an asset of MI6, British counter-espionage, and of the intelligence division of the Air Ministry. His was one of the first masks of the mummery: he had been posing as an 'admirer' of the regime – as a staunch appeaser – since the first Nazi electoral breakthrough, and by now he had gained the complete confidence of his hosts. *The Nazis told him everything*: they told him how, together with England, they would have destroyed Communism, and how zealously they were preparing for Operation Otto, *later codenamed 'Barbarossa,'* that is, the invasion of Russia.[113]

On July 25, 1934, a hapless vanguard of Austrian Nazis, trained by the SS with the approval of Hitler, botched a coup in Vienna: they assassinated the premier, Dolfuss, but could not go any further. The Italian leader, Mussolini, who acted as the protector of Austria, alerted his divisions on the common frontier; he then turned to France and Britain for coordinating a disciplinary maneuver against the brash savagery of the new German regime. France turned to Britain, *and Britain said 'no'*: no military castigation of Germany – it was not worth it. Britain, the French concluded, had written off Austria.[114] And she had: Mussolini would not forget Britain's betrayal, nor would Hitler – gratefully: with Austria, he would try again later.

In the same month, Conservative leader Stanley Baldwin, the fox who would soon become Prime Minister (June 1935–May 1937), had 'defended Germany's right to recreate and air force: "She has every argument in her favor, from her defenseless position in the air, to make herself secure".'[115]

And in the summer of 1934, Churchill resurfaced from the parliamentarian swamp with an important agenda: he wooed the Soviet Ambassador in London, Maisky, singing to him of his love for the British empire – his 'be-all and end-all' – and truncated the ode by inviting the Russians to join forces with Britain against Hitler.[116] Immediately thereafter, Churchill stormed the House to diffuse a series of alarmist speeches, in which he 'prophesied' that in one seven-day attack on London by the German Luftwaffe, 30,000 people would be killed or maimed. Lloyd George would then be charged by Baldwin to rebuke Churchill for ignoring how critical it was for Britain to have Germany as a bulwark against Communism.[117]

Splendid maneuver: now a fourth mask was added to the British panoply (Figure 5.2) – an anti-Nazi, pro-Russian nucleus coagulated round Churchill, while the pacifiers behind Lloyd George rose in influence. It

* See Chapter 4, pp. 194–5.

was a democratic, taut face that Britain was now showing to the world – a face upon which expressions of cynical pragmatism (appeasement) were somewhat tempered by the moderation of the Milner fraternity and the open dissent of Churchill. It was the wholesome visage of pluralism.

In January 1935, Baron Wilhelm de Ropp, a Balt double agent working in Berlin for Winterbotham's team, met with two of King George V's four sons in London: Edward VIII, the Prince of Wales, and Prince George, the Duke of Kent, to 'give them a complete picture of the qualities of Hess, Rosenberg, and the other leaders.'[118]

This was the overture of the masquerade's most picturesque visual effect: the dressing of a pro-Nazi Peace Party crowned by a royal candidate. The intelligence services were now casting for a suitable foil among the regal offspring, someone to play the role of the antagonist in the hypothetical scenario whereby Britain would be split into a dominant anti-German War Party and an underground pro-Nazi Peace Party. Edward, then living easy as the world's ageless teenage idol, seemed to fit the role to a T: his German was fluent, and he was always eager to evoke the sweetest summers of his childhood spent in the company of his favorite 'Uncle Willi,' the former Kaiser Wilhelm II, his father's cousin.[119] Edward passed the audition.

On March 6, 1935, in the face of German rearmament, France reinstituted military conscription. Ten days later, adducing the French decision as a pretext, Hitler did likewise – again, in violation of the provisions of Versailles. Britain 'protested,' though, curiously, she did not omit to enquire with the Nazi authorities: 'Would the German government be still willing to receive Sir Eric Simon and Anthony Eden of the Foreign Office, as previously scheduled?' – hardly the concern of an enemy. On March 25, the two British statesmen landed in Berlin. The German interpreter Paul Schmidt recalled Simon's large brown eyes gazing paternally upon the Führer, with fondness. Eden was more circumspect.

Before them, Hitler expatiated once more on the need to form a common front against Bolshevism, and – the novelty – he foreshadowed the possibility of coming to an understanding on rearmament ratios: say, to begin by allowing a tonnage for the German fleet 35 percent as large as that of the Royal Navy. The British did not say no.

The talks had been a success. They were concluded by a festive brunch at the British embassy, where the ambassador, Sir Eric Phipps, had lined up his children to give Hitler and his train the Nazi salute, shouting '*Sieg Heil!*' – a choreographic effort, so thought the German interpreter, that was 'a little shameful.'[120] All would have been perfect had Eden not taken leave to continue on to Moscow.

This was the earliest instance of the Foreign Office's duplicitous mime; the Germans were shown two faces: the congenial countenance of Simon, and the skeptical brow of Eden; the former being presented in a higher position of authority, and the latter flying subsequently to Nazism's enemy. The display was as much for the consumption of Germany as it was for that of European diplomacy: poised on this perennial ambivalence, Britain was best situated to carry out her plan.

As the follow-up to the March encounter, Hitler delegated the Anglophile Joachim von Ribbentrop, a former champagne dealer who had married into a wine dynasty and joined Nazism via von Papen, to seal in London the '35 percent deal' for the German navy.

'Never Forget,' Ribbentrop was warned before the negotiation by the military attaché of the Japanese embassy in London, Navy Captain Arata Oka, 'that the British are the most cunning people on earth, and that they graduated to absolute masters in the art of negotiation as well as in that of manipulating the press and public opinion.'[121] But neither Ribbentrop nor any other Nazi had the faintest idea of what sort of cunning they would be dealing with.

Talks commenced on May 24 at the Foreign Office in the presence of the benevolent Simon. Ribbentrop, as expected, demanded that the British acquiesce to the ratio advanced by Hitler in March. But Simon turned red; he glowed with fury: he found the request outrageous and such dilettante bluster unacceptable. That ended the discussion. Ribbentrop and his team were, to say the least, confused. Two days later, however, the German legation was conveyed to the wainscoted halls of the Admiralty, where Simon's Deputy, Sir Robert Craigie, announced with composure that Britain accepted the German offer: Ribbentrop's associates were speechless at their good fortune.[122] Thereupon Hitler phoned Ribbentrop: 'Good job,' he thundered, 'this is the most beautiful day of my life.'[123] All would have been perfect had the Fellows not subsequently refused to admit Ribbentrop's son to Eton.[124]

*In the space of six months, spanning between the Norman-inspired Anglo-German Payments Agreement of late 1934, and the Naval Pact, officially signed on June 18, 1935, Hitler won from Britain no less than her official financial and military support. The Führer was exultant.*

And France, disheveled, didn't know where to turn: in mid May 1935, in despair, she concluded pacts of mutual assistance with Russia and Czechoslovakia.

On June 19, 1935, Edward VIII made his debut as the pro-Nazi candidate when at Queen's Hall he delivered a speech to the ex-combatants of the

Legion inviting them to bury the animosity of the Great War between Britain and Germany forever. He was showered with a standing ovation, while all around the Union Jack mingled with the gamma-crossed standards of the German veterans. The speech made a splash, and King George was quite appropriately disturbed.[125] A month later, it was Hitler who received the British combatants at the Chancellery: together they evoked the days of the trenches, reminiscing with passion, as if they had been brothers-in-arms firing from the same dugout.[126]

The biennium 1936–37 represented the apogee of appeasement. Its beginning was of promise: on January 19, 1936, King George V sank into his final sleep, which was shortened by an injection of morphine and cocaine, so that he might be declared dead in the morning edition of *The Times*.[127] He was succeeded by Edward, Prince of Wales, the Nazi candidate himself. The ceremony of the coronation was fixed for May of the following year.

*Then in March 1936, Germany locked irreversibly into the path to war*; she was ready to play her first gambit: the occupation of the demilitarized zone of the Rhineland. As seen earlier, the clause in the Versailles Treaty contemplated the consequences of such a move in no ambiguous language. If a single German soldier trespassed on the Rhineland buffer, *it was war*: Britain, Italy, and Belgium would have rushed at once with swords drawn to back up France.

The half-baked 1936 Wehrmacht of Hitler was in no case a match to France's tested *force de frappe*: 'France,' General Jodl would confess at Nuremberg, 'could have blown us into pieces.'[128]

Regardless, the Führer 'gambled.' On March 7, denouncing the Franco-Soviet agreements, Hitler ordered three meager battalions to cross the Rhine. France's wall, the Maginot Line, was on full alert; her North African troops massed on the border – all she needed was a signal from London. Von Neurath, Germany's Foreign Secretary, was terrified; Hitler, trembling with emotion no less than his minister, spoke words of strength for them both: fear not, he whispered, Britain shall not budge.

And indeed she did not: by the evening of the seventh, her stewards were scrambling all over to shield the Nazi advance. The press magnates, Lord Beaverbrook of the *Daily Express*, who was also courting the Russians since June 1935 on behalf of his intimate Churchill,[129] and Lord Rothermere of the *Daily Mail*, cheered loudly for Hitler and Germany. '[Hitler:] All the Beaverbrook-Rothermere circle came to me and said: "In the last war we were on the wrong side."'[130]

From London, Lord Lothian and Lord Astor, intoning the usual refrain that Germany was the dam against Bolshevism, scolded their French colleagues for being so 'quarrelsome'[131] about Germany's understandable desire to walk into 'her own backyard.'[132] Thereafter Eden and Lord Halifax flew to Paris to deliver France a double blow. Upon arrival, Eden enjoined: 'refrain from any act conducive to war, England wants peace.' And Halifax doubled: 'settle the issue with negotiation.' Flandin, France's Foreign Minister, did not understand; 'if England acts,' he insisted, 'she will lead Europe...this is her last chance. If she does not stop Germany now, all is lost...'

France had not read Mackinder.

All the British gave France after this decisive Nazi sortie, as a sop, was a public session in London at the Council of the League of Nations on March 14. On this occasion, Eden, in a perfect construct of Foreign Office double-speak phrased for the pleasure of Nazism, averred that *the occupation of the Rhineland was a violation of the Treaty of Versailles, but did not represent a threat to peace. It compromised the power of France, but not her security.* The French were stupefied.

Britain had flagrantly dishonored her pledge to guarantee the security of Europe. The following day, Eden, as if nothing had happened, invited Ribbentrop for breakfast to pore over some maps and canvass German geopolitics. On March 29, without wasting an instant, Goebbels appealed to the Rhineland with one more referendum to suffrage its incorporation into the Reich: 99 percent favorable.[133]

For the British set-up, the appeasing thrust could not but elicit an opposite reaction: after the Rhineland coup, the anti-Nazi faction led by Churchill was turned with Jewish funding into a faster, more articulate and most secret outfit known as The Focus. As was the expressed wish of its leader, no detailed record of the group's formation and activities has ever been divulged.[134]

But Hitler was not in the least worried by Churchill's party which, to him, was just an annoyance capable of nothing more than words. After March, the Nazis were ever more willing to indulge their British infatuation – with torrents of champagne, feasts, conferences, summer and winter Olympics, and the disclosure of military secrets. Yet the Führer yearned for something of heavier symbolism – an encounter at the very top, say, with the Prime Minister, Baldwin. Baldwin knew better, and courteously declined the invitation.[135] Instead, the Prime Minister fished Lloyd George from the extras of Britain's appeasement and sent him off to meet the Führer in his Eagle's Nest in the Bavarian Alps.

Thus the event was charged with a symbolism of a different valence: on September 4, 1936, Hitler clasped hands not with his British opposite, but with one of Nazism's most accomplished midwives: that same Lloyd George that had cut the deal in Versailles. The two conversed animatedly about the war, politics, and labor issues. Hitler, overawed by his guest, whom he described as a 'genius,' wished to display him at the party convention in a few days, but Lloyd George, with caution, refused, though he did not refrain from bad-mouthing the Czechs[136] – a hint.

In sum, the encounter was another success, and Lloyd George would thereafter extol the Führer in the press, acknowledging him as the 'greatest German of the age.'

With regard to this episode, the question has been raised: 'Who fooled whom?'[137] That the British government fooled the Germans is hardly disputable; whether Lloyd George was a conscious or an unconscious tool of such a manipulation is irrelevant – and the only striking certainty is that Hitler and the Nazis never fooled anyone.

And the foolery went on, ever more imaginatively. At this time Edward, the new king, had an American mistress: Mrs. Wallis Simpson.

In the last months of 1936, the Prime Minister, Stanley Baldwin, with the complicit act of Edward, was about to carry off a phenomenal show. The Prince of Wales was most likely instructed to go about reciting the mantra 'No marriage, no coronation,' whereby he publicly conditioned his coronation on making Wallis, a twice-divorced American commoner, his Queen. Baldwin would have then seen to it that a press campaign and a query submitted to the Dominions as to appropriateness of the choice of bride would have gone against the marriage.[138] And so it did on November 16; afterwards Edward faced three choices: (1) give up Mrs. Simpson and keep the throne, (2) dismiss Baldwin and his Cabinet, (3) abdicate.

Although Wallis implored the Prince to keep his throne, and her as his concubine almighty,[139] Edward, for 'love,' chose the least sensible option and abdicated on December 10, 1936. 'God save the King,' he shouted at the end of his speech. Albert, the Duke of York, ascended to the throne as George VI: thus the royalty was split between a conventional regent and his brother, the 'pro-Nazi' Edward, who would thenceforth acquire the title of Duke of Windsor.

The Nazis mistook the abdication for the result of an inner struggle to purge the royalty of its alleged 'pro-German' sympathizers, which did not exist, and though the Führer was distressed by the event,[140] the aim of the ploy was to keep him always hanging with a tantalizing game of wink and brush-off – which was working perfectly.

In June 1937, Edward and Wallis married in France, and in October they were invited to Germany for a grand tour of the Reich: everywhere the Duke and Duchess were hailed, and Edward requited the salute. On October 12, 1937, the day following their arrival, Edward was introduced in the house of Robert Ley, the Nazi Labor Secretary, to Himmler, Goebbels, and Hess[141] – an encounter for which the intelligence services had prepared him two and half years previously.

Finally, in November 1937, after all this profusion of geniality on the part of Britain, the time came to thrust the Führer forward on to war. *The mission of Lord Halifax on November 19 to the alpine residence of Hitler was the turning point in the dynamics leading to World War II.* By this time, the broad aggregation of the appeasers dissolved into the two main 'parties' of Britain:[142] the anti-Bolsheviks, who had regained the helm with Neville Chamberlain, and the Round Table, the two being relayed by the propaganda of the Peace Party, which fluctuated in their midst (Figure 5.2). The Nazis now stared at three different facets of a single front urging them to expand their European stronghold before aggressing the Soviets.

In synthesis, Halifax told Hitler that: (1) Britain considered Germany the bastion against Communism; (2) Britain had no objection to the German acquisition of Austria, Czechoslovakia, and Danzig; and (3) Germany should not use force to achieve her aims in Europe.

In the light of (1) the agenda set in *Mein Kampf*, which all British stewards had studied carefully, (2) the world's full-fledged rearmament, (3) the steady and intense supply of British and American weapons the Nazis had received during the past four years, and (4) the Reich's notorious preparations for Barbarossa, Hitler was justified in disregarding entirely the specious warning not to use force: in brief, Britain was urging him to go ahead. Ordinary Britons, and the rest of the world, were told nothing of this autumnal pact.

'*So oder so,*' 'in one way or another,' Hitler decided in January 1938 'to achieve self-determination for the Austrians': in other words, he was going to annex the country. In February, the Prime Minister, Neville Chamberlain, and the Secretary of the Treasury, Sir Eric Simon, announced in the House of Commons that Great Britain could not be expected to support Austrian independence. This was the signal.

On March 12, Hitler marched into Austria and asked the Austrians thereafter to sanction the deed with a referendum: 99.7 percent swung to his side in favor of *grossdeutsch* unity – the Push to the East had begun. Czechoslovakia was next.

On April 21, 1938, General Keitel received orders from Hitler 'to draft plans for invading Czechoslovakia.'[143]

It is important to emphasize that at this point not a single maneuver on the path to war was the fruit of Hitler's strategy or imagination; the schemers of Versailles had prepared the route for him long ago, and the British stewards were now facilitating the progression.

By sequestering the 3.4 million Sudeten Germans (22 percent of the population) into the artificial creation of Czechoslovakia in 1918–20,[*] the old treaty furnished the Führer with the beautiful pretext of claiming these back into the Reich in the name of 'ethnic self-determination' – and so Hitler did.

The British press – again, the *Daily Mail* of the appeasing Rothermere – opened fire with a leader on May 6 denouncing Czechoslovakia as a hateful country, inhabited by rascals, whose treatment of the German-speaking Sudeten was an outrage that Britain could not tolerate.[144]

Once more, France, the helpless Marianne forsaken by Britain, scurried around frantically to patch up some kind of belated common front against this Nazi juggernaut – whose 15-year incubation France's mischievous pride had ultimately favored.

In May she supplicated the Russians to intervene on her side against Germany. She appeared to be utterly unaware that both Britain and Russia, who always seemed to be playing in tandem, had no intention whatever of stopping Hitler at this point.

Russia replied that she would do so as long as Poland and Romania afforded her the passage of Soviet troops in their territory (see Figure 5.3). Which was a bluff, because the Soviet Union did nothing to dissipate the rancor and seething hostility that divided her from Poland on one hand, and Romania on the other. France then implored both countries, but they refused: they did not trust the Russians, least of all in their home – 'Give up,' said Poland to France, 'Czechoslovakia is dead.'

As France insisted, on May 20, 1938, Litvinov, Russia's cunning Foreign Secretary, torpedoed once and for all France's endeavors to convey Soviet divisions westward by raising the prospect of Russia attacking Poland: Russia might have to do so, fibbed Litvinov, to protect Czechoslovakia from the greed of Poland, which wanted to rob the former of the coal-rich district of Teschen. Thus the Soviets hamstrung France's tangled skein of alliances. And once again, by the end of May, the ball was in Britain's court.[145]

Poland was the keystone of the pre-war crisis because: (1) thanks to Versailles, by means of the Corridor, she might be set at variance with Germany; (2) she was allied to France; (3) but she was indeed hostile to Czechslovakia, who was an ally of France; (4) she was temporarily allied to

---

[*]   See Chapter 2, p. 65.

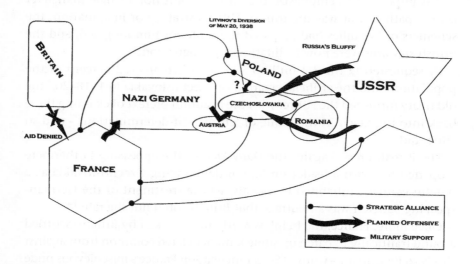

*Figure 5.3*   Alliances and threats on the eve of the Czechoslovak crisis, 1938

Germany, the enemy of France, and (5) she was sharply hostile to the USSR, the mortal enemy of Germany. Poland's buffer position allowed Britain to buy precious time to direct the march of the Hitlerites.

The combined forces of Britain, Russia, Czechoslovakia, and France would have literally pulverized the Wehrmacht in 1938: all the powers involved knew this.[146] Especially Britain, who, within two weeks of Hitler's annexation of Austria, moved to emasculate Czechoslovakia and allow Hitler and herself to complete military preparations.

Already on March 24, Neville Chamberlain, sending another smoke signal to the Nazis, announced that Britain would refuse to lend assistance to the Czechs if they were attacked or to France is she went to their rescue.

At the end of May 1938, Hitler marked the date for striking at Czechoslovakia: October 1. Then a group of generals clustered round the Chief of the General Staff, General Ludwig Beck, hatched a plot in three phases: (1) they would attempt to dissuade the Führer from his plan; (2) they enjoined Britain to stand firmly by Czechoslovakia and promised Hitler that she would fight him; and (3) if Hitler persisted in his resolve to wage war, they would proceed to assassinate him – the date was set for September 28, 1938. 'Although message after message was sent to Britain in the first two weeks of September...the British refused to cooperate.'[147]

Instead, the stewards – Halifax, Simon, Hoare, the British Ambassador in Berlin, Henderson, and the whole set – launched a disinformation/

terror campaign in grand style: they began interminable and most intricate negotiations by which they sought to persuade the Czechs to surrender to the Reich the German-speaking Sudeten districts, upon which, most importantly, were erected first-class fortifications that would have posed a serious obstacle to a Nazi advance.

The argument they peddled for the purpose declared that: (1) Czechoslovakia would have been irremediably smashed in a war against Germany (which was false); (2) Russia's military value was nil (which was false); (3) the Soviet Union wouldn't have honored her alliance with the Czechs (which was true only insofar as Britain herself did not intervene); and (4) Germany would have been merely satisfied with the Sudeten regions (false) and with the Polish Corridor (true). 'To make their aims more appealing they emphasized the virtues of "autonomy" and "self-determination."'[148]

The British plan, clearly, was to dismember Czechoslovakia which, with 34 sterling divisions, 1 million men, well trained, and with a high morale, could very well stall Hitler in the middle of Europe.

Meanwhile, to sell these catastrophic lies to the public, the stewards unleashed a bogus terror campaign, *which the Peace Party amplified*, by grossly exaggerating Germany's bellicose potential, misrepresenting the fighting assets of the Czechs, and presaging the absurd threat of an aerial attack by the Luftwaffe, accompanied by gas attacks: in the first weeks of September, Londoners were fitted with gas masks and were taught air raid shelter drills.[149]

Then, to shield Hitler from General Beck's conspiracy, in September Chamberlain flew to Germany twice, on the 15th and 22nd, to reach an agreement that would prevent the Nazis from going to war over Czechoslovakia – for their own good. An elderly British Prime Minister boarding a plane for the first time in his life...to rush to Germany. Unheard of. '[During the Czech crisis, Chamberlain] used secret messengers to let Hitler know that he should ignore tough official statements that might emerge in the next few days from Britain and France regarding Czechoslovakia.'[150]

The talks would lead to Chamberlain's infamous radio speech of September 27: 'How horrible, fantastic, incredible it is that we should be digging trenches and trying on gas masks here because of a quarrel in a far-away country between people of whom we know nothing.'

The following day, the day the generals were going to pull the trigger on the Führer, France, Germany, England, and Italy convened in Munich to carve up Czechoslovakia, without consulting anyone, least of all the

Czechs: the homeland that the Anglo-French had granted the Czechs in 1919 as a reward for their provocation in Siberia they now took away. In four stages, Germany occupied the designated and fortified areas, while the rump of Czechoslovakia was to be guaranteed by France and Britain – the guarantee would never be given. The Czech army disbanded, and on October 10, the Czechs surrendered another piece of their mangled estate to the Poles.

On October 21, Hitler issued orders to invade the rump and turn it into a protectorate, which punctually came to pass on March 14, 1939 – the Czechs offered no resistance. And Montagu Norman, picking the pockets of the senseless victims, remitted to the Reichsbank, treacherously, £6 million of Czech gold held in custody at the Bank of England. That Norman was in close contact with the Chamberlain faction is certain (it couldn't have been otherwise), but the nature and content of their interaction have never been revealed.[151]

Now, to finish off Versailles, only Poland remained – and after that, Germany would be at the gates of the Soviets: Captain Winterbotham, the British spy, had recently returned from Eastern Prussia, where the district leader had confided to him that Barbarossa should have been operational by May 1941.[152] There was *nothing* that England did not know.

The stewards changed costumes once more (Figure 5.2). Appeasement, as a public stance, was finished: after the Czech invasion, it could no longer be 'sold' to the masses. So a different configuration emerged: the pro-Nazi Peace Party took the back-seat to posture as an elitist den of frondeurs, while the Round Table and the anti-Bolsheviks fused in an informal 'diarchy,' whereby the visible front, led by Halifax, made a pretense of enforcing tough-dealing with the Nazis, while the secret front, staffed with the Chamberlain group, continued to bestow upon Hitler concessions and 'friendly' assurances that Britain wouldn't fight.[153]

Hitler had gone as far as he had been allowed, and it was time for Britain to set him up on the Western Front and thus precipitate the war. On March 31, 1939, 'Exactly half-way between the public break-off and the secret resumption of…economic negotiations with Germany,'[154] Chamberlain informed the House of Commons that 'in the event of any action which clearly threatened Polish independence, His majesty's Government would feel themselves bound at once to lend the Polish Government all support in their power.'

This was an extraordinary assurance. The British government since 1918 had resolutely refused any bilateral agreement guaranteeing any state in

Europe. Now they were making a *unilateral* declaration in which they obtained nothing but in which they guaranteed a state in *eastern* Europe, and they were giving that state the responsibility of deciding when the guarantee would take effect, something quite unprecedented.[155]

No matter how shrewd as to realization and timing, the strategy of Britain was always the same: that is, pit foe against foe and secure her own involvement by priming satellite nations like land mines encircling the enemy of choice – in this case, the Germans. What she had done by guaranteeing Belgium on the eve of World War I, she now replayed with Poland.

Hitler had begun talks with Poland in October 21, 1938, by asking, predictably, for the city of Danzig and a kilometer-wide strip across the Polish Corridor to provide a highway and a four-track railroad under German sovereignty. These, indeed modest, requests were made to the Polish ally in an atmosphere as cordial as possible; they were the last, paltry shreds of Germany lost at Versailles: Hitler had no desire to overrun Poland, but rather to engage her in the forthcoming onslaught against Russia.[156] Yet by late March, Poland turned litigious, and at first, the Führer, not realizing that Britain had made clandestine overtures to Warsaw, could not fathom 'Poland's newfound resilience.'[157]

Not content with duping the Nazis, the British inveigled the Poles as well by making them believe that Britain and France would have unbridled a full-scale offensive against Germany, should the latter have decided to strike at Poland. But in the late spring of 1939 no aid worthy of the name, consisting of either men or munitions, was seen traveling from the Allied countries to Poland: 'Britain had stalled when Poland requested economic help and military equipment to prepare to deal with a German invasion.'[158] By May, Hitler readied his generals to consider Britain, for a time, the proximate enemy.

From London, the Chamberlain group continued to dance with the Nazis, promising as late as August a 'full-bodied political partnership' in exchange for peace,[159] while the Round Table persisted in urging the Poles not to back down.

Hitler refused to believe that the Anglo-French were in earnest – it was a put-on, he concluded. He was fully armed, he had lost the Poles, he needed to strike – he was going to have the war that he wanted.

In the spring of 1939, Roosevelt's clandestine emissary, Supreme Court judge Felix Frankfurter – who was close to the American Jewish Committee, which, in turn, stood 'at one or two removes' behind The Focus – visited

London. Soon after his departure an extravagant publicity campaign began on Chuchill's behalf.[160] The War Party was thus catapulted to the vanguard of British policy (Figure 5.2), eager to meet Hitler on the battlefield. In May 1937, when Germany had dismissed Churchill as a political lightweight, the bulldog had warned Ribbentrop: 'Do not underrate England…She is very clever. If you plunge us all into another Great War she will bring the whole world against you.'[161]

Before commencing, however, the Führer had to think the unthinkable: to sign a truce with none other than Bolshevik Russia to sweep Poland out of the way.

### A Soviet tale of madness and sacrifice

All appeased the Nazis: the Pope for fear, the British by design, and the Russians to buy time. Stalin, too, had read *Mein Kampf*[162] – he harbored no illusions: the Nazis would come to him sooner or later.

Russia underwent her first Five-Year Plan in October 1928, four years later than Germany's: from the latter the Soviets imported large amounts of capital equipment and machine tools; Krupp and the aircraft-maker Junkers possessed installations in anti-capitalist Russia, as did such jewels of corporate enterprise as Standard Oil, the enthusiastic Nazi-phile Henry Ford, and a variety of other Anglo-American concerns involved in the extraction of gold and oil. Stalin planned on trebling the production of iron, coal, and oil. To justify the forced industrialization of the country, he raised the spook of a forthcoming aggression from the West, and proceeded to consummate the endeavor at the expense of 25 million peasant households – the Kulaks. Five million of them were obliterated while their estates were shattered and collectivized. The environmental and economic repercussions, let alone the human strain of such a sacrifice led Stalin's Russia by 1930 to such a disastrous impasse that only the capitalist rescue of the West enable him to tide over his dictatorial caravan to the next and last stage of the great pre-war mummery. For instance, the dam on the Dniepr – the greatest of such salvaging investments – was funded by US money and fitted by a British concern.[163]

When Hitler came to power, Stalin observed. He watched the suppression of the German Communists with utter detachment – such was the deserved fate of what had been all along an expendable crew since the early 1920s. And in June when the Führer purged the dissenters in his bosom, then Stalin realized that the incubation was terminated, and that Adolf Hitler was indeed the piper conjured at Versailles who would be leading the German hordes into Russia.

Presently, he too had to appease. Britain's game was transparent: as in World War I, she wanted Russia to win the war in Eurasia for her by swallowing the Nazis into the steppes and devour them, like the Whites, in a drawn-out and prolonged effusion of blood. To Churchill, Baldwin would thus sum it up in July 1936: 'If there is any fighting in Europe to be done, I should like to see the Bolshies and the Nazis doing it.'[164]

It was understood that the fighting should have been to the detriment of Germany rather than Russia, as Veblen had wrongly assumed. And the USSR, ever the imaginary foe of the Anglo-American oligarchy, would oblige. For that, though, the path had to be cleared of any kind of disagreement, of any kind of old Bolshevik talk – the talk, say, of Trostky and of all those who wanted to fight too soon and too far afield, overstepping the present entrenchment of Russia, which was in line with the designs of the Sea Powers, and in the name of junkyard bywords such as 'world revolution' or 'Socialist brotherhood.' A corps not of doctrinaires, but of two-faced tacticians was what was needed in the Red Army and the Politburo. And Hitler, with his fire and night of the long knives, provided the Red Czar with the inspiration.

In the wake of the holocaust of the Kulaks and the ensuing catastrophes, the majority of the army, the peasantry, the commissars, and 90 percent of the party machine had come to stand foursquare against Stalin's regime.[165]

The pressure was about to reach breaking point when, suddenly, on December 1, 1934, the Stalinist nomenklature moved to head off the opposition. Laying hold of another useful idiot, the secret police of Leningrad 'oriented' this obscure and allegedly 'hysterical'[166] student by the name of Nikolaev into the corridors of the Smolny Institute.* There, Sergei Kirov, Stalin's old comrade, and at the time his leading rival, was shot dead by the young unknown: twice Nikolaev had been found by the local police wandering around the Institute, *armed*, and twice upon higher and veiled orders he had been released, till Kirov fell.

Stalin rushed to Leningrad to find, as Hitler did in Berlin the year before, that the intelligence services were serving him a 'fire' and 'the arsonist' on a silver platter. And the arsonist, as the Russian public was subsequently disinformed, was but the tip of a vast terrorist network woven by a gang of Trostkyite saboteurs, in cahoots with the German Reaction – a variation on

---

* The school for noblewomen from which Lenin directed the Bolshevik *coup d'état* on 25 October 1917, and which was later taken over by the Communist Party of Leningrad.

the usual 'terrorist lie' that generally inaugurates a coup carried from within by the most conservative and unscrupulous fringe of a despotic regime.

Two days after the assassination, Nikolaev 'accidentally' perished in a Leningrad police van while the first wave of the great Stalinist purge washed over the apparatus of the Soviets: hundreds were immediately rounded up, laboriously tortured and killed; hundreds of thousands were shipped off to Siberia. This was only the beginning of a five-year slaughter, which shaded off into delirium during the great Show Trials of the Stalinist era.

Not coincidentally, the first season of such theatrical trials was produced by Stalin within a few days after the German occupation of the Rhineland, in March 1936: before the much aroused audiences of the world, the former apparatchiks first accused themselves and one other of being foul, shifty vermin, and then shambled to the wall. Face to face with the firing squad, they died shouting hails for Stalin and the Revolution – as if echoing the mutinous SA, who had fallen in June 1934 yelling '*Sieg Heil!*'

By such ways, the old Leninist Guard was flushed down the drain, one faction after another standing trial to betray the next with false accusations planted in pre-packaged scripts recited by a chorus of inquisitors methodically cast for the role. The peak of British appeasement, 1937, marked the paroxysm of the Stalinist Terror, which was but the second cycle of the cleansing mass sacrifices inaugurated by Lenin after the Civil War to keep the conquered beehive of Russia chronically malleable.

As one of Trotsky's men, Radek, too, was doomed. The sinuous propagandist of much Russo-German incestuous dealing and one of the privileged few selected to accompany Lenin in that famous voyage across Germany arranged by Parvus in 1917, Radek was called to the dock, and as all the others before him had done to shield their own families, he lent himself to the sham. On January 23, 1937, in the course of his 'confession,' Radek, summoned by the prosecutor to shed light on his alleged network of 'complicity,' dropped the names of Putna and Tukhachevsky.

Putna was a little known general, but Tukhachevsky was a celebrity. The former was in fact one of the top brains of the Red Army, serving at this time as the military attaché at the Russian embassy in London, whereas the latter was the Red Army's most prestigious commander – the glorious Tukhachevsky. Born a Muscovite patrician in 1893, he joined the Great War as a czarist officer. Captured twice by the enemy in 1915 and 1916, he managed to escape from his German captors by improvising such utterly reckless getaways that romanesque tales of the boldness and soldierly brilliance of this Slav Monte Cristo preceded his return to Russia. It was with the profoundest dismay that Tukhachevsky witnessed the collapse of the

Russian armies during the Kerensky intermezzo, and when the Bolsheviks seized power, he was one of those officers who, unlike the Whites, pitched their sabers in the water and donned the Red Star, resigned in their hearts that the world they had known would never come back, and that Russia had to be created anew.

At only 26, he was made a general in Trotsky's converted divisions – thereupon he would lash at the Whites like Nemesis incarnate, thrashing in sequence the Czech legion and Kolchak in Siberia, and finally dealing the decisive blow in the South to Denikin's loyalist armies. On the home front, he brought to heel rebellious peasant formations even by using poisonous gas. And by the mid 1920s he emerged as the unrivaled prince of the *spets*, the new vanguard of young 'specialists' that dreamt of transforming the old imperial army into a new mechanized fighting device. It was not by chance that he would be chosen to form the strongest link of that subterranean connection that tied the Red Army to the German military–industrial complex from 1926 to 1932. The Russians learned much from the Germans: revolutionary theories on tank warfare from General Guderian, and many other prized secrets from the rest of the Reichswehr's top brass: Schleicher, Bredow, Blomberg...

By 1935, the *spets* had so advanced the metamorphosis of the old Russian army into the hierarchized Moloch of their dreams that Stalin conferred upon the ambitious Tukhachevsky, whom he nicknamed 'Napoleonchik,'[167] and a handful of other 'Kommandirs' the title of Marshal of the Soviet Union – Tukhachevsky being, at 42, the youngest.

By this time, knowledgeable as he was of Germany after nesting for the best part of the Nazi incubation within her officer caste, Tukhachevsky guessed correctly, point by point, the objectives and the timetable of the Hitlerites. There was not an instant to lose: Russia, France, Czechoslovakia, and Britain had to unite and crush Nazism in a major offensive.

In January 1936, following the death of George V, Tukhachevsky was sent to London as Stalin's representative to attend the funeral of the king. Magnificent opportunity: thereafter, in fact, he counted on meeting exponents of the British General Staff, whom Putna had contacted on his behalf. Utterly deceived like everyone else as to the nature and aims of the British empire, he believed that he would need little time to seduce the British generals with what appeared to be an irresistible proposal.[168]

Citing precise numbers, Tukhachevsky invited the British to consider that by 1937 the rearmament pace of Germany would find itself significantly behind the joint production of weaponry by France and Czechoslovakia. And what was more, Russia's scaled-up manufacture of fighter planes, tanks, and cannons, which could have been deployed in Czechoslovakia by means of a spectacular 'aerial bridge' across Poland and Romania, would have made the Allied defense arsenal such that even a pre-emptive blitz against Germany could have neutralized the Nazis without excessive damage.

And the British? They listened politely and shook their heads – not interested. To justify the snub, they would craft the lie that Tukhachevsky had inflated his numbers, the same lie that the stewards upheld when in 1938 they moved to declaw the Czechs. And hadn't Lord Lothian in 1935 confidently assured a group of visiting Ministers from Germany that 'they would cut through Russia as through butter'?

Disheartened, Tukhachevsky left London. And tried again in Paris. But the French showed no inclination to fight at this time, and preferred to repose behind their fortified lines. 'But it'll be too late,' expostulated Tukhachevsky. Only two months later, after the Rhineland coup, France's Foreign Secretary, Flandin, would cry out to the British the exact same words.

Defeated, the young Marshal returned to Moscow – in time to partake in the reunion of the Soviet Supreme. Listening to the speeches of the Foreign Secretary, Litvinov, and of the Prime Minister, Molotov, he was literally struck, if not provoked by the mild, and almost kind words that were spoken towards Germany.

Then Tukhachevsky took the stand and slung around barbs that were meant to cut deep: trenchant words aimed not just at the Nazis, but also at the party grandees that inexplicably soothed them. He spoke exuding the assurance of a general backed by the whole of a powerful army.

If there ever was anybody Stalin should have feared amongst the warriors, Napoleonchik was always the one: temerarious and naturally situated to attract any coherent build-up of insubordination, Tukhachevsky was now putting the whole of Stalin's and Britain's, appeasement at risk.

According to a story, dismissed by some as fantastic, through the White central of Russian émigrés in Paris, the Soviet secret police (the GPU) obtained a dossier falsified by the conniving Nazi intelligence services (the Gestapo), which provided Stalin with 'crushing evidence' that Tukhachevsky, Putna, and their confederates had not ceased to betray Russia for more than a decade by passing on to Germany Soviet classified information.[169]

On June 12, 1937, a laconic communiqué featured on the last page of the press organs reported that Tukhachevsky and Putna had been executed. There followed the liquidation of 35,000 additional officers – about half the commanding corps. All in all, the Stalinists cannibalized with the purges two-thirds of the governing class – roughly 1 million individuals.

Legend has it that Stalin decapitated the Red Army with a view to repelling from Russia the eventual Nazi onslaught and diverting it towards the West – Britain and France – where, as he hoped, the Wehrmacht would crumble, prostrate. But if that were so, why was he so keen on making the Nazi war machine as strong as possible by pursuing doggedly since 1935 a policy of economic cooperation with the Reich?

In fact, while Anthony Eden reached Moscow from Berlin in March 1935, Soviet envoys were in Berlin negotiating with Schacht a long-term loan of 200 million marks, which Stalin would have flaunted as 'his greatest triumph.'[170] On the basis of this and further, larger availments of credit, the Nazis extended technical know-how for a steady and much more significant counterpart of Russian oil, grain, rubber, and manganese, without which, as is widely recognized, the Wehrmacht would have never been in a position to strike in 1939.[171] The collusion was so intense that in April 1937, Kandelaki, Stalin's chief economic legate, was received by the Führer in person. Russian convoys laden with war supplies would be regularly sent to Germany until the very day of the Nazi attack, Operation Barbarossa', June 22, 1941.[172]

In sum, Britain from the right and the USSR from the left had been fitting and rousing this Nazi construction since 1919: the former with diplomatic cunning, American loans, appeasement, the imperial markets, and the support of the Bank of England; the latter with the Red Terror, the sabotage of the Left opposition and vital materials in the run-up to war. Russia and Britain did move in sync. Alone the Nazis would have gone nowhere.

In March 1938, the Soviets acknowledged the *Anschluss* without protest, and in May, as seen, they undermined France's belated efforts to assemble a coalition against Germany. On March 10, 1939, as he broached the question of its late annexations, Stalin displayed such good humor toward the Nazi Reich that three days later Hitler despoiled the rump of Czechoslovakia.

And in the spring of 1939 the masquerade spiraled into the last act.

On one side were the appeasing schemers of Britain, who kept on making all sorts of alluring promises to the Nazis, and who renewed their deceitful oaths on March 16, 1939, by ratifying a master commercial agreement with Germany.[173] On the other was the Churchillian War Party, which pushed for an immediate entente with Russia and France: but it was out of office, and its antics, thus far, were for display only.

On May 19, Chamberlain, responding to Churchill, refused officially to bind Britain in *any* alliance, and seized the moment to laud Poland, grotesquely – Poland, that 'virile nation,' he orated with a straight face, that 'is bound to give us all the aid...it can.'

While the deceptive lure of a British partnership was kept dangling before the eyes of the Nazis until early August (and beyond), from April 1939 Britain conducted mock negotiations with Russia and France – mock negotiations, whose sole intent was to hoodwink the French into believing that Britain was serious about confronting Hitler in the immediate future, and which Britain would finally sap by conveying to Moscow on August 11 a legation of second-rank generals devoid of decisional power.[174]

Russia was no fool to any of these games – in fact she readied herself to deal directly with the Nazis in early May, when Molotov was appointed Foreign Secretary to replace Litvinov, who was Jewish, and was therefore not suitable for negotiating with a Nazi envoy.

Things came to a head on August 19. On that day, Poland, ever more heedless, refused once and for all to allow the passage of Russian troops in her territory, although Romania had agreed to do so; Germany and Russia signed a commercial pact, and Ribbentrop's visit to Moscow was announced.

On August 23, 1939, Hitler's new Foreign Secretary landed in Moscow, and by the late evening it was done: *Nazi Germany and Bolshevik Russia undersigned the stunning Ribbentrop-Molotov Pact of Non-Aggression.* The gem of the document was the secret protocol that envisioned the partition of Poland between the two signatories – just a respite before the great butchery.

Then, in the presence of his Nazi guests, the Red Czar drank to the health of the Führer, waited for Ribbentrop to depart, and finally muttered to the intimate circle: 'Of course, it's all a game to see who can fool whom. I know what Hitler's up to. He thinks he's outsmarted me but actually it's I who tricked him...War would passes us by a little longer...'[175]

World War II was less than a week away.

On August 12, a mere fortnight before the Russo-German truce, Ernst Jünger completed the final draft of *On the Marble Cliffs*, which would be published later in the fall. This was the central novel of the Third Reich, written by the rhapsodist of its warrior caste.[176] Reading it allegorically, the book disclosed an esoteric narrative of the German vicissitudes from the end of the Great War until the vigil of World War II, whose symbolism the Hitlerites would temporarily turn to political use.

*On the Marble Cliffs* told the story of two brothers, who, after taking part as knights in the campaign of Alta Plana gave up the sword and retired to a life of contemplation within the walls of a monastic retreat. The sanctum of the cloister – the venue of rituals untold – was matted by vipers that periodically untangled to form the blazon of the flaming fire-wheel – the swastika.

The brothers had once been initiated into a fraternity, called the Order of the Mauretanians.[177] Power was the principle worshipped in their lodges, and the brotherhood demanded that domination be exercised dispassionately, whether in insurrection or in order – no surprise then if members of parties otherwise mortally hostile were seen conversing amicably in the underground walkways of Mauretania: all of them were pupils of the same master. Such a master was the Chief Ranger, an ogre larger than life, half-giant, half-beast – a tyrant terrible, earthly yet seduced by the ways of 'technique'.

Nestled into the marble cliffs, which looked down upon the prosperous counties of the Marina, the hermitage afforded a vista over Burgundy to the south, and the isle of Alta Plana, enveloped by glaciers. To the north, at the back of the cliffs, ran the marches of the Campagna, which turned into marshland as they neared the long sickle-shaped thickets of the Ranger's sylvan domains. There, in what was known as Flayer's Copse, the monstrous retinue of the Ranger might be espied dispatching sacrificial victims in ways indescribable.

The war on the borders of Alta Plana had forever disrupted the order that reigned over the coastal dominions: gone was the rough core of honor. The Marina was now ridden by crime, and agents and spies, who had descended upon it from the northern dark woods. Biedenhorn, the chief of the army, thus acquired significant clout. In the turmoil, the clans sought him out, as did the woodland riffraff, with whom he compromised by ceding to them the control of several districts. Evil blood thus spread from the forests in the veins of the world and the weak rebelled against the laws that had been issued for their very protection. Resisting the rebellious rage whipped up by the huntsmen and the even cruder foresters stood the proud Belovar, a chief herdsman of the Campagna often seen in the cloister, whose farm was a home to many sons of the land bent on opposing these powers of darkness.

One day, Braquemart, a Mauretanian obsessed by dreams of resurrecting the sun temples of an old race of gods, reached the hermitage, accompanied by a silent young prince, to speak of a plan. Braquemart confided to his hosts his desire to embark on an adventure, to the north, where he would put into practise his theory that in the new hive masters were to be separated from slaves and never allowed to cross-breed again.

Against the counsel of a mysterious priest, the head of a matriarchal church hovering behind the scenes, Braquemart and the prince, joined by the brothers, pushed on and invaded the demoniacal forest. They were backed by Belovar and Sombor – his corpulent son – who sicked on the mastiffs of the Ranger their two packs of snarling molossi, roused by blood they had licked off the flags of their masters.

The hounds of Belovar – the pride of the old man – fought bravely across the ungodly brushes, but the red dogs of the Ranger, whose chilling laugh might be heard from afar, had numbers on their side. Chiffon Rouge, the enormous molossus leading the red pack, came rumbling down upon Belovar and his dogs in charges so violent that soon ill-omened signs of cracking could be seen in the ranks of the herdsmen. They were overwhelmed: one by one they were slain. As they retreated, the brothers discovered the severed heads of Braquemart and the prince impaled upon spikes in a clearing bordering the Copse. When they repaired to the Marina, it was too late: a spectacle of devastation opened before the narrator, who cast a long, lewd glance upon the ruins of the cities that lay smoldering, sparkling with fire like a necklace of rubies.

In the twilit finale of Jünger's fantasia, Chiffon Rouge led the conclusive attack against the hermitage perched on the cliffs, but as the dogs from hell fumbled into the crypt, the sanctuary's snakes wrapped the beasts into their coils and strangled them all.

Meanwhile the villagers hustled in droves to abandon the ravaged Marina in ships overladen headed to Burgundy and to Alta Plana. On one of these vessels the brothers embarked and reached the ice ring of the visible isle, where they were received in the farmstead of hospitable friends – friends that once had been knights whom the brothers had fought in that distant campaign. On seeing their shelter, the narrator concluded, 'we felt we had come home.'

The narrator was Ernst Jünger himself and 'Brother Otho' was his younger sibling Friedrich Georg, both of whom had fought with conviction as commissioned officers on the Western Front during World War I, the 'campaign' against Britain – the icy Albion depicted as Alta Plana, which faced Burgundy, that is, France. The Marina was Germany, and the hermitage was something of a Thule Lodge: the elitist, and occultist, vantage point secured by the counter-initiates of the New Germany – the proto-Nazis like Jünger, who had been originally inducted into the great network of power. The order of Mauretania appeared to be an antipodal Freemansonry, which bred tyranny in all its forms, hence the possibility of chancing in its corridors upon Nationalists slumming with Bolsheviks and professional revolutionaries: possibly men, say, like Parvus and Trebitsch.

The state of decay in which the Marina found itself after the war was a transparent allusion to the corruption of the puppet republic of Weimar: Germany had been turned overnight into a house of sin, where delinquents mixed with the helots, the huntsmen, and foresters. The huntsmen were the Socialists, with whom Biedenhorn, the Chief of the Reichswehr (Groener, Seeckt, Schleicher…), sealed on behalf of the clans (the upper classes) the lurid compact for the suppression of the Councils' Republics. These Councils were in turn infiltrated by the foresters, that is, the Communist agents that had descended from the forests – the sickle-shaped and bloody woods of Bolshevik Russia – into the plains of the Campagna: Central Europe.

Standing guard against these hellish hordes was Belovar, with his son Sombor and their *two* packs of hounds: that is, Hitler, the honorary member of Thule, the portly Göring, and the SA and the SS, who marched behind banners maculated with the blood of the martyrs of November 9, 1923[*] – a consecratory ritual introduced by Hitler in 1926.[178]

The setting was thus laid for the coming expedition of Braquemart and the prince: the invasion of Russia – Operation Barbarossa – led by the top echelons of the SS (Braquemart and his fixation with ancestral archeology), and the Junkers of the Wehrmacht, symbolized by the mute prince, whose silence was the tragic presentiment of a forthcoming doom. Jünger, seeing it as his duty to join this brigade,[†] was yet certain that the 'herdsmen' of Germany would be routed in the deep maws of Stalin – Chiffon Rouge – who appeared to be cheered by the Devil himself – the Chief Ranger. In the end, the Bolsheviks laid waste the whole of Europe while the Nazi initiates forsook the marble cliffs and 'came home' to the oak groves of their knightly brethren in Britain. The defeatist narration of the coming battle against Stalin prompted several party censors, including Goebbels,

---

[*] 'On Sunday morning took place the most singular ceremony of the Third Reich, that of the consecration of the flags. One would bring before the Führer "the flag of blood," that which was carried by the militants killed at the time of the aborted putsch of 1923, in front of the Feldherrenhalle of Munich…With one hand, the Chancellor clasped the banner of blood, and the pennants to be consecrated with the other. He supposedly acted as the vector of a fluid unknown, and thus the blessings of the martyrs were bestowed upon the new symbols of the German Fatherland. Purely symbolic ceremony? I don't think so. There truly lives in the thought of Hitler as in that of the Germans the idea of a sort of mystical transfiguration, analogous to that of the benediction of the water by the priest, – if not to the Eucharist. Whoever fails to discern in the consecration of the flags the analogue of the consecration of the bread is not likely to understand anything about Nazism. I don't know what was the Germany of yore. She is today a great, strange country, more removed from us than either India or China. The flag itself accentuates thus stunning oriental impression…' (Robert Brasillach, *Les sept couleurs* (Paris: Plon, 1939) pp. 123–4).

[†] He would indeed be re-enlisted in World War II as an officer, who would see active duty first in occupied Paris and then briefly on the Eastern Front.

to demand that the book be banned and the author punished, but Hitler intervened personally in the matter, forbidding anyone to molest the bard. Such an allegory, painted by a writer who was at the time imposing himself as one of the greatest literary talents of the twentieth century, with its emphasis on: (1) the religious hatred for the Red Empire in the East, (2) the certainty of spiritual victory over the enemy – the snake smothering the hound – and (3) the hand conclusively outstretched towards the racial brethren of Britain, was precisely the sort of coded message the Führer wished to diffuse in the direction of what he believed to be the British allies of the Peace Party. As they were to take their preliminary steps towards war in a most uncertain environment, whose shifting sands were the work of Britain's unceasing dissimulation, the Nazis endeavored to the best of their ability to secure this elusive partnership with the British empire, which they saw as the fundamental prerequisite for founding their Aztec beehive in the plains of Ukraine.

But even the metaphors of Jünger were powerless to alter a decision made long before Stalin would reach the marble cliffs, by men that never had and never would befriend the Germans.

## Fake war in the West, true push in the East

Poland refused to negotiate and Germany declared war on her on September 1, 1939. On September 27 Warsaw surrendered. As agreed by her barbarous invaders, the country was torn in the middle and its population treated like refuse – the Germans did what they did, and the Russians applied their methods by a preliminary round-up of 22,000 members of the Polish intelligentsia – officers, intellectuals, officials – whom they shot, one after the other, in the nape of the neck before dumping them in the ditches of Katyn.

And with its trumpeted unilateral promise to guarantee the independence of this 'virile nation,' what did noble Britain do? Nothing. She watched impassively.

Everything repeated itself: when war broke out, Churchill was summoned by Chamberlain to resume the command of the Admiralty – the very same post from which in 1915 no less impassively he had let the *Lusitania* sink in the hope of drawing the United States into the conflict.

Formally, Britain was now bound to declare war upon Russia too, but of course, she didn't. And Joseph Kennedy, the American Ambassador in London, who was fascinated by the twisted pattern of British diplomacy, asked Churchill why. The latter replied: 'The danger to the world is Germany, and not Russia...'[179]

During the Polish campaign, the Franco-British contingent numbered 1.5 million troops on the Western Front, where Hitler had stationed a mere 350,000 men – clearly there was no willingness to fight the Nazis. Instead of bombs, leaflets were dropped from planes assuring the German population that the Allies had no quarrel with them, but only with their rulers.[180] Strict orders were issued to the Royal Air Force not to bomb any German land forces – such orders would remain unchanged until April 1940: 'When some Members of Parliament put pressure on the government to drop bombs on German munitions factories in the Black Forest, Sir Kingsley Wood [the Air Minister] rejected the suggestion with asperity: "Are you aware it is private property?"'[181]

And this time the blockade round Germany was perfunctory: throughout the war the Nazi regime would restock its facilities via countless channels from all over the world.

On October 12, Hitler addressed the first of his peace speeches to Britain: along with the desire to come to an understanding, he envisaged the possibility of relegating the Jews in the Polish rump under German control. Britain rejected the overture.

On February 10, 1939, Pope Pius XI died; Pacelli, the diplomatic fox of the Vatican and former nuncio to Germany, succeeded him as Pius XII on March 12.

In late November, Pacelli decided to redeem somewhat the damning mistakes of the past. And he went far. He consented to serve as the liaison between the Catholic resistance in Germany and the British Foreign Office for what was another serious attempt to assassinate the Führer. 'The hazardous nature of such a plot for the Pope, the Curia, and all those associated with the Vatican can be hardly exaggerated.'[182] On December 5 he summoned the British Minister, Osborne, to the Vatican and passed on to him the following information from the German anti-Nazis: (1) in the coming spring Hitler was about to launch a major campaign in the West, and (2) this offensive would not occur if a nucleus of Wehrmacht generals succeeded in overthrowing the Hitlerites – for that, the German rebels conditioned, it was imperative that Britain guaranteed an honorable peace for Germany.

Osborne relayed this to the Foreign Secretary, Lord Halifax, who in turn reported to the Prime Minister, Neville Chamberlain. These plots to assassinate Hitler were always a nuisance and a source of embarrassment to Britain: she did not want the fruit of her conjuration dead just yet;

certainly not at this early stage. And so the stewards sabotaged this plot as well. Osborne complained to the Pope that the coup was 'hopelessly vague,' and Halifax, as disingenuous as could be, lamented that Britain would not collaborate unless the German conspirators showed their faces and submitted a definitive program outlining their intentions. The Pope persisted, but Osborne, cued by his superiors, cut the secret talks short: 'If you want to proceed with a change of government,' he retorted curtly to Pacelli, 'get on with it. I don't see how we can make peace so long as the German military machine remains intact.'[183]

And still no fighting from the Allies – the people called it the '*drôle de guerre*,' the 'funny,' 'phoney,' or 'sitting' war – *Sitzkrieg*.

Between April and May 1940, Hitler occupied Norway and Denmark. And on May Day he launched the invasion of France and the Low Countries. The nine months of the *Sitzkrieg* came to an end.

At long last the War Party, which had been pining for action since 1934, was picked as the first mask of the masquerade: the time of Winston Churchill had arrived (Figure 5.2). Contrary to what transpired from the public debate, the changing of the guard between Chamberlain and Churchill was smoothest: it was indeed a conspiracy of these two to bring about what had been a foregone conclusion for years:[184] On May 10, 1940, Winston Churchill took the helm of the empire as Prime Minister and chief stalwart of the anti-Nazi crusade. Surprisingly, the vast majority of Liberal historians have seldom if ever wondered: if all such fights and feuds within the British Establishment about Germany were real and not feigned, why would Churchill, the staunch anti-German, retain in the Cabinet and in key Intelligence positions most of Chamberlain's entourage?[185] In fact, he kept the very appeasers, the alleged pro-Nazis of yesteryear, many of whom were always 'his men' (for example, Sam Hoare), to do what they had continually done for years with unsurpassed ability, that is, delude the Nazis with the prospect of an alliance – a delusion designed to redirect the Reich towards Russia and gain time before the Americans were drawn into the war.

On May 15 Holland fell. With clemency, on May 24 Hitler allowed the evacuation to Britain of the drifting Franco-British contingent at Dunkirk – 375,000 men, a third of whom were French. Belgium surrendered on the 27th, and the Nazis marched into Paris on June 14, 1940.

After dynamiting the commemorative car at Compiègne near Paris, in which Erzberger had signed Germany's humiliating surrender in November 1918, the Germans proceeded to occupy the north of France so as to keep Britain in watchful view, and surrender the remainder of the country to their French *Collabos* under General Pétain, possibly as a reward for making the victory of the Nazis so suspiciously speedy.

As Prime Minister, Churchill also became the chief choreographer of the masquerade: with over three decades of intelligence operations behind him and an extraordinary talent for theatrical mendacity, he was eminently qualified to direct the final and riskiest steps of the dance. Now was the time to play the Windsor trump card again.

The plot was to create a counterfeit zone of British appeasement in the Iberian peninsula. Windsor would be the bait. Edward was presently serving as Major General of the British Army in the Allied Command stationed in Paris. On May 16, he 'suddenly deserted his post without authorization – a court-martial offense – and took the Duchess to the South of France.'[186] What looked like a mad scramble to escape from the advancing Nazi divisions was instead a secret mission to the neutral terrain of Spain. On June 20, Edward was in Barcelona.

Meanwhile, on May 19 Churchill had dispatched Samuel Hoare as British Ambassador to Madrid: a former 'appeaser' whom the Nazis did trust.

Furthermore, by way of Sweden, the British disinformed the Hitlerites in late May that a core of pacifiers, opposed to Churchill was coalescing around Halifax.[187] The counterfeit bisection of the British establishment into adversary clans, which had been employed for the Trebitsch dupery of 1920, was presently readapted on a giant scale to the last stage of Britain's great deception of the Third Reich (Figure 5.2) – and, not by chance, the same man, Churchill, was behind both operations.

At that time the Nazis were told by double-agents like de Ropp that not until after a major battle, which 'left no doubt about German military might,' would the Peace Party be in a position to topple the Churchill Cabinet.[188]

And the Nazis believed everything: for years they had looked into the eyes of this party, a party which appeared to cast an enormous shadow over the whole of British society: the diplomatic corps, the intelligence services, the intelligentsia, the upper class. All of them seemed engulfed in an assortment of Fascist movements bent on overthrowing the throne should Britain have been invaded and sued for peace. At the grassroots, these groups were variously called The Link, The Right Club, The Nordic League...[189] Few, if any, were genuine.

On July 3 Windsor was in Lisbon – there he lay in wait for the Nazis. He was hosted by rich Portuguese friends, who were linked to the spying web of the Germans. The prince talked much, and the German embassy in Lisbon relayed the conversation to Ribbentrop in Berlin. On July 12, Edward was allegedly heard recommending that the Nazis bomb Britain severely to make her ready for signing an immediate peace with Hitler.[190]

Since July 10, the Luftwaffe had been bombing British ports and logistic positions. Appealing 'once more to reason and common sense', Hitler offered Britain peace in his address of July 19, 1940. And once more Britain rejected it. Three days earlier, the Führer had alerted his generals, theatrically, to 'prepare' for the cross-Channel invasion of England – that great Nazi hoax referred to as Operation Sea Lion (*Seelöwe*): naturally, Hitler would never make good on it. And Churchill knew it.[191]

And then, towards the end of July, the high-level Nazi envoys landed in Lisbon. The documentation pertaining to this mission was suppressed by Churchill himself;[192] only a few coded records survived. From one creditable reconstruction, it emerges that Walter Schellenberg, one of the top agents of the Nazi intelligence services, was joined in Lisbon by his chief, Reinhardt Heydrich, to escort none other than the Deputy Führer, Rudolf Hess, who had flown from Germany to complete a round of secret preliminary negotiations with the Duke – Hess' old acquaintance from 1937.[193]

What they negotiated on July 28 is not known, though it might be easily guessed from the subsequent developments of the war and the further declarations of the Duke to his entourage: namely, that he was not willing to risk civil war in Britain by reclaiming his throne just yet, but that bombing sense into Britain at this stage might have prepared the terrain for his swift return from the Bahamas, whose governorship he had for the time being accepted at the suggestion of Churchill. On August 1, 1940, the Windsors embarked in Lisbon on a liner headed for the Caribbean and stepped down from the stage.

'Unhappy with the Luftwaffe's limited results, [on that very day, Hitler] announced his intention to accelerate the campaign and ordered a massive and continuous onslaught, which he code-named *Adlerangriff*, or Eagle Attack'.[194] This was staged as some kind of thundering preamble to the imaginary land-invasion of Britain, which, having always been in the nature of a *bluff*, was accordingly postponed by the Führer *sine die*. The aerial battle over Britain, which Hitler patently undertook with the greatest reluctance, began on August 13. He had never wanted to fight Britain, nor was he obviously prepared to do so at this time: Germany had but ten submarines in the Atlantic and her bombers were wholly unsuited for independent warfare against Britain. 'Clearly [her] aircraft had never been designed for that purpose.'[195] Not surprisingly, Eagle Attack was a fiasco – it was aborted on September 17, just 36 days after its beginning, and *de facto* terminated on May 10, 1941, after a swap of desultory air raids between enemies.

Windsor had served his purpose in the hands of Chuchill perfectly: he had provoked Hitler into triggering those 'air massacres' that Churchill had been invoking like manna from heaven since 1934, and that since the fall of 1939 he held up to the Americans as the chief lure to drag them into the war. For almost two years Chuchill tried to blackmail the United States, threatening that Britain might have had to surrender her fleet to Hitler if the latter had bombed her into submission. 'Every hour will be spent by the British,' US Ambassador Kennedy predicted, 'in trying to figure out how we can be gotten in.'[196]

The truth was also that the war was costing Britain $1.5 billion per month – this was World War I all over again: America had to be stirred to join, once more, Britain's Eurasian intrigues. But Roosevelt and the clubs behind him needed no persuasion – they had rearmed on a colossal scale since 1938; whatever the New Deal could not do was solved by rearmament: after playing the Russian roulette with Montagu Norman in 1929, America reaped in the subsequent decade 10 million men without work. Eventually, it picked them up, one at a time, and clothed them in khaki, so that by 1940 the reserve army of the jobless had become a drilled fighting corps of 11 million GIs. The United States was dying to fight.

After the inglorious end of the German Reparations in 1932, the Americans had sworn they would sell no weapons to belligerents, and whatever they sold, they would sell for cash. In 1939, however, they revised the legislation and resumed the sale of arms to warring nations; and by the end of 1940, pressured by the British, who were nearly insolvent, they agreed to do so on credit. 'Suppose my neighbor's house catches fire,' Roosevelt tauntingly addressed the American public on December 17, 1940, 'I don't say to him..."my hose cost me $15...I don't want $15 – I want my garden hose back after the fire is over".'[197] This piece of fireside wisdom was turned into law on January 6 1941, as the Lend-Lease Agreement and ratified two months later by Congress – Churchill, immensely pleased, would categorize it as 'the most unsordid act in the history of our nation.' 'We must be,' Roosevelt concurred, 'the great arsenal of democracy.'[198]

Afterwards, the US Administration did not even bother to deviate from the routine of 1916: it insisted, in fact, on establishing American naval escort of supply ships to Britain with a view to setting off a 'shooting war' with the Nazi U-boats.[199] This, however, would not be necessary, for Hitler would declare war on the United States four days after Pearl Harbor, on December 11, 1941.

Meantime, between January and April 1941, the fake Peace Party in England continued to signal to the Nazis.[200]

The preparation for Barbarossa was completed by December 18, 1940; the tentative date for the invasion was set for mid May 1941.

In April 1941, the British informed Stalin of the coming German storm. 'Let them come,' replied the Red Czar, 'we will be ready for them!'[201]

Yet between March and June 1941, the German maneuver in the Mediterranean basin was so successful that the British Foreign Office was seriously preoccupied by the eventuality of a wholesale collapse of its Middle Eastern defensive apparatus. In May 1941, victorious with Rommel in Cyrenaica,[*] and in Crete, the Germans landed aircraft in Iraq: a further deployment by Germany of airborne troops across Syria, Iraq, and Iran would have cut off Britain from her oil supply, and thereby afforded the Reich, by way of India, a much feared connection to the Japanese armies battling in the theaters of Asia.

But on May 10, 1941, Rudolf Hess disappeared.

Where he vanished, and how, and what happened to him afterwards, is not known. The story that fearing a war on two fronts and furiously jealous of the blooming intimacy between his deputy Bormann, and Hitler, the lunatic Hess on a whim flew a ponderous jet over Scotland to rendezvous a cabal of appeasers, strayed off course, ejected himself perilously from the cockpit, landed on a field nearby, twisted his ankle, and presented himself as Captain Alfred Horn to a bewildered Scottish plowman, is a cheap myth. A fabrication which neither the Nazis nor the British, or their loyal archivists, ever endeavored to dispel.

In fact, there appear to be two Hesses,[202] two planes leaving from different locations,[203] two uniforms,[204] an alleged impostor in the prison of Spandau,[205] and an amnesiac, stuporous defendant at Nuremberg,[206] who was alternatively classified by the Allied staff psychiatrists as a 'dull-witted, autistic psychopath,' a 'sham,' an 'enigma,' or 'a schizoid.'[207] A man who refused to see his wife for 28 years, and who died mysteriously – most probably strangled by 'specialists'[208] – the day before his release in 1987.

Whatever the truth of the case, the facts speak clearly. After Hess vaporized:

1. The German deployment in the Far East ceased – Rommel was forsaken at the gates of Egypt; the directive to march to the southeast and the expeditions against Malta and Cyprus were rescinded, definitively. All available German forces were hastily conveyed towards Russia.

---

[*]   Eastern Libya.

Had Rommel succeeded in North Africa...had he reached Suez and penetrated the Near East to make juncture with Japanese forces...The global strategy of the Nazi General Staff would have been immensely advanced towards its goal of global victory...The failure of the Nazi campaign in North Africa must take its place among the great 'ifs' of history.[209]

2.  The night of Hess's disappearance coincided with the final aerial raid conducted by the Luftwaffe against Britain.

On June 22, 1941, a little over a month after the event, at 3:30 am, while German planes bombed Byelorussia, Hitler's 'herdsmen' invaded the Russian forest – they made up a highly mechanized legion of 3 million Germans, Croats, Finns, Romanians, Hungarians, and Italians – with the SS sting in the tail. Awaiting them was an equally large pack of 'red dogs', which in the heat of the clash would grow to be four times as numerous.

*The Nazis surrendered Hess as some form of collateral, and the British 'appeasers' appeared to keep their end of the bargain. Churchill and his military staff would prevent the Americans from opening a western front for a period of three years of unspeakable carnage: they granted the Nazis their yearned 'free hand' in the East.*[210] They gave the Germans some time to sink in the Russian quagmire, before coming with the Americans to finish them off and conquer at last the prized booty of the German Fatherland.[211]

Already on July 26, 1941, Stalin requested an immediate Allied intervention in Western Europe. Churchill refused.[212] In April of 1942, General Marshall of the US Army was in London to discuss the plan of a cross-Channel invasion; Churchill was 'reluctant.' In January 1943, at Casablanca, the American generals again pressed the British to act. Not even in November 1943, when the 'big three'* met in Teheran, would Churchill allow discussion of the western closure before mooting territorial tradeoffs.[213]

Sir Alan Brooks, the Chief of the Imperial Staff, opposed all plans for such an assault, while others, like Churchill, wanted to postpone such an attack indefinitely...The Americans...advocated a [cross-Channel attack] on the largest possible scale at the earliest possible time.[214]

Instead, from the Allies the Russians would get $10 billion worth of guns, and afterwards, as Baldwin had explained to Churchill, who needed no

* Roosevelt, Churchill, and Stalin.

explication, one was to let the 'Bolshies' slowly blow the Nazis to pieces. The deception was sustained unabatedly for the whole duration of Barbarossa: in January 1942 Hitler might still be heard wishing that Hoare would take power,[215] or hoping in the autumn of 1943 that Windsor would overthrow his brother.[216] The Führer would remain a victim of the most astounding illusions till the end.

Not until May 1944 would the British agree to open the Western Front with the cross-Channel operation (Overlord), which had been timidly prefaced by the Mafia-assisted debarkation of the Americans in Sicily – Operation Husky of July 1943. By then the Nazis' invading corps had been so ravaged that 'it became obvious that the Soviet Union was capable of destroying Nazi Germany on her own.'[217]

Then and then only did Britain deem that the time had finally come to dispatch this Nazi creature, by now mortally wounded, that she had nurtured for over a quarter of a century for the sake of her Eurasian ambition.

# 6 Conclusion

Yet it is necessary…to feign, greatly, and to dissemble, for men are so simple, and so prone to obey the exigencies of the moment, that he who deceives will always find someone ready to be deceived.

Machiavelli, *The Prince* (XVIII, 3)

### '*E sono tanto semplici gli uomini…*'

The elimination of the German menace of 1900 cost Britain dearly: her empire, her military and economic strength. Yet the English-speaking idea, the imperial creed, and the cultivation of the oligarchic bent were all traits that she bequeathed upon her natural, insular heir: they live on in the American establishment. Britain's was a conscious decision; she knew the risks involved.

The present geopolitical policy of the United States is a direct and wholly consistent continuation of the old imperial strategy of Britain. It is that unmistakable cocktail of aggression, subversion and mass murder waged at the vital nodes of the landmass, from Palestine and Central Asia to the gates of China, in Taiwan and Korea, that seeks to undermine any movement towards a confederation of nations capable of turning the continental base into a Eurasian league of socio-political cooperation and defense (against Anglo-American assault).

It took two world conflicts to destroy the German threat. World War I was a conventional siege in which the British empire sacrificed roughly 1 million men – the first bloodletting that shook the establishment to its foundations. In the second round, which was necessary given that World War I had in fact left the Fatherland unscathed, no such effusion would have been tolerable – Britain would sacrifice 400,000 soldiers in World War II. So deception was employed on a major scale to trip the Nazis into the inescapable war on two fronts.

That such was the intention at Versailles may not be doubted – the astonishing prophecy of Veblen is there to attest it. Though this is not to say that schemers of the Round Table expected the engineers of the Final Solution. As has been argued throughout this book, they rather conjured a reactionary movement that could then be attracted into the Russian swamp. Which was sinister enough.

The position of Bolshevik Russia is assuredly one of the greatest enigmas of the affair. Even its origin is most mysterious. But one thing is certain: never, either during the interwar period or even in the course of the Cold War, did the Soviet Union play *directly* against the West – that is why Egyptian President Anwar Sadat thought it 'an imaginary foe.' Rather, it appeared to mimic the slow motions of an enormous circus bear, whose tamer was elsewhere – a buttress in the Orient that slumped studiously, shifting its weight around to keep the Eurasian union in check. Otherwise the Trebitsch affair, the German-Bolshevik 'secret' entente, the terrorist agitprop of the KPD, the sabotage of the common front with the German Socialists for the ultimate benefit of Hitler, the extraordinary massacre of the leadership of the Red Army, and Stalin's appeasement, are inexplicable: Stalin played always in line with the geopolitical designs of Britain. Besides, the Bolsheviks owed virtually everything to the West: the deposition of the Czar, the timing of Rasputin's death, the political void after Kerensky, the slush funds – German and otherwise – the double-crossing of the Whites, capital equipment, giant investments, military know-how...

When the hyperinflation climaxed in 1923 the natural candidate for leading the *Radikalisierung* at home came in full view. Of all the rabble-rousers of Germany, Hitler was not only the most charismatic but also the most fervently pro-British: for Britain he was almost too good to be true. That Professor Karl Haushofer was the inspiration for Hitler's British fancy is by no means unwarranted. And Haushofer was himself a mysterious character, of whom we should know infinitely more.* What is certain, however, is the idiocy behind the claim that Hitler assembled the Nazi philosophy and geopolitical plans in the raving solitude of his disarrayed bedroom.

The Wall Street Crash triggered by Norman was the signal that Germany had in fact completed her first informal Five-Year-Plan; thereafter it became a foregone matter that Hitler would become Chancellor. Yet Germany was more resilient than what the British stewards could have imagined: throughout Weimar she would *never* give the Nazis more than 1 out of 3 votes, and that only under the most catastrophic of social circumstances. But by 1933, with further 'tightening from outside,' the circle was closed.

The weave of Britain's interaction with the Nazis consisted in fact of one of history's most astounding exploits of choral dissimulation, which unraveled for more than a decade (1931–43). The problem, however, was

---

* Like Prisoner No. 7 of the Spandau fortress – the man said to be Rudolf Hess – in 1987, Haushofer, too, seemed to have been assassinated, along with his wife, by the British Secret Services on the ides of March of 1946 (for instance, this presumption has reappeared in Martin Allen's *The Hitler/Hess Deception*, p. xviii).

that this was no swanky gimmick but a deliberate tampering with forces that were 'other' – and Veblen, again, intuited this eerie drift as early as 1915. Britain courted fire and in the end wished for a holocaust – which came. That of the war, and that of the Jews.

The 'Bolshies' took the shock of the German offensive and paid with 20 million dead, half of them civilians. This was probably a price that Tukhachevsky was not willing to see his people pay. Nor should it ever be forgotten that 3.5 million German civilians had perished by the end of this game.

If it is true that the British stewards intrigued at Versailles to conjure a reactionary movement that would feed on radicalism and be prone to seek war in the East; if it is true that the Anglo-Americans traded heavily with and offered financial support to the Nazis, continuously and deliberately from the Dawes loans of 1924 to the conspicuous credits via the Bank of International Settlements in Basle of late 1944;[1] if it is true that the encounter in Cologne of January 4, 1933, in von Schröder's manse was the decisive factor behind Hitler's appointment as Chancellor; if it is true that such financial support was accorded to make Nazism an enemy target so strong as to elicit in war a devastating response – retribution that would make the Allied victory clear-cut and definitive; if it is true that appeasement was a travesty since 1931; if it is true that Churchill refused deceitfully to open a western front for three years, during which the expectation was that the Germans would find themselves so hopelessly mired in the Russian bog as to make the British closing onslaught from the West as painless as possible; and if it is true that Hess brought with him to Britain plans for evacuating the Jews to the island of Madagascar, for such was the last policy pursued by the German government before adopting the Final Solution – [2] a plan which clearly was given no sequitur; if all the foregoing is true, then it is just to lay direct responsibility for incubating Nazism and planning World War II, and indirect responsibility for the Holocaust of the Jews, at the door of the Anglo-American establishment.

Clearly, the last 60 years have been devoted by the restless and most faithful archivists of the empire, seconded by a legion of no less devout academics, publicists and film-makers, to deny each of the above statements in the most categorical fashion.

To begin, Veblen's review is literally ignored: on Versailles Keynes is still the adopted 'classic.'

'It is of course an exaggeration,' we read in textbooks, 'to claim that the Dawes loans set in motion foreign lending by the United States...';[3] rather, these loans are depicted as a yet another wave of little nest eggs from America in search of a good yield, and some 'corporate greed' on the side – but nothing more.

The Crash and the crisis? Those, intimated an acclaimed Nobel Prize winner, were but the product of the 'somewhat *fortuitous* combination of structural factors and monetary policy *errors.*'[4]

On the other hand, we are also told that the collapse of the gold-exchange standard and the surreal devaluation of the pound were due to 'an inescapable *error*...of the British who knew [not] the size of the problem they labored under':[5] that is to say that the British Governor was too 'intermittently ill' to be able to look after his messy construction, and 'even when well, [he was] distracted by other pressing matters...'[6] Yet one wonders what those 'other pressing matters' could be...

Thus of Montagu Norman – admittedly the greatest central banker of the modern era, who spent a quarter of a century leading the most powerful financial outfit of his age – we should be satisfied with a caricature featuring him as psychopathic Scrooge of the old school, with only a shaky grasp of modern financial dynamics.

Von Schröder? Schröder counts for nothing, we hear: 'he was merely a partner in a medium-sized *provincial* bank...'[7]

As to that revolting show known as British 'appeasement' (of Hitler), they tell us it was the misguided policy of an 'imbecile Foreign Office'[8] that sought to combine 'morality and expediency' in reaching an agreement with what, alas, proved to be an intractable interlocutor.[9] And the latter-day trumps of the Peace Party who deliberately prolonged the war to gain time? Their cynicism is excused on the grounds that the empire was fighting for its own survival, [10] when in fact it was sacrificing millions to extricate itself from the bloody mess it had forged since 1919.

And the Wehrmacht: was it indeed a strong, luxury item, fitted to its teeth with materials of the highest quality? Of course not, retorted the 'American' Schacht: 'Foreign investigations – some conducted with extreme accuracy– on Germany's financing of warlike expenditure have shown unanimously how thoroughly inadequate our rearmament, and thereby how insubstantial the attending financial outlay has been.'[11] This is from the self-apologetic post-war production of the individual who, for his sixtieth birthday in 1937, had been hailed by the hebdomadary publication of the German army, the *Militär-Wochenblatt,* as 'the man who made the reconstruction of the Wehrmacht possible.'[12] And the damage the Wehrmacht could inflict did not escape the record, irrespective of the falsehoods that Schacht hawked, lying and recanting ignominiously at Nuremberg to save his skin and the name of his protectors. He hid behind the following lies: (1) The Nazis came to power by means of self-financing, (2) the army was of a shoddy make, (3) the Hitlerites violated the economy, and (4) the Nazi economic experiment was a failure as a whole.

The professional literature on the topic has latched onto the Schachtian fabrications with fervor: of the German army it is still said that it was 'a chaos of competing organizations,' worsened by 'Hitler's paranoid style.'[13] Nazi work creation, instead, is described as a 'fragmented' and 'decentralized' endeavor, which owed nothing to Nazi leadership other than 'coercion.'[14] Even the obvious commentary to the steep, sudden boost that Germany experienced after January 1933 in employment, production, and welfare – namely, that such an exceptional recovery after so much misery was a willed feat propitiated by the financial elites of Germany and Anglo-America in collusion with the Hitlerites – has been drowned in a preposterous and interminable debate as to whether, in fact, the Nazi boom was more the bitter fruit of *luck* than of deliberate intervention and efficient economics.[15]

It naturally behooves the establishment to circulate the old superstition that there had been a 'fortuitous turnaround in the second semester of 1932,'[16] a 'natural economic upswing,' whose wind, so the fantasy goes, Hitler luckily caught in his own sails. This noxious fable disposes in one blow of all the thorny issues that bristle in the biennium of 1932–33: namely, the foreign financing of the Nazis, their rigged election to the Chancellery, and the decisional forces behind the full-blown resumption of economic activity under the Third Reich.

Moreover, Nazi economics, fueled by its potent blend of free enterprise, communitarian appeal, industrial brilliance, deep ecology, redistributive policies, anti-plutocratic invective, hi-tech virtuosity, tight regulation, monetary swiftness, and efficient planning, is clearly a phenomenon that comforts no one: neither the Liberal apologists of business nor the doctrinaires of the Left, and not even the anarcho-reformers of regionalism – it is a deep embarrassment for it features too many traits that are dear to them all and is thus better left unmentioned, or at the very least, distorted.

All the more so as the Allies had sunk massive investments in the Third Reich. And this was not done for the cynical sake of profits, but in view of the future reconstruction of Germany under the American aegis – the clubs were already gazing two steps ahead. That Hitler, in time, would lose the war, was understood – and this despite the reprieve the Nazis were afforded by such economic 'help.' Eventually, in 1949, when Germany was torn along the East–West divide, the new Federal Republic was not asked to pay any reparations in cash: it surrendered in kind a mere 4 percent of its industrial capacity. The securities of the German absentees were temporarily sequestered by the occupying Command; the giant industrial combines of the past were broken into smaller concerns and reintegrated into the Common Market of Europe, which was, by way of the new clearings, the IMF, and Marshall Aid, solidly anchored to the outlets of the American empire. Now Washington had Germany *and* the Meditarranean, along with the Pope, whose absolution it bought by refurbishing the bank of the Vatican with millions of dollars earmarked for pro-American action.[17]

And the Shoah? The Anglo-American elites vetoed the Schacht Plan of late 1938. In May 1939, the United States – the future home of much Holocaust museology – would not even offer sanctuary to 1,000 wealthy Jews whom Hitler had allowed to ship out of Hamburg.[18] Nothing came out of the Madagascar Plan, and when the SS penetrated the Russian forests, Churchill allowed them in fact, for his own ends, three long, uninterrupted years to set out on their 'task,' presumably knowing the intentions of the black squads *even before* they began.[19]

The sheer amount of lies perpetrated by the Anglo-American establishment against its public in order to preserve the myth that World War II was a 'good' war, won for a just cause, is incalculable. The proof lies in the myriad of classified files documenting the vital phases of this intrigue, which to this day remain unavailable to the public eye – for reasons of 'national security,' they say.

In sum, the Allied elites have told a story. The story that the Germans have always been disturbers of the peace; they disturbed it once and were punished for it, although a little too harshly. Out of such blundering castigation, an evil force materialized out of nowhere – a force whose evil greatly exceeded the petty severity of the Allies that caused such evil to emerge despite themselves. And, the story goes, the evil of this force grew to be such that a violent global conflict became necessary to uproot it.

More than a cock-and-bull story, this is an insult. And what is worse, every day more and more people, for the sake of psychological tranquillity, choose to believe it. Because individuals, as the loathsome Machiavelli put it in his 'classic' vademecum for subhuman conduct, are 'simple' and willing to trust the word of the constituted authorities. Constituted authorities, which we think embody our will, when in truth they are nothing but high battlements hiding oligarchy and lies, both of which must come to an end.

# Notes

## Chapter 1

1. Robert Deacon, *John Dee. Scientist, Astrologer & Secret Agent to Elizabeth I* (London: Frederick Muller, 1968), pp. 92, 94.
2. Thorstein Veblen, *Imperial Germany and the Industrial Revolution* (London: Macmillan & Co., 1915), pp. 50–84.
3. David Fromkin, *A Peace to End All Peace. The Fall of the Ottoman Empire and the Creation of the Modern Middle East* (New York: Avon Books, 1989), p. 27.
4. Paul M. Kennedy, *The Rise of Anglo-German Antagonism, 1860–1914* (London: Ashfield Press, 1980), pp. 41–58.
5. Michael Balfour, *The Kaiser and His Times* (New York: W. W. Norton & Co., 1972), pp. 54–5.
6. Paolo Giordani, *L'impero coloniale tedesco* (Milano: Fratelli Treves, 1915), pp. 30, 89ff.
7. Balfour, *The Kaiser.*
8. Kennedy, *Anglo-German Antagonism,* p. 110.
9. Bernhard von Bülow, *La Germania Imperiale* (Prodenone: Edizioni Studio Tesi, 1994 [1914]), p. 87.
10. Veblen, *Imperial Germany,* pp. 231–2.
11. Michael Stürmer, *L'impero inquieto, 1866–1918* (*Das ruhelose Reich,* Bologna: Il Mulino, 1993 [1983]), p. 326.
12. Kennedy, *Anglo-German Antagonism,* p. 362.
13. S. L. A. Marshall, *World War I* (Boston: Houghton Mifflin Company, 1992), p. 114.
14. Andreas Dorpalen, *The World of General Haushofer. Geopolitics in Action* (New York: Farrar & Rinehart Inc., 1942), p. 52.
15. Ibid., pp. 194, 196, 198, 200; emphasis added.
16. Carlo Jean, *Geopolitica* (Bari: Laterza, 1995), pp. 29–31.
17. F. von Bernhardi, *Germany and the Next War* (New York: Longmans, Green & Co., 1914 [1911]), pp. 18, 25, 52, 90ff.
18. Niall Ferguson, *The Pity of War* (New York: Basic Books, 1999), pp. 169–73.
19. Robert L. Owen, *The Russian Imperial Conspiracy [1892–1914]* (New York: Albert and Charles Boni, 1927), p. vii.
20. Ibid., pp. 3, 25–6.
21. See for instance, Donald Kagan, *On the Origins of War, and the Preservation of Peace* (New York: Doubleday, 1995), pp. 206–12.
22. Evgheni Tarle, *Breve storia d'Europa* (Bologna: Editori Riuniti, 1959 [1928]), p. 354.
23. Stürmer, *Impero inquieto,* p. 440.
24. T. H. Meyer (ed.), *Light for the New Millennium. Rudolf Steiner's Association with Helmuth von Moltke. Letters, Documents and After-Death Communications* (London: Rudolf Steiner Press, 1997), p. 3.
25. Carroll Quigley, *Tragedy and Hope. A History of the World in Our Time* (New York: Macmillan Company, 1966), p. 100.
26. Dmitri Volkogonov, *Trotsky, the Eternal Revolutionary* (New York: The Free Press 1996), p. 42.
27. Tarle, *Breve storia,* p. 143.
28. A. S. Erusalimskij, *Da Bismarck a Hitler. L'imperialismo tedesco nel XX secolo* (Roma: Editori Riuniti, 1974), p. 185.

29. Greg King, *The Man Who Killed Rasputin. Prince Felix Youssoupov and Murder That Helped Bring Down the Russian Empire* (New York: Citadel Press, 1995), p. 27.
30. Fromkin, *Peace*, p. 31.
31. Erusalimskij, *Bismarck*, p. 198.
32. Balfour, *The Kaiser*, p. 328.
33. Ibid., p. 203.
34. Quigley, *Tragedy*, pp. 226, 228.
35. Léon Degrelle, *Hitler: Born at Versailles* (Costa Mesa: Institute for Historical Review, 1987), p. 111.
36. Erusalimskij, *Bismarck*, p. 255.
37. Quigley, *Tragedy*, p. 221.
38. Owen, *Russian Imperial Conspiracy*, p. 15.
39. Leon De Poncins, *The Secret Powers Behind Revolution* (San Pedro, CA: GSG Publishers, 1996 [1929]), p. 78.
40. Degrelle, *Hitler*, pp. 14–15.
41. Such was one of the several attributes wherewith Timothy McVeigh (the man convicted of bombing the FBI building in Oklahoma City, April 19, 1995), a modern-day Princip in his own right, was labeled in the public discussion of his case (Gore Vidal, *Perpetual War for Perpetual Peace: How We Got to Be So Hated* New York: Thunder's Mouth Press, 2002, p. 121).
42. Erusalimskij, *Bismarck*, p. 234.
43. Ibid., p. 235.
44. The philosopher Bertrand Russell wrote: 'I had noticed during the previous years how carefully Sir Edward Grey lied in order to prevent the public from knowing the methods by which he was committing us to the support of France in the event of war' (Fromkin, *Peace*, p. 125).
45. Tarle, *Breve storia*, p. 279.
46. Quigley, *Tragedy*, pp. 316–17.
47. Owen, *Russian Imperial Conspiracy*, p. 14.
48. Erusalimskij, *Bismarck*, p. 269.
49. Balfour, *The Kaiser*, p. 351.
50. Quoted in Geminello Alvi, *Dell'estremo occidente. Il secolo americano in Europa. Storie economiche* (Firenze: Marco Nardi Editore, 1993), p. 75.
51. Degrelle, *Hitler*, p. 86.
52. Fromkin, *Peace*, p. 125.
53. Erusalimskij, *Bismarck*, pp. 255–56.
54. Adolf Hitler, *Mein Kampf* (Boston: Houghton Mifflin Company, 1971 [1924–26]), pp. 163–4.
55. Meyer, *Millennium*, p. 89.
56. Quigley, *Tragedy*, p. 230.
57. Dennis Wheatley, *Red Eagle. The Story of the Russian Revolution* (London: Book Club, 1938), p. 103.
58. B. H. Liddell Hart, *The Real War, 1914–1918* (Boston: Little, Brown, & Company, 1930), p. 113.
59. Richard Pipes, *A Concise History of the Russian Revolution* (New York: Vintage Books, 1995), p. 77.
60. John Maynard, *Russia in Flux* (New York: Macmillan Company, 1948), p. 173.
61. King, *Rasputin*, pp. 148–62.
62. R. H. Bruce Lockart, *British Agent* (London: G. P. Putnam & Sons, 1933), p. 161.
63. For a GNP of 20 billion rubles in 1913 (Paul Gregory, *Russian National Income (1885–1913)* (Cambridge: Cambridge University Press, 1982), p. 56), at 17.3 rubles to the pound in 1917 (Angiolo Forzoni, *Rublo. Storia civile e monetaria della Russia da Ivan a Stalin* (Roma: Valerio Levi Editore, 1991), p. 226). Britain by then owed the United States £497 million (Alvi, *Occidente*, p. 75).

64.  Alvi, *Occidente*, p. 75.
65.  Pietro Zveteremich, *Il grande Parvus* (Milano: Garzanti, 1988), p. 195.
66.  Alvi, *Occidente*, pp. 77ff.
67.  Degrelle, *Hitler*, p. 271.
68.  Henri Vibert, *Fronte a l'Inghilterra* (Firenze: Beltrami Editore, 1936), p. 111.
69.  Z. A. B. Zeman and W. B. Scharlan, *The Merchant of Revolution. The Life of Alexander Israel Helphand (Parvus), 1867–1924* (London: Oxford University Press, 1965), p. 151.
70.  Ibid., p. 152.
71.  Ibid., pp. 182, 199.
72.  Pipes, *Concise History*, p. 122.
73.  Alvi, *Occidente*, p. 79.
74.  Leon Trotsky, *The Russian Revolution. The Overthrow of Tzarism & the Triumph of the Soviets* (New York: Doubleday Anchor Books, 1959 [1930]), pp. 131–47.
75.  Ibid., p. 84.
76.  Zveteremich, *Parvus*, p. 249.
77.  Anthony C. Sutton, *Wall Street and the Bolshevik Revolution* (New Rochelle, NY: Arlington House Publishers, 1981), pp. 25–8.
78.  N. Gordon-Levin Jr., *Woodrow Wilson and World Politics. America's Response to War and Revolution* (Oxford: Oxford University Press, 1968), p. 60.
79.  Alfred Döblin, *Karl & Rosa* (New York: Fromm International Publishing Corporation, 1983 [1950]), p. 50.
80.  Sutton, *Bolshevik Revolution*, pp. 72, 82.
81.  Maynard, *Russia*, p. 190.
82.  Pipes, *Concise History*, p. 120.
83.  Maynard, *Russia*, p. 195.
84.  Quigley, *Tragedy*, p. 250.
85.  'The *Lusitania* was a British merchant vessel…carrying a cargo of 2,400 cases of rifle cartridges and 1,250 cases of shrapnel, and with orders to attack German submarines whenever possible. Seven hundred and eighty-five of 1,257 passengers, including 128 of 197 Americans, lost their lives. The incompetence of the acting captain contributed to the heavy loss, as did also a mysterious "second explosion" after the German torpedo struck. The vessel, which had been declared "unsinkable", went down in eighteen minutes. The captain was on a course he had orders to avoid; he was running at reduced speed; he had an inexperienced crew; the portholes had been left open; the lifeboats had not been swung out, and no lifeboat drills had been held…' (Quigley, *Tragedy*, pp. 250–1).
86.  Degrelle, *Hitler*, p. 267.
87.  Tarle, *Breve storia*, p. 362.
88.  Liddell Hart, *Real War*, p. 386.
89.  Quigley, *Tragedy*, pp. 249–50.
90.  Edward House, *The Intimate Papers of Colonel House, Arranged as a Narrative by Charles Seymour* (Boston: Houghton Mifflin Company, 1926), p. 60.
91.  Thorstein Veblen, 'Dementia Pracox,' in Thorstein Veblen, *Essays in Our Changing Order* (New York: Augustus M. Kelley, 1964 [1922]), p. 424.
92.  Thorstein Veblen, *An Inquiry into the Nature of Peace and the Terms of Its Perpetuation* (New Brunswick: Transaction Books, 1998 [1917]), p. 38.
93.  Veblen, 'Dementia,' p. 434.
94.  Degrelle, *Hitler*, p. 244.
95.  Carroll Quigley, *The Anglo-American Establishment. From Rhodes to Cliveden* (San Pedro, CA: GSGS & Associates Publishers, 1981), pp. 10, 130, 131.
96.  Fromkin, *Peace*, p. 271.
97.  Ibid., pp. 281–2. Five years later, Winston Churchill, taking office as Colonial Secretary, would reiterate that 'A Jewish State under the protection of the British

Crown...would be especially in harmony with the truest interest of the British Empire' (ibid., p. 519).

98.  Fromkin, *Peace*, p. 217.
99.  Ibid., pp. 217, 312.
100. Quigley, *Tragedy*, p. 236.

## Chapter 2

1.  Christopher Marlowe, *The Tragedy of Doctor Faustus* (New York: Washington Square Press, 1959 [1588]), pp. 26–7.
2.  Volker Berghahn, *Imperial Germany, 1871–1914* (Providence, RI: Berghahn Press, 1994), p. 336.
3.  Sebastian Haffner, *The Failure of a Revolution. Germany, 1918–1919* (Chicago: Banner Press, 1986 [1969]), p. 16.
4.  D. Authier and J. Barriot, *La sinistra comunista in Germania* (Milano: La Salamandra, 1981 [1976]), p. 40.
5.  Thorstein Veblen, *The Theory of the Leisure Class* (New York: Penguin Books, 1979 [1899]), p. 198.
6.  Ibid, p. 204.
7.  Thorstein Veblen, *The Vested Interests and the Common Man (The Modern Point of View and the New Order)* (New York: B. W. Huebsch, Inc., 1919), p. 165.
8.  Thorstein Veblen, 'The Economics of Karl Marx II,' in Thorstein Veblen, *The Place of Science in Modern Civilization* (New York: Capricorn Books, 1969 [1907]), pp. 453–4.
9.  Haffner, *Failure*, p. 16.
10. Ibid., p. 28.
11. Ibid., p. 57.
12. Bernhard von Bülow, 'Revolution in Berlin,' in A. Kaes, M. Jay and E. Dimendberg (eds), *The Weimar Republic Sourcebook* (Berkeley: University of California Press, 1994), pp. 56–7.
13. Morgan Philips Price, *Dispatches from the Weimar Republic. Versailles and German Fascism* (London: Pluto Press, 1999 [1919–29]), p. 23.
14. Ernst Toller, *I was a German. The Autobiography of Ernst Toller* (New York: William Morrow and Company, 1934), pp. 141–2.
15. Klaus Epstein, *Matthias Erzberger and the Dilemma of German Democracy* (Princeton: Princeton University Press,1959), pp. 274–82.
16. Adolf Hitler, *Mein Kampf* (Boston: Houghton Mifflin Company, 1971 [1925]), pp. 204–6.
17. George F. Kennan, *Russia and the West under Lenin and Stalin* (Boston: Little, Brown & Co., 1960), p. 155.
18. Tacitus, *Agricola, Germania, Dialogus* (Cambridge, MA: Harvard University Press, Loeb Classical Library, 1992 [98 AD]), p. 152.
19. Kennan, *Russia*, p. 158.
20. Ernst Jünger, 'Fire' (1922), in Kaes et al., *Weimar Sourcebook*, p. 19.
21. Ernst Von Salomon, *I proscritti (Die Geächteten)* (Parma: Edizioni all'insegna del veltro, 1979 [1930]), p. 49.
22. Ibid., pp. 36–40, 86.
23. Haffner, *Failure*, p. 161.
24. Freya Eisner, *Kurt Eisner: die Politik des libertären Sozialismus* (Frankfurt am Main: Suhrkamp Verlag, 1979), p. 110.
25. I. Benoist-Méchin, *Histoire de l'armée allemande* (Paris: Éditions Albin Michel, 1966), Vol. 1, p. 270.

26. Rudolf Von Sebottendorff, *Prima che Hitler venisse. Storia della Società Thule (Bevor Hitler kam)* (Torino: Edizioni Delta-Arktos, 1987 [1933]), pp. 73–143.
27. Eugene Lunn, *Prophet of Community. The Romantic Socialism of Gustav Landauer* (Berkeley: University of California Press, 1973), p. 331. Gustav Landauer introduced his reforms as Commissioner for Enlightenment and Public Instruction. Silvio Gesell, a former businessman turned anarchist guru and monetary reformer, was appointed to Munich's Soviet as Finance Minister to launch his radical proposal for stamped scrip (paper certificates with a maturity date) (Silvio Gesell, *The Natural Economic Order* (San Antonio: Free-Economy Publishing Co., 1920), pp. 130ff.).
28. Kennan, *Russia*, p. 160.
29. Walt Whitman, *Leaves of Grass* (New York: Penguin Books, 1986 [1855]), p. 42.
30. Von Sebottendorff, *Hitler*, pp. 121ff.
31. Ian Kershaw, *Hitler: 1889–1936: Hubris* (New York: W. W. Norton & Co., 1998), p. 120.
32. Douglas Reed, *Nemesi? La storia di Otto Strasser* (Roma: Edizioni delle catacombe, 1944), p. 55.
33. Kershaw, *Hubris*, p. 126.
34. Joachim Fest, *Hitler* (New York: Vintage Books, 1975 [1973]), p. 118.
35. Kershaw, *Hubris*, p. 140.
36. Benoist-Méchin, *Armée allemande*, Vol. 2, pp. 225–6.
37. Gustav Meyrink, *The Golem* (Sawtry, Cambs: Dedalus, 1995 [1915]), p. 59.
38. Jean-Michel Angebert, *The Occult and the Reich. The Mystical Origins of Nazism and the Search for the Holy Grail* (New York: Macmillan Publishing, 1974 [1971]), p. 165.
39. Fest, *Hitler*, p. 116, and René Alleau, *Hitler et les sociétés secrètes. Enquête sur les sources occultes du nazisme* (Paris: Éditions Bernard Grasset, 1969), p. 139.
40. Nicholas Goodrick-Clarke, *The Occult Roots of Nazism. Secret Aryan Cults and Their Influence on Nazi Ideology* (New York: New York University Press, 1985), p. 151.
41. Werner Gerson, *Le Nazisme société secrète* (Paris: J'ai lu, 1969), pp. 176–7.
42. Ernst Jünger, *Das abenteurliche Herz. Figuren und Capriccios* (Hamburg: Hanseatische Verlaganstalt, 1938), pp. 75–6.
43. Kershaw, *Hubris*, p. 155.
44. Jünger, *Herz*, p. 66.
45. Dietrich Eckart, 'Jewishness In and Around Us: Fundamental Reflections,' in B. Miller Lane and L. Rupp (eds), *Nazi Ideology Before 1933. A Documentation* (Austin: University of Texas Press, 1978 [1919]), pp. 23–5.
46. Von Sebottendorff, *Hitler*, p. 55.
47. Ibid., p. 208.
48. Goodrick-Clarke, *Occult Roots*, p. 152.
49. Ernst Jünger, *On the Marble Cliffs* (Norfolk, CT: New Directions, 1947 [1939]), p. 28.
50. N. Gordon-Levin Jr., *Woodrow Wilson and World Politics. America's Response to War and Revolution* (Oxford: Oxford University Press, 1968), pp. 91–5.
51. Ibid., p. 219.
52. Angiolo Forzoni, *Rublo. Storia civile e monetaria delle Russia da Ivan a Stalin* (Roma: Valerio Levi Editore, 1991), p. 342.
53. Richard Pipes, *A Concise History of the Russian Revolution* (New York: Vintage Books, 1995), p. 235.
54. Gordon-Levin, *Woodrow Wilson*, pp. 78–80.
55. Peter Fleming, *The Fate of Admiral Kolchak* (New York: Harcourt, Brace & World, Inc., 1963), p. 49.
56. Ibid., p. 51.
57. George Stewart, *The White Armies of Russia: A Chronicle of Counter-Revolution and Allied Intervention* (New York: Macmillan Company, 1933), pp. 83–91.

58. Pipes, *Concise History*, p. 92.
59. Stewart, *White Armies*, pp. 137–8.
60. Kennan, *Russia*, p. 108.
61. Stewart, *White Armies*, pp. 135–6.
62. In Siberia, Britain, France and Italy fielded 1,400, 1,400, and 1,200 men respectively (ibid., p. 226).
63. Jonathan Smele, *Civil War in Siberia. The Anti-Bolshevik Government of Admiral Kolchak, 1918–1920* (Cambridge: Cambridge University Press, 1996), pp. 72, 97–9, 418.
64. Stewart, *White Armies*, p. 153.
65. Richard Luckett, *The White Generals. An Account of the White Movement in Russia and the Russian Civil War* (New York: Viking Press, 1971), p. 231.
66. Pipes, *Concise History*, p. 235.
67. 'There must be no attempt to conquer Bolshevik Russia by force of arms...The anti-Bolshevik armies must not be used to restore the old tsarist regime...[and] reimpos[e] on the peasants the old feudal conditions [!] under which they held their land...' (Lloyd George, quoted in ibid., p. 250).
68. Carroll Quigley, *Tragedy and Hope. A History of the World in Our Time* (New York: Macmillan Company, 1966), p. 261.
69. The high tide of the White movement against the Soviets was reached in September 1919.
70. Stewart, *White Armies*, p. 166.
71. Pipes, *Concise History*, p. 252.
72. Léon Degrelle, *Hitler: Born at Versailles* (Costa Mesa; Institute for Historical Review, 1987), p. 430.
73. Stewart, *White Armies*, p. 173.
74. Luckett, *White Generals*, p. 257.
75. Stewart, *White Armies*, p. 162.
76. Gordon-Levin, *Woodrow Wilson*, p. 224.
77. Geminello Alvi, *Dell'estremo occidente. Il secolo americano in Europa. Storie economiche* (Firenze: Marco Nardi Editore, 1993), p. 158.
78. Smele, *Civil War*, pp. 419–20.
79. Luckett, *White Generals*, p. 226.
80. Stewart, *White Armies*, p. 296.
81. Ibid., p. 286.
82. Ibid., p. 314.
83. Smele, *Civil War*, p. 201.
84. Niall Ferguson, *The Pity of War* (New York: Basic Books, 1999), p. 337.
85. Margaret Macmillan, *Paris 1919. Six Months that Changed the World* (New York: Random House, 2002), p. 222.
86. Stewart, *White Armies*, p. 243.
87. Forzoni, *Rublo*, p. 342.
88. Fleming, *Kolchak*, p. 71.
89. As such did Anwar Sadat, Nasser's lieutenant, and later Egyptian President, refer to the USSR, whenever the alleged hostility of Russia was factored into any form of geopolitical analysis (John K. Cooley, *Unholy Wars. Afghanistan, America, and International Terrorism* (London: Pluto Press, 2000), p. 33).
90. Gordon-Levin, *Woodrow Wilson*, p. 231.
91. Ibid., p. 230.
92. Pipes, *Concise History*, p. 250.
93. Ibid., p. 270.
94. Ibid., p. 250.
95. R. H. Bruce Lockart, *British Agent* (London: G. P. Putnam & Sons, 1933), p. 222.

96. Anthony Sutton, *Wall Street and the Bolshevik Revolution* (New Rochelle, NY: Arlington House Publishers, 1981), p. 158.
97. Edward Jay Epstein, *Dossier: The Secret Story of Armand Hammer* (New York: Random House, 1996), pp. 45–85.
98. Giovanni Preziosi, *Giudaismo, bolscevismo, plutocrazia e massoneria* (Torino: Arnoldo Mondadori, 1941), p. 127.
99. Kennan, *Russia*, p. 113.
100. Ibid., pp. 117–18.
101. John Maynard Keynes, *The Economic Consequences of the Peace* (New York: Penguin Books, 1995 [1920]), p. 153.
102. Ibid., p. 165.
103. Macmillan, *Paris 1919*, p. 181.
104. Ibid., p. 192.
105. Charles L. Mee Jr., *The End of Order, Versailles 1919* (New York: E. P. Dutton, 1980), pp. 209–210.
106. Quigley, *Tragedy*, p. 272.
107. Ibid.
108. Macmillan, *Paris 1919*, p. 466.
109. Ibid., p. 472.
110. Epstein, *Erzberger*, p. 323.
111. Quigley, *Tragedy*, p. 277.
112. Bernhard von Bülow, *Le memorie del Principe di Bülow, Volume III, 1901–1920* (Milano: Arnoldo Mondadori, 1931), p. 322.
113. One million Germans were allotted to Poland, 3 million to Czechoslovakia, half a million to Hungary and Yugoslavia, and 700,000 to Romania (Quigley, *Tragedy*, p. 280).
114. Hans Mommsen, *The Rise & Fall of the Weimar Democracy* (Chapel Hill: University of North Carolina Press, 1989), p. 110.
115. Mee, *End of Order*, p. 222.
116. Keynes, *Economic Consequences*, p. 146.
117. Erich Eyck, *Storia della repubblica di Weimar, 1918–1933 (Geschichte der weimarer Republik)* (Torino: Giulio Einaudi Editore, 1966 [1956]), p. 131.
118. Keynes, *Economic Consequences*, p. 200.
119. Mee, *End of Order*, p. 256.
120. Keynes, *Economic Consequences*, pp. 289–90, 294.
121. Ibid., pp. 296–7.
122. Alvi, *Occidente*, p. 141.
123. Keynes, *Economic Consequences*, pp. 269.
124. Graham Hutton, *Is it Peace?* (New York: Macmillan Company, 1937), pp. 73–4.
125. Hamilton Armstrong, *Peace and Counterpeace. From Wilson to Hitler* (New York: Harper & Row Publishers, 1971), p. 98.
126. Thorstein Veblen, *Imperial Germany and the Industrial Revolution* (London: Macmillan & Co., 1915), p. 69.
127. E. W. Jorgensen and H. I. Jorgensen, *Thorstein Veblen. Victorian Firebrand* (Armonk, NY: M. E. Sharpe, 1999), p. 149.
128. Thorstein Veblen, *The Nature of Peace and the Terms of its Perpetuation* (New Brunswick: Transaction Books, 1998 [1917]) p. 277.
129. Veblen, *Imperial Germany*, pp. 54–5.
130. Ibid., p. 58, emphasis added.
131. Jorgensen and Jorgensen, *Thorstein Veblen*, p. 150.
132. Veblen, *Nature of Peace*, p. 142.
133. Ibid., p. 150.
134. Ibid., p. 270.
135. Ibid., p. 280

136. Ibid., p. 295.
137. Thorstein Veblen, *The Engineers and the Price System* (New York: Harcourt, Brace & World, Inc., 1963 [1921]).
138. Thorstein Veblen, 'Bolshevism is a Menace – to Whom?' (1919), in Thorstein Veblen, *Essays in Our Changing Order* (New York: Augustus M. Kelley, 1964), p. 400.
139. Thorstein Veblen, 'The Economic Consequences of the Peace' (1920), in Veblen, *Essays*, pp. 462–3; emphasis added.
140. Ibid., p. 466.
141. Ibid., p. 468; emphasis added.
142. Ibid., p. 469; emphasis added.
143. Ibid.
144. Ibid., p. 470.
145. Quigley, *Tragedy*, p. 312.
146. Veblen, 'Economic Consequences,' p. 470.
147. Gerald Feldman, *The Great Disorder. Politics, Economics and Society in the German Inflation, 1914–1924* (Oxford: Oxford University Press, 1997), p. 148.

## Chapter 3

1. Friedrich Hölderlin, *Hyperion, Empedokles* (Weimar: Erich Liechenstein Verlag, 1922 [1799]), p. 207.
2. Friedrich Hölderlin, *Hymns and Fragments* (trans. Richard Siebuhr) (Princeton: Princeton University Press, 1984 [1801–06]), pp. 61–3.
3. Carroll Quigley, *Tragedy and Hope. A History of the World in Our Time* (New York: Macmillan Company, 1966), p. 418.
4. Peter Gay, *Weimar Culture. The Insider as Outsider* (New York: W. W. Norton & Company, 2001), pp. 1–2.
5. I. Benoist-Méchin, *Histoire de l'armée allemande*, (Paris: Éditions Albin Michel, 1966) Vol. 3, p. 105.
6. Harry Kessler, *Rathenau* (Bologna: Il Mulino, 1995 [1928]), p. 314.
7. George Kennan, *Russia and the West under Lenin and Stalin* (Boston: Little, Brown & Co., 1960), p. 203.
8. Quigley, *Tragedy*, p. 422.
9. Arthur Moeller van den Bruck, *Il Terzo Reich* (*Das dritte Reich*) (Roma: Edizioni Settimo Sigillo, 2000 [1923]), p. 152.
10. D. J. Goodspeed, *Ludendorff. Soldier, Dictator, Revolutionary* (London: Rupert Hart-Davis, 1966), pp. 223–4.
11. Paul von Hindenburg, 'The Stab in the Back,' in A. Kaes, M. Jay and E. Dimendberg (eds), *The Weimar Republic Sourcebook* (Berkeley: University of California Press, 1994), p. 15.
12. Klaus Epstein, *Matthias Erzberger and the Dilemma of German Democracy* (Princeton: Princeton University Press, 1959), p. 54.
13. Ibid., p. 323.
14. F. W. Henning, *Das industrialisierte Deutschland 1914 bis 1972* (Paderborn: Ferdinand Schöningh, 1974), pp. 42–3.
15. Matthias Erzberger, *Reden zu Neuordnung des deutschen Finanzwesens* (Berlin: Verlag von Reimar Hobbing, 1919), pp. 4–6.
16. Ludwig Holtfrerich, *L'inflazione tedesca 1914–1923* (*Die deutsche Inflation*) (Bari: Laterza, 1989 [1980]), p. 280.
17. Epstein, *Erzberger*, pp. 336–43.
18. Costantino Bresciani-Turroni, *The Economics of Inflation* (New York: Augustus M. Kelley Publishers, 1968 [1931]), p. 55.
19. Ibid., pp. 357–9.

20. Johannes Erger, *Der Kapp-Lüttwitz Putsch. Ein Beitrag zur deutschen Innenpolitik.* (Düsseldorf: Droste Verlag, 1967), p. 77.
21. Ibid., p. 78.
22. Epstein, *Erzberger*, p. 342.
23. Erich Eyck, *Storia della repubblica di Weimar, 1918–1933 (Geschichte der Weimarer Republik)* (Torino: Giulo Einaudi Editore, 1966 [1956]), p. 152.
24. Epstein, *Erzberger*, p. 367.
25. Ernst Troeltsch, *La democrazia improvvisata, la Germania dal 1918 al 1922* (Napoli: Guida Editori, 1977 [1924]), p. 111.
26. Arthur Rosenberg, *Storia della repubblica tedesca (Deutsche Republik)* (Roma: Edizioni Leonardo, 1945 [1934]), pp. 99–100.
27. Edward Hallett Carr, *The Bolshevik Revolution 1917–1923, Vol. 3* (London: Macmillan & Co. Ltd., 1953), p. 310.
28. Eyck, *Weimar*, p. 150.
29. Morgan Philips Price, *Dispatches from the Weimar Republic. Versailles and German Fascism* (London: Pluto Press, 1999 [1919–29]), p. 66.
30. Erger, *Kapp-Lüttwitz Putsch*, p. 41.
31. Ibid., p. 42.
32. Erwin Könnemann, 'Kapp-Putsch gegen die weimarer Republik. Ein Spiel mit den Roten und den weissen Russen,' in *Der Tagesspiel* (March 14, 2000), p. 2.
33. E. J. Feuchtwanger, *From Weimar to Hitler. Germany, 1918–1933* (New York: St. Martin's Press, 1995), p. 73.
34. Könnemann, 'Kapp-Putsch,' p. 2.
35. Bernard Wasserstein, *The Secret Lives of Trebitsch-Lincoln* (New York: Penguin Books, 1988), chapters 1–8.
36. Ibid.
37. Werner Gerson, *Le Nazisme société secrète* (Paris: J'ai lu), p. 278.
38. Donald McCormick, *The Mask of Merlin. A Critical Study of David Lloyd George* (London: Macdonald, 1963), p. 75.
39. Ibid., p. 80.
40. Wasserstein, *The Secret Lives*, p. 343.
41. Maurice Laporte, *Bouddha contre l'Intelligence Service* (Paris: Alexis Redier Éditeur, 1933), p. 82.
42. Imre Gyomaï, *Trebitsch-Lincoln. Le plus grand aventurier du siècle* (Paris: Les Éditions de France, 1939), p. 100.
43. Wasserstein, *The Secret Lives*, p. 148.
44. Laporte, *Bouddha*, p. 82.
45. Felix Gross, *I Knew Those Spies* (London: Hurst & Blackett, 1940), pp. 81–2.
46. Wasserstein, *The Secret Lives*, pp. 155, 166.
47. David Lampe and Lazlo Szenasi, *The Self-made Villain. A Biography of I. T. Trebitsch-Lincoln* (London: Cassell, 1961), p. 110.
48. Wasserstein, *The Secret Lives*, p. 336.
49. Sidney T. Felstead, *German Spies at Bay. Being an Actual Record of the German Espionage in Great Britain during the Years 1914–1918 (Compiled from Official Sources)* (London: Hutchinson & Co., 1920), p. 61.
50. Wasserstein, *The Secret Lives*, p. 166, and Gyomaï, *Trebitsch*, pp. 150–151.
51. Louis Dupeux, *National-Bolchévisme en Allemagne, sous la République de Weimar (1919–1933)* (Paris: Librairie Honoré Champion, 1974), p. 147.
52. Ibid., p. 148.
53. Erger, *Kapp-Lüttwitz Putsch*, p. 105.
54. Könemann, 'Kapp-Putsch,' p. 5.
55. Benoist-Méchin, *Armée allemande*, Vol. 2, pp. 79–81.
56. Könnemann, 'Kapp-Putsch,' p. 6.

57. John Wheeler-Bennett, *The Nemesis of Power. The German Army in Politics 1918–1945* (London: Macmillan & Co., 1961), p. 73.
58. Alex De Jonge, *The Weimar Chronicle. Prelude to Hitler* (New York: Meridian Books, 1978), p. 64.
59. Benoist-Méchin, *Armée allemande*, Vol. 2, p. 96.
60. Wheeler-Bennett, *Nemesis of Power*, p. 76.
61. Anton Golecki (ed.), *Das Kabinett Bauer (21 Juni 1919 bis 27 März 1920). Akten der Reichkanzlei weimarer Republik* (Boppard am Rhein: Harald Boldt Verlag, 1980), p. 687.
62. Heinrich August Winkler, *La repubblica di Weimar, 1918–1933: storia della prima repubblica tedesca* (Roma: Donzelli Editore, 1998 [1993]), p. 135
63. Carr, *Bolshevik Revolution*, p. 172.
64. Hagen Schulze, *La repubblica di Weimar, la Germania dal 1918 al 1933* (*Weimar, Deutschland 1918–1933*) (Bologna: Il Mulino, 1993 [1983]), pp. 262–3.
65. Wasserstein, *The Secret Lives*, p. 185.
66. Ian Kershaw, *Hitler: 1889–1936: Hubris* (New York: W. W. Norton & Co., 1998), p 153.
67. Gerson, *Nazisme*, p. 84.
68. Wasserstein, *The Secret Lives*, p. 186.
69. Ibid., p. 189.
70. Feuchtwanger, *From Weimar to Hitler*, p. 77.
71. Rosenberg, *Republica tedesca*, p. 117.
72. L. Riddell, *Intimate Diary of the Peace Conference and After, 1918–1923* (New York: Reynal & Hitchcock, 1934), p. 177.
73. Lampe and Szenasi, *Self-made Villain*, p. 139.
74. Gerson, *Nazisme*, p. 83.
75. Dupeux, *National-Bolchévisme*, p. 129.
76. Benito Mussolini, *Opera omnia, Vol. XIV (1919–1920)* (Firenze: La Fenice, 1954), pp. 374–5.
77. Dupeux, *National-Bolchévisme*, p. 150.
78. Wasserstein, *The Secret Lives*, p. 182.
79. Sigrid Schultz, *Germany Will Try It Again* (New York: Reynal & Hitchcock, 1944), pp. 58–9.
80. Carr, *Bolshevik Revolution*, p. 160.
81. Dupeux, *National-Bolchévisme*, p. 149.
82. Wasserstein, *The Secret Lives*, p. 191.
83. Ibid., p. 183.
84. David Stafford, *Churchill and the Secret Service* (New York: Overlook Press, 1999), p.24.
85. Riddel, *Intimate Diary*, p. 177.
86. Dupeux, *National-Bolchévisme*, p. 168.
87. Ibid., p. 157.
88. Lampe and Szenasi, *Self-made Villain*, p. 148.
89. Ibid., p. 166, and Wasserstein, *The Secret Lives*, p. 324.
90. Kershaw, *Hubris*, p. 140.
91. Epstein, *Erzberger*, p. 387.
92. Quigley, *Tragedy*, p. 305.
93. Gerald Feldman, *The Great Disorder. Politics, Economics and Society in the German Inflation, 1914–1924* (Oxford: Oxford University Press, 1997), p. 400.
94. Geminello Alvi, *Dell'estremo occidente. Il secolo americano in Europa. Storie economiche* (Firenze: Marco Nardi Editore, 1993), p. 177.
95. Quigley, *Tragedy*, p. 306.
96. Holtfrerich, *Inflation*, p. 128.
97. Feldman, *Great Disorder*, p. 449.

98. Alvi, *Occidente*, p. 175.
99. Feldman, *Great Disorder*, p. 333.
100. Robert Musil, *The Man Without Qualities* (*Der Mann ohne Eigenschaften*) (New York: Vintage books, 1995 [1930–52]), p. 206.
101. Feldman, *Great Disorder*, p. 345.
102. Kessler, *Rathenau*, p. 275.
103. Benoist-Méchin, *Armée allemande*, Vol. 2, p. 208.
104. Musil, *Man Without Qualities*, p. 203.
105. Quigley, *Tragedy*, pp. 231, 235, and Kessler, *Rathenau*, p. 169.
106. Walther Rathenau, *In Days to Come* (*Von kommenden Dingen*) (London: George Allen & Unwin, 1921[1917]), p. 158.
107. Kennan, *Russia*, p. 212.
108. Ibid., p. 213.
109. Ibid., p. 219.
110. Kessler, *Rathenau*, p. 303.
111. Ibid., pp. 280, 305, 306.
112. Von Salomon, *Die Geächteten*, p. 234.
113. Ibid., 176.
114. Ibid., p. 242.
115. Benoist-Méchin, *Armée allemande*, Vol. 2, p. 214.
116. Ibid., p. 217.
117. Von Salomon, *Die Geächteten*, p. 249.
118. Richard Hanser, *Putsch!* (New York: Pyramid Books, 1970), p. 256.
119. Ibid., p. 257.
120. Ernst von Salomon, *The Answers of Ernst von Salomon. The 131 Questions in the Allied Military Government. 'Fragebogen'* (London: Putnam, 1954 [1951]), p. 56.
121. Hanser, *Putsch!*, p. 259.
122. Hebert Helbig, *Die Träger der Rapallo Vertrag* (Göttingen: Vandenhoeck & Ruprecht, 1958), p. 123.
123. Carr, *Bolshevik Revolution*, pp. 310–11.
124. Cecil F. Melville, *The Russian Face of Germany* (London: Wishart & Co., 1932), pp. 86–97, and Hans W. Gatzke, 'Russo-German Military Collaboration During the Weimar Republic', in H. W. Gatzke (ed.), *European Diplomacy Between Two Wars, 1919–1933* (Chicago: Quadrangle Books, 1972), pp. 50–4.
125. Walther Goerlitz, *History of the German General Staff 1657–1945* (New York: Frederick A. Praeger Publishers, 1962), pp. 231–3.
126. Quigley, *Tragedy*, p. 425.
127. Stephanie Salzmann, *Great Britain, Germany and the Soviet Union. Rapallo and After, 1922–1934* (Woodbridge, Suffolk: Boydell Press, 2003), p. 21.
128. Gatzke, 'Russo-German Military Collaboration,' p. 59.
129. Rosenberg, *Republica tedesca*, p. 126.
130. Benoit-Méchin, *Armée allemande*, Vol. 2, p. 205, and André Fourgeaud, *La dépréciation et la revalorisation du Mark allemand, et les enseignements de l'experience monétarire allemande* (Paris: Payot, 1926), p. 11.
131. Max Hermant, *Les paradoxes économiques de l'Allemagne moderne 1918–1931* (Paris: Librarie Armand Collin, 1931), pp. 31–3.
132. Holtfrerich, *Inflation*, p. 14.
133. Ibid., p. 149.
134. Quigley, *Tragedy*, p. 307.
135. Rosenberg, *Republica tedesca*, p. 152.
136. Bresciani-Turroni, *Inflation*, p. 329.
137. Rosenberg, *Republica tedesca*, p. 155.
138. Fritz K. Ringer, *The German Inflation of 1923* (New York: Oxford University Press, 1969), p. 94; emphasis added.

139.  Viscount D'Abernon, *The Diary of an Ambassador* (New York: Doubleday, Doran & Company Inc., 1929), p. 329; emphasis added.
140.  Holtfrerich, *Inflation*, p. 132.
141.  F. D. Graham, *Exchange, Prices and Production in Hyper-Inflation Germany, 1920–1923* (Princeton: Princeton University Press, 1930), pp. 52ff.
142.  Fourgeaud, *Dépréciation*, pp. 93–4.
143.  Germany's GDP in 1923, in terms of 1913 prices, was 34.9 billion marks; $2 billion correspond, at the rate of 4.2 marks per dollar, to approximately 9 billion marks, that is, 25 percent of 1923 GDP.
144.  Fourgeaud, *Dépréciation*, pp. 94–6.
145.  Jan Van Zanden, *The Economic History of the Netherlands, 1914–1995* (London: Routledge, 1997), pp. 102–4.
146.  Ibid., p. 118.
147.  Bresciani-Turroni, *Inflation*, p. 58.
148.  Fourgeaud, *Dépréciation*, p. 13.
149.  Alvi, *Occidente*, p. 181, and Hermant, *Paradoxes*, pp. 54–5.
150.  Holtfrerich, *Inflation*, pp. 290–5.
151.  Hermann Jacques, *Allemagne, société à responsabilité limitée* (Paris: Éditions de la revue mondiale, 1932), pp. 118, 141.
152.  Riddell, *Intimate Diary*, p. 40.
153.  The origin of the meltdown can be discerned from the following statistics:

*Table 3.2*   Germany's inflationary meltdown

| Year | Repayment of funded debt (Graham) | Interest burden of the Reich (Henning) | Interest service + debt repayment | Expenses of the Reichs (Henning) | Increase in Discounted bills (Bresciani-Turroni) |
|------|------|------|------|------|------|
| 1919 | – | 10.4 | 10.4 | 54.9 | 31.2 |
| 1920 | 10.8 | 36.2 | 47.0 | 145.3 | 66.4 |
| 1921 | 20.0 | 30.0 | 50.0 | 298.8 | 94.3 |
| 1922 | 23.0 | 33.0 | 56.0 | 327.9 | 1247.9 |

All figures are in billions of current marks. The first column is obtained by multiplying the data in gold marks (Graham, *Hyper-Inflation*, pp. 40–1, Table IV) by the yearly average exchange rate of the gold mark expressed in paper marks (Bresciani-Turroni, *Inflation*, p. 441). In 1922, 23 billion additional marks of the funded debt were repaid, but by that time, inflation had rendered this last installment insignificant. So altogether, from 1920 to 1922, 50 percent of the *Kriegsanleihe* had been cashed in. The second and fourth columns are derived from two sets of data provided by Henning (*Industrialisierte Deutschland*, pp. 59–60), whereas the net variation in the Reich's discounted bills, reproduced in the fifth column, is taken from Bresciani-Turroni (*Inflation*, pp. 439–40). The third column is the sum of the first and second. After 1922, the private sector, which until then had absorbed about 50 percent of every issue of state bonds, shunned government paper altogether, and left the Reichsbank alone in shouldering the Reich's bills, which the economy was redeeming en masse (Graham, *Hyper-Inflation*, pp. 60–1, and Fourgeaud, *Dépréciation*, p. 118). In 1923, the de-cumulation of Reich bills had definitively taken over the dynamics of the inflation, and by 1923 the redemption of bills for cash would surpass the discounting thereof and liquefy the German mark into annihilation. Thus the sum of interest and refunded debt (that is, the cashing in of the war loan) between 1919 and 1920 (that is, 57.4 billion marks – the sum of the first two data in column 3) *tallied up to circa 30 percent (28.7) of the Reich's total outlay* (the sum of the first two data in column 4) and *corresponded roughly to 60 percent (58.8) of the total amount of money created during that time* (that is, the bills discounted by the Reichsbank: 97.6 billion marks; the sum of the the first two data in column 5, assuming that no part of this debt could have been covered with taxes).

154. Marcel Mauss, *Écrits politiques* (Paris: Librairie Arthème Fayard, 1997 [1924]), p. 665.
155. Adolf Hitler, *Hitler's Secret Conversations 1941–1944* (New York: Farrar, Straus & Young, 1953), p. 54.
156. Holtfrerich, *Inflation*, p. 155.
157. Quigley, *Tragedy*, p. 312.
158. W. G. Krivitsky, *In Stalin's Secret Service* (New York: Enigma Books, 2000 [1941]), pp. 28–38.
159. Konrad Heiden, *Der Fuehrer. Hitler's Rise to Power* (Boston: Houghton Mifflin Company, 1944), pp. 130–1.
160. Von Salomon, *The Answers*, p. 242.
161. Quoted in Louis Kilzer, *Churchill's Deception. The Dark Secret that Destroyed Germany* (New York: Simon & Schuster, 1994), p. 100.
162. Hitler, *Mein Kampf*, (Boston: Houghton Mifflin Company, 1971 [1925]), pp. 687.
163. Claus-Ekkehard Bärsch, *Die politische Religion des Nationalsozialismus* (München: Wilhelm Fink Verlag, 1998), pp. 63–70.
164. Ibid., p. 90.
165. Adolf Hitler, *Mein Kampf*, pp. 131–43; emphasis added.
166. David Irving, *The War Path: Hitler's Germany, 1933–1939* (London: Michael Joseph, 1978), p. 56.
167. Ian Kershaw, *Hubris*, p. 151.
168. Arthur Moeller van den Bruck, *L'uomo politico (Der politische Mensch)* (Roma: Settimo Sigillo, 1997 [1918]), p. 93.
169. Paul Harrison Silfen, *The Völkisch Ideology & The Roots of Nazism. The Early Writings of Artur Moeller van den Bruck* (New York: Exposition Press, 1973), p. 11.
170. Ernst Hanfstaengl, *Hitler: The Missing Years* (New York: Arcade Publishing, 1994 [1957]), p. 64.
171. Alfred Rosenberg, *Der Mythus des 20. Jahrhunderts. Eine Wertung der seelisch-geistigen Gestaltenkampfe unserer Zeit* (München: Honeichen-Verlag, 1934), p. 640.
172. See for instance, Detlev Rose, *Die Thule-Gesellschaft. Legende, Mythos, Wirklichkeit.* (Tübingen: Grabert Verlag, 1994), pp. 176–7.
173. Karl Haushofer, *Weltmeere und Weltmächte.* (Berlin: Zeitgeschichte Verlag, 1937), p. 284.
174. Woodruff D. Smith, *The Ideological Origins of Nazi Imperialism* (Oxford: Oxford University Press, 1986), p. 223.
175. Hitler, *Mein Kampf*, p. 610.
176. Ibid. pp. 615–19.
177. Ibid., pp. 662, 663.
178. Ibid., pp. 660–2.
179. Ibid., pp. 664.

## Chapter 4

1. Louis-Ferdinand Céline, *Voyage au bout de la nuit* (Paris: Gallimard, 1952 [1932]), p. 26.
2. Erich Kästner, *Lärm im Spiegel* (Berlin: Deutsche Verlag-Anstalt, 1929), pp. 70, 71.

3. Erich Kästner, *Fabian: The Story of a Moralist* (Evanston: Northwestern University Press, 1990 [1931]), p. 44.
4. Silvio Gesell, *The Natural Economic Order* (San Antonio: Free Economy Publishing Co., 1920), Part I.
5. Ibid., pp. 275–8.
6. Jacques Rueff, *De l'aube au crépuscule. Autobiographie de l'auteur.* (Paris: Librairie Plon, 1977), p. 307.
7. Webster G. Tarpley, and Anton Chaitkin, *George Bush. The Unauthorized Biography* (Washington DC: Executive Intelligence Review, 1992), p. 31.
8. Francis Williams, *A Pattern of Rulers* (London: Longman, 1965), p. 201.
9. Ibid., p. 199.
10. Ibid., p. 203.
11. Henry Clay, *Lord Norman* (London: Macmillan & Co., 1957), p. 475.
12. Williams, *Pattern*, p. 203.
13. Andrew Boyle, *Montagu Norman* (London: Cassell, 1967), p. 67.
14. Ibid., p. 85.
15. Williams, *Pattern*, p. 204.
16. Ibid.
17. Percy Arnold, *The Bankers of London* (London: Hogarth Press, 1938), pp. 9, 16–17.
18. Ibid., p. 11.
19. Boyle, *Norman*, pp. 129–30.
20. Ibid., p. 133.
21. Ibid., p. 131.
22. Carroll Quigley, *Tragedy and Hope. A History of the World in Our Time* (New York: Macmillan Company, 1966), p. 326.
23. Boyle, *Norman*, pp. 133–4, 137–8; emphasis added.
24. William Adams Brown Jr., *England and the New Gold Standard, 1919–1926* (New Haven: Yale University Press, 1929), p. 55.
25. Boyle, *Norman*, p. 217.
26. Ibid. p. 185
27. G. Balachandran, *John Bullion's Empire: Britain's Gold Problem and India Between the Wars* (Richmond, Surrey: Curzon Press, 1996), p. 64.
28. Maxwell S. Stewart, 'Silver – Its International Aspects,' *Foreign Policy Reports*, Vol. VII, No. 13 (1931), p. 242.
29. Adams Brown, *England*, p. 84.
30. Balachandran, *John Bullion's Empire*, p. 91.
31. Ibid., p. 89.
32. Ibid., pp. 98, 100.
33. Ibid., p. 202.
34. Boyle, *Norman*, p. 138.
35. Stanley Lebergott, *The Americans. An Economic Record* (New York: Norton & Co., 1984), p. 396.
36. Clay, *Lord Norman*, p. 129.
37. Boyle, *Norman*, p. 68.
38. Clay, *Lord Norman*, p. 135.
39. Ibid., p. 132.
40. Barry Eichengreen, *Golden Fetters. The Gold Standard and the Great Depression, 1919–1939* (New York: Oxford University Press, 1992), p. 118.
41. Charles O. Hardy, *Is There Enough Gold?* (Washington DC: Brookings Institution, 1936), pp. 103, 153.
42. Ibid., p. 154.
43. Marcello De Cecco, *Moneta e impero. Il sistema finanziario internazionale dal 1890 al 1914* (Torino: Piccola biblioteca Einuadi, 1979), p. 157.
44. Balachandran, *John Bullion's Empire*, p. 92.

45. William Adams Brown Jr., *The International Gold Standard Reinterpreted, 1914–1934* (New York: National Bureau of Economic Research, Inc., 1940), p. 295.
46. Hardy, *Enough Gold?*, p. 93.
47. Adams Brown, *Gold Standard*, p. 294.
48. Ibid., p. 290.
49. Ibid., p. 301.
50. Eichengreen, *Golden Fetters*, p. 164.
51. Boyle, *Norman*, pp. 147–8.
52. Melchior Palyi, *The Twilight of Gold 1914–1936. Myths and Realities* (Chicago: Henry Regnery Company, 1972), p. 144.
53. Hjalmar Schacht, *My First Seventy-six Years. The Autobiography of Hjalmar Schacht* (London: Allen Wingate, 1955), p. 131.
54. Ibid.
55. Anton Chaitkin, *Treason in America, from Aaron Burr to Averell Harriman.* (New York: New Benjamin Franklin House, 1985), p. 545.
56. Ibid., p. 546; emphasis added.
57. Schacht, *Autobiography*, p. 188.
58. Clay, *Lord Norman*, p. 197.
59. Bank of England, G1/44–419, p. 123, quote from an article of Carl von Ossietzky on the *Weltbühne*, November 27, 1928.
60. Boyle, *Norman*, p. 169.
61. Ibid., p. 171.
62. Schacht, *Autobiography*, p. 194.
63. Boyle, *Norman*, p. 171.
64. Charles L. Mowat, *Britain Between the Wars, 1918–1940* (Chicago: University of Chicago Press, 1955), p. 373.
65. Boyle, *Norman*, p. 159.
66. Geminello Alvi, *Dell'estremo occidente. Il secolo americano in Europa. Storie economiche* (Firenze: Marco Nardi Editore, 1993), p. 195.
67. Ibid., p. 197.
68. Paul R. Leach, *That Man Dawes* (Chicago: Reilly & Lee Co., 1930), pp. 206–7.
69. Ibid., p. 194.
70. Quigley, *Tragedy*, p. 308.
71. Alvi, *Occidente*, pp. 197–8.
72. Ibid., p. 199.
73. Maurice Callot, *Le mark allemand depuis 1924* (Paris: Librairie Arthur Rousseau, 1934), p. 20.
74. Boyle, *Norman*, p. 197.
75. Alvi, *Occidente*, p. 208.
76. Démètre Delivanis, *La politique des banques allemandes, en matière de crédit à court terme* (Paris: Librairie du Recueil Sirey, 1934), p. 53.
77. Alvi, *Occidente*, p. 198.
78. Louis T. McFadden, *Collected Speeches of Congressman Louis T. McFadden, as Compiled from the Congressional Record* (Hawthorne, CA: Omni Publications, 1970), p. 204.
79. Quigley, *Tragedy*, p. 308.
80. Theo Balderston, *The Origins and Causes of the German Economic Crisis, November 1923 to May 1932* (Berlin: Haude & Spener, 1993), p. 134.
81. Carl T. Schmidt, *German Business Cycles, 1924–1933* (New York: National Bureau of Economic Research, 1934), p. 71.
82. Balderston, *Origins and Causes*, p. 140.
83. Garet Garrett, *The Rescue of Germany & As Noble Lenders* (New York: The Chemical Foundation, 1931), p. 3.
84. McFadden, *Collected Speeches*, p. 57.

85. Derek Aldcroft, *From Versailles to Wall Street, 1919–1929* (New York: Penguin Books, 1978), p. 90, and Quigley, *Tragedy*, p. 309.
86. Paul Oesterfeld, *La leggende dell'oro* (Roma: Casa Editrice Mediterranea, 1943), pp. 171, 182–3.
87. Garrett, *Rescue of Germany*, pp. 36–40.
88. Arthur Rosenberg, *Storia della repubblica tedesca (Deutsche Republik)* (Roma: Edizioni Leonardo, 1945 [1934]), p. 193.
89. Kästner, *Fabian*, p. 33.
90. Rosenberg, *Storia della repubblica tedesca*, pp. 198, 199, 210.
91. Delivanis, *Politique des banques*, p. 52.
92. Joseph Borkin, *The Crime and Punishment of I. G. Farben* (New York: The Free Press, 1978), p. 7.
93. Richard Sasuly, *I. G. Farben* (New York: Boni & Gear, 1947), p. 40.
94. Borkin, *Crime and Punishment*, p. 21.
95. Ibid., p. 1.
96. Ibid., p. 28.
97. Anthony C. Sutton, *Wall Street and the Rise of Hitler* (Sudbury, Suffolk: Bloomfield Books, 1976), p. 33.
98. William Manchester, *The Arms of Krupp, 1857–1968* (Boston: Little, Brown and Company, 1968), pp. 348–50.
99. Borkin, *Crime and Punishment*, p. 45.
100. Ibid., p. 54.
101. Sasuly, *I. G. Farben*, p. 148.
102. Sutton, *Rise of Hitler*, p. 35.
103. Sasuly, *I. G. Farben*, p. 149.
104. Sutton, *Rise of Hitler*, pp. 35, 36.
105. Ibid., p. 22; emphasis added.
106. Andrej Gromyko, *L'espansione internazionale del capitale, storia e attualità* (Roma: Editori Riuniti, 1985 [1982]), p. 139.
107. Sutton, *Rise of Hitler*, pp. 51–66.
108. Palyi, *Twilight of Gold*, p. 155.
109. Quigley, *Tragedy*, p. 308.
110. Garrett, *Rescue of Germany*, p. 29.
111. Stephen V. O. Clarke, *Central Bank Cooperation, 1924–1931* (New York: Federal Reserve Bank of New York, 1967), p. 85.
112. Adams Brown, *England*, p. 206.
113. Ibid., pp. 213–14, 220–1, and Adams Brown, *Gold Standard*, 1940, p. 368.
114. As a result of the particular dispositions of the Gold Act of 1925 with regard to convertibility, gold in circulation would amount by 1928 to 8 percent of the total monetary stock worldwide, whereas, barring Chinese and Indian hoards, it had been 45 percent in 1913 (Edwin F. Gay, 'The Gold Problem,' *Foreign affairs*, Vol. 9, January 1931, p. 198).
115. Quigley, *Tragedy*, p. 322.
116. Rueff, *De l'aube au crépuscule*, p. 313.
117. Hardy, *Enough Gold?*, p. 101; emphasis added.
118. Emile Moreau, *Souvenirs d'un Gouverneur de la Banque de France, histoire de la stabilisation du franc (1926–1928)*. Paris: Librairie de Médicis, 1954), p. 48.
119. Boyle, *Norman*, p. 194.
120. Quigely, *Tragedy*, p. 326.
121. Felix Somary, *Die Ursache der Krise* (Tübingen: J. C. B. Mohr, 1932), p. 11.
122. Ibid., pp. 4, 11–13.
123. Moreau, *Souvenirs d'un Gouverneur*, p. 40; 'Norman is a very tough businessman, and very astute.'
124. Ibid., pp. 48–9.

125. Alfred Sauvy, *Histoire économique de la France entre les deux guerres* (Paris: Fayard, 1965), p. 158.
126. McFadden, *Collected Speeches*, p. 158.
127. Moreau, *Souvenirs d'un Gouverneur*, p. 308.
128. Boyle, *Norman*, p. 228.
129. Clay, *Lord Norman*, p. 486.
130. Boyle, *Norman*, p. 135.
131. Ibid., p. 228.
132. Moreau, *Souvenirs d'un Gouverneur*, pp. 329–31.
133. Ibid., p. 333.
134. Aldcroft, *From Versailles to Wall Street*, pp. 165–6.
135. Clay, *Lord Norman*, p. 484.
136. Clarke, *Central Bank Cooperation*, p. 124.
137. George B. Robinson, *Monetary Mischief* (New York: Columbia University Press, 1935), p. 30.
138. Hardy, *Enough Gold?*, p. 155.
139. Adams Brown, *Gold Standard*, p. 487.
140. Clarke, *Central Bank Cooperation*, pp. 130, 134.
141. Moreau, *Souvenirs d'un Gouverneur*, p. 383.
142. Diane Kunz, *The Battle for Britain's Gold Standard in 1931* (London: Croom Helm, 1987), p. 18.
143. Bank of England, G1/453, Norman to Schacht, 11 December 1928.
144. Clarke, *Central Bank Cooperation*, p. 157.
145. Robinson, *Monetary Mischief*, p. 43.
146. J. R. Levien, *Anatomy of a Crash – 1929* (New York: Traders Press, 1966), p. 45.
147. Alexander Dana Noyes, *The Market Place. Reminiscences of a Financial Editor* (Boston: Little, Brown & Company, 1938), pp. 329, 330.
148. Francis W. Hirst, *Wall Street and Lombard Street. The Stock Exchange Slump of 1929 and the Trade Depression of 1930* (New York: Macmillan Company, 1931), pp. 6, 9.
149. Robinson, *Monetary Mischief*, p. 37.
150. Frank Simonds, *Can Europe Keep the Peace?* (New York: Blue Ribbon Books, Inc., 1934), p. 307.
151. Lago Gil Aguado, 'The Creditanstalt Crisis of 1931 and the Failure of the Austro-German Customs Union Project,' *Historical Journal*, Vol. 44, No. 1 (2001), p. 201.
152. Lionel Robbins, *The Great Depression* (New York: Macmillan Company, 1934), p. 28, and Rueff, *De l'aube au crépuscule*, p. 301.
153. R. J. Truptil, *British Banks and the London Money Market* (London: Jonathan Cape, 1936), p. 289.
154. Walter A. Morton, *British Finance, 1930–1940* (New York: Arno Press, 1978), pp. 32–4.
155. Clay, *Lord Norman*, p. 396.
156. Boyle, *Norman*, p. 263.
157. Clarke, *Central Bank Cooperation*, p. 203.
158. Kunz, *The Battle*, p. 84.
159. McFadden, *Collected Speeches*, p. 229.
160. Kunz, *The Battle*, p. 91.
161. Ibid., pp. 122, 130.
162. Paul Einzig, *The Tragedy of the Pound* (London: Kegan, Paul, Trench, Trubner & Co., Ltd., 1932), pp. 90–1.
163. Adams Brown, *Gold Standard*, p. 1015.
164. Clarke, *Central Bank Cooperation*, p. 214.
165. Ibid.
166. Palyi, *Twilight of Gold*, p. 155.

167. D. E. Moggridge, *British Monetary Policy, 1924–1931. The Norman conquest of $ 4.86* (Cambridge: Cambridge University Press, 1972), pp. 184, 185.
168. Morton, *British Finance*, p. 45; emphasis added.
169. Williams, *Pattern*, p. 210.
170. Morton, *British Finance*, p. 46.
171. Boyle, *Norman*, p. 275.
172. Palyi, *Twilight of Gold*, p. 272.
173. Kindleberger, *The World in Depression, 1929–1939* (New York: Penguin Books, 1987), p. 157.
174. Robert Wolff, *Économie et finances de la France, passé et avenir* (New York: Brentano's, 1943), p. 175.
175. Hardy, *Enough Gold?*, p. 92.
176. Francis W. Hirst, *Money, Gold, Silver and Paper* (New York: Charles Scribner's Sons, 1934), p. 162, and Balachandran, *John Bullion's Empire*, p.152.
177. Balachandran, *John Bullion's Empire*, p. 177.
178. Alvi, *Occidente*, p. 376.
179. Balachandran, *John Bullion's Empire*, p. 181.
180. Clarke, *Central Bank Cooperation*, p. 218.
181. John Hargrave, *Montagu Norman* (New York: Greystone Press, 1942), pp. 308–10.
182. I. Benoist-Méchin, *Histoire del'armée allemande* (Paris: Éditions Albin Michel, 1966), Vol. 3, p. 11.
183. Chaitkin, *Treason in America*, p. 541.
184. Martin Broszat, *Hitler and the Collapse of Weimar Germany* (Leamington Spa: Berg, 1987 [1984]), p. 65.
185. Schacht, *Autobiography*, pp. 230–1.
186. Broszat, *Hitler and the Collapse*, p. 66.
187. Ian Kershaw, *Hitler: 1889–1936: Hubris* (New York: W. W. Norton & Co., 1998), p. 318.
188. Edward H. Carr, *German-Soviet Relations between the Two World Wars, 1914–1939* (Baltimore: Johns Hopkins University Press, 1951), p. 36.
189. Dimitri Volkogonov, *Trotsky, the Eternal Revolutionary* (New York: The Free Press), p. 270–2.
190. George F. Kennan, *Russia and the West under Lenin and Stalin* (Boston: Little, Brown & C., 1960), p. 286.
191. Ibid.
192. Simonds, *Can Europe Keep the Peace?*, p. 306.
193. Hjalmar Schacht, *Das Ende der Reparationen* (Oldenburg: Gerhard Stalling, 1931), pp. 97–127.
194. Alvi, *Occidente*, p. 318.
195. Rosenberg, *Storia della repubblica tedesca*, p. 204.
196. Broszat, *Hitler and the Collapse*, p. 83.
197. Balderston, *Origins and Causes*, p. 313.
198. Eichengreen, *Golden Fetters*, p. 272.
199. Simonds, *Can Europe Keep the Peace?*, pp. 151–2.
200. Karl Erich Born, *Die deutsche Bankenkrise 1931, Finanzen und Politik* (München: R. Piper & Co. Verlag, 1967), p. 100.
201. Boyle, *Norman*, p. 260.
202. Clarke, *Central Bank Cooperation*, p. 196.
203. Adams Brown, *Gold Standard*, p. 1045.
204. Alvi, *Occidente*, pp. 512–13, and René Alleau, *Hitler et les sociétés secrètes. Enquête sur les sources occulted du nazisme* (Paris: Éditions Bernard Grasset, 1969), p. 209.
205. Eustace Mullins, *Secrets of the Federal Reserve. The London Connection* (Staunton, VA: Bankers Research Institute, 1991), pp. 81, 98.

206. Paul M. Kennedy, *The Rise of Anglo-German Antagonism, 1860–1914* (London: Ashfield Press, 1980), p. 304.
207. Arnold, *The Bankers*, p. 23.
208. Truptil, *British Banks*, p. 148.
209. David Williamson, *The British in Germany, 1918–1933. The Reluctant Occupiers* (New York: Berg Publishers, 1991), p. 43.
210. Broszat, *Hitler and the Collapse*, p. 90.
211. Leon Trotsky, *The Struggle Against Fascism in Germany* (New York: Pathfinder Press, 1971 [1931–33]), p. 338.
212. Aldcroft, *From Versailles to Wall Street*, p. 95.
213. Garrett, *The Rescue of Germany*, p. 72.
214. Hans Mommsen, *The Rise & Fall of the Weimar Democracy* (Chapel Hill: University of North Carolina Press, 1989), p. 339.
215. Udo Kissenkoetter, *Gregor Straßer und die NSDAP* (Stuttgart: Deutsche Verlags-Anstalt, 1978), p. 120.
216. Quigley, *Tragedy*, p. 433.
217. Henry A. Turner Jr., *German Big Business and the Rise of Hitler* (Oxford: Oxford University Press, 1985), p. 117.
218. Quigley, *Tragedy*, pp. 429–30.
219. Tarpley and Chaitkin, *Bush Biography*, pp. 29–31; information recently reconfirmed in the *Sarasota Herald Tribune*, November 12, 2000.
220. Robert Dell, *Germany Unmasked* (London: Martin Hopkins Ltd., 1934), pp. 61–70.
221. Kershaw, *Hubris*, p. 404.
222. Benoist-Méchin, *Armée allemande*, Vol. 3, p. 77.
223. Heinrich August Winkler, *La repubblica di Weimar, 1918–1933: storia della prima repubblica tedesca* (Roma: Donzelli Editore, 1998 [1993]), pp. 651–652
224. Ivan Maisky, *Who Helped Hitler?* (London: Hutchinson, 1964 [1962]), pp. 16, 19.
225. Quigley, *Tragedy*, p. 433.
226. James Pool and Suzanne Pool, *Who Financed Hitler. The Secret Funding of Hitler's Rise to Power, 1919–1933* (London: MacDonald and Jane's), p. 444.
227. Karl R. Bopp, *Hjalmar Schacht: Central Banker* (University of Missouri Studies, 1939), p. 62.
228. Stewart A. Stehlin, *Weimar and the Vatican, 1919–1933* (Princeton: Princeton University Press, 1983), p. 365.
229. Winkler, *Weimar*, p. 671.
230. John Gunther, *Inside Europe* (New York: Harper and Brothers, 1938), p. 41.
231. Hargrave, *Montagu Norman*, pp. 219–20.

## Chapter 5

1. Reinhold Hoops, *Englands Selbst-täuschung* (Berlin: Zentralverlag NSDAP Franz Eher Nachfolger Gmbh, 1940), p. 37.
2. Adolf Hitler, *Hitler's Secret Conversations 1941–1944* (New York: Farrar, Straus & Young, 1953), pp. 166, 259, 534, 507.
3. Ernst Jünger, *On the Marble Cliffs* (Norfolk, CT: New Directions, 1947), p. 93.
4. Johann Wolfgang von Goethe, *Goethe's Faust Part Two* (Prose translation by Max Dietz) (Pennsylvania: Bryn Mawr, 1949), p. 191.
5. Klaus Fischer, *Nazi Germany. A New History* (New York: Continuum, 1996), p. 268.
6. Carroll Quigley, *Tragedy and Hope. A History of the World in Our Time* (New York: Macmillan Company, 1966), p. 430.
7. I. Benoist-Méchin, *Histoire del'armée allemande* (Paris: Éditions Albin Michel, 1966), Vol. 3, p. 87.

8. Jacques Delarue, *Gestapo. A History of Horror* (New York: Dell, 1964), p. 65.
9. Ibid.
10. John Toland, *Adolf Hitler* (Garden City, NY: Doubleday & Co., 1976), p. 569.
11. Fischer, *Nazi Germany*, p. 272.
12. Joseph Borkin, *The Crime and Punishment of I. G. Farben* (New York: The Free Press, 1978), p. 56.
13. John Cornwell, *Hitler's Pope. The Secret History of Pius XII* (New York: Viking, 1999), p. 154.
14. Hans Mommsen, 'The Reichstag Fire and Its Political Consequences,' in Hajo Holborn (ed.), *Republic to Reich. The Making of the Nazi Revolution. Ten Essays* (New York: Vintage, 1972), p. 147.
15. André François-Poncet, *The Fateful Years. Memoirs of a French Ambassador in Berlin, 1931–1938* (London: Victor Gollancz, 1949), p. 55.
16. Mommsen, 'Reichstag Fire,' p. 150.
17. Delarue, *Gestapo*, p. 67.
18. Max Gallo, *The Night of the Long Knives* (New York: Da Capo Press, 1997 [1972]), pp. 41–2.
19. John Weitz, *Hitler's Banker: Hjalmar Horace Greeley Schacht* (Boston: Little, Brown & Company, 1997), p. 140.
20. Delarue, *Gestapo*, pp. 70–71.
21. François-Poncet, *Fateful Years*, p. 55.
22. Fischer, *Nazi Germany*, p. 285.
23. Ibid.
24. Gallo, *Long Knives*, p. 100.
25. Delarue, *Gestapo*, p. 141.
26. Douglas Reed, *The Prisoner of Ottawa, Otto Strasser* (London: Jonathan Cape, 1953).
27. Ian Kershaw, *Hitler: 1889–1936: Hubris* (New York: W. W. Norton & Co., 1998), p. 515.
28. François-Poncet, *Fateful Years*, p. 133.
29. Ibid., p. 153.
30. Edmond Vermeil, *Germany's Three Reichs. Their History and Culture* (London: Andrew Dakers Limited, 1945), p. 291.
31. Paul Maquenne, *L'hérésie économique allemande* (Paris: Guerre 39, Union Latine, 1940), p.115.
32. François-Poncet, *Fateful Years*, p. 221.
33. Hans Ulrich Thamer, *Il Terzo Reich* (*Verführung und Gewalt, Deutschland 1933–1945*) (Bologna: Il Mulino, 1993 [1986]), p. 222.
34. Hjalmar Schacht, *My First Seventy-six Years: The Autobiography of Hjalmar Schacht* (London: Allen Wingate, 1955), p. 295.
35. Karl Erich Born, *Die Deutsche Bankenkrise 1931, Finanzen und Politik* (München: R. Piper & Co. Verlag, 1967), p. 118.
36. N. J. Johannsen, *A Neglected Point in Connection with Crises* (New York: Augustus M. Kelley Publishers, 1971 [1908]), pp. 35, 80; emphasis added.
37. Born, *Deutsche Bankenkrise*, pp. 174ff.
38. Karl Schiller, *Arbeitsbeschaffung und Finanzordnung in Deutschland* (Berlin: Junker und Dünnhaupt Verlag, 1936), pp. 35–67.
39. Jan Marczewski, *Politique monétaire et financière du IIIe Reich* (Paris: Librairie du Recueil Sirey, 1941), p. 58.
40. Kenyon Poole, *German Financial Policies 1932–1939* (Cambridge, MA: Harvard University Press, 1939), p. 37.
41. Marczewski, *Politique monétaire*, pp. 32–3.
42. Poole, *German Financial Policies*, p. 47.
43. Schacht, *Autobiography*, p. 297.

44. Gallo, *Long Knives*, p. 158.
45. Schacht, *Autobiography*, p. 320.
46. Weitz, *Hitler's Banker*, p. 157.
47. Norbert Mühlen, *Schacht: Hitler's Magician. The Life and Loans of of Dr. Hjalmar Schacht* (New York: Alliance Book Corporation, 1939), p. 157.
48. Schacht, *Autobiography*, p. 302.
49. Peter Padfield, *Himmler, Reichsführer-SS* (London: Macmillan, 1990), p. 115.
50. Hitler, *Secret Conversations*, p. 350.
51. Edward Norman Peterson, *Hjalmar Schacht: For and Against Hitler* (Boston: Christopher Publishing House, 1954), p. 149; emphasis added.
52. Poole, *German Financial Policies*, p. 29.
53. R. J. Overy, *War and Economy in the Third Reich* (Oxford: Clarendon Press, 1994), p. 38.
54. Otto Nathan, *Nazi War Finance and Banking* (NBER Paper No. 20, 1944), p. 43.
55. Samuel Lurie, *Private Investment in a Controlled Economy* (New York: Columbia University Press, 1947), p. 15.
56. Ibid., pp. 58–9.
57. Thamer, *Terzo Reich*, p. 414.
58. Avraham Barkai, *Nazi Economics. Ideology, Theory and Policy* (New Haven: Yale University Press, 1990), p. 165.
59. Hitler, *Secret Conversations*, p. 372.
60. Poole, *German Financial Policies*, p. 111.
61. Lurie, *Private Investment*, p. 36, and Barkai, *Nazi Economics*, p. 255.
62. Marczewski, *Politique monétaire*, p. 88.
63. Poole, *German Financial Policies*, pp. 118–20.
64. Lurie, *Private Investment*, p. 158.
65. Ibid., p. 59.
66. Ibid., pp. 57–8, 154.
67. Barkai, *Nazi Economics*, p. 158.
68. Bank of England, OV 34/9, from two memoranda, respectively, by G. H. S. Pinsent, 6 December 1938 (p. 79), and C. F. Cobbold, 24 August 1939 (p. 231).
69. Overy, *War and Economy*, p. 42.
70. David Schoenbaum, *Hitler's Social Revolution. Class and Status in Nazi Germany, 1933–1939* (New York: W. W. Norton & Company, Inc., 1980 [1966]), pp. 145–8.
71. Schacht, *Autobiography*, p. 317.
72. Fischer, *Nazi Germany*, p. 377.
73. Stephen Roberts, *The House That Hitler Built* (New York: Harper & Brothers Publishers, 1938), p. 172.
74. H. W. Arndt, *The Economic Lessons of the Nineteen Thirties* (London: Oxford University Press, 1944), pp. 187–8.
75. Bruno Bettelheim, *L'économie allemande sous le nazisme: un aspect de la décadence du capitalisme* (Paris: Librairie Marcel Rivière et Cie., 1946), p. 180.
76. Mühlen, *Schacht*, pp. 120–35.
77. Weitz, *Hitler's Banker*, p. 206.
78. Neil Forbes, *Doing Business With the Nazis. Britain's Economic and Financial Relations With Germany, 1931–1939* (London: Frank Cass, 2000), p. 97.
79. Ibid., p. 107.
80. Cleona Lewis, *Nazi Europe and World Trade* (Washington DC: Brookings Institution, 1941), p. 16.
81. Forbes, *Doing Business*, p. 181.
82. Bank of England, OV 34/201, p. 10, a memorandum dated October 14, 1934, speaks of 'Standstill bills' being drawn *'under credit lines* granted before July 1931' (emphasis added), which can only be understood as a provision for initiating a

new cycle of fresh lending to German importers by these specific short-term bills, which were renewed as soon as they were paid off.

83.  John Gunther, *Inside Europe* (New York: Harper & Brothers, 1938), p. 99.
84.  Forbes, *Doing Business*, pp. 113, 116.
85.  Ibid., pp. 173, 174.
86.  Mühlen, *Schacht*, p. 35.
87.  Martin Gilbert, *The Roots of Appeasement* (New York: New American Library, 1966), p. 155.
88.  Henry Clay, *Lord Norman* (London: Macmillan & Co., 1957), pp. 318–22.
89.  Dorothy Woodman, *Hitler Rearms. An Exposure of Germany's War Plans* (London: John Lane; Bodley Head Limited, 1934), p. 201.
90.  John Hargrave, *Montagu Norman* (New York: Greystone Press, 1942), p. 218.
91.  Ernst Hanfstaengl, *Hitler: The Missing Years* (New York: Arcade Publishing, 1994 [1957]), p. 204.
92.  Anthony Sutton, *Wall Street and the Rise of Hitler* (Sudbury: Suffolk: Bloomfield Books, 1976), pp. 15–16.
93.  William Dodd, *Ambassador Dodd's Diary, 1933–1938* (New York: Harcourt, Brace and Company, 1941), pp. 166, 170, 176.
94.  Bettelheim, *L'économie allemande*, p. 78.
95.  Charles Higham, *Trading With the Enemy: An Exposé of the Nazi-American Money Plot, 1933–1949* (New York: Delacorte Press, 1983), p. xvi.
96.  Andrej Gromyko, *L'espansione internazionale del capitale, storia e attualità* (Roma: Editori Riuniti, 1985 [1982]), p. 151.
97.  Padfield, *Himmler*, p. 206.
98.  Schacht, *Autobiography*, p. 370.
99.  Ibid. pp. 366ff.
100. Padfield, *Himmler*, p. 208.
101. Hitler, *Secret Conversations*, pp. 514–15.
102. Weitz, *Hitler's Banker*, p. 240.
103. Schacht, *Autobiography*, pp. 383–4.
104. Ron Chernow, *The Warburgs. The Twentieth-Century Odyssey of a Remarkable Jewish Family* (New York: Random House, 1993), pp. 480–5.
105. Gilbert, *Appeasement*, pp. 138–50.
106. Quigley, *Tragedy*, p. 581.
107. Gunther, *Inside Europe*, p. 278.
108. Carroll Quigley, *The Anglo-American Establishment. From Rhodes to Cliveden* (San Pedro, CA: GSG & Associates Publishers, 1981), pp. 227–8.
109. Quigley, *Tragedy*, p. 653.
110. Ibid., p. 582.
111. Gilbert, *Appeasement*, pp. 79–80.
112. Ibid., p. 120.
113. Louis Kilzer, *Churchill's Deception. The Dark Secret that Destroyed Germany* (New York: Simon & Schuster, 1994), p. 117.
114. François-Poncet, *Fateful Years*, pp. 152–3.
115. Quoted in Clement Leibovitz and Alvin Finkel, *In Our Time. The Chamberlain-Hitler Collusion* (New York: Monthly Review Press, 1998), p. 23.
116. Ivan Maisky, *Who Helped Hitler?* (London: Hutchinson, 1964 [1962]), p. 55.
117. David Irving, *Churchill's War: Vol. 1, The Struggle for Power* (Bullsbrook, Australia: Veritas Publishing Company, 1987), pp. 39–40.
118. Charles Higham, *The Duchess of Windsor. The Secret Life* (New York: McGraw & Hill, 1988), p. 109.
119. Peter Allen, *The Windsor Secret. New Revelations of the Nazi connections* (New York: Stein & Day Publishers, 1984), p. 34.
120. Paul Schmidt, *Da Versaglia a Norimberga* (Roma: L'arnia, 1951), pp. 271–80.

121. Benoist-Méchin, *Armée allemande*, Vol. 3, p. 263.
122. Schmidt, *Da Versaglia*, p. 291.
123. Benoist-Méchin, *Armée allemande*, Vol. 3, p. 267.
124. Hanfstaengl, *Missing Years*, p. 228.
125. Higham, *Duchess of Windsor*, p. 117.
126. Schmidt, *Da Versaglia*, p. 293.
127. Higham, *Duchess of Windsor*, p. 130.
128. Allen, *Windsor Secret*, p. 68.
129. Maisky, *Who Helped Hitler?*, p. 57.
130. Hitler, *Secret Conversations*, pp. 556–7.
131. Hajo Holborn, *A History of Modern Germany* (Princeton: Princeton University Press, 1969), p. 769.
132. Allen, *Windsor Secret*, p. 69.
133. Benoist-Méchin, *Armée allemande*, Vol. 3, pp. 286–95.
134. Irving, *Churchill's War*, pp. 54–5.
135. Alfred Smith, *Rudolf Hess and Germany's Reluctant War, 1939–1941* (Sussex: Book Guild Ltd., 2001), p. 61.
136. George Lentin, *Lloyd George and the Lost Peace. From Versailles to Hitler, 1919–1940* (Basingstoke: Palgrave Macmillan, 2001), p. 103.
137. Ibid., p. 99.
138. Lord Beaverbrook, *The Abdication of King Edward VIII* (New York: Atheneum, 1966), p. 63.
139. Higham, *Duchess of Windsor*, p. 188.
140. Allen, *Windsor Secret*, p. 97.
141. Greg King, *The Duchess of Windsor. The Uncommon Life of Wallis Simpson* (New York: Citadel Press, 1999), p. 280.
142. Quigley, *Tragedy*, p. 583.
143. Ibid., p. 777.
144. Benoist-Méchin, *Armée allemande*, Vol. 5, p. 307.
145. Ibid., Vol. 5, pp. 340–5.
146. Quigley, *Anglo-American Establishment*, pp. 286–8.
147. Quigley, *Tragedy*, p. 631.
148. Ibid., p. 627.
149. Ibid., p. 633.
150. Leibovitz and Finkel, *In Our Time*, p. 144.
151. Ibid., p. 182.
152. Allen, *Windsor Secret*, p. 253.
153. Quigley, *Tragedy*, pp. 642–3.
154. Ibid., p. 646.
155. Ibid., p. 648.
156. Benoist-Méchin, *Armée allemande*, Vol. 6, p. 179.
157. David Irving, *The War Path: Hitler's Germany, 1933–1939* (London: Michael Joseph, 1978), p. 193.
158. Leibovitz and Finkel, *In Our Time*, p. 208.
159. Ibid., pp. 256, 232.
160. Irving, *Chuchill's War*, pp. 167–8.
161. Kilzer, *Churchill's Deception*, p. 124.
162. Simon S. Montefiore, *Stalin, the Court of the Red Tsar* (New York: Alfred Knopf, 2004), p. 307.
163. Angiolo Forzoni, *Rublo. Storia civile e monetaria delle Russia da Ivan a Stalin* (Roma: Valerio Levi Editore, 1991), p. 533.
164. Irving, *Chuchill's War*, p. 61.
165. Ibid., p. 162.
166. Edvard Radzinsky, *Stalin* (New York: Doubleday, 1996), p. 323.

167. Montefiore, *Stalin*, p. 222.
168. Benoist-Méchin, *Armée allemande*, Vol. 4, pp. 210–70.
169. W. G. Krivitsky, *In Stalin's Secret Service* (New York: Enigma Books, 2000 [1941]), pp. 205–8.
170. Ibid., p. 12.
171. Edward E. Ericson, *Feeding the German Eagle. Soviet Economic Aid to Nazi Germany, 1933–1941* (Westport, CA: Praeger, 1999), p. 182, and Thamer, *Terzo Reich*, p. 793.
172. David Irving, *Hitler's War* (New York: Avon Books, 1990), p. 360.
173. Quigley, *Anglo-American Establishment*, p. 298.
174. Maisky, *Who Helped Hitler?*, p. 171.
175. Montefiore, *Stalin*, p. 312.
176. Jünger, *Marble Cliffs*, 1947.
177. For a study of Jünger's Mauretanians, see Julien Hervier, *Deux individus contre l'histoire: Pierre Drieu la Rochelle, Ernst Jünger* (Paris: Editions Klincksieck, 1978), p. 191.
178. Benoist-Méchin, *Armée allemande*, Vol. 3, p. 23.
179. Irving, *Chuchill's War*, p. 193.
180. Smith, *Rudolf Hess*, p. 109.
181. Quigley, *Tragedy*, p. 667.
182. Cornwell, *Hitler's Pope*. p. 236.
183. Ibid., p. 238.
184. Smith, *Rudolf Hess*, p. 138.
185. Leibovitz and Finkel, *In Our Time*, p. 231.
186. Higham, *Duchess of Windsor*, p. 276.
187. Kilzer, *Churchill's Deception*, p. 231.
188. Ibid., p. 229.
189. Higham, *Duchess of Windsor*, p. 265.
190. Allen, *Windsor Secret*, p. 200.
191. Irving, *Churchill's War*, p. 379; Irving, *Hitler's War*, p. 306.
192. Irving, *Churchill's War*, p. 376.
193. Allen, *Windsor Secret*, pp. 224–33, and Smith, *Rudolf Hess*, p. 245.
194. Michael Veranov (Ed.), *The Mammoth Book of the Third Reich at War* (New York: Carroll & Graf Publishers Inc. 1997), p. 141.
195. Smith, *Rudolf Hess*, p. 55.
196. Irving, *Churchill's War*, p. 193.
197. Quigley, *Tragedy*, p. 715.
198. Irving, *Churchill's War*, pp. 483–9.
199. Quigley, *Tragedy*, p. 720.
200. Kilzer, *Churchill's Deception*, p. 270.
201. Irving, *Hitler's War*, p. 358.
202. Hugh Thomas, *The Murder of Rudolf Hess* (New York: Harper & Row Publishers, 1979).
203. Richard Deacon, *A History of the British Secret Service* (London: Frederick Muller, 1969), p. 319.
204. Allen, *Windsor Secret*, p. 261.
205. Gordon Thomas, *Journey into Madness. The True story of Secret CIA Mind Control and Medical Abuse* (New York: Bantam Books, 1989), pp. 152–3.
206. International Military Tribunal, *Trial of the Major War Criminals, 14 November 1945–1 October 1946, Vol. XXII* (Nuremberg, 1948), pp. 368–72.
207. John K. Lattimer, *Hitler & the Nazi Leaders. A Unique Insight into Evil* (New York: Hippocene Books, Inc., 2001), pp. 109–17.
208. Smith, *Rudolf Hess*, pp. 457–8.

209. Edmund Walsh, *Total Power. A Footnote to History* (New York: Doubleday & Company, 1948), p. 9.
210. Kilzer, *Churchill's Deception*, p. 283.
211. A recent book by Martin Allen entitled *The Hitler/Hess Deception* (London: HarperCollins, 2004) claims to have at long last solved the Hess mystery. We wish it were so. Allen has 'discovered' additional archival documents that prove that the Peace Party that signaled to the Germans until the departure of Hess was indeed a pretense, the creation of Britain's Secret Service. Allen further argues that all the diplomatic feints, shams, and wiles performed in 1940 and 1941 by 'eminent marionettes' (p. 219) such as Hoare, Halifax & Co. to entice the Nazis formed the essential complement to the deception orchestrated from the secret retreat at Woburn Abbey, the headquarters of a shady branch of the intelligence division for Special Operations. The deception was in fact aimed at diverting the Nazis' urge for devastation away from the Middle East and the Mediterranean seaboard, and reorienting it towards Soviet Russia. So it appears that Allen's findings do nothing but confirm what had been an *easy* supposition in this field of research for at least a couple of decades. For instance, Louis Kilzer had already guessed this much in *Churchill's Deception*, which Allen duly ignores. Moreover, Kilzer, most importantly, wondered whether those three terrible years of unhampered Nazi activity in the East (1941–44) were not in fact the British reward for the surrender of Hess. Allen broaches none of these key problems, nor does he explain how the Nazis were in fact duped if the Hess mission in the end proved to be a failure, which is what the author, not deviating from the standard account of Hess's Scottish impromptu, contends. In other words, it is not at all clear why Hitler resolved nonetheless to push ahead with Barbarossa, even though he had not received any token reassurance from Britain that his back would be covered in the West if he attacked in the East. We don't know why the author has dragged us one more time into a retelling of the story of 'the Nazi bigwig that parachuted himself over the Dungavel estate' if we are to rate that episode, ever anew, as a diplomatic fiasco. Finally, Allen is careful to circumscribe this admittedly horrible deception (it would cost the lives of tens of millions of people) to the 'desperate' circumstances afflicting the British empire in the spring of 1941; we are to take it as the cynical policy of self-defense resorted to by the stewards of the empire to 'survive the fighting season' (pp. 72, 140). The thesis of *The Hitler/Hess Deception* appears to be that such a deception, which worked god knows how, was the worthy price to pay for keeping the British empire standing until Nazism, other than which nothing is worse (the ever-present tacit caption), would be defeated with the prop of America in the West, and that, somewhat less willing, of Russia in the East. To this we may respond that even if the situation in 1941 had been truly critical for the British empire, it was nonetheless a situation entirely of Britain's making – and clearly not an accidental one. It was a terrifying turn of events that had arisen from a mad bet placed at Versailles in 1919, and which Britain managed as best as she could (very well indeed), until she finally crowned her western ambition by destroying Germany and subjecting Europe to Anglo-American domination.
212. Dmitri Volkogonov, *Stalin. Triumph and Tragedy* (New York: Grove Weidenfeld, 1991), p. 485.
213. Radzinsky, *Stalin*, p. 497.
214. Quigley, *Tragedy*, p. 758.
215. Hitler, *Secret Conversations*, p. 208.
216. Michael Bloch, *Operation Willi. The Plot to Kidnap the Duke of Windsor, July 1940* (London: Weidenfeld and Nicolson, 1984), p. 223.
217. Volkogonov, *Stalin*, p. 485.

## Chapter 6

1. Charles Higham, *Trading With the Enemy: An Exposé of the Nazi-American Money Plot, 1933–1949* (New York: Delacorte Press, 1983), pp. 8–20.
2. Alfred Smith, *Rudolf Hess and Germany's Reluctant War, 1939–1941* (Sussex: Book Guild Ltd., 2001), pp. 341–391.
3. Charles Kindleberger, *The World in Depression, 1929–1939* (New York: Penguin Books, 1987), p. 39.
4. Paul Samuelson quoted in Kenneth Mouré, *The Gold Standard Illusion. France, the Bank of France, and the International Gold Standard, 1914–1939* (Oxford: Oxford University Press, 2002), p. 4; emphasis added.
5. Kindleberger, *World in Depression,* pp. 32, 52; emphasis added.
6. Stephen Clarke, *Central Bank Cooperation, 1924–1931* (New York: Federal Reserve Bank of New York, 1967), p. 142.
7. Henry Ashby Turner Jr., *German Big Business and the Rise of Hitler* (Oxford: Oxford University Press, 1987), pp. 314–15; emphasis added.
8. R. H. Knickerbocker, *Is Tomorrow Hitler's?* (New York: Reynal & Hitchcock, 1941), p. 271.
9. Martin Gilbert, *The Roots of Appeasement* (New York: New American Library, 1966), p. 187.
10. Martin Allen, *The Hitler/Hess Deception* (London: HarperCollins, 2004), pp. xviii, 72.
11. Hjalmar Schacht, *1933: Wie eine Demokratie stirbt* (Düsseldorf: Econ-Verlag, 1968), p. 88.
12. Peter Allen, *The Windsor Secret. New Revelations of the Nazi Connections* (New York: Stein & Day Publishers, 1984), p. 98.
13. Klaus Fischer, *Nazi Germany. A New History* (New York: Continuum, 1996), p. 443.
14. Dan P. Silverman, *Hitler's Economy. Nazi Work Creation Programs, 1933–1936* (Cambridge, MA: Harvard University Press, 1998), pp. 146, 243.
15. F. W. Henning, 'Die zeitliche Einordnung der Überwindung der Wirtschaftskrise in Deutschland,' in Harald Winkel (ed.), *Finanz- und Wirschaftspolititische Fragen der Zwischenkriegszeit,* Band 73 (Berlin: Duncker & Humblot, 1973).
16. Pierre Ayçoberry, *The Social History of the Third Reich, 1933–1945* (New York: The New Press, 1999), p. 158.
17. John Cornwell, *Hitler's Pope. The Secret History of Pius XII* (New York: Viking, 1999), p. 328.
18. John Weitz, *Hitler's Banker: Hjalmar Horace Greeley Schacht* (Boston: Little, Brown & Company, 1997), p. 243.
19. According to the American military attaché at the London embassy, who claimed to have spoken with Hess after the latter arrived in England, the Deputy Führer supposedly confessed to a British psychiatrist sent to examine him that the Nazis were on the verge of obliterating the Jews (Louis Kilzer, *Churchill's deception. The Dark Secret that Destroyed Germany* (New York: Simon & Schuster, 1994), pp. 60–2). Moreover, author Alfred Smith relates that on May 13, 1941, only three days after Hess landed, Churchill sent a memo to his colleague, Anthony Eden...It concludes with the words 'Like other Nazi leaders this man is potentially a war criminal and he and his confederates may well be declared outlaws at the close of the war. In this his repentance stands him in good stead.' Smith raises the question: 'Why did Churchill describe Hess as a *potential* war criminal?...The "Crimes against humanity," and in particular the Holocaust, did not take place until after the launch of Operation Barbarossa in June 1941, a month after Hess's flight.' Smith concludes: 'The only construction that makes sense of Churchill's remarks is that he was aware of the war crimes *that were going to be committed in the future*' (Smith, *Rudolf Hess,* p. 341).

# Select Bibliography

Adams Brown, William Jr. 1929. *England and the New Gold Standard, 1919–1926*. New Haven: Yale University Press.

Adams Brown, William Jr. 1940. *The International Gold Standard Reinterpreted, 1914–1934*. New York: National Bureau of Economic Research, Inc.

Aguado, Lago Gil. 2001. 'The Creditanstalt Crisis of 1931 and the Failure of the Austro-German Customs Union Project,' *Historical Journal*, Vol. 44, No. 1.

Aldcroft, Derek A. 1978. *From Versailles to Wall Street, 1919–1929*. New York: Penguin Books.

Alleau, René. 1969. *Hitler et les sociétés secrètes. Enquête sur les sources occultes du nazisme*. Paris: Éditions Bernard Grasset.

Allen, Martin. 2004. *The Hitler/Hess Deception*. London: HarperCollins.

Allen, Peter. 1984. *The Windsor Secret. New Revelations of the Nazi Connections*. New York: Stein & Day Publishers.

Alvi, Geminello. 1993. *Dell'estremo occidente. Il secolo americano in Europa. Storie economiche*. Firenze: Marco Nardi Editore.

Angebert, Jean-Michel. 1974. *The Occult and the Reich. The Mystical Origins Nazism and the Search for the Holy Grail*. New York: Macmillan Publishing [1971].

Armstrong, Hamilton F. 1971. *Peace and Counterpeace. From Wilson to Hitler*. New York: Harper & Row Publishers.

Arndt, H. W. 1944. *The Economic Lessons of the Nineteen Thirties*. London: Oxford University Press.

Arnold, Percy. 1938. *The Bankers of London*. London: Hogarth Press.

Authier, D., and Barriot, J. 1981. *La sinistra comunista in Germania*. Milano: La Salamandra [1976].

Ayçoberry, Pierre. 1999. *The Social History of the Third Reich, 1933–1945*. New York: The New Press.

Balachandran, G. 1996. *John Bullion's Empire: Britain's Gold Problem and India Between the Wars*. Richmond, Surrey: Curzon Press.

Balderston, Theo. 1993. *The Origins and Causes of the German Economic Crisis, November 1923 to May 1932*. Berlin: Haude & Spener.

Balfour, Michael. 1972. *The Kaiser and His Times*. New York: W. W. Norton & Co.

Bank of England. Archives of the Bank of England.

Barkai, Avraham. 1990. *Nazi Economics. Ideology, Theory and Policy*. New Haven: Yale University Press.

Bärsch, Claus-Ekkehard. 1998. *Die politische Religion des Nationalsozialismus*. München: Wilhelm Fink Verlag.

Beaverbrook, Lord. 1966. *The Abdication of King Edward VIII*. New York: Atheneum.

Beck, Earl. 1955. *Verdict on Schacht: A Study in the Problem of Political Guilt*. Tallahassee: Florida State University Press.

Benoist-Méchin, I. 1966. *Histoire de l'armée allemande*. Paris: Éditions Albin Michel.

Berghahn, Volker R. 1994. *Imperial Germany, 1871–1914*. Providence, RI: Berghahn Press.

Bettelheim, Bruno. 1946. *L'économie allemande sous le nazisme: un aspect de la décadence du capitalisme*. Paris: Librairie Marcel Rivière et Cie.

Bloch, Michael. 1984. *Operation Willi. The Plot to Kidnap the Duke of Windsor, July 1940*. London: Weidenfeld and Nicolson.

Bopp, Karl R. 1939. *Hjalmar Schacht: Central Banker*. University of Missouri Studies.

Borkin, Joseph. 1978. *The Crime and Punishment of I. G. Farben*. New York: The Free Press.

Born, Karl Erich. 1967. *Die deutsche Bankenkrise 1931, Finanzen und Politik*. München: R. Piper & Co. Verlag.

Boyle, Andrew. 1967. *Montagu Norman*. London: Cassell.

Bresciani-Turroni, Costantino. 1968. *The Economics of Inflation*. New York: Augustus M. Kelley [1931].

Broszat, Martin. 1987. *Hitler and the Collapse of Weimar Germany*. Leamington Spa: Berg [1984].

Bruce Lockart, R. H. 1933. *British Agent*. London: G. P. Putnam & Sons.

Callot, Maurice. 1934. *Le mark allemand depuis 1924*. Paris: Librairie Arthur Rousseau.

Carr, Edward Hallett. 1951. *German-Soviet Relations Between the Two World Wars, 1914–1939*. Baltimore: Johns Hopkins University Press.

Carr, Edward Hallett. 1953. *The Bolshevik Revolution 1917–1923, Vol. 3*. London: Macmillan & Co. Ltd.

Chaitkin, Anton. 1985. *Treason in America, from Aaron Burr to Averell Harriman*. New York: New Benjamin Franklin House.

Chernow, Ron. 1993. *The Warburgs. The Twentieth-Century Odyssey of a Remarkable Jewish Family*. New York: Random House.

Clarke, Stephen V. O. 1967. *Central Bank Cooperation, 1924–1931*. New York: Federal Reserve Bank of New York.

Clay, Henry. 1957. *Lord Norman*. London: Macmillan and Co.

Cornwell, John. 1999. *Hitler's Pope. The Secret History of Pius XII*. New York: Viking.

D'Abernon, Viscount. 1929. *The Diary of an Ambassador*. New York: Doubleday, Doran & Company, Inc.

Dana Noyes, Alexander. 1938. *The Market Place. Reminiscences of a Financial Editor*. Boston: Little, Brown & Company.

Deacon, Richard. 1968. *John Dee. Scientist, Geographer, Astrologer & Secret Agent to Elizabeth I*. London: Frederick Muller.

Deacon, Richard. 1969. *A History of the British Secret Service*. London: Frederick Muller.

De Cecco, Marcello. 1979. *Moneta e impero. Il sistema finanziario internazionale dal 1890 al 1914*. Torino: Piccola Biblioteca Einaudi.

Degrelle, Léon. 1987. *Hitler: Born at Versailles*. Costa Mesa: Institute for Historical Review.

De Jonge, Alex. 1978. *The Weimar Chronicle. Prelude to Hitler*. New York: Meridian Books.

Delarue, Jacques. 1964. *The Gestapo. A History of Horror*. New York: Dell.

Delivanis, Démètre J. 1934. *La politique des banques allemandes, en matière de crédit à court terme*. Paris: Librairie du Recueil Sirey.

Dell, Robert. 1934. *Germany Unmasked*. London: Martin Hopkins Ltd.

De Poncins, Leon. 1996. *The Secret Powers Behind Revolution*. San Pedro, CA: GSG Publishers [1929].

Döblin, Alfred. 1983. *Karl & Rosa*. New York: Fromm International Publishing Corporation [1950].

Dodd, William. 1941. *Ambassador Dodd's Diary, 1933–1938*. New York: Harcourt, Brace and Company.

Dorpalen, Andreas. 1942. *The World of General Haushofer. Geopolitics in Action*. New York: Farrar & Rinehart Inc.

Dupeux, Louis. 1974. *National-Bolchévisme en Allemagne, sous la République de Weimar (1919–1933)*. Paris: Librairie Honoré Champion.

Eckart, Dietrich. 1978. 'Jewishness In and Around Us: Fundamental Reflections,' in Barbara Miller Lane and Leyla J. Rupp (eds.), *Nazi Ideology Before 1933. A Documentation* [1919]. Austin: University of Texas Press.

Eichengreen, Barry. 1992. *Golden Fetters. The Gold Standard and the Great Depression, 1919–1939.* New York: Oxford University Press.

Eisner, Freya. 1979. *Kurt Eisner: die Politik des libertären Sozialismus.* Frankfurt am Main: Suhrkamp Verlag.

Einzig, Paul. 1932. *The Tragedy of the Pound.* London: Kegan, Paul, Trench, Trubner & Co., Ltd.

Epstein, Edward Jay. 1996. *Dossier. The Secret Story of Armand Hammer.* New York: Random House.

Epstein, Klaus. 1959. *Matthias Erzberger and the Dilemma of German Democracy.* Princeton: Princeton University Press.

Erger, Johannes. 1967. *Der Kapp-Lüttwitz Putsch. Ein Beitrag zur deutschen Innenpolitik.* Düsseldorf: Droste Verlag.

Ericson, Edward E. 1999. *Feeding the German Eagle. Soviet Economic Aid to Nazi Germany, 1933–1941.* Westport, CT: Praeger.

Erusalimskij. A.S. 1974. *Da Bismarck a Hitler. L'imperialismo tedesco nel XX secolo.* Roma: Editori Riuniti.

Erzberger, Matthias. 1919. *Reden zu Neuordnung des deutschen Finanzwesens.* Berlin: Verlag von Reimar Hobbing.

Eyck, Erich. 1966. *Storia della repubblica di Weimar, 1918–1933 (Geschichte der weimarer Republik).* Torino: Giulio Einaudi Editore [1956].

Feldman, Gerald. 1997. *The Great Disorder. Politics, Economics and Society in the German Inflation, 1914–1924.* Oxford: Oxford University Press.

Felstead, Sidney Theodore. 1920. *German Spies at Bay. Being an Actual Record of the German Espionage in Great Britain during the Years 1914–1918 (Compiled from Official Sources).* London: Hutchinson & Co.

Ferguson, Niall. 1999. *The Pity of War.* New York: Basic Books.

Fest, Joachim. 1975, *Hitler.* New York: Vintage Books [1973].

Feuchtwanger, E. J. 1995. *From Weimar to Hitler. Germany, 1918–1933.* New York: St. Martin's Press.

Fischer, Klaus P. 1996. *Nazi Germany. A New History.* New York: Continuum.

Fleming, Peter. 1963. *The Fate of Admiral Kolchak.* New York: Harcourt, Brace & World, Inc.

Forbes, Neil. 2000. *Doing Business With the Nazis. Britain's Economic and Financial Relations With Germany, 1931–1939.* London: Frank Cass.

Forzoni, Angiolo. 1991. *Rublo. Storia civile e monetaria delle Russia da Ivan a Stalin.* Roma: Valerio Levi Editore.

Fourgeaud, André. 1926. *La dépréciation et la revalorisation du Mark allemand, et les enseignements de l'experience monétarire allemande.* Paris: Payot.

François-Poncet, André. 1949. *The Fateful Years. Memoirs of a French Ambassador in Berlin, 1931–1938.* London: Victor Gollancz.

Fromkin, David. 1989. *A Peace to End all Peace. The Fall of the Ottoman Empire and the Creation of the Modern Middle East.* New York: Avon Books.

Gallo, Max. 1997. *The Night of the Long Knives.* New York: Da Capo Press [1972].

Garrett, Garet. 1931. *The Rescue of Germany & As Noble Lenders.* New York: The Chemical Foundation.

Gatzke, Hans W. 1972. 'Russo-German Military Collaboration During the Weimar Republic', in H. W. Gatzke (ed.), *European Diplomacy Between Two Wars, 1919–1933.* Chicago: Quadrangle Books.

Gay, Edwin F. 1931. 'The Gold Problem,' in *Foreign Affairs,* January, Vol. 9.

Gay, Peter. 2001. *Weimar Culture. The Insider as Outsider.* New York: W. W. Norton & Company.

Gerson, Werner. 1969. *Le Nazisme société secrète.* Paris: J'ai lu.

Gesell, Silvio. 1920. *The Natural Economic Order.* San Antonio: Free-Economy Publishing Co.

Gilbert, G. M. 1995. *Nuremberg Diary.* New York: Da Capo Press [1947].
Gilbert, Martin. 1966. *The Roots of Appeasement.* New York: New American Library.
Giordani, Paolo. 1915. *L'Impero coloniale tedesco.* Milano: Fratelli Treves Editori.
Goerlitz, Walther. 1962. *History of the German General Staff 1657–1945.* New York: Frederick A. Praeger Publishers.
Goethe, Johann Wolfgang. 1949. *Goethe's Faust, Part Two* (Prose translation by Max Dietz). Pennsylvania: Bryn Mawr [1831].
Golecki, Anton (ed.). 1980. *Das Kabinett Bauer (21 Juni 1919 bis 27 März 1920). Akten der Reichkanzlei weimarer Republik.* Boppard am Rhein: Harald Boldt Verlag.
Goodrick-Clarke, Nicholas. 1985. *The Occult Roots of Nazism. Secret Aryan Cults and Their Influence on Nazi Ideology.* New York: New York University Press.
Goodspeed, D. J. 1966. *Ludendorff. Soldier, Dictator, Revolutionary.* London: Rupert Hart-Davis.
Gordon Levin, N. Jr. 1968. *Woodrow Wilson and World Politics. America's Response to War and Revolution.* Oxford: Oxford University Press.
Graham, F. D. 1930. *Exchange, Prices and Production in Hyper-Inflation Germany, 1920–1923.* Princeton: Princeton University Press.
Gregory, Paul. 1982. *Russian National Income (1885–1913).* Cambridge: Cambridge University Press.
Gromyko, Andrej. 1985. *L'espansione internazionale del capitale, storia e attualità.* Roma: Editori Riuniti [1982].
Gross, Felix. 1940. *I Knew Those Spies.* London: Hurst & Blackett.
Gunther, John. 1938. *Inside Europe.* New York: Harper & Brothers.
Gyomaï, Imre. 1939. *Trebitsch-Lincoln. Le plus grand aventurier du siècle.* Paris: Les Éditions de France.
Haffner, Sebastian. 1986. *Failure of a Revolution. Germany, 1918–1919.* Chicago: Banner Press [1969].
Hanfstaengl, Ernst. 1994. *Hitler: The Missing Years.* New York: Arcade Publishing [1957].
Hanser, Richard. 1970. *Putsch!* New York: Pyramid Books.
Hardy, Charles O. 1936. *Is There Enough Gold?* Washington DC: Brookings Institution.
Hargrave, John. 1942. *Montagu Norman.* New York: Greystone Press.
Haushofer, Karl. 1937. *Weltmeere und Weltmächte.* Berlin: Zeitgeschichte Verlag.
Heiden, Konrad. *Der Fuehrer. Hitler's Rise to Power.* Boston: Houghton Mifflin Company.
Helbig, Herbert. 1958. *Die Träger der Rapallo Vertrag.* Göttingen: Vandenhoeck & Ruprecht.
Henning, F. W. 1973. 'Die zeitliche Einordnung der Überwindung der Wirtschaftskrise in Deutschland,' in Harald Winkel (ed.), *Finanz- und Wirschaftspolititische Fragen der Zwischenkriegszeit,* Band 73. Berlin: Duncker & Humblot.
Henning, F. W. 1974. *Das industrialisierte Deutschland 1914 bis 1972.* Paderborn: Ferdinand Schöningh.
Hermant, Max. 1931. *Les paradoxes économiques de l'Allemagne moderne 1918–1931.* Paris: Librarie Armand Collin.
Hervier, Julien. 1978. *Deux individus contre l'histoire: Pierre Drieu la Rochelle, Ernst Jünger.* Paris: Editions Klincksieck.
Higham, Charles. 1983. *Trading With the Enemy: An Exposé of the Nazi-American Money Plot, 1933–1949.* New York: Delacorte Press.
Higham, Charles. 1988. *The Duchess of Windsor. The Secret Life.* New York: McGraw & Hill.
Hirst, Francis W. 1931. *Wall Street and Lombard Street. The Stock Exchange Slump of 1929 and the Trade Depression of 1930.* New York: Macmillan Company.
Hirst, Francis W. 1934. *Money, Gold, Silver and Paper.* New York: Charles Scribner's Sons.
Hitler, Adolf. 1953. *Hitler's Secret Conversations 1941–1944.* New York: Farrar, Straus & Young.
Hitler, Adolf. 1971. *Mein Kampf.* Boston: Houghton Mifflin Company [1925].

Holborn, Hajo. 1969. *A History of Modern Germany*. Princeton: Princeton University Press.

Hölderlin, Friedrich. 1922. *Hyperion, Empedokles*. Weimar: Erich Liechenstein Verlag [1799].

Hölderlin, Friedrich. 1984. *Hymns and Fragments* (trans. Richard Sieburth). Princeton: Princeton University Press [1801–06].

Holtfrerich, Ludwig. 1989. *L'inflazione tedesca, 1914–1923 (Die deutsche Inflation)*. Bari: Laterza [1980].

Hoops, Reinhold. 1940. *Englands Selbst-täuschung*. Berlin: Zentralverlag NSDAP Franz Eher Nachfolger Gmbh.

House, Edward. 1926. *The Intimate Papers of Colonel House, Arranged as a Narrative by Charles Seymour*. Boston: Houghton Mifflin Company.

Hutton, Graham. 1937. *Is it Peace?* New York: Macmillan Company.

International Military Tribunal. 1948. *Trial of the Major War Criminals, 14 November 1945– 1 October 1946, Vol. XXII*. Nuremberg.

Irving, David. 1978. *The War Path: Hitler's Germany, 1933–1939*. London: Michael Joseph.

Irving, David. 1987. *Churchill's War: Vol. 1, The Struggle for Power*. Bullsbrook, Australia: Veritas Publishing Company.

Irving, David. 1990. *Hitler's War*. New York: Avon Books.

Jaques, Hermann. 1932. *Allemagne, société à responsabilité limitée*. Paris: Éditions de la revue mondiale.

Jean, Carlo. 1995. *Geopolitica*. Bari: Laterza.

Johannsen, N. J. 1971. *A Neglected Point in Connection with Crises*. New York: Augustus M. Kelley Publishers [1908].

Jorgensen, Elizabeth W., and Jorgensen, Henry I. 1999. *Thorstein Veblen. Victorian Firebrand*. Armonk, NY: M. E. Sharpe.

Jünger, Ernst. 1938. *Das abenteurliche Herz. Figuren und Capriccios*. Hamburg: Hanseatische Verlaganstalt.

Jünger, Ernst 1947. *On the Marble Cliffs*. Norfolk, CT: New Directions.

Kaes, A., Jay, M., and Dimendberg, E. (eds.). 1994. *The Weimar Republic Sourcebook*. Berkeley: University of California Press.

Kästner, Erich. 1990. *Fabian: The Story of a Moralist*. Evanston: Northwestern University Press [1931].

Kennan, George F. 1960. *Russia and the West under Lenin and Stalin*. Boston: Little, Brown & Co.

Kennedy, Paul M. 1980. *The Rise of Anglo-German Antagonism, 1860–1914*. London: Ashfield Press.

Kershaw, Ian. 1998. *Hitler: 1889–1936: Hubris*. New York: W. W. Norton & Co.

Kessler, Harry. 1995. *Rathenau*. Bologna: Il Mulino [1928].

Keynes, John Maynard. 1995. *The Economic Consequences of the Peace*. New York: Penguin Books [1920].

Kilzer, Louis. 1994. *Churchill's Deception. The Dark Secret that Destroyed Germany*. New York: Simon & Schuster.

Kindleberger, Charles P. 1987. *The World in Depression, 1929–1939*. New York: Penguin Books.

King, Greg. 1995. *The Man Who Killed Rasputin. Price Felix Youssoupov and the Murder That Helped Bring Down the Russian Empire*. New York: Citadel Press.

King, Greg. 1999. *The Duchess of Windsor. The Uncommon Life of Wallis Simpson*. New York: Citadel Press.

Kissenkoetter, Udo. 1978. *Gregor Straßer und die NSDAP*. Stuttgart: Deutsche Verlags-Anstalt.

Knickerbocker, H. R. 1941. *Is Tomorrow Hitler's?* New York: Reynal & Hitchcock.

Könnemann, Erwin. 2000. 'Kapp-Putsch gegen die weimarer Republik. Ein Spiel mit den roten und den weissen Russen,' *Der Tagesspiel* (March 14, 2000).

Krivitsky, W. G. 2000. *In Stalin's Secret Service*. New York: Enigma Books [1941].

Kunz, Diane. 1987. *The Battle for Britain's Gold Standard in 1931*. London: Croom Helm.

Lampe, David, and Szenasi, Lazlo. 1961. *The Self-made Villain. A Biography of I. T. Trebitsch-Lincoln*. London: Cassell.

Laporte, Maurice. 1933. *Bouddha contre l'Intelligence Service*. Paris: Alexis Redier Éditeur.

Lattimer, John K. 2001. *Hitler & the Nazi Leaders. A Unique Insight into Evil*. New York: Hippocene Books, Inc.

Leach, Paul R. 1930. *That Man Dawes*. Chicago: Reilly & Lee Co.

Lebergott, Stanley. 1984. *The Americans. An Economic Record*. New York: Norton & Co.

Lee, Marshall M., and Michalka, Wolfgang. 1987. *German Foreign Policy, 1917–1933: Continuity or Break?* Leamington Spa: Berg.

Leibovitz, Clement, and Finkel, Alvin. 1998. *In Our Time. The Chamberlain-Hitler Collusion*. New York: Monthly Review Press.

Lentin, Anthony. 2001. *Lloyd George and the Lost Peace. From Versailles to Hitler, 1919–1940*. Basingstoke: Palgrave Macmillan.

Levien, J. R. 1966. *Anatomy of a Crash – 1929*. New York: Traders Press.

Lewis, Cleona. 1941. *Nazi Europe and World Trade*. Washington DC: Brookings Institution.

Liddell Hart, B. H. 1930. *The Real War, 1914–1918*. Boston: Little, Brown & Company.

Luckett, Richard, 1971. *The White Generals. An Account of the White Movement in Russia and the Russian Civil War*. New York: Viking Press.

Lunn, Eugene. 1973. *Prophet of Community. The Romantic Socialism of Gustav Landauer*. Berkeley: University of California Press.

Lurie, Samuel. 1947. *Private Investment in a Controlled Economy*. New York: Columbia University Press.

Macmillan, Margaret. 2002. *Paris 1919. Six Months that Changed the World*. New York: Random House.

Maisky, Ivan. 1964. *Who Helped Hitler?* London: Hutchinson [1962].

Manchester, William. 1968. *The Arms of Krupp, 1857–1968*. Boston: Little, Brown and Company.

Maquenne, Paul. 1940. *L'hérésie économique allemande*. Paris: Guerre 39, Union Latine.

Marczewski, Jan. 1941. *Politique monétaire et financière du IIIᵉ Reich*. Paris: Librairie du Recueil Sirey.

Marlowe, Christopher. 1959. *The Tragedy of Doctor Faustus*. New York: Washington Square Press [1588].

Marshall, S. L. A. 1992. *World War I*. Boston: Houghton Mifflin Company [1964].

Mauss, Marcel. 1997. *Écrits politiques*. Paris: Librairie Arthème Fayard [1924].

Maynard, John. 1948. *Russia in Flux*. New York: Macmillan Company.

McCormick, Donald. 1963. *The Mask of Merlin. A Critical Study of David Lloyd George*. London: Macdonald.

McFadden, Louis T. 1970. *Collected Speeches of Congressman Louis T. McFadden, as Compiled from the Congressional Record*. Hawthorne, CA: Omni Publications.

Mee, Charles L. Jr. 1980. *The End of Order, Versailles 1919*. New York: E. P. Dutton.

Melville, Cecil F. 1932. *The Russian Face of Germany*. London: Wishart & Co.

Meyer, T. H. (Ed.). 1997. *Light for the New Millennium. Rudolf Steiner's Association with Helmuth von Moltke, Letters, Documents and After-Death Communications*. London: Rudolf Steiner Press.

Meyrink, Gustav. 1995. *The Golem*. Sawtry, Cambs: Dedalus [1915].

Moeller van den Bruck, Arthur. 1997. *L'uomo politico (Der politische Mensch)*. Roma: Settimo Sigillo [1918].

Moeller van den Bruck, Arthur. 2000. *Il terzo Reich (Das dritte Reich)*. Roma: Edizione Settimo Sigillo [1923].

Moggridge, D. E. 1972. *British Monetary Policy 1924–1931. The Norman Conquest of $ 4.86.* Cambridge: Cambridge University Press.

Mommsen, Hans. 1972. 'The Reichstag Fire and Its Political Consequences,' in Hajo Holborn (ed.), *Republic to Reich. The Making of the Nazi Revolution. Ten Essays.* New York: Vintage.

Mommsen, Hans. 1989. *The Rise & Fall of the Weimar Democracy.* Chapel Hill: University of North Carolina Press.

Montefiore, Simon S. 2004. *Stalin, the Court of the Red Tsar.* New York: Alfred Knopf.

Moreau, Emile. 1954. *Souvenirs d'un Gouverneur de la Banque de France, histoire de la stabilisation du franc (1926–1928).* Paris: Librairie de Médicis.

Morton, Walter A. 1978. *British Finance, 1930–1940.* New York: Arno Press.

Mowat, Charles Loch. 1955. *Britain Between the Wars, 1918–1940.* Chicago: University of Chicago Press.

Mühlen, Norbert. 1939. *Schacht: Hitler's Magician. The Life and Loans of Dr. Hjalmar Schacht.* New York: Alliance Book Corporation.

Mullins, Eustace. 1991. *Secrets of the Federal Reserve. The London Connection.* Staunton, VA: Bankers Research Institute.

Musil, Robert. 1995. *The Man Without Qualities (Der Mann ohne Eigenschaften).* New York: Vintage books [1930–52].

Mussolini, Benito. 1954. *Opera omnia, Vol. XIV (1919–1920).* Firenze: La Fenice.

Nathan, Otto. 1944. *Nazi War Finance and Banking.* NBER Paper No. 20.

Noakes, J., and Pridham, G. 1984. *Nazism 1919–1945, Vol. 2: State, Economy and Society, 1933–1939.* Exeter: University of Exeter Press.

Oesterfeld, Paul. 1943. *La leggenda dell'oro.* Roma: Casa Editrice Mediterranea.

Overy, R. J. 1994. *War and the Economy in the Third Reich.* Oxford: Clarendon Press.

Owen, Robert. L. 1927. *The Russian Imperial Conspiracy [1892–1914].* New York: Albert and Charles Boni.

Padfield, Peter. 1990. *Himmler, Reichsführer-SS.* London: Macmillan.

Palyi, Melchior. 1972. *The Twilight of Gold 1914–1936. Myths and Realities.* Chicago: Henry Regnery Company.

Peterson, Edward Norman. 1954. *Hjalmar Schacht: For and Against Hitler.* Boston: Christopher Publishing House.

Philips Price, Morgan. 1999. *Dispatches from the Weimar Republic. Versailles and German Fascism.* London: Pluto Press [1919–29].

Pipes, Richard. 1995. *A Concise History of the Russian Revolution.* New York: Vintage Books.

Pool, James, and Pool, Suzanne. 1978. *Who Financed Hitler. The Secret Funding of Hitler's Rise to Power, 1919–1933.* London: MacDonald and Jane's.

Poole, Kenyon. 1939. *German Financial Policies 1932–39.* Cambridge, MA: Harvard University Press.

Preziosi, Giovanni. 1941. *Giudaismo, bolscevismo, plutocrazia e massoneria.* Torino: Arnoldo Mondadori.

Quigley, Carroll. 1966. *Tragedy and Hope. A History of the World in Our Time.* New York: Macmillan Company.

Quigley, Carroll. 1981. *The Anglo-American Establishment. From Rhodes to Cliveden.* San Pedro, CA: GSG & Associates Publishers.

Radzinsky, Edvard. 1996. *Stalin.* New York: Doubleday.

Rathenau, Walther. 1921. *In Days to Come (Von kommenden Dingen).* London: George Allen & Unwin [1917].

Rathenau, Walther. 1964. *Schriften und Reden.* Frankfurt am Main: S. Fischer Verlag.

Reed, Douglas. 1944. *Nemesi? La storia di Otto Strasser (Nemesis? The History of Otto Strasser).* Roma: Edizioni delle catacombe.

Reed, Douglas. 1953. *The Prisoner of Ottawa, Otto Strasser.* London: Jonathan Cape.

Riddell, L. 1934. *Intimate Diary of the Peace Conference and After, 1918–1923*. New York: Reynal & Hitchcock.

Ringer, Fritz K. 1969. *The German Inflation of 1923*. New York: Oxford University Press.

Robbins, Lionel. 1934. *The Great Depression*. New York: Macmillan Company.

Roberts, Stephen H. 1938. *The House That Hitler Built*. New York: Harper & Brothers Publishers.

Robinson, George Buchan. 1935. *Monetary Mischief*. New York: Columbia University Press.

Rose, Detlev. 1994. *Die Thule-Gesellschaft. Legende, Mythos, Wirklichkeit*. Tübingen: Grabert Verlag.

Rosenberg Alfred. 1934. *Der Mythus des 20. Jahrhunderts. Eine Wertung der seelisch-geistigen Gestaltenkampfe unserer Zeit*. München: Honeichen-Verlag.

Rosenberg, Arthur. 1945. *Storia della repubblica tedesca (Deutsche Republik)*. Roma: Edizioni Leonardo [1934].

Rueff, Jacques. 1977. *De l'aube au crépuscule. Autobiographie de l'auteur*. Paris: Librairie Plon.

Salzmann, Stephanie. 2003. *Great Britain, Germany and the Soviet Union. Rapallo and After, 1922–1934*. Woodbridge, Suffolk: Boydell Press.

Sasuly, Richard. 1947. *I. G. Farben*. New York: Boni & Gear.

Sauvy, Alfred. 1965. *Histoire économique de la France entre les deux guerres*. Paris: Fayard.

Schacht, Hjalmar. 1931. *Das Ende der Reparationen*. Oldenburg: Gerhard Stalling.

Schacht, Hjalmar. 1955. *My First Seventy-Six Years. The Autobiography of Hjalmar Schacht*. London: Allen Wingate.

Schacht, Hjalmar. 1968. *1933: Wie eine Demokratie stirbt*. Düsseldorf: Econ-Verlag.

Schiller, Karl. 1936. *Arbeitsbeschaffung und Finanzordnung in Deutschland*. Berlin: Junker und Dünnhaupt Verlag.

Schmidt, Carl T. 1934. *German Business Cycles, 1924–1933*. New York: National Bureau of Economic Research.

Schmidt, Paul. 1951. *Da Versaglia a Norimberga*. Roma: L'arnia.

Schoenbaum, David. 1980. *Hitler's Social Revolution. Class and Status in Nazi Germany, 1933–1939*. New York: W. W. Norton & Company, Inc. [1966].

Schulze, Hagen. 1993. *La repubblica di Weimar, la Germania dal 1918 al 1933 (Weimar, Deutschland 1918–1933)*. Bologna: Il Mulino [1983].

Schultz, Sigrid. 1944. *Germany Will Try It Again*. New York: Reynal & Hitchcock.

Silfen, Paul Harrison. 1973. *The Völkisch Ideology & The Roots of Nazism. The Early Writings of Artur Moeller van den Bruck*. New York: Exposition Press.

Silverman, Dan P. 1998. *Hitler's Economy. Nazi Work Creation Programs, 1933–1936*. Cambridge, MA: Harvard University Press

Simonds, Frank H. 1934. *Can Europe Keep the Peace?* New York: Blue Ribbon Books, Inc.

Smele, Jonathan. 1996. *Civil War in Siberia. The Anti-Bolshevik Government of Admiral Kolchak, 1918–1920*. Cambridge: Cambridge University Press.

Smith, Alfred. 2001. *Rudolf Hess and Germany's Reluctant War, 1939–1941*. Sussex: Book Guild Ltd.

Smith, Woodruff D. 1986. *The Ideological Origins of Nazi Imperialism*. Oxford: Oxford University Press.

Somary, Felix. 1932. *Die Ursache der Krise*. Tübingen: J. C. B. Mohr.

Stafford, David. 1999. *Churchill and the Secret Service*. New York: Overlook Press.

Stehlin, Stewart A. 1983. *Weimar and the Vatican, 1919–1933*. Princeton: Princeton University Press.

Stewart, George. 1933. *The White Armies of Russia: A Chronicle of Counter-Revolution and Allied Intervention*. New York: Macmillan Company.

Stewart, Maxwell S. 1931. 'Silver – Its International Aspects,' *Foreign Policy Reports*, Vol. VII, No. 13.

Stürmer, Michael. 1993. *L'impero inquieto, 1866–1918* (*Das ruhelose Reich, 1866–1918*). Bologna: Il Mulino [1983].

Sutton, Anthony C. 1981. *Wall Street and the Bolshevik Revolution*. New Rochelle, NY: Arlington House Publishers.

Sutton, Anthony C. 1976. *Wall Street and the Rise of Hitler*. Sudbury, Suffolk: Bloomfield Books.

Tacitus. 1992. *Agricola, Germania, Dialogus*. Cambridge, MA: Harvard University Press (Loeb Classical Library) [98 AD].

Tarle, Evgheni V. 1959. *Storia d'Europa, 1871–1919*. Bologna: Editori Riuniti [1928].

Tarpley, Webster Griffin, and Chaitkin, Anton. 1992. *George Bush. The Unauthorized Biography*. Washington DC: Executive Intelligence Review.

Thamer, Hans Ulrich. 1993. *Il Terzo Reich* (*Verführung und Gewalt, Deutschland 1933–1945*). Bologna: Il Mulino [1986].

Thomas, Gordon. 1989. *Journey into Madness. The True story of Secret CIA Mind Control and Medical Abuse*. New York: Bantam Books.

Thomas, Hugh. 1979. *The Murder of Rudolf Hess*. New York: Harper & Row Publishers.

Toland, John. 1976. *Adolf Hitler*. Garden City, NY: Doubleday & Co.

Toller, Ernst. 1934. *I Was a German. The Autobiography of Ernst Toller*. New York: William Morrow and Company.

Troeltsch, Ernst. 1977. *La democrazia improvvisata, la Germania dal 1918 al 1922*. Napoli: Guida Editori [1924].

Trotsky, Leon. 1959. *The Russian Revolution. The Overthrow of Tzarism & the Triumph of the Soviets*. New York: Doubleday Anchor Books [1930].

Trotsky, Leon. 1971. *The Struggle Against Fascism in Germany*. New York: Pathfinder Press [1931–33].

Truptil, R. J. 1936. *British Banks and the London Money Market*. London: Jonathan Cape.

Turner, Henry Ashby Jr. 1985. *German Big Business and the Rise of Hitler*. Oxford: Oxford University Press.

Van Zanden, Jan. 1997. *The Economic History of the Netherlands, 1914–1995*. London: Routledge.

Veblen, Thorstein. 1915. *Imperial Germany and the Industrial Revolution*. London: Macmillan & Co.

Veblen, Thorstein. 1919. *The Vested Interests and the Common Man (The Modern Point of View and the New Order)*. New York: B. W. Huebsch, Inc.

Veblen, Thorstein, 1963. *The Engineers and the Price System*. New York: Harcourt, Brace & World, Inc. [1921].

Veblen, Thorstein. 1964. *Essays in Our Changing Order*. New York: Augustus M. Kelley [1915].

Veblen, Thorstein. 1969. *The Place of Science in Modern Civilization*. New York: Capricorn Books [1907].

Veblen, Thorstein. 1979. *The Theory of the Leisure Class*. New York: Penguin books [1899].

Veblen, Thorstein. 1998. *The Nature of Peace*. New Brunswick: Transaction Books [1917].

Veranov, Michael (ed.). 1997. *The Mammoth Book of the Third Reich at War*. New York: Carroll & Graf Publishers Inc.

Vermeil, Edmond. 1945. *Germany's Three Reichs. Their History and Culture*. London: Andrew Dakers Limited.

Vibert, Henri. 1936. *Fronte a l'Inghilterra*. Firenze: Beltrami Editore.

Volkogonov, Dmitri. 1996. *Trotsky, the Eternal Revolutionary*. New York: The Free Press.

Volkogonov, Dmitri. 1991. *Stalin. Triumph and Tragedy*. New York: Grove Weidenfeld.

Von Bernhardi, F. 1914. *Germany and the Next War*. New York: Longmans, Green & Co. [1911].

von Bülow, Bernhard. 1931. *Le memorie del Principe di Bülow, Volume III, 1901–1920*. Milano: Arnoldo Mondadori.

von Bülow, Bernhard. 1994. *La Germania imperiale*. Prodenone: Edizioni Studio Tesi [1914].

Von Salomon, Ernst. 1954. *The Answers of Ernst von Salomon. The 131 Questions in the Allied Military Government. 'Fragebogen.'* London: Putnam [1951].

Von Salomon, Ernst. 1979. *I proscritti (Die Geächteten)*. Parma: Edizioni all'insegna del veltro [1930].

Von Sebottendorff, Rudolf. 1987. *Prima che Hitler venisse. Storia della Società Thule (Bevor Hitler kam)*. Torino: Edizioni Delta-Arktos [1933].

Walsh, Edmund A. 1948. *Total Power. A Footnote to History*. New York: Doubleday & Company, Inc.

Wasserstein, Bernard. 1988. *The Secret Lives of Trebitsch-Lincoln*. New York: Penguin Books.

Weitz, John. 1997. *Hitler's Banker: Hjalmar Horace Greeley Schacht*. Boston: Little, Brown & Company.

Wheatley, Dennis. 1938. *Red Eagle. The Story of the Russian Revolution*. London: The Book Club.

Wheeler-Bennett, John. 1961. *The Nemesis of Power. The German Army in Politics 1918–1945*. London: Macmillan & Co.

Williams, Francis. 1965. *A Pattern of Rulers*. London: Longman.

Williamson, David G. 1991. *The British in Germany, 1918–1930. The Reluctant Occupiers*. New York: Berg Publishers.

Winkler, Heinrich August. 1998. *La repubblica di Weimar, 1918–1933: storia della prima repubblica tedesca*. Roma: Donzelli Editore [1993].

Wolff, Robert. 1943. *Économie et finances de la France, passé et avenir*. New York: Brentano's.

Woodman, Dorothy. 1934. *Hitler Rearms. An Exposure of Germany's War Plans*. London: John Lane, Bodley Head Limited.

Zeman, Z. A. B., and Scharlan, W. B. 1965. *The Merchant of Revolution. The Life of Alexander Israel Helphand (Parvus), 1867–1924*. London: Oxford University Press.

Zveteremich, Pietro. 1988. *Il grande Parvus*. Milano: Garzanti.

# Index

A.E.G. (Germany's General Electrics), 115, 170
Albert, Duke of York, *see* George VI
Allenby, Sir Edmund, British general, 40
Anglo-German Naval Treaty, 234
Anglo-German Payments Agreement, 223, 234
Appeasement, xviii, 78, 117, 228–44, 266
Arco-Valley, Anton von, murderer of K. Eisner, 22, 55–6
Artamanov, Colonel Victor, Russia's military attaché in Bosnia, 21
Asquith, Herbert H., British Prime Minister, 39–40
Astor, Lord, British appeaser, 235
Austria, as Germany's ally, 7, 22–3, 27, 110, Norman's bailout of, 139, 140, 158, 159, collapse of the Creditanstalt, 181, 194, and the *Zollverein*, 193, and the 1934 coup, 232, and the *Anschluss* (annexation), 238, 249
Avalov-Bermondt, Russian White adventurer, 98, 103
Axelrod, Tobias, Russian subversive, 56

Baden, Max von, Weimar Chancellor, 47, 50
Baldwin, Stanley, British Prime Minister, 232, 236, 237, 245, 261
Bank of England, 69, 139–41, 148–58, 182–4, 222, 224, 242, 249
Bank of France, 162, 176, 182
Barbarossa, directive for the Nazi invasion of Soviet Russia, 87, 113, 232, 238, 242, 249, 253, 260–2, 293, 294
Bauer, Colonel Max, Kapp putschist, 99–100, 103–9, 110
Beaverbrook, Lord (William M. Aitken), director of the *Daily Express*, 194, 235
Bebel, August, SPD leader, 44
Beck, General Ludwig, Chief of Staff of the *Wehrmacht*, 240, 241
Beerhall Putsch, *see* Hitler
Bell, Johannes, Weimar Minister, 78
Bethmann-Hollweg, Theobald von, Imperial Chancellor, 17
Bin Laden, Osama, Saudi professional subversive, 21n
Bismarck, Herbert, 4

Bismarck, Otto von, Imperial Chancellor, 2–5, 7, 17, 207
Björkö, aborted Russo-German treaty, 16–17
Blomberg, General Werner von, Defense Minister of the Third Reich, 209, 247
'Bloody Sunday' (Russian uprising of 1905), 16, 32
BMW, German corporation, 226
Bormann, Martin, Nazi hierarch, 260
Bosch, Carl, I. G. Farben's chief engineer, 168–9
Bredow, General Kurt von, Schleicher's aide, 210, 247
Brest-Litvosk, Russo-German peace treaty, 37, 51, 62
British Petroleum (BP), 224
Brockdorff-Rantzau, Ulrich von, German diplomat and Minister, 30–2, 75–6, 108
Brooks, Sir Alan, Commander in Chief of the British Army, 261
Brown Brothers & Co., US bank, 147, 170
Brown Shipley, London branch of Brown Brothers, 147–8, 149, 159
Brüning, Heinrich, Weimar Chancellor, 192, 194–6, 205, 207, 213
Brusilov, General Alexei, Russian commander in WWI, 27
Buchanan, Lord George, British ambassador, 28–9, 31, 36
Bülow, Bernhard von, Imperial Chancellor, 4, 49
Bush, Prescott, fiduciary of America's Anglophile clubs, 198

Cambon, Paul, French ambassador, 19
Central Intelligence Agency (CIA), 21n, 195
Chamberlain, Neville, British Prime Minister, 228, 238–44, 249, 255–6
Chase National, US bank, 170
Churchill, Winston, 194, 202, 235, 245, in WWI, 25, on the Russian civil war, 65, 72, and Trebitsch, 101, 108–10, and Norman, 187, as anti-Nazi leader, 227, 231, 232–3, 236, 244, 249, in WWII, 254, 256–9, 261, 265, 268, on

Palestine, 271, and the Hess affair, 293, 294

Clémenceau, Georges, French Prime Minister, 68, 75, 78

Cockayne, Brian, Governor of the Bank of England, 148–9

Craigie, Sir Robert, British Foreign vice-Secretary, 234

Cunliffe, Walter, Governor of the Bank of England, 149, 150

Cuno, Wilhelm, industrialist and Weimar Chancellor, 123

Czech Legion, 64–5, 69–70, 247

Czechoslovakia, created, 65, and Versailles, 77, and the 1938 crisis, 238–42, 247–8, 249, 275

D'Abernon, Lord, British ambassador, 124–5, 229

*Daily Express*, 194, 235

*Daily Mail*, 28, 235, 239

DAP (German Workers' Party), 58–60

Dawes, Charles C., banker and US vice-President, 163, 165

Dawes Plan, 162–72, 176, 179, 181, 187, 199, 212, 224, 230, 231, 265

Dawson, Geoffrey, editor of *The Times*, 194, 229

Dee, John, Elizabethan occultist, 7

Denikin, General Anton, White commander, 67–8, 71, 72, 98, 111, 247

De Ropp, Wilhelm, Balt double-agent, 232, 257

Dodd, William, US ambassador, 225, 226

Dollfuss, Engelbert, Austrian Chancellor, 232

Dresdner Bank, 159, 160

Drexel, Anton, founder of the DAP, 58, 59

Dulles, Allan, late Cold War director of the CIA, 195

Dulles, John Foster, Allied overseer in Germany, 75, 160–1, 167, 195, 211, 215

Dunlop Rubber, British corporation, 224

DuPont, US chemical corporation, 225

Eagle Attack (*Adlerangriff*), German aerial offensive against Britain, 258

Ebert, Friedrich, SPD leader and Weimar President, 49, 50–3, 74, 76, 104, 187, 196

Eckart, Dietrich, Nazi ideologue, 58, 60, 106, 133, 134, 135

Eden, Sir Anthony, British Minister, 233, 236, 249, 294

Edward VIII, Prince of Wales, 233, 234–5, 237–8, 257–8, 262

Ehrhardt, Captain Hermann, *Freikorps* commander, 53, 104, 106, 110, 119

Eisner, Kurt, Socialist radical, 22, 55

*Entente cordiale*, Franco-British alliance, 15, 17

Epp, Captain Franz Xaver von, *Freikorps* Commander, 53, 57

*Erfüllungspolitik* ('policy of fulfillment'), 112, 116, 117, 123

Erzberger, Matthias, German Catholic parliamentarian, 89, 90, 91, 102, 104, 113, 115, 118, 119, 125, 126, 129, 161, 207, 256, and the German surrender, 50, 51, 55, and Versailles, 76, as Finance Minister, 93–7, death of, 112

*Faust*, 203

February Revolution (Russian Liberal putsch of 1917), 29, 33–4

Feder, Gottfried, Hitler's early economics mentor, 58, 60

Federal Reserve Board, 36, 150, 154–6, 159, 172, 178, 179, 180

Ferdinand, Archduke of Austria, 20, 78

Ferry Abel, French vice-Minister, 24

Final Solution, *see* Holocaust

Fischer, Hermann, assassin of W. Rathenau, 22, 118–19

Flandin, Pierre-Etienne, French Foreign Secretary, 236, 248

Foch, Ferdinand, French Marshal, 50

Focus, the, Churchill's anti-Nazi faction, 236, 243

Ford, Edsel, 169

Ford, Henry, 244

Ford Motor Company, 169, 226

Fourteen Points, *see* Woodrow Wilson

France, hostility towards Germany, 5, 9, 14–19, 80, and WWI, 24–6, and the Russian Civil War, 61, 64, 65, 68, 71, and Versailles, 75–7, and the reparations, 114, 166, and Rapallo, 116–17, invades the Ruhr, 123, in Mein Kampf, 136–7, and financial engagement with Britain, 162–3, 176–7, facing Hitler, 231–2, 250, and the Rhineland, 235–6, and the Czech crisis, 238–49, and Poland, 76, 243, her fall in WWII, 256–7

François-Poncet, André, French ambassador to the Third Reich, 211

Frank, Hans, Nazi hierarch, 60

Frankfurter, Felix, US Supreme Court judge, 243
*Frankfurter Zeitung* (newspaper), 73, 108, 109
Franz Josef, Austrian Emperor, 23, 27
French, Sir John, British general, 19
Frick, Wilhelm, Nazi Minister, 201

Gandhi, 186
Gapon, Russian pope, 16
Gardiner, Rolf, early Nazi sympathizer, 231
General Electrics, US corporation 170, 191
George V, King of England, 233, 235, 247
George VI, King of England, 237, 262
George, Duke of Kent, 233
*Germanenorden*, Order that spawned the Thule Society, 59
Gesell, Silvio, monetary reformer and Finance Minister of the Bavarian Soviet, 272
Gessler, Otto, Weimar Defense Minister, 121
Gilbert, Parker Seymour, Morgan agent, 163, 176
GM (General Motors), US corporation, 226
Goebbels, Josef, Nazi hierarch, 188, 200, 205, 206, 208, 211, 236, 238, 253
Gold-exchange standard, 139–41, 172–87
Goltz, General Kolmar von, WWI and Kapp putschist, 71, 98, 106
Göring, Hermann, Nazi hierarch, 201, 206, 208, 227, 253
Graves, General William, Chief of the US corps in Siberia, 64, 69, 73
'Great Crash' (Wall Street collapse of 1929), 139, 140, 175, 189, 264, 266
Grey, Lord Edward, British Foreign Secretary, 17, 19, 22, 270
Groener, General Wilhelm, Chief of the General Staff, 47, 51, 52, 53, 76, 98, 253
Guderian, General Hans, *Wehrmacht* commander, 247

Halifax, Lord (Edward Wood), British steward, 202, 228, 229, 236, 238, 240, 242, 255–7, 293
Hall, Captain Reginald, Director of British Naval Intelligence, 101
Hammer, Armand, Russo-American captain of industry, 72
Hanfstaengl, Ernst, early Nazi maecenas, 136

Hanussen, Jan, fortuneteller, 206, 207
Harrer, Karl, journalist and founder of the DAP, 59
Harriman & Co., US bank, 170, 198
Harrison, George, Federal Reserve Governor, 180, 182
Harvey, Ernst, vice-Governor of the Bank of England, 182–5
Haushofer, General Karl, Professor of geopolitics, 135–6, 264
Havenstein, Rudolf, Reichsbank Governor, 106, 124–5, 126, 129, 161, 189, 194
Helfferich, Karl, Imperial Minister and Nationalist stalwart, 94, 96–7, 102, 103, 108, 161, 162, 189
Helphand, Alexander Israel ('Parvus'), 1, 29–33, 36, 75, 101, 189, 246, 252
Henderson, Sir Nevile, British ambassador, 240
Hess, Rudolf, 57, 60, 112, 133, 136, 233, 238, 258, 260, 261, 264n, 265, 293, 294
Heydrich, Reinhardt, chief of Nazi intelligence, 258
Himmler, Heinrich, Reichsführer SS, 238
Hindenburg, General Paul von, 26, 51, 93, 98, 140, 187, 191, 195, 196, 198–201, 203, 205, 210, 216
Hirschfeld, Oltwig von, aggressor of M. Erzberger, 22, 96
Hitler, Adolf, xviii, 41, 42, 44, 78, 90, 122–3, 128, 131, 140, 170, 190, 203, 204, 225, 226, 227, 245, 249, 250, 254, 264, 265, 267, 268, 293, in WWI, 25, at War's end, 51, in post-revolutionary Munich, 57–60, and the Kapp Putsch, 106, organizes the NSDAP, 111–12, and the Beerhall Putsch, 90, 132–3, 151, 161, during Weimar's 'Golden Years', 186–8, and the bid to power, 192, 195, 196–201, establishes the Third Reich, 205–11, and the Nazi boom, 215–17, 220, 222, 223, 224, and Appeasement, 228–44, as character of *On the Marble Cliffs*, 253, in WWII, 255–62, *see also Mein Kampf*
Hoare, Samuel, British statesman, 229, 240, 256, 257, 262, 293
Hoffmann, Johannes, Bavarian SPD leader, 56, 107
Holocaust, 265, 268
Hoover, Herbert, US President, 150, 193
Houghton, Alanson, US ambassador, 162

House, Edward ('Colonel'), councilor of US President Wilson, 20, 35, 78

Hugenberg, Alfred, Krupp director and late Nationalist leader, 97

I.G. Farben, industrial conglomerate, 165–9, 206, 224, 225, 227

India, 139, 152–4, 157, 185–6

International Harvester Company, 225

ITT (International Telephone & Telegraph), US corporation, 226

Jagow, Gottlieb von, Imperial Foreign Secretary, 32

Janin, General Maurice, Commander-in-Chief of the Allied troops in Siberia, 69–70

Jodl, General Alfred, Wehrmacht commander, 235

J. P. Morgan Banking Interests, 36, 150, 161, 162, 163, 166, 172, 226

Jung, Carl Gustav, Swiss psychiatrist, 148

Jünger, Ernst, German novelist, 43, 60, 119, 250–4

Kahr, Gustav von, Bavarian commissioner, 107, 132–3, 210

Kandelaki, David, Soviet trade envoy, 249

Kapp, Wolfgang, Nationalist exponent and putschist, 100, 104, 106–9, 111

Kapp–Lüttwitz Putsch, 98–111, 117, 120, 132n

Keitel, General Wilhelm, Field Marshal of the Wehrmacht, 238

Kennan, George F., US diplomat and historian, 73

Kennedy, Joseph, US ambassador, 254, 259

Kerensky, Aleksandr, barrister and figurehead of the Liberal experiment in Russia, 1, 35–6, 63, 68, 247, 264

Kern, Erwin, assassin of W. Rathenau, 22, 118–19

Keynes, John M., British economist, 43, 74, 77–9, 84–5, 87, 231, 265

Kilgore, Harley M, US senator, 169

Kipling, Rudyard, 147

Kirov, Sergei, Soviet leader, 22, 245

Kitchener, Lord Horatio H., British War Minister, 39–40

Knox, Sir Alfred, chief of the British mission in Russia, 65

Knox, Frank, US Navy Secretary, 226

Kolchak, Aleksandr, White commander, 65, 68–70, 72, 98, 111, 158, 247

Kopp, Vigdor, Soviet envoy to Berlin, 103, 105, 106, 120

KPD (German Communist Party), 43, 52, 103, 104, 107–9, 206, 264

Kristallnacht, 228

Krivitsky, Walter. G., Soviet Intelligence chief, 131

Krupp, steel-making potentate, 168, 220, 223, 225, 244

Kuhn, Loeb & Co., US bank, 150

Lamont, Thomas, J.P. Morgan fiduciary, 161

Landauer, Gustav, literatus and Education Minister in the Bavarian Soviet, 272

Lansing, Robert, US State Secretary, 72, 74

Lawrence, Sir Herbert, chairman of Vickers, 225

Lenin, 32–7, 52, 63, 68, 72, 76, 103, 189, 245n, 246

Ley, Robert, Nazi Labor Minister, 238

Levien, Max, Russian subversive, 56, 57

Leviné, Eugene, Russian subversive, 56, 57

Liebknecht, Karl, KPD leader, 52, 53, 105

Litvinov, Maxim, Soviet Foreign Secretary, 199, 239, 248, 250

Lloyd George, David, 14, 29, 40, 66, 72, 75, 78, 100, 101, 109, 116–17, 127, 232, 236–7

Lodge, Henry Cabot, US Senator, 80

Long Island (meeting of central bankers), 178

Lossow, General Otto von, Bavarian secessionist, 132–3

Lothian, Lord (Philip Kerr), British Minister, 229, 235, 248

Lubbe, Martin van der, arsonist of the Reichstag, 22, 208–9

Ludendorff, General Erich von, 24, 26, 40, 47, 48, 92–3, 99–100, 102, 103, 106–9, 111, 133, 187

Lusitania, British ocean liner, 37, 254, 271

Luther, Hans, Reichsbank Governor, 194, 195, 271

Lüttwitz, General Walther von, Kapp conspirator, 104–5, 106, 108

Luxemburg, Rosa, KPD leader, 52, 53, 105

Machiavelli, Niccoló, 263, 268

Mackinder, Halford, British geographer, 8–15,

Macmillan Report, 182

Maercker, Captain Georg, Freikorps commander, 53

Maisky, Ivan, Soviet ambassador, 199, 232
Malcolm, General N., Chief of the British
   command in Weimar, 92, 104, 108–10
Maltzan, Ago von, German diplomat,
   117
*Manchester Guardian*, 39, 198
Marne, western theater of WWI, 15, 25
Marshall, General George C., Chief of
   Staff of the US Army, 261
Masurian Lakes, eastern theater of WWI,
   25–6
Mayr, Captain Karl, Hitler's instructor,
   58, 106
McKinley, William, US President, 163
McVeigh, Timothy, 270
*Mein Kampf*, 133–7, 140, 192, 194, 238,
   244
Michael, Grand Duke, *see* Romanovs
Milner, Lord Alfred, British imperial
   administrator, 39–40, 74
Mitchell, C. E., banker, 169
Moeller van den Bruck, Arthur,
   conservative ideologue, 135
Möhl, Ritter von, German general, 107
Molotov, Vyacheslav, Soviet hierarch,
   248, 250
Moltke, Helmuth von, Chief of the
   German General Staff, 15, 19, 24–6
Moreau, Emile, Governor of the Bank of
   France, 176–7
Moret, Clément, Governor of the Bank of
   France, 183, 185
Müller, Hermann, Weimar Minister, 78
Munich Conference, 241–2, *see also*
   Czechoslovakia
Mussolini, Benito, 232

Neurath, Konstantin Freiherr von,
   Foreign Minister of the Third Reich,
   235
*New York Times*, 125, 180
Nicholas II, Czar of Russia, xviii, 16, 17,
   27–9, 30, 32–4, 43, 62, 64, 264 *see also*
   Romanovs
Nikolaiev, Alexei, murderer of S. Kirov,
   22, 245, 246
Norman, Montagu, Governor of the Bank
   of England, xviii, 139–41, 147–53, 188,
   211, 259, 264, 266, and the crunch of
   1920, 154–9, and Schacht, 162, and
   the German bailout, 162–4, crashes the
   Gold-exchange standard, 171–87, and
   the end of Weimar, 194, and the Nazi
   boom, 201, 224, 228, 231, 242

Noske, Gustav, SPD leader and Weimar
   Minister, 52–3, 56, 105, 108
Noyes, Alexander Dana, financial editor
   of the *New York Times*, 180
NSDAP (National-Socialist Party of the
   German Workers, the Nazi Party), xvi,
   90, 111, 131, 140, 189, 197, 210

October Revolution (Bolshevik coup), 36,
   68, 84
Oka, Captain Arata, Japanese military
   attaché in Britain, 234
*On the Marble Cliffs*, E. Jünger's novel,
   250–4
'Organization Consul', alleged terrorist
   central in Weimar Germany, 119
Osborne, Francis d'Arçy, British diplomat,
   255–6
Overlord, Allied directive for the cross-
   Channel attack of Germany, 261–2
Owen, Robert, U.S. Senator, 13

Pabst, Captain Waldemar, *Freikorps*
   commander, 53, 105, 110
Pacelli, Monsignor Eugenio, pontifical
   nuncio and late Pope Pius XII, 200,
   207, 255–6, 268
Palestine, 2, 39, 263
Papen, Franz von, Weimar Chancellor,
   197–20, 203, 205, 212, 213, 214, 217,
   234
Parvus, *see* Helphand
Pasternak, Boris, Russian novelist, 25
Pearl Harbor, 259
Pershing, General John J., US Army Chief
   in WWI, 37, 163
Pétain, Marshal Philippe, Nazi
   collaborationist, 257
Phipps, Sir Eric, British ambassador, 226,
   233
Plekhanov, George, Russian Marxist
   politician, 34
Poincaré, Raymond, President of France,
   176
Poland, 68, 71, 158, 248, 275  in WWI,
   26, created at Versailles, 76–7, in the
   light of Rapallo, 120, allied with
   Germany, 231, and the Czech Crisis,
   239–42,and the pre-war crisis, 242–4,
   249, 250 in WWII, 254, 255
Pourtalès, Friedrich von, German
   ambassador, 23,
Princip, Cabrinovic and Grabez, Sarajevo
   assassins, 20–2, 78

Putna, General Vitovt, Soviet Military attaché in Britain, 246, 247, 248

Radek, Karl, Soviet publicist, 103, 105, 108, 120, 246
Rapallo Treaty (Russo-German pact), 116–17, 119–21, 131, 138
Rasputin, Gregori, 17, 22, 24, 28, 31, 32, 231, 264
Rathenau, Walther, Reich industrialist and Weimar Minister, 22, 90, 93, 112–21, 122, 123, 128, 160, 161
Reichsbank, 106, 124, 129, 139, 161, 165, 167, 181, 192, 211–13, 215–21, 242
Reichstag Fire, 203, 206, 208, 210
Reparations, 74–5, 77, 79, 85–7, 96, 112, 113–14, 115, 124, 129–30, 138, 164, 166, 174, 176, 191, 197, 259, see also Versailles
Rhineland Settlement, Versailles provision, 77, re-militarization of, 235–6, 246
Ribbentrop, Joachim von, Nazi Minister, 234, 244, 250, 258
Ridell, Lord, British press representative, 107, 127
Rist, Charles, vice-Governor of the Bank of France, 178
Robins, Raymond, Wall Street operator, 72
Rockefeller corporate Interests, 170
Röhm, Ernst, SA commander, 57, 187, 192, 209–10, 215, 217
Romanovs, Russian Imperial family, 16, 64, czarina Alexandra, 16–17, 27–8 czarevitch Alexei, 16–17, Grand Duke Michael, 33–4, see also Nicholas II
Rommel, General Erwin, Field Marshal of the Wehrmacht, 260–1
Roosevelt, Franklin Delano, US President, 225, 259, 261n
Rosenberg, Alfred, Nazi theorist of the race, 58, 60, 134, 136, 194–5, 232, 233
Rosenberg, Arthur, German historian, 107
Rote Fahne ('The Red Flag', press organ of the KPD), 53, 107, 109
Rothermere, Viscount (Harold Harmsworth), director of the Daily Mail, 235, 239
Round Table, British imperialist club, 39, 74, 229–31, 242, 263
Rowntree, Benjamin, entrepreneur and Trebitsch's early patron, 101
Ruhr, invasion of, 123, 158, 163, 166, 174
Russell, Bertrand, 270

Ryan, Colonel, British military superintendent in Köln, 99–100

SA (Sturm Abteilung, Hitler's shock troops), 112, 131, 196, 206, 207, 208–10, 217, 246, 253,
Sadat, Anwar, President of Egypt, 264, 274
Salomon, Ernst von, Freikorps bard, 22, 118–19
Sauerbruch, Ferdinand, renowned surgeon, 219
Sazanov, Sergei, Russian Foreign Minister, 23
Schacht, Hjalmar, Governor of the Reichsbank, xviii, 159–62, 164, 178, 180, 188, 191–2, 194, 195, 200, 211, 214–21, 223, 224, 225, 226–8, 249, 266, 268
Scheidemann, Philip, Weimar Chancellor, 76
Schellenberg, Walter, Nazi intelligence officer, 258
Schleicher, General Kurt von, Weimar Chancellor, 52, 120, 196–201, 205, 209, 210, 214–15, 247, 253
Schlieffen Plan, 19, 23–5
Schmidt, Paul, Hitler's interpreter, 233
Schmitt, Kurt, Economics Minister of the Third Reich, 215, 216
Schröder, Baron Kurt von, banker, 200, 209, 265, 266
Schröders, London banking house, 194, 200
Sea Lion (Seelöwe), feigned Nazi directive for the land-invasion of Britain, 258
Sebottendorff, Rudolf von, occultist and founder of the Thule Society, 59, 60
Seeckt, General Hans von, Chief of the Army Command, 100, 104, 105, 120, 132, 196, 253
Seisser, Hans von, Munich's Police Chief, 133
Semenov, Cossack chief, 63
Siemens, industrial conglomerate, 220, 226
Simon, Sir Eric, British Minister, 229, 233, 234, 238
Simpson, Wallis (Duchess of Windsor), 237–8, 257–8
Smuts, Jan, South African fiduciary of the British Empire, 74, 77, 229
Snowden, Philip, British Secretary of the Treasury, 185
Somary, Felix, Swiss banker, 175, 193

SPD (German Socialist Party), 44–7, 49, 52, 112, 140, 167, 201, 207

SS (*Schutzstaffel*, the Führer's protection squad), 131, 196, 210, 253, 261, 268

Stalin, 189–90, 202, 244–9, 253, 260, 261, 264

Standard Oil, US corporation, 169, 225, 226, 244

Stephani, Major Franz von, *Freikorps* commander, 53, 110

Strasser, Gregor, leader of Nazi Left Wing, 187–8, 197, 200, 210, 217

Strasser, Otto, leader of the Nazi Left Wing and late organizer of the Blackfront, 187–8, 210, 217

Stresemann, Gustav, Weimar Chancellor, 132

Strong, Benjamin, Governor of the Federal Reserve, 150, 151, 155–7, 172, 178, 179, 180

Sullivan & Cromwell, Wall Street law firm, 160, 194

Tacitus, 53

Teagle, Walter, CEO of Standard Oil, 169

Thälmann, Ernst, KPD leader, 190

Thucydides, xvi

Thule Society, 56, 57, 59–60, 134, 252, 253

Thyssen, Alfred, German steel potentate, 170, 198

Tiarks, Frank C., Schröders' fiduciary, 195

Tillesen and Schultz, assassins of M. Erzberger, 22, 112

*Times*, 194, 229, 235

Tirpitz, Alfred von, Reich Admiral, 5, 102, 103

Trebitsch-Lincoln, Ignatz, 90, 100–12, 252, 257, 264

Triple Entente, alliance of Britain, France and Russia, 17, 19

Trotsky, Leon, 16, 33, 37, 63, 72, 120, 189–90, 196, 245, 246, 247

Tukhachevsky, General Mikhail, Field Marshal of the Red Army, 71, 120, 246–8, 265

Turner, General, envoy to the Baltic region, 98

Twentieth Century Fox, 197

Unilever, British chemical conglomerate, 224

USPD (Independent Socialist Party of Germany), 46, 55

Vanderlip, Frank, banker, 73

Vatican, 140, 189, 207

Veblen, Thorstein, 4, 43, 44, 46, 80–8, 90, 91, 94, 130, 140, 151, 197, 207, 229, 245, 263, 265

Versailles Treaty, xviii, 42, 43, 74–80, 84–6, 89, 90, 92, 94, 98, 103, 108, 113, 120, 121, 123, 124, 127, 130, 151, 160, 163, 168, 170, 191, 205, 230, 231, 233, 235, 236, 237, 239, 242, 265, 293

Vickers-Armstrong, British arms manufacturer, 224–5

Victoria, Queen of England, 5, 103

Vissering Gerard, Governor of the Netherland Bank, 185

*Völkischer Beobachter*, Nazi press organ, 60, 132, 189

'War guilt clause' (*Kriegsschuldfrage*), 75

Warburg, Paul, banker, 169

*Washington Post*, 36

Weber, Max, German sociologist, 76

Whitman, Walt, American poet, 56

Wilhelm II, German Kaiser, 5, 6, 13, 14, 17–19, 23, 24, 28, 42, 45, 47, 50, 93, 102–3, 233

Willingdon, Lord (George Freeman Thomas), Viceroy of India, 186

Wilson, Woodrow, US President, 20, 29, 37, 47, 64, 72, 74, 75, 78, 80, his Fourteen Points, 47, 74, 75, 76, 80

Windsor, Duke of, *see* Edward VIII

Winterbotham, Captain Frederick, British spy, 231–2, 241

Wood, Sir Kingsley, British Minister, 255

Wrangel, Peter, White commander, 71, 98

Young, Owen, director of General Electrics, 191

Young Plan, 191

Yudenitch, General Nicholas, White commander, 71, 111

Yussupov, Felix, murderer of Rasputin, 22, 28

*Zentrum* (German Catholic Center Party), 112, 207

*Zürcher Zeitung* (newspaper), 97

Zyklon B, the lagers' asphyxiating gas, 169